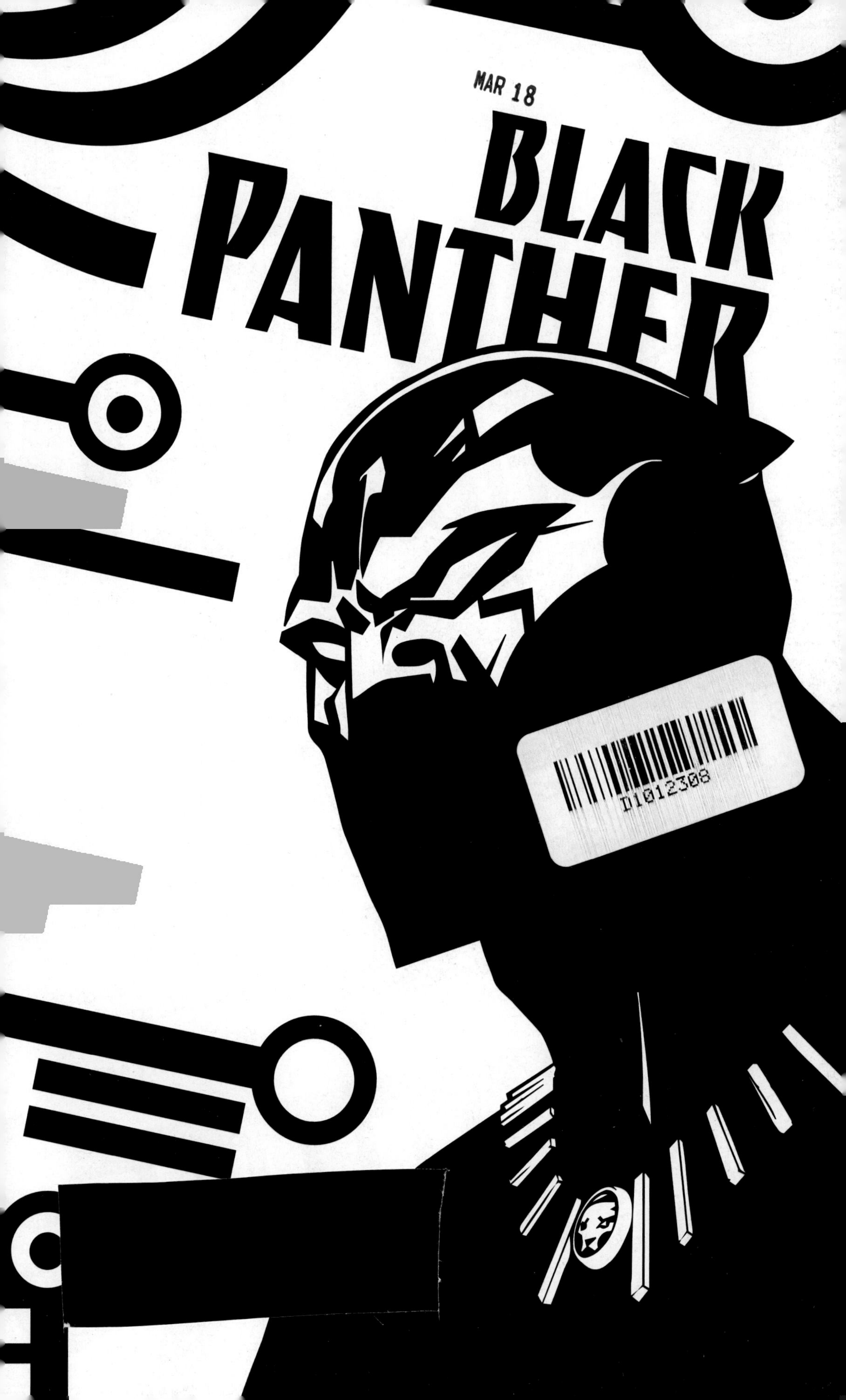
BLACK
PANTHER

BLACK PANTHER

A NATION UNDER

Writer/**Ta-Nehisi Coates**

ISSUE #9

Artist/**Brian Stelfreeze**
Color Artist/**Laura Martin**

ISSUE #10

Layouts/**Chris Sprouse**
Finishes/**Karl Story**
Color Artist/**Laura Martin**

ISSUE #11

Layouts/**Chris Sprouse**
Finishes/**Goran Sudžuka, Walden Wong,**
Karl Story & Roberto Poggi
Color Artists/**Laura Martin**
with **Matt Milla, Larry Molinar,**
Rachelle Rosenberg & Paul Mounts

ISSUE #12

Pencils/**Brian Stelfreeze & Chris Sprouse**
Inks/**Brian Stelfreeze, Karl Story**
& Scott Hanna
Color Artists/**Laura Martin & Matt Milla**

Since Thanos's attack on Wakanda, **Shuri** — former queen, former Black Panther, and sister to T'Challa—had been trapped in a petrified state known as **The Living Death**. Her spirit was driven to **The Djalia**, the plane of Wakandan memory. While there, she learned of Wakanda's past, present, and future from a Griot wearing the aspect of her mother, Ramonda. Meanwhile, the real Ramonda is under intensive medical care due to injuries she received during a suicide bombing.

After months of agonizing research and experimentation in an effort to revive his sister, **T'Challa** constructed a transverse dimensional brace to augment **Manifold's** teleportation abilities and send their spirits to The Djalia to retrieve her. Shuri returned to the physical plane with Wakanda's collective knowledge and new abilities.

Meanwhile, a rebellion ravages Wakanda. A faction known as **The People**, led by **Tetu** and **Zenzi**, gathers forces to topple T'Challa's regime. The *Dora Milaje*, formerly the protection service to the crown, have broken away under the direction of **The Midnight Angels — Ayo** and **Aneka** — to protect and serve ignored Wakandans while T'Challa's attention has been spread thin. The People and the *Dora Milaje* agree that Wakanda needs new leadership, but have not yet made a formal alliance...

R FEET BOOK THREE

Letterer/**VC's Joe Sabino**
Logo Design/**Rian Hughes**
Cover Art/**Brian Stelfreeze & Laura Martin**
Assistant Editor/**Chris Robinson**
Editor/**Wil Moss**
Executive Editor/**Tom Brevoort**

BLACK PANTHER CREATED BY **STAN LEE** & **JACK KIRBY**

COLLECTION EDITOR/**JENNIFER GRÜNWALD**
ASSISANT EDITOR/**CAITLIN O'CONNELL**
ASSOCIATE MANAGING EDITOR/**KATERI WOODY**
EDITOR, SPECIAL PROJECTS/**MARK D. BEAZLEY**
VP PRODUCTION & SPECIAL PROJECTS/**JEFF YOUNGQUIST**
SVP PRINT, SALES & MARKETING/**DAVID GABRIEL**
BOOK DESIGNERS/**JAY BOWEN** & **MANNY MEDEROS**
SPECIAL THANKS TO JESS HAROLD

EDITOR IN CHIEF/**AXEL ALONSO**
CHIEF CREATIVE OFFICER/**JOE QUESADA**
PRESIDENT/**DAN BUCKLEY**
EXECUTIVE PRODUCER/**ALAN FINE**

BLACK PANTHER: A NATION UNDER OUR FEET BOOK 3. Contains material originally published in magazine form as BLACK PANTHER #9-12; and NEW AVENGERS #18, #21 and #24. First printing 2017. ISBN# 978-1-302-90191-2. Published by MARVEL WORLDWIDE, INC., a subsidiary of MARVEL ENTERTAINMENT, LLC. OFFICE OF PUBLICATION: 135 West 50th Street, New York, NY 10020. Copyright © 2017 MARVEL. No similarity between any of the names, characters, persons, and/or institutions in this magazine with those of any living or dead person or institution is intended, and any such similarity which may exist is purely coincidental. Printed in the U.S.A. DAN BUCKLEY, President, Marvel Entertainment; JOE QUESADA, Chief Creative Officer; TOM BREVOORT, SVP of Publishing; DAVID BOGART, SVP of Business Affairs & Operations, Publishing & Partnership; C.B. CEBULSKI, VP of Brand Management & Development, Asia; DAVID GABRIEL, SVP of Sales & Marketing, Publishing; JEFF YOUNGQUIST, VP of Production & Special Projects; DAN CARR, Executive Director of Publishing Technology; ALEX MORALES, Director of Publishing Operations; SUSAN CRESPI, Production Manager; STAN LEE, Chairman Emeritus. For information regarding advertising in Marvel Comics or on Marvel.com, please contact Vit DeBellis, Integrated Sales Manager, at vdebellis@marvel.com. For Marvel subscription inquiries, please call 888-511-5480. Manufactured between 2/17/2017 and 3/21/2017 by QUAD/GRAPHICS WASECA, WASECA, MN, USA.

10 9 8 7 6 5 4 3 2 1

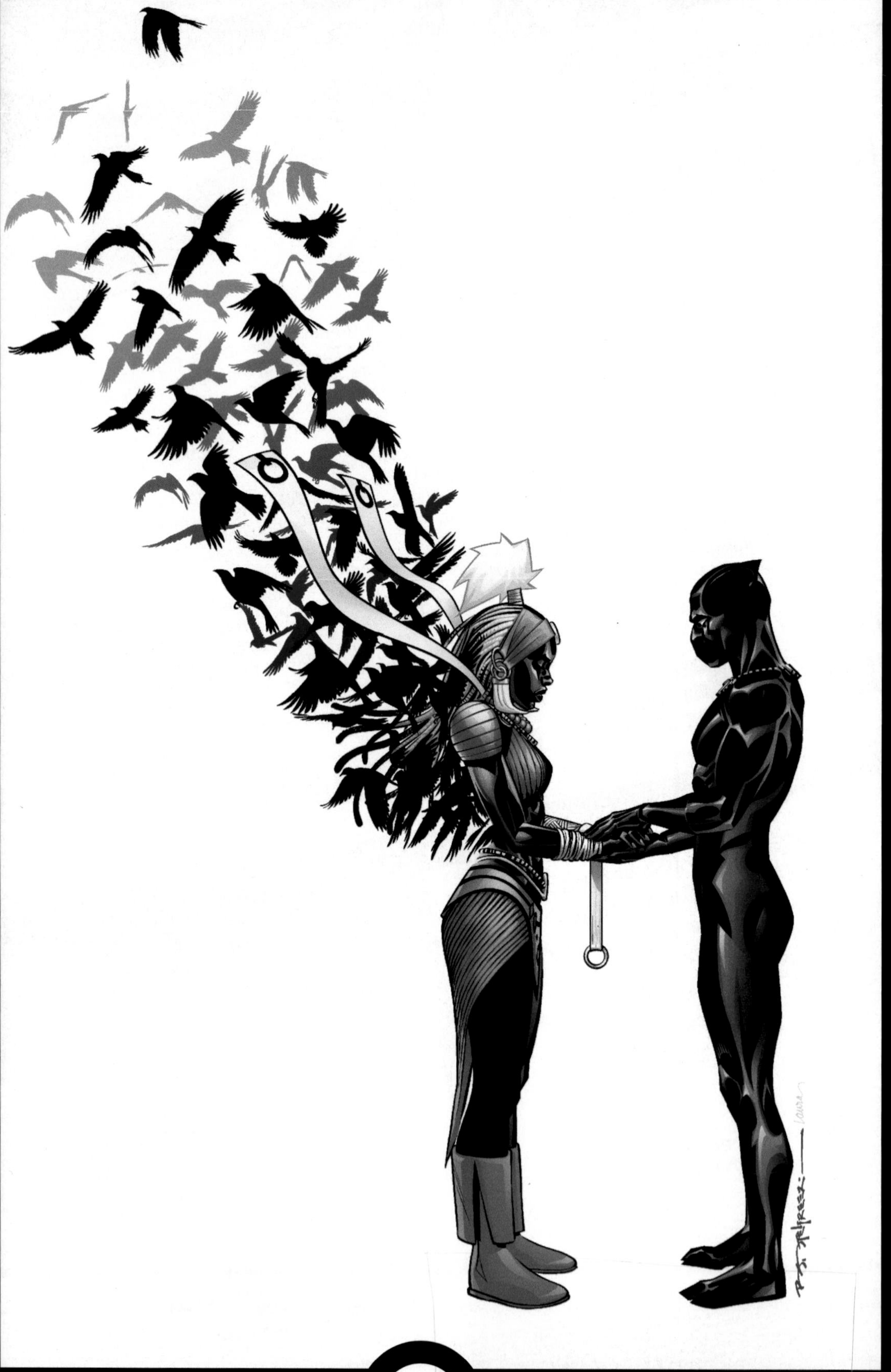

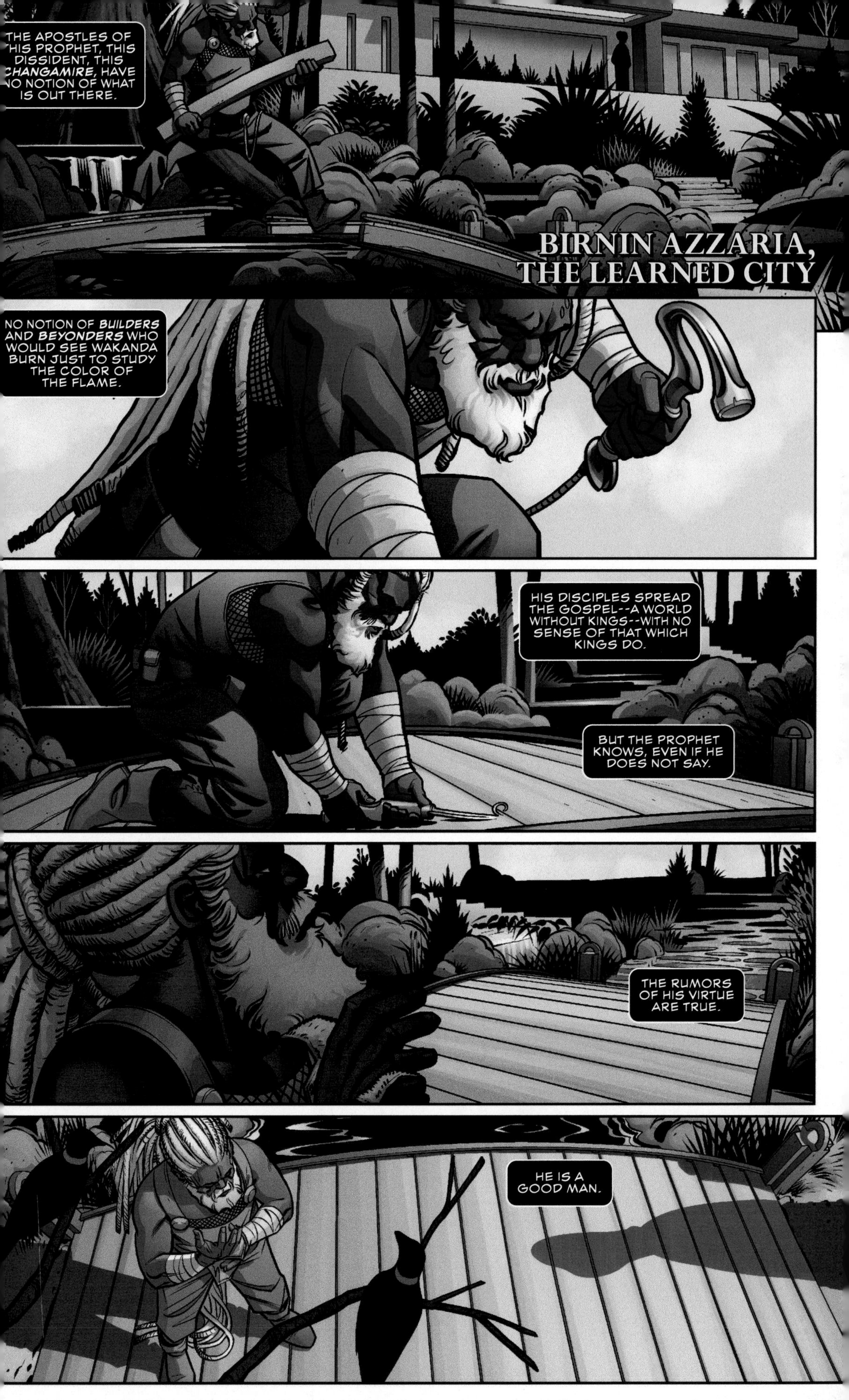
THE APOSTLES OF THIS PROPHET, THIS DISSIDENT, THIS CHANGAMIRE, HAVE NO NOTION OF WHAT IS OUT THERE.
BIRNIN AZZARIA, THE LEARNED CITY
NO NOTION OF BUILDERS AND BEYONDERS WHO WOULD SEE WAKANDA BURN JUST TO STUDY THE COLOR OF THE FLAME.
HIS DISCIPLES SPREAD THE GOSPEL--A WORLD WITHOUT KINGS--WITH NO SENSE OF THAT WHICH KINGS DO.
BUT THE PROPHET KNOWS, EVEN IF HE DOES NOT SAY.
THE RUMORS OF HIS VIRTUE ARE TRUE.
HE IS A GOOD MAN.

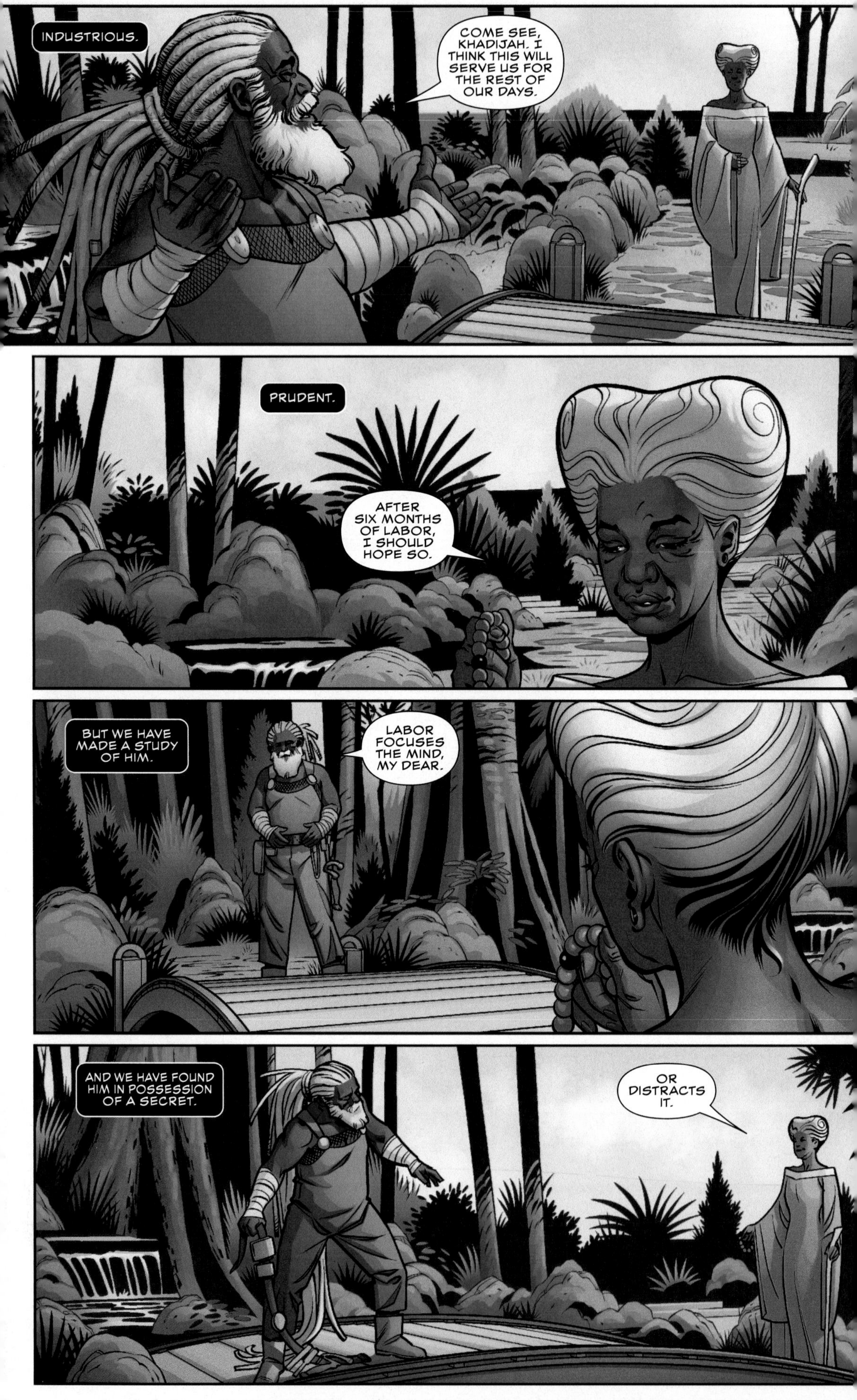
INDUSTRIOUS.
COME SEE, KHADIJAH. I THINK THIS WILL SERVE US FOR THE REST OF OUR DAYS.
PRUDENT.
AFTER SIX MONTHS OF LABOR, I SHOULD HOPE SO.
BUT WE HAVE MADE A STUDY OF HIM.
LABOR FOCUSES THE MIND, MY DEAR.
AND WE HAVE FOUND HIM IN POSSESSION OF A SECRET.
OR DISTRACTS IT.

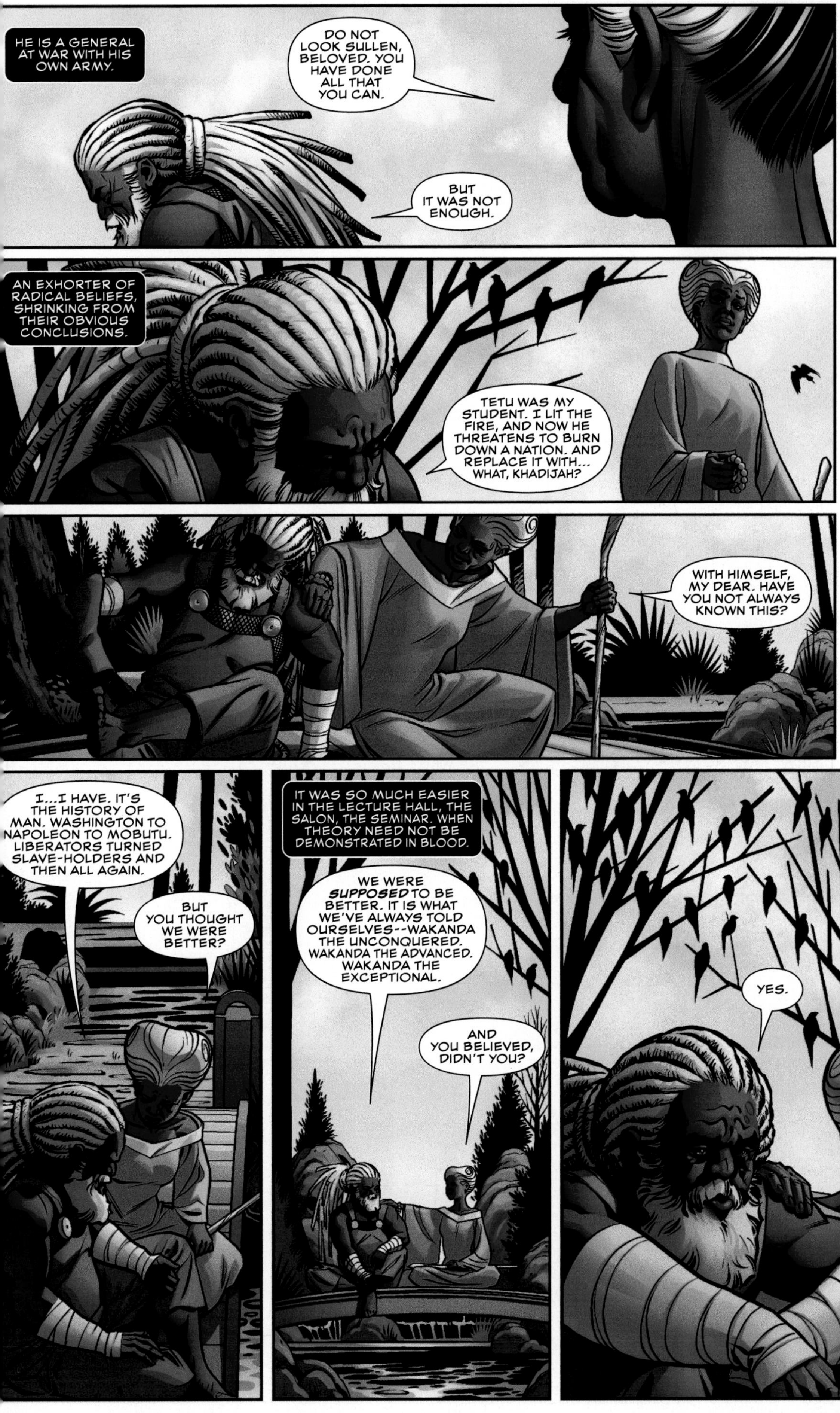
HE IS A GENERAL AT WAR WITH HIS OWN ARMY.
DO NOT LOOK SULLEN, BELOVED. YOU HAVE DONE ALL THAT YOU CAN.
BUT IT WAS NOT ENOUGH.
AN EXHORTER OF RADICAL BELIEFS, SHRINKING FROM THEIR OBVIOUS CONCLUSIONS.
TETU WAS MY STUDENT. I LIT THE FIRE, AND NOW HE THREATENS TO BURN DOWN A NATION. AND REPLACE IT WITH... WHAT, KHADIJAH?
WITH HIMSELF, MY DEAR. HAVE YOU NOT ALWAYS KNOWN THIS?
I...I HAVE. IT'S THE HISTORY OF MAN. WASHINGTON TO NAPOLEON TO MOBUTU. LIBERATORS TURNED SLAVE-HOLDERS AND THEN ALL AGAIN.
BUT YOU THOUGHT WE WERE BETTER?
IT WAS SO MUCH EASIER IN THE LECTURE HALL, THE SALON, THE SEMINAR. WHEN THEORY NEED NOT BE DEMONSTRATED IN BLOOD.
WE WERE *SUPPOSED* TO BE BETTER. IT IS WHAT WE'VE ALWAYS TOLD OURSELVES--WAKANDA THE UNCONQUERED. WAKANDA THE ADVANCED. WAKANDA THE EXCEPTIONAL.
AND YOU BELIEVED, DIDN'T YOU?
YES.

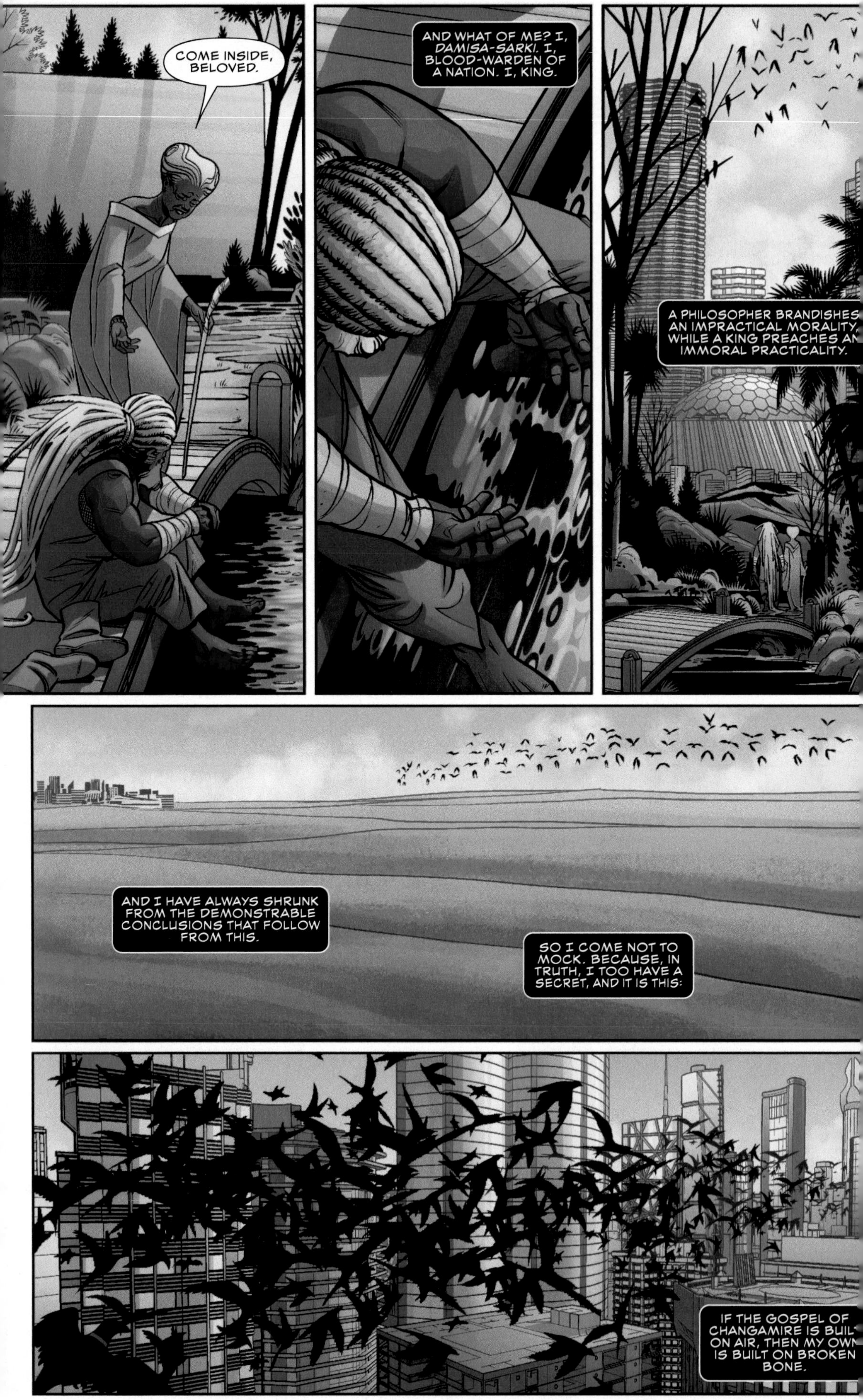
COME INSIDE, BELOVED.
AND WHAT OF ME? I, DAMISA-SARKI. I, BLOOD-WARDEN OF A NATION. I, KING.
A PHILOSOPHER BRANDISHES AN IMPRACTICAL MORALITY, WHILE A KING PREACHES AN IMMORAL PRACTICALITY.
AND I HAVE ALWAYS SHRUNK FROM THE DEMONSTRABLE CONCLUSIONS THAT FOLLOW FROM THIS.
SO I COME NOT TO MOCK. BECAUSE, IN TRUTH, I TOO HAVE A SECRET, AND IT IS THIS:
IF THE GOSPEL OF CHANGAMIRE IS BUILT ON AIR, THEN MY OWN IS BUILT ON BROKEN BONE.

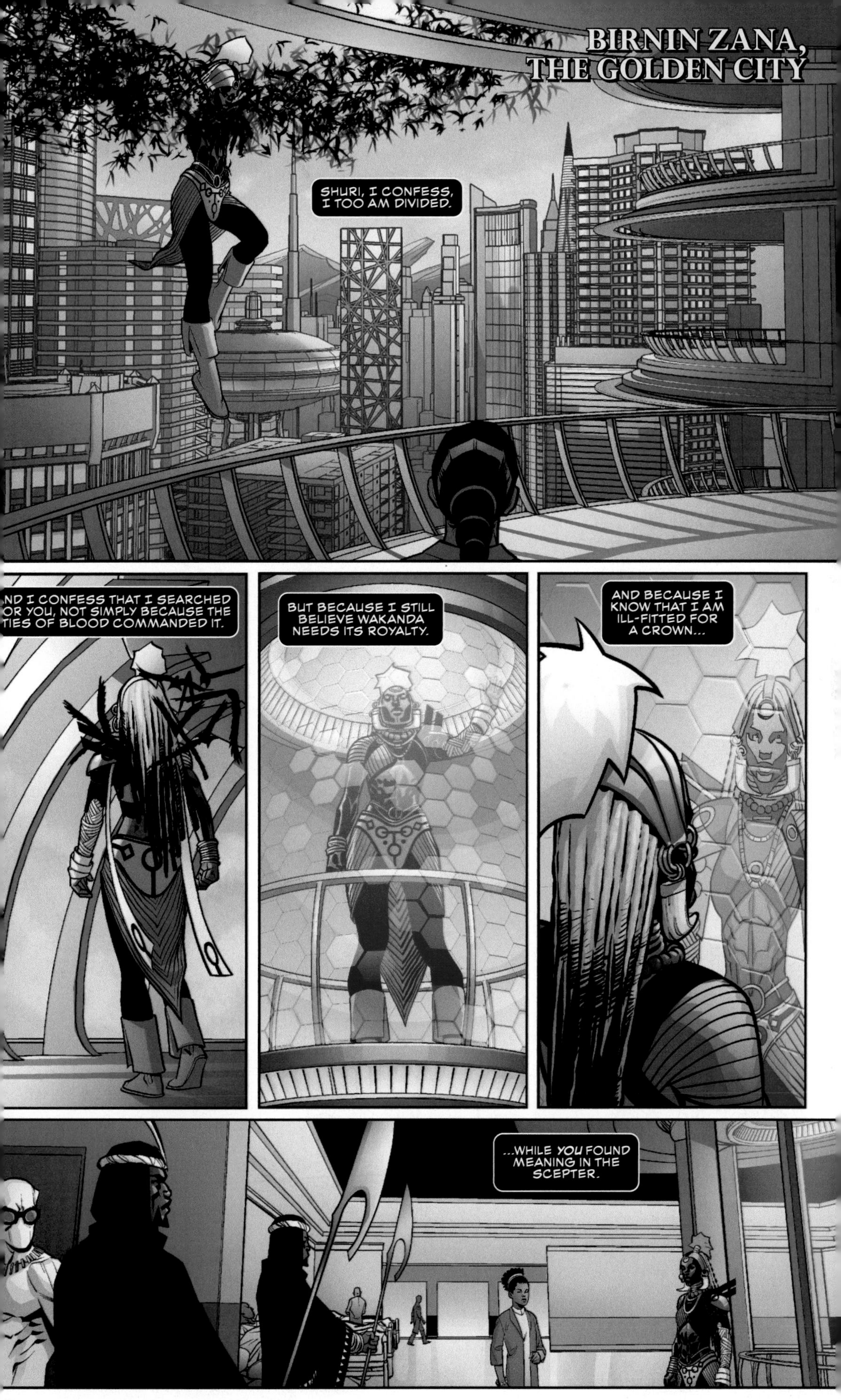
BIRNIN ZANA, THE GOLDEN CITY
SHURI, I CONFESS, I TOO AM DIVIDED.
ND I CONFESS THAT I SEARCHED OR YOU, NOT SIMPLY BECAUSE THE TIES OF BLOOD COMMANDED IT.
BUT BECAUSE I STILL BELIEVE WAKANDA NEEDS ITS ROYALTY.
AND BECAUSE I KNOW THAT I AM ILL-FITTED FOR A CROWN...
...WHILE *YOU* FOUND MEANING IN THE SCEPTER.

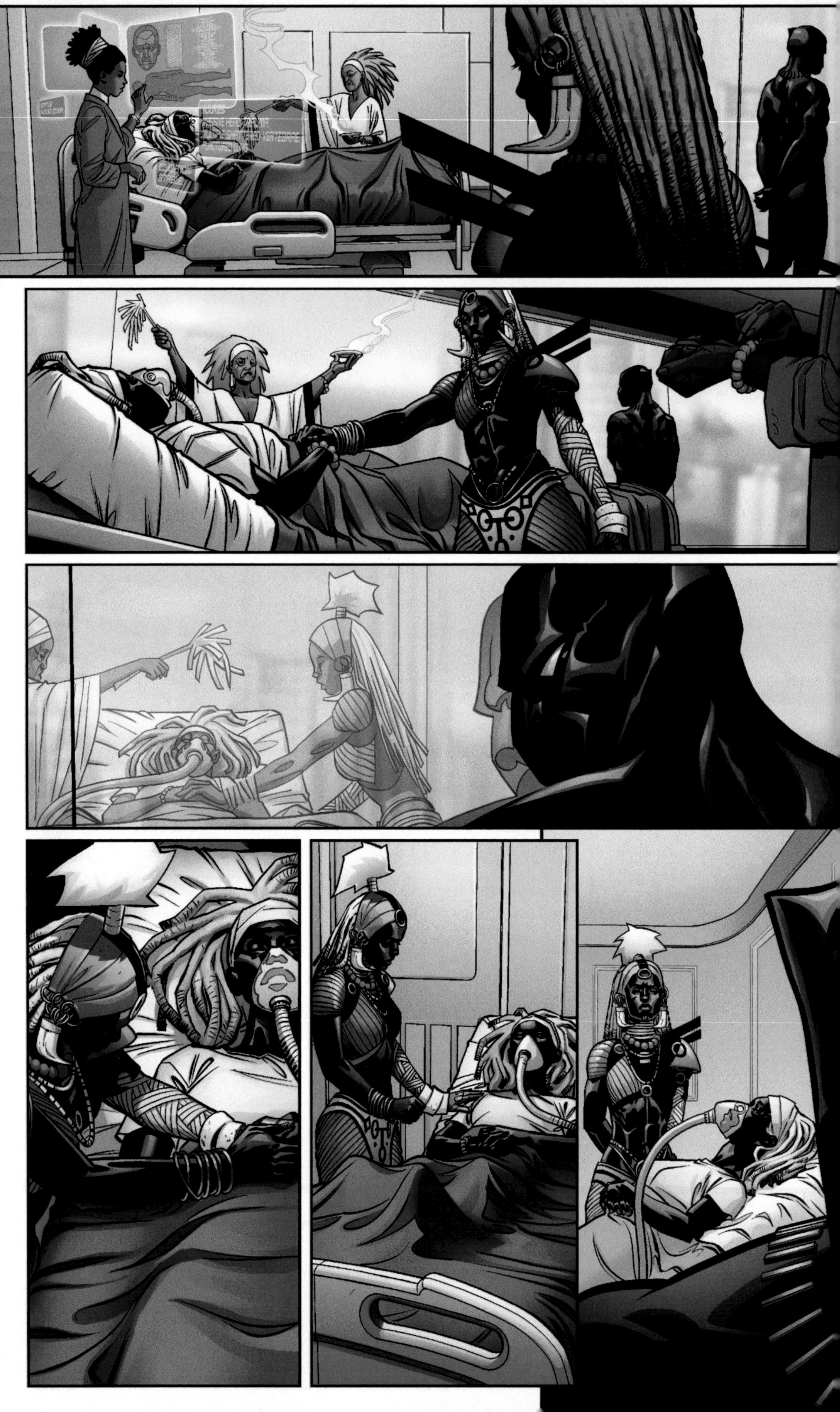
STABLE

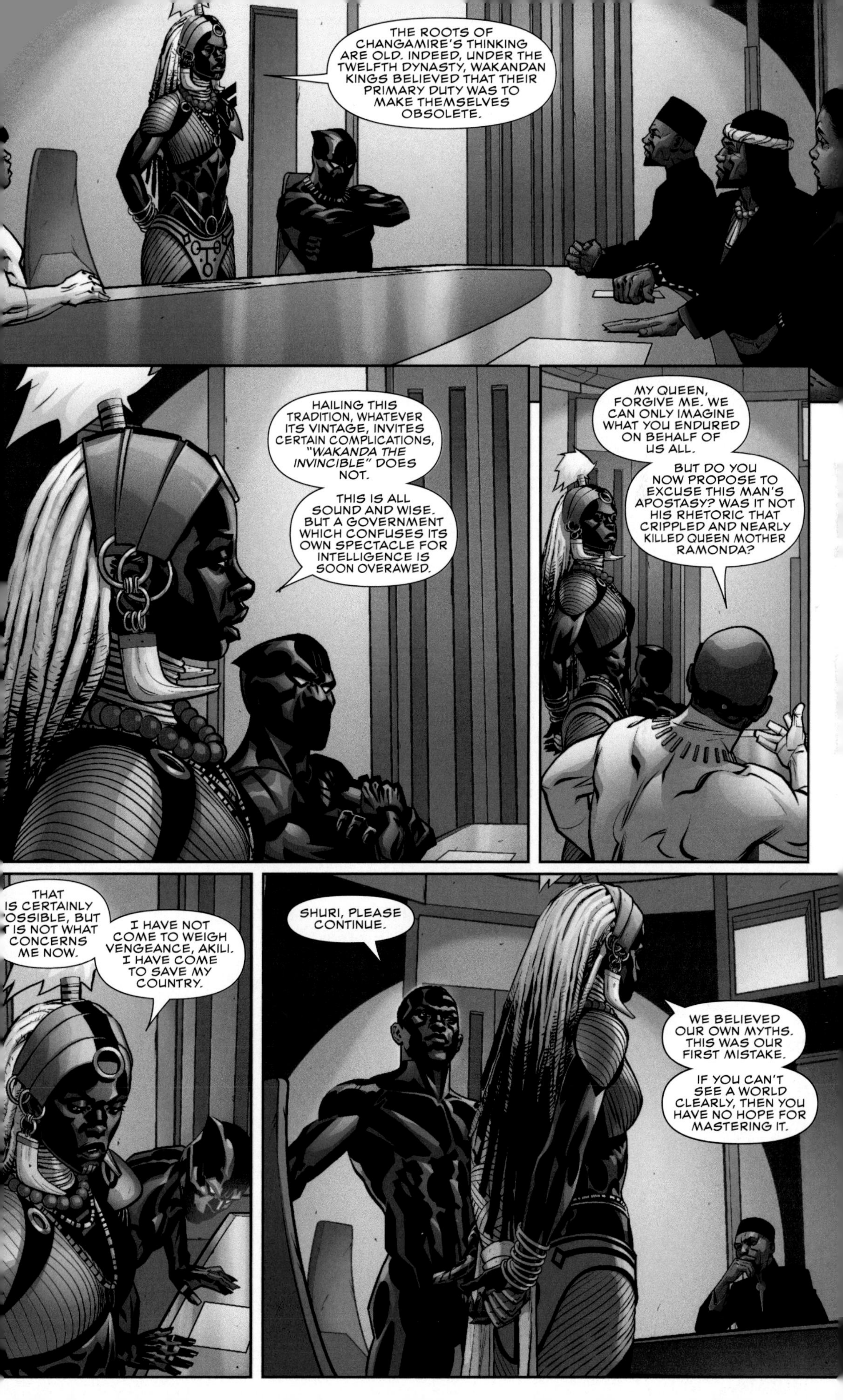
THE ROOTS OF CHANGAMIRE'S THINKING ARE OLD. INDEED, UNDER THE TWELFTH DYNASTY, WAKANDAN KINGS BELIEVED THAT THEIR PRIMARY DUTY WAS TO MAKE THEMSELVES OBSOLETE.
HAILING THIS TRADITION, WHATEVER ITS VINTAGE, INVITES CERTAIN COMPLICATIONS. "WAKANDA THE INVINCIBLE" DOES NOT.
THIS IS ALL SOUND AND WISE. BUT A GOVERNMENT WHICH CONFUSES ITS OWN SPECTACLE FOR INTELLIGENCE IS SOON OVERAWED.
MY QUEEN, FORGIVE ME. WE CAN ONLY IMAGINE WHAT YOU ENDURED ON BEHALF OF US ALL.
BUT DO YOU NOW PROPOSE TO EXCUSE THIS MAN'S APOSTASY? WAS IT NOT HIS RHETORIC THAT CRIPPLED AND NEARLY KILLED QUEEN MOTHER RAMONDA?
THAT IS CERTAINLY POSSIBLE, BUT IT IS NOT WHAT CONCERNS ME NOW.
I HAVE NOT COME TO WEIGH VENGEANCE, AKILI. I HAVE COME TO SAVE MY COUNTRY.
SHURI, PLEASE CONTINUE.
WE BELIEVED OUR OWN MYTHS. THIS WAS OUR FIRST MISTAKE.
IF YOU CAN'T SEE A WORLD CLEARLY, THEN YOU HAVE NO HOPE FOR MASTERING IT.

SEEN CLEARLY, CHANGAMIRE IS NO APOSTATE. INDEED, HE IS THE BEARER OF A TRADITION AS OLD, AND AS WAKANDAN, AS OUR OWN.

WHAT GOOD IS THIS, MY QUEEN? WE ARE AT WAR! A REGIMENT OF *HATUT ZERAZE* ARE IMPRISONED IN THE NORTH. TETU AMASSES FORCES TO THE SOUTH. HOW CAN WE SIT HERE IN CONFERENCE WITH OUR NATION, OUR HONOR, ON THE BRINK?

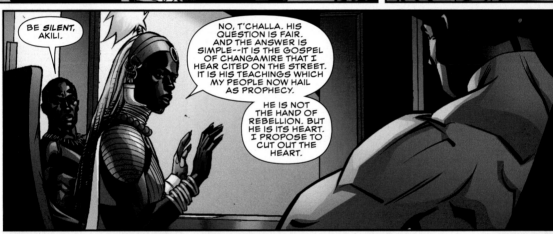

BE *SILENT*, AKILI.

NO, T'CHALLA. HIS QUESTION IS FAIR. AND THE ANSWER IS SIMPLE--IT IS THE GOSPEL OF CHANGAMIRE THAT I HEAR CITED ON THE STREET. IT IS HIS TEACHINGS WHICH MY PEOPLE NOW HAIL AS PROPHECY.

HE IS NOT THE HAND OF REBELLION. BUT HE IS ITS HEART. I PROPOSE TO CUT OUT THE HEART.

THIS WILL NOT BE HARD. CHANGAMIRE IS NOW BEING FORCED TO ACKNOWLEDGE THAT WHICH ALWAYS FOLLOWS REVOLUTION.

HE TOO BELIEVED HIS OWN MYTHS. AND NOW ALL HIS PHILOSOPHY IS CRACKING UNDER THE WEIGHT OF REALITY.

CHANGAMIRE IS NOT REBELLING. HE IS *MOURNING*.

I UNDERSTAND. BUT HOW THEN DO YOU SUGGEST WE HANDLE THIS MOURNER?

IN THE SAME WAY YOU WOULD HANDLE ANY OTHER MAN IN MOURNING...

...BY CONSOLING HIM, OF COURSE.

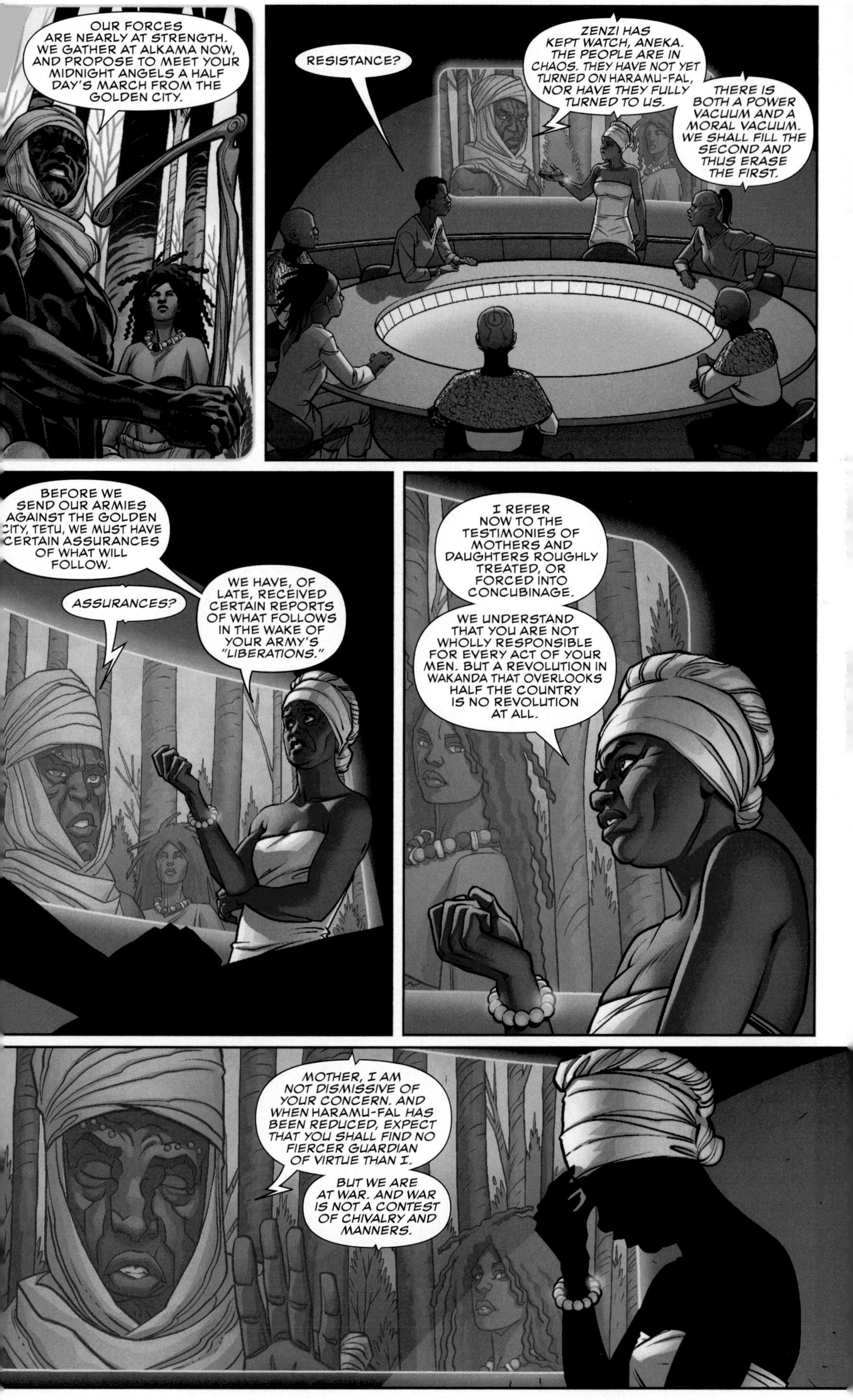
OUR FORCES ARE NEARLY AT STRENGTH. WE GATHER AT ALKAMA NOW, AND PROPOSE TO MEET YOUR MIDNIGHT ANGELS A HALF DAY'S MARCH FROM THE GOLDEN CITY.
RESISTANCE?
ZENZI HAS KEPT WATCH, ANEKA. THE PEOPLE ARE IN CHAOS. THEY HAVE NOT YET TURNED ON HARAMU-FAL, NOR HAVE THEY FULLY TURNED TO US.
THERE IS BOTH A POWER VACUUM AND A MORAL VACUUM. WE SHALL FILL THE SECOND AND THUS ERASE THE FIRST.
BEFORE WE SEND OUR ARMIES AGAINST THE GOLDEN CITY, TETU, WE MUST HAVE CERTAIN ASSURANCES OF WHAT WILL FOLLOW.
ASSURANCES?
WE HAVE, OF LATE, RECEIVED CERTAIN REPORTS OF WHAT FOLLOWS IN THE WAKE OF YOUR ARMY'S "LIBERATIONS."
I REFER NOW TO THE TESTIMONIES OF MOTHERS AND DAUGHTERS ROUGHLY TREATED, OR FORCED INTO CONCUBINAGE.
WE UNDERSTAND THAT YOU ARE NOT WHOLLY RESPONSIBLE FOR EVERY ACT OF YOUR MEN. BUT A REVOLUTION IN WAKANDA THAT OVERLOOKS HALF THE COUNTRY IS NO REVOLUTION AT ALL.
MOTHER, I AM NOT DISMISSIVE OF YOUR CONCERN. AND WHEN HARAMU-FAL HAS BEEN REDUCED, EXPECT THAT YOU SHALL FIND NO FIERCER GUARDIAN OF VIRTUE THAN I.
BUT WE ARE AT WAR. AND WAR IS NOT A CONTEST OF CHIVALRY AND MANNERS.

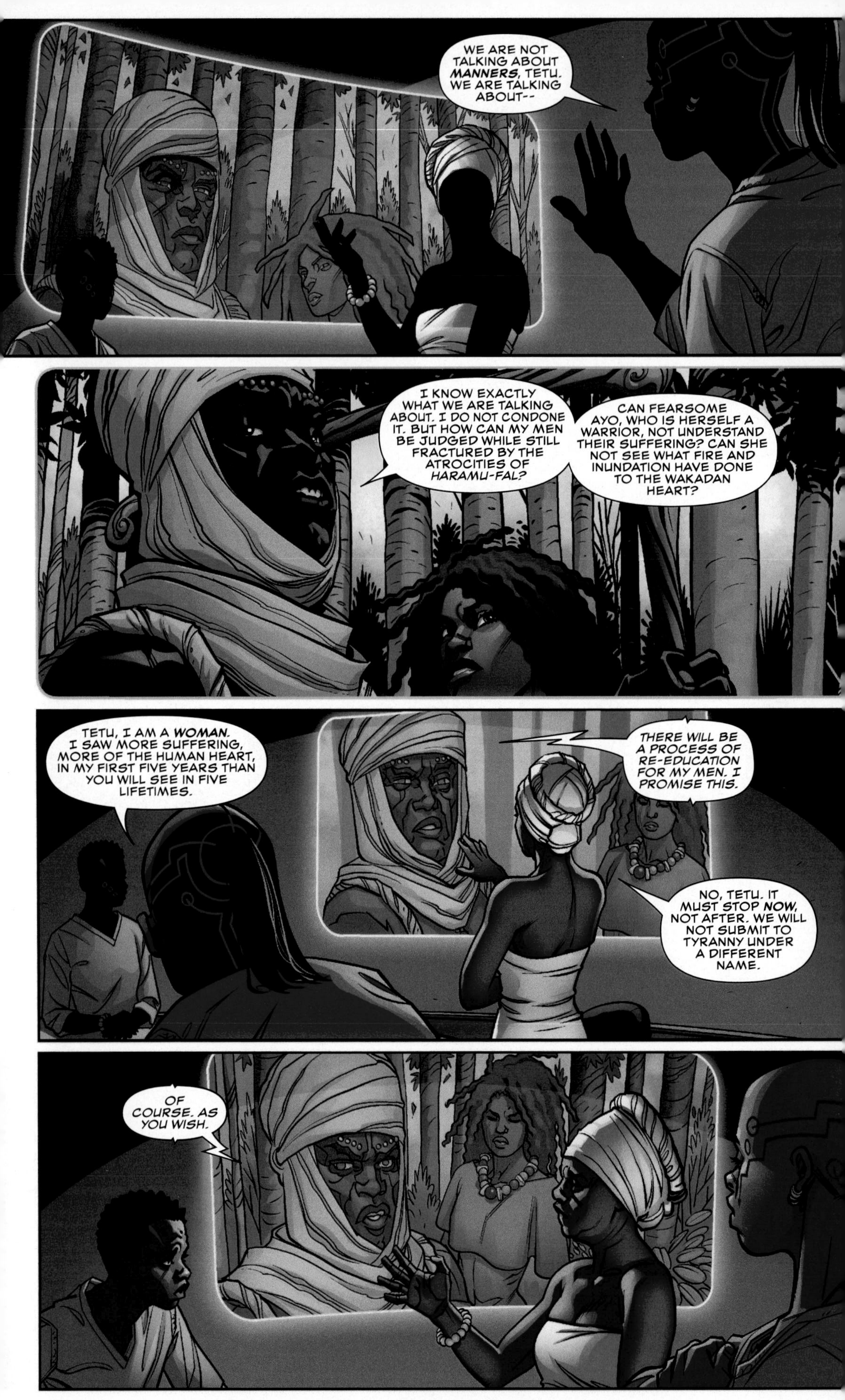
WE ARE NOT TALKING ABOUT *MANNERS*, TETU. WE ARE TALKING ABOUT--
I KNOW EXACTLY WHAT WE ARE TALKING ABOUT. I DO NOT CONDONE IT. BUT HOW CAN MY MEN BE JUDGED WHILE STILL FRACTURED BY THE ATROCITIES OF *HARAMU-FAL*?
CAN FEARSOME AYO, WHO IS HERSELF A WARRIOR, NOT UNDERSTAND THEIR SUFFERING? CAN SHE NOT SEE WHAT FIRE AND INUNDATION HAVE DONE TO THE WAKADAN HEART?
TETU, I AM A *WOMAN*. I SAW MORE SUFFERING, MORE OF THE HUMAN HEART, IN MY FIRST FIVE YEARS THAN YOU WILL SEE IN FIVE LIFETIMES.
THERE WILL BE A PROCESS OF RE-EDUCATION FOR MY MEN. I PROMISE THIS.
NO, TETU. IT MUST *STOP NOW*, NOT AFTER. WE WILL NOT SUBMIT TO TYRANNY UNDER A DIFFERENT NAME.
OF COURSE. AS YOU WISH.

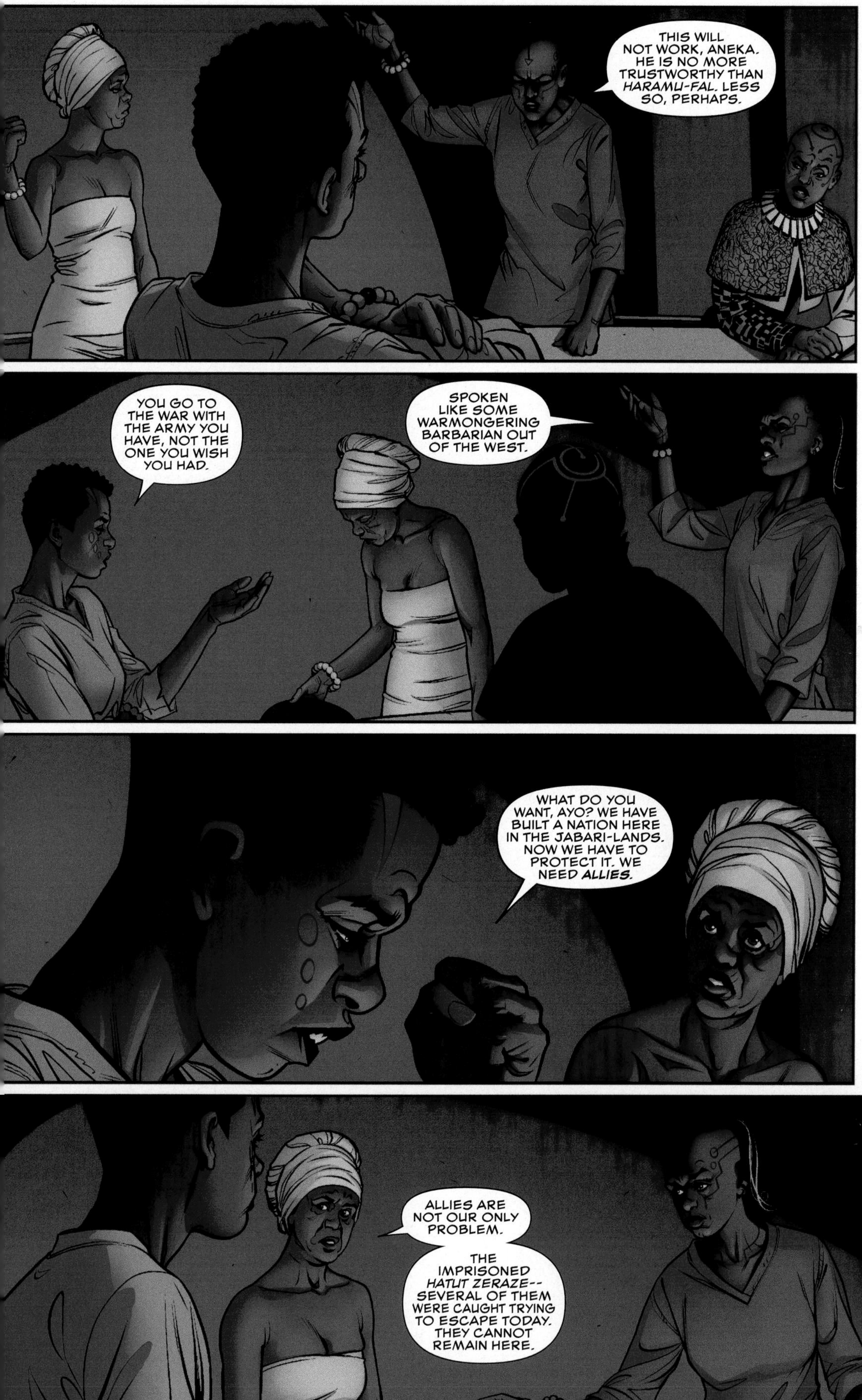
THIS WILL NOT WORK, ANEKA. HE IS NO MORE TRUSTWORTHY THAN *HARAMU-FAL*. LESS SO, PERHAPS.
YOU GO TO THE WAR WITH THE ARMY YOU HAVE, NOT THE ONE YOU WISH YOU HAD.
SPOKEN LIKE SOME WARMONGERING BARBARIAN OUT OF THE WEST.
WHAT DO YOU WANT, AYO? WE HAVE BUILT A NATION HERE IN THE JABARI-LANDS. NOW WE HAVE TO PROTECT IT. WE NEED *ALLIES*.
ALLIES ARE NOT OUR ONLY PROBLEM.
THE IMPRISONED *HATUT ZERAZE*-- SEVERAL OF THEM WERE CAUGHT TRYING TO ESCAPE TODAY. THEY CANNOT REMAIN HERE.

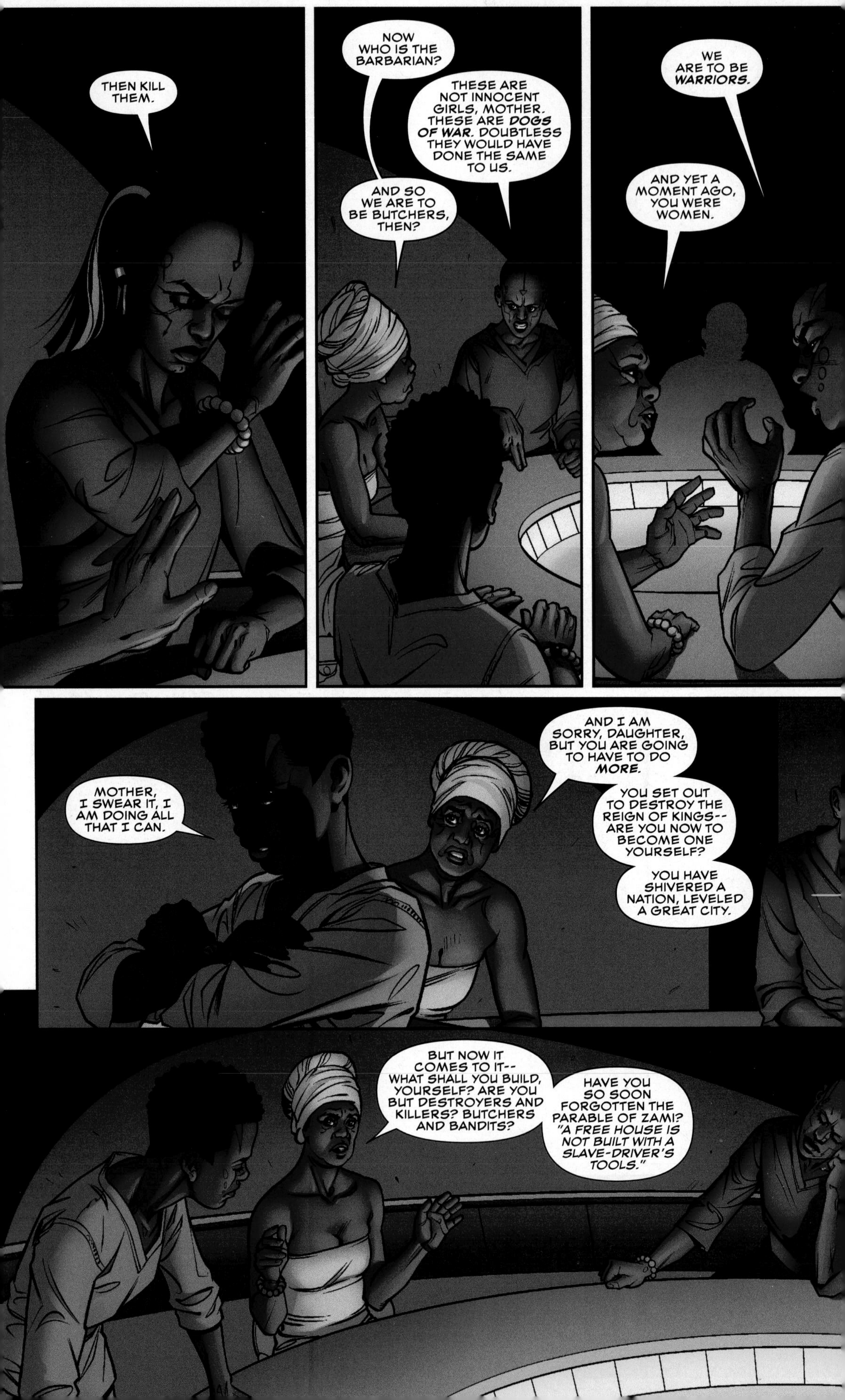
THEN KILL THEM.
NOW WHO IS THE BARBARIAN?
THESE ARE NOT INNOCENT GIRLS, MOTHER. THESE ARE DOGS OF WAR. DOUBTLESS THEY WOULD HAVE DONE THE SAME TO US.
AND SO WE ARE TO BE BUTCHERS, THEN?
WE ARE TO BE WARRIORS.
AND YET A MOMENT AGO, YOU WERE WOMEN.
MOTHER, I SWEAR IT, I AM DOING ALL THAT I CAN.
AND I AM SORRY, DAUGHTER, BUT YOU ARE GOING TO HAVE TO DO MORE.
YOU SET OUT TO DESTROY THE REIGN OF KINGS-- ARE YOU NOW TO BECOME ONE YOURSELF?
YOU HAVE SHIVERED A NATION, LEVELED A GREAT CITY.
BUT NOW IT COMES TO IT-- WHAT SHALL YOU BUILD, YOURSELF? ARE YOU BUT DESTROYERS AND KILLERS? BUTCHERS AND BANDITS?
HAVE YOU SO SOON FORGOTTEN THE PARABLE OF ZAMI? "A FREE HOUSE IS NOT BUILT WITH A SLAVE-DRIVER'S TOOLS."

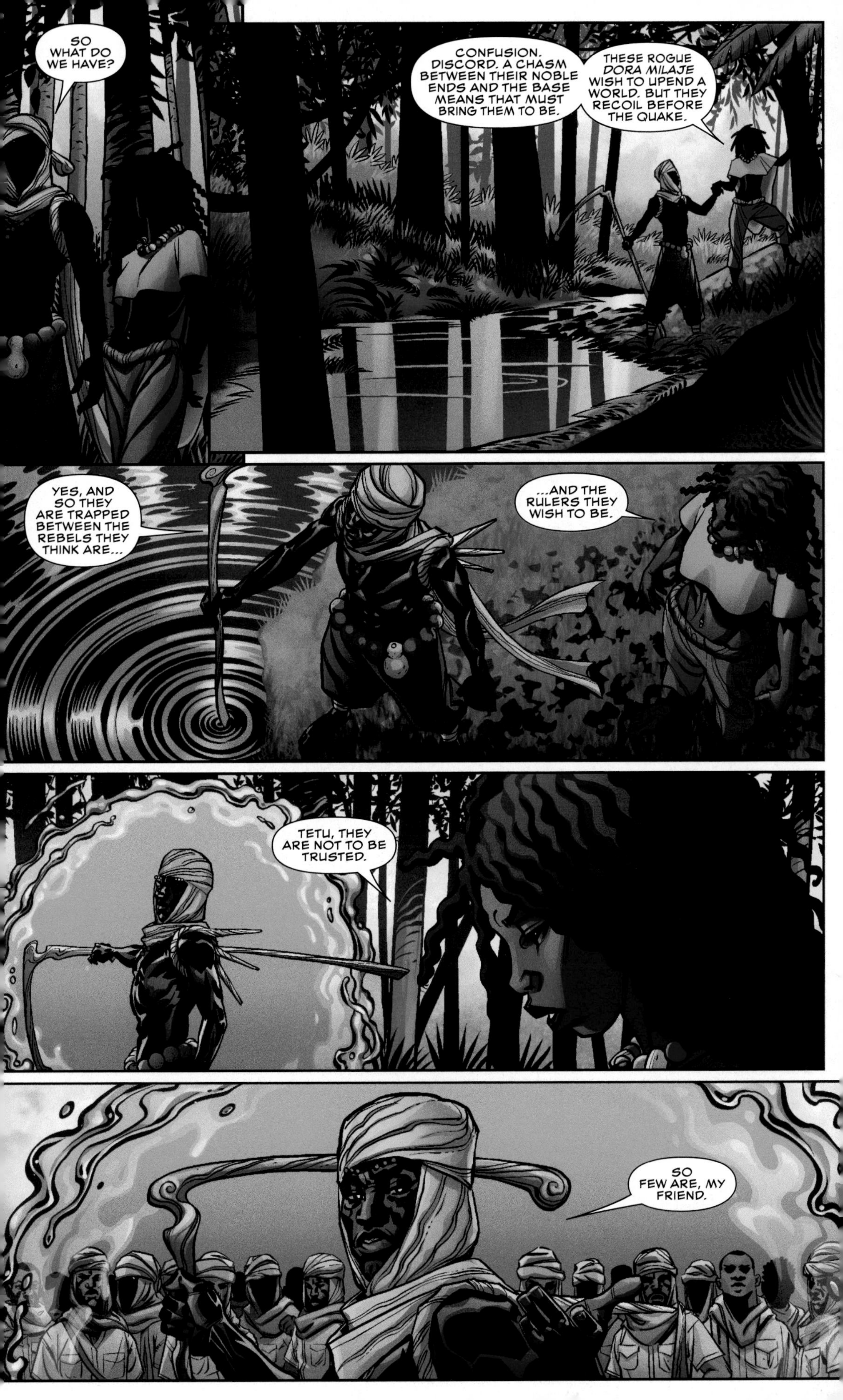
SO WHAT DO WE HAVE?
CONFUSION. DISCORD. A CHASM BETWEEN THEIR NOBLE ENDS AND THE BASE MEANS THAT MUST BRING THEM TO BE.
THESE ROGUE *DORA MILAJE* WISH TO UPEND A WORLD. BUT THEY RECOIL BEFORE THE QUAKE.
YES, AND SO THEY ARE TRAPPED BETWEEN THE REBELS THEY THINK ARE...
...AND THE RULERS THEY WISH TO BE.
TETU, THEY ARE NOT TO BE TRUSTED.
SO FEW ARE, MY FRIEND.

AT ALL EVENTS, TRUST IS NO FOUNDATION FOR OUR NEW COUNTRY. FOR THAT, WE SHALL REQUIRE SOMETHING MORE.

YES. SO LET US BEGIN WITH *RAGE*.

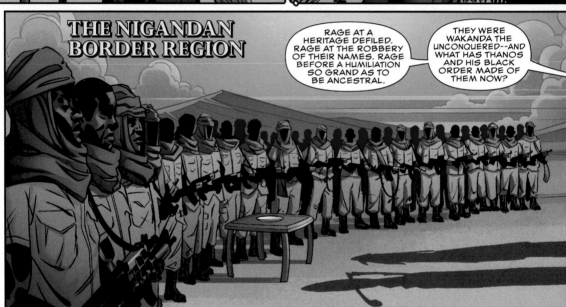

THE NIGANDAN BORDER REGION

RAGE AT A HERITAGE DEFILED. RAGE AT THE ROBBERY OF THEIR NAMES. RAGE BEFORE A HUMILIATION SO GRAND AS TO BE ANCESTRAL.

THEY WERE WAKANDA THE UNCONQUERED--AND WHAT HAS THANOS AND HIS BLACK ORDER MADE OF THEM NOW?

BUT RAGE ALONE IS AIMLESS, UNTAMED, INEPT. WHEN WHAT WE NEED IS *HOPE*.

HOPE FOR A WORLD WHERE THEY ARE THEIR ONLY MASTERS, AND THEIR HEADS ARE HELD HIGH IN THE PRESENCE OF THEIR DAUGHTERS.

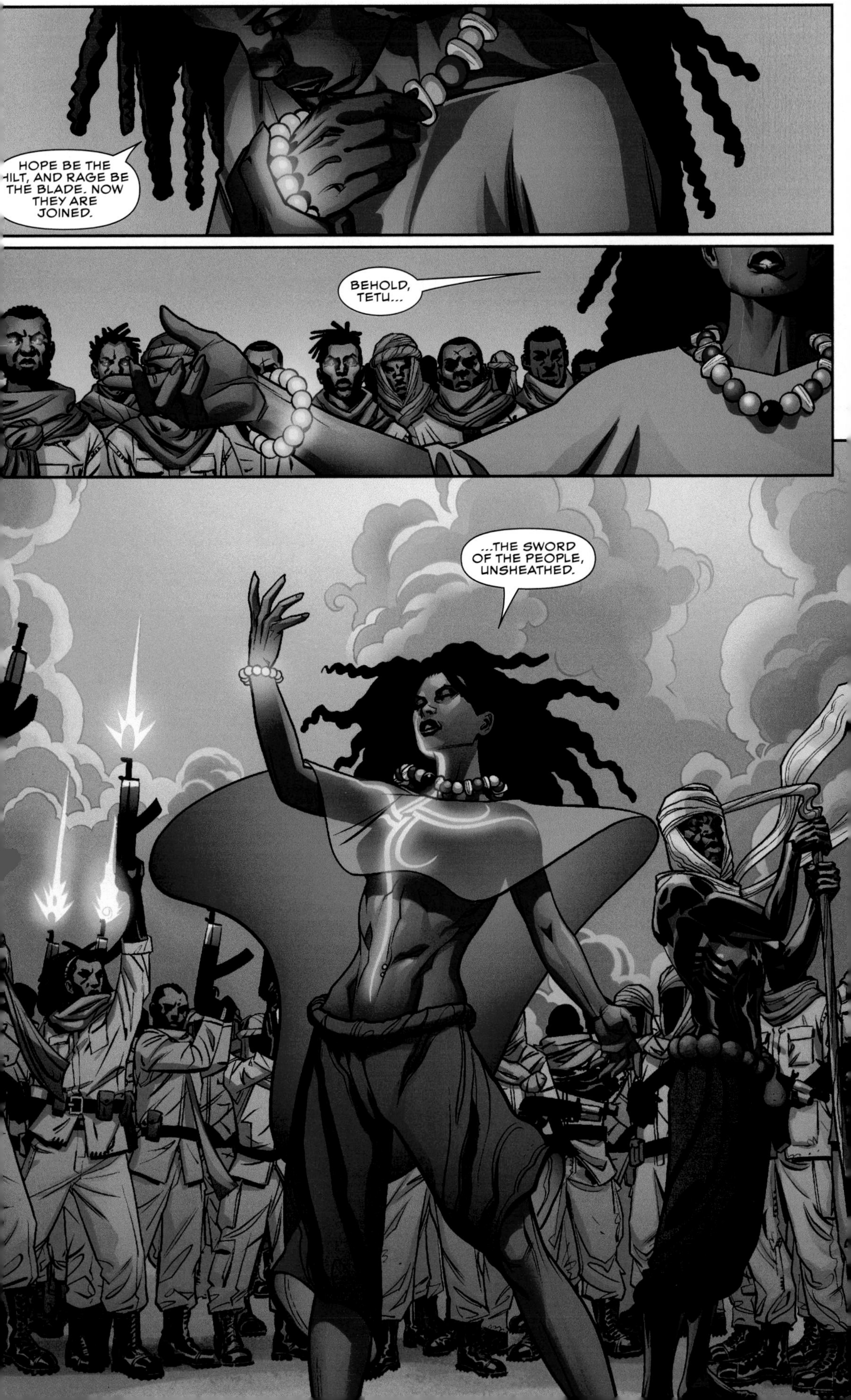
HOPE BE THE HILT, AND RAGE BE THE BLADE. NOW THEY ARE JOINED.
BEHOLD, TETU...
...THE SWORD OF THE PEOPLE, UNSHEATHED.

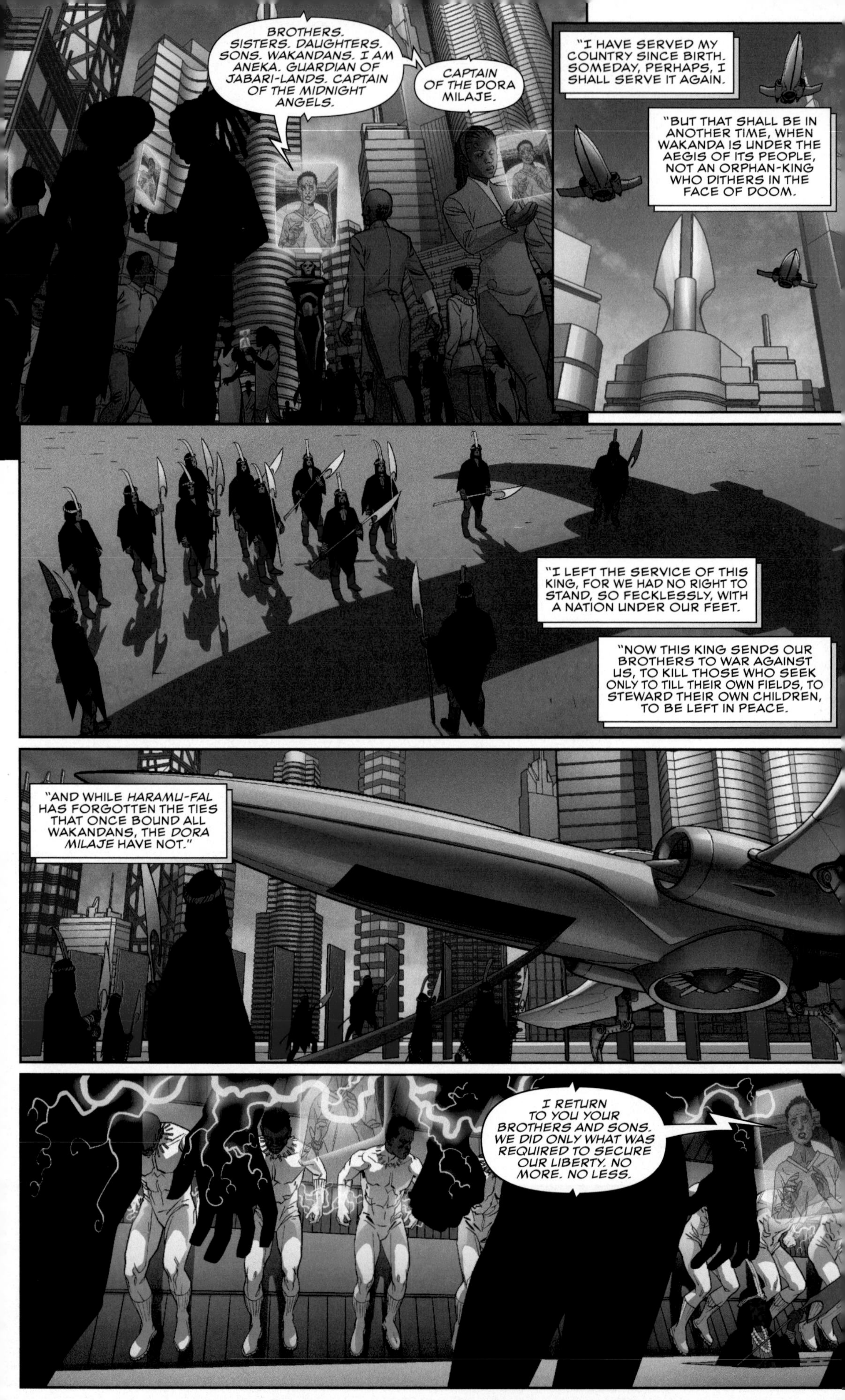

BROTHERS. SISTERS. DAUGHTERS. SONS. WAKANDANS. I AM ANEKA. GUARDIAN OF JABARI-LANDS. CAPTAIN OF THE MIDNIGHT ANGELS.
CAPTAIN OF THE DORA MILAJE.
"I HAVE SERVED MY COUNTRY SINCE BIRTH. SOMEDAY, PERHAPS, I SHALL SERVE IT AGAIN.
"BUT THAT SHALL BE IN ANOTHER TIME, WHEN WAKANDA IS UNDER THE AEGIS OF ITS PEOPLE, NOT AN ORPHAN-KING WHO DITHERS IN THE FACE OF DOOM.
"I LEFT THE SERVICE OF THIS KING, FOR WE HAD NO RIGHT TO STAND, SO FECKLESSLY, WITH A NATION UNDER OUR FEET.
"NOW THIS KING SENDS OUR BROTHERS TO WAR AGAINST US, TO KILL THOSE WHO SEEK ONLY TO TILL THEIR OWN FIELDS, TO STEWARD THEIR OWN CHILDREN, TO BE LEFT IN PEACE.
"AND WHILE HARAMU-FAL HAS FORGOTTEN THE TIES THAT ONCE BOUND ALL WAKANDANS, THE DORA MILAJE HAVE NOT."
I RETURN TO YOU YOUR BROTHERS AND SONS. WE DID ONLY WHAT WAS REQUIRED TO SECURE OUR LIBERTY. NO MORE. NO LESS.

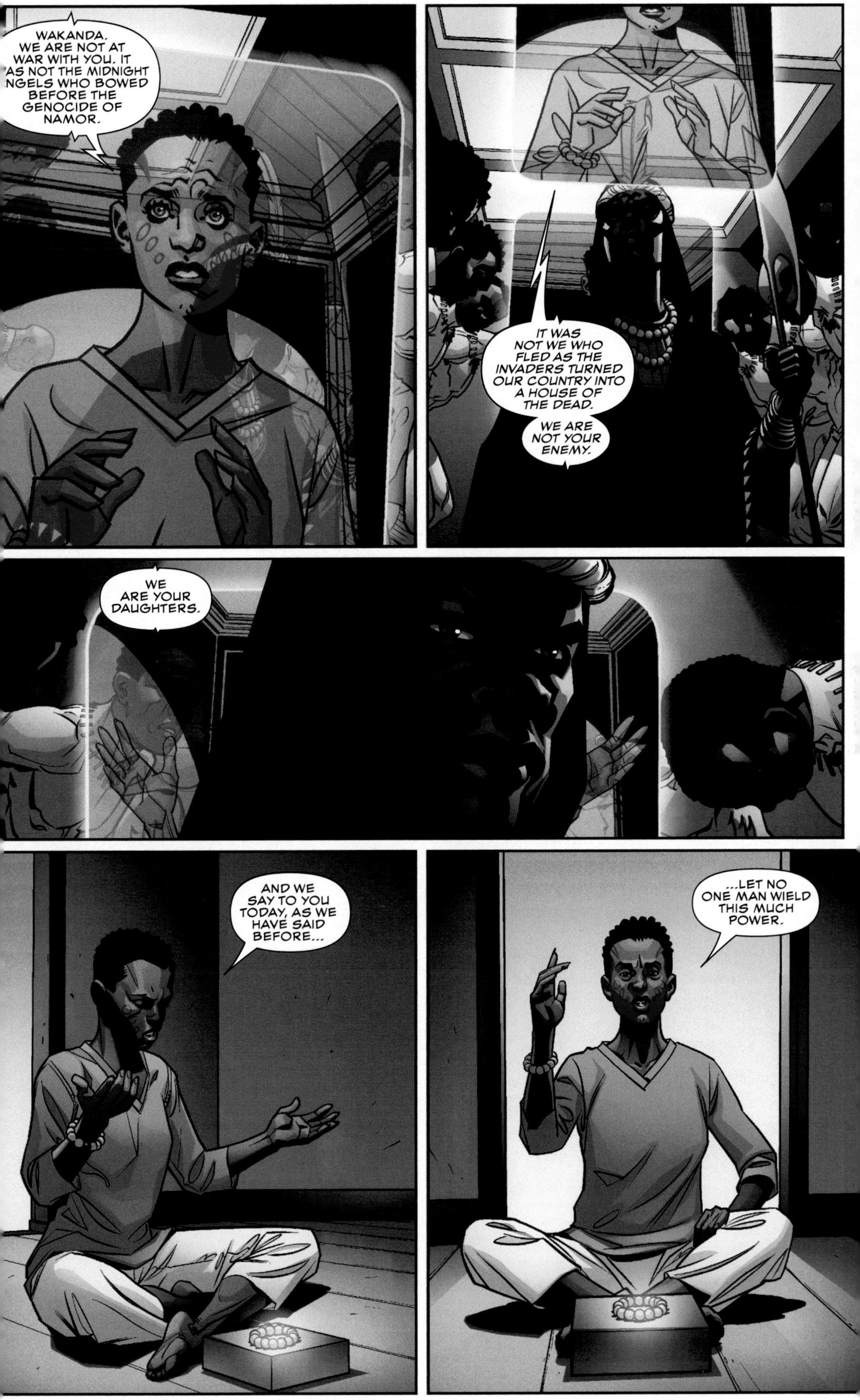
WAKANDA. WE ARE NOT AT WAR WITH YOU. IT AS NOT THE MIDNIGHT NGELS WHO BOWED BEFORE THE GENOCIDE OF NAMOR.
IT WAS NOT WE WHO FLED AS THE INVADERS TURNED OUR COUNTRY INTO A HOUSE OF THE DEAD.
WE ARE NOT YOUR ENEMY.
WE ARE YOUR DAUGHTERS.
AND WE SAY TO YOU TODAY, AS WE HAVE SAID BEFORE...
...LET NO ONE MAN WIELD THIS MUCH POWER.

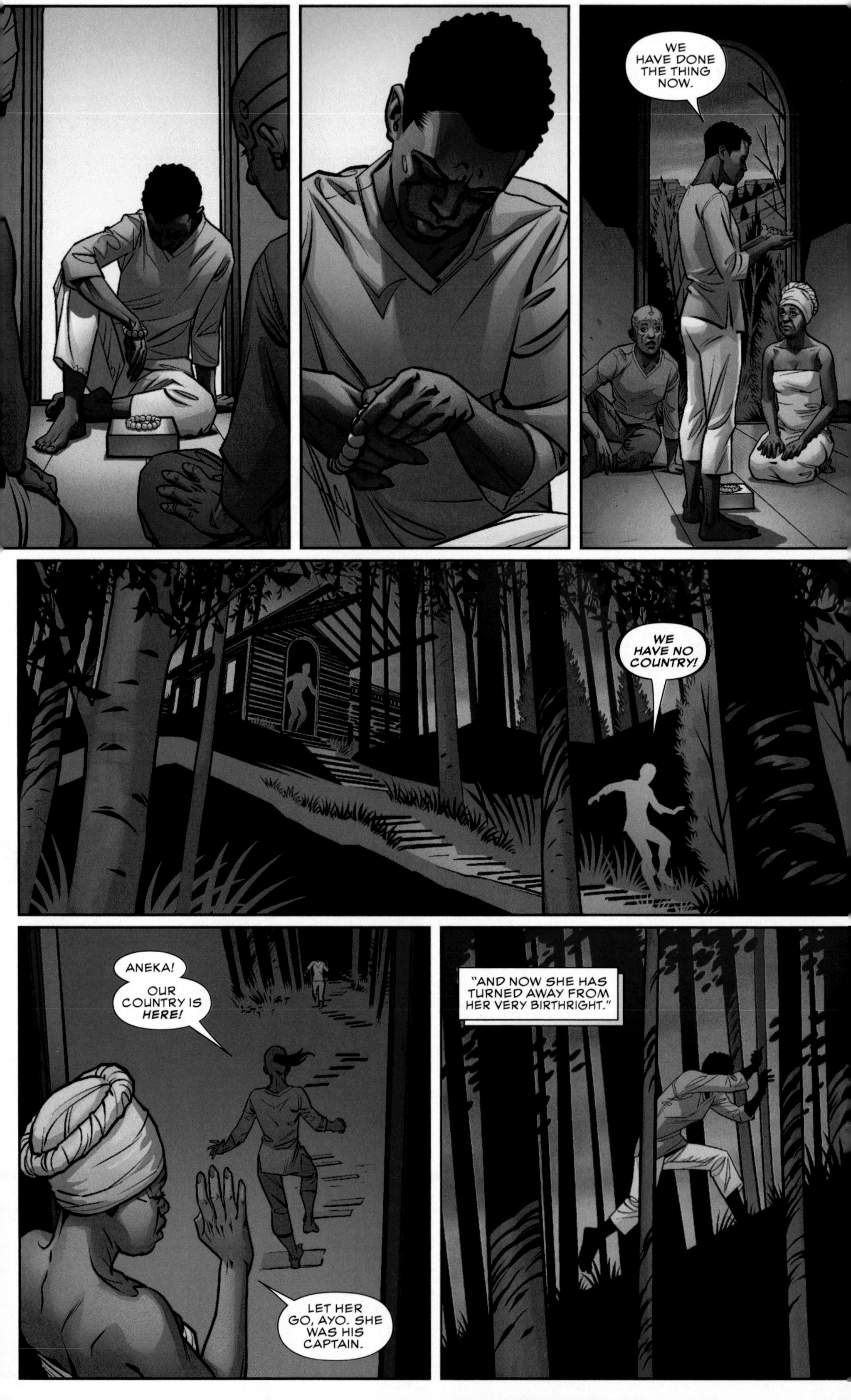
WE HAVE DONE THE THING NOW.
WE HAVE NO COUNTRY!
ANEKA!
OUR COUNTRY IS *HERE!*
LET HER GO, AYO. SHE WAS HIS CAPTAIN.
"AND NOW SHE HAS TURNED AWAY FROM HER VERY BIRTHRIGHT."

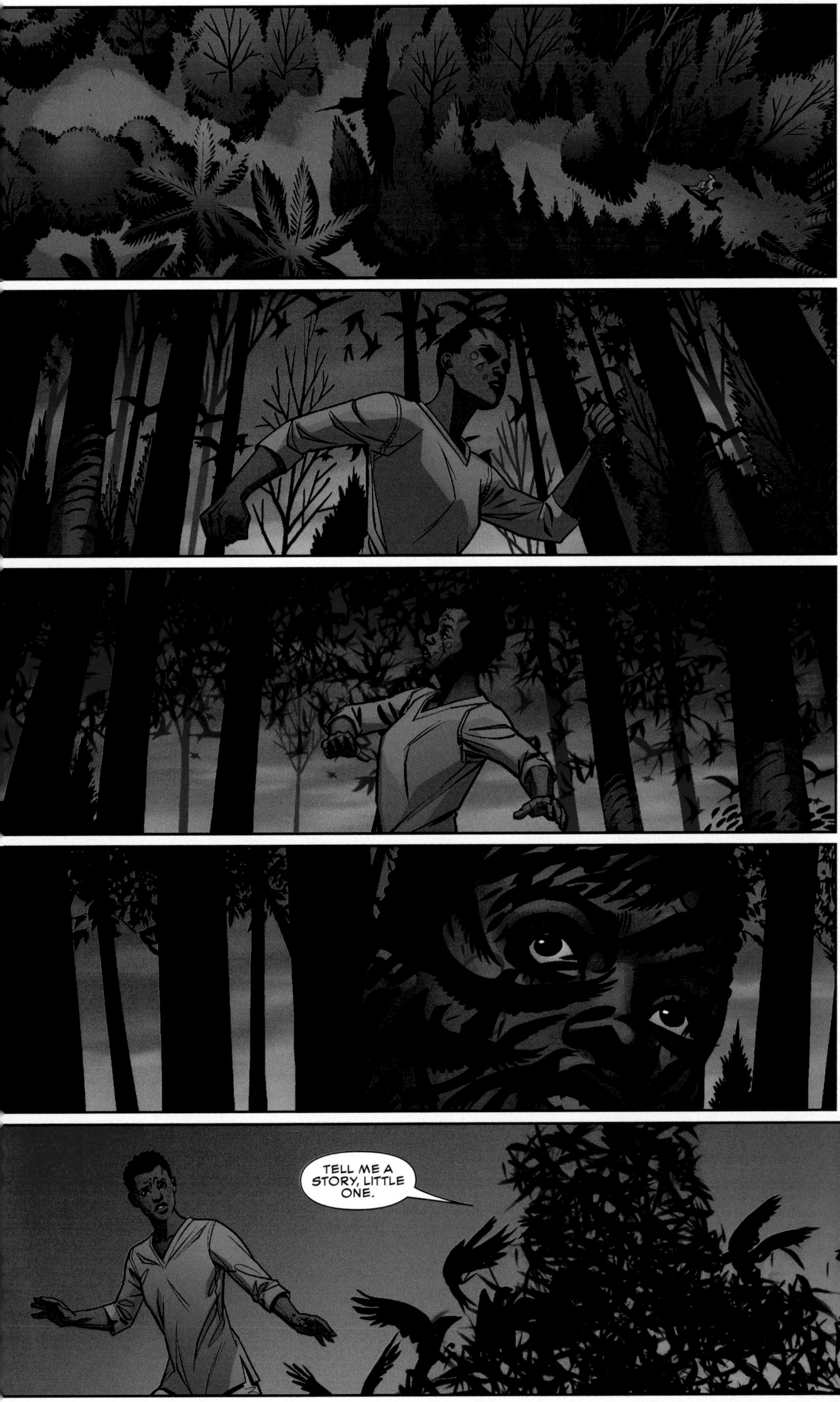
TELL ME A STORY, LITTLE ONE.

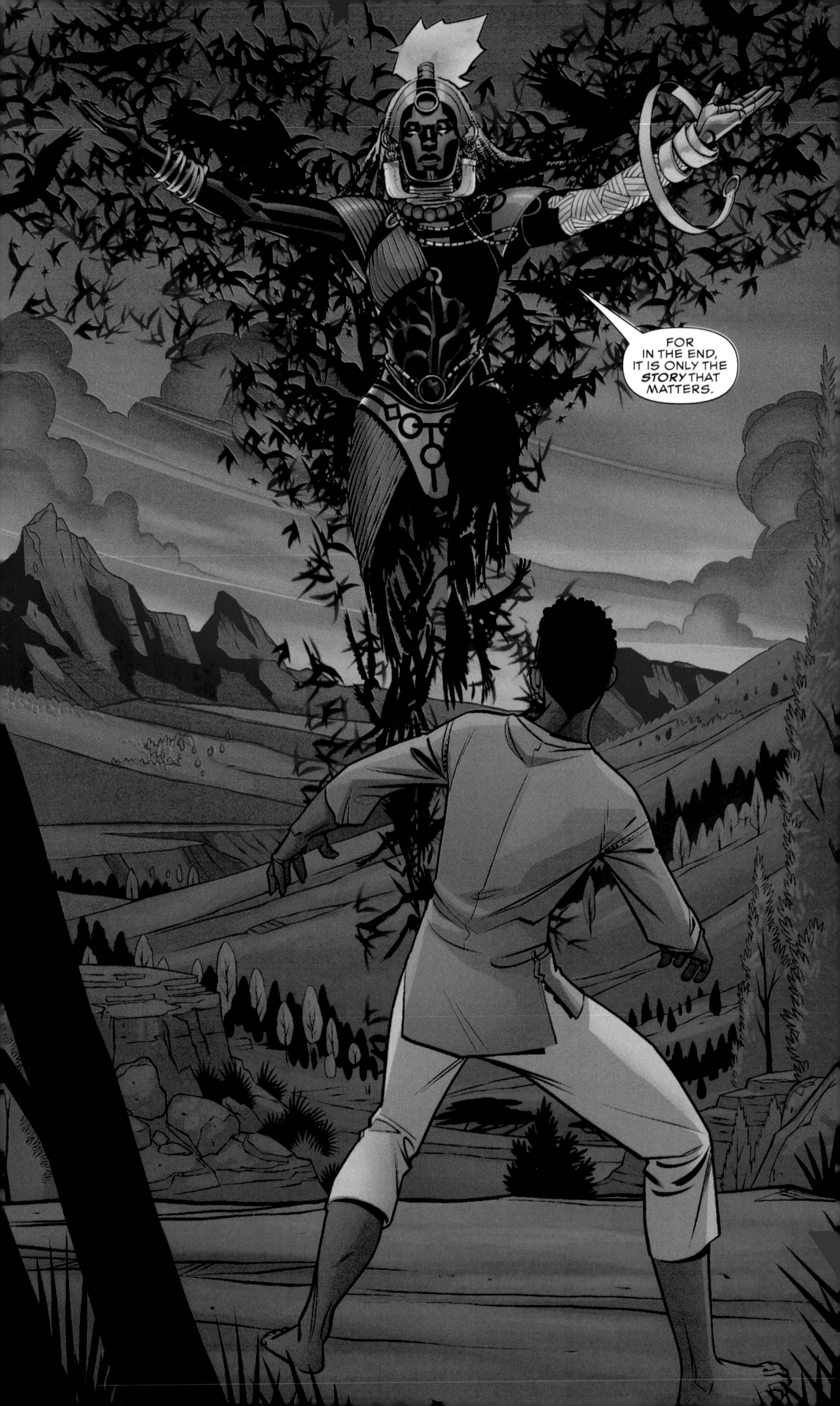
FOR IN THE END, IT IS ONLY THE STORY THAT MATTERS.

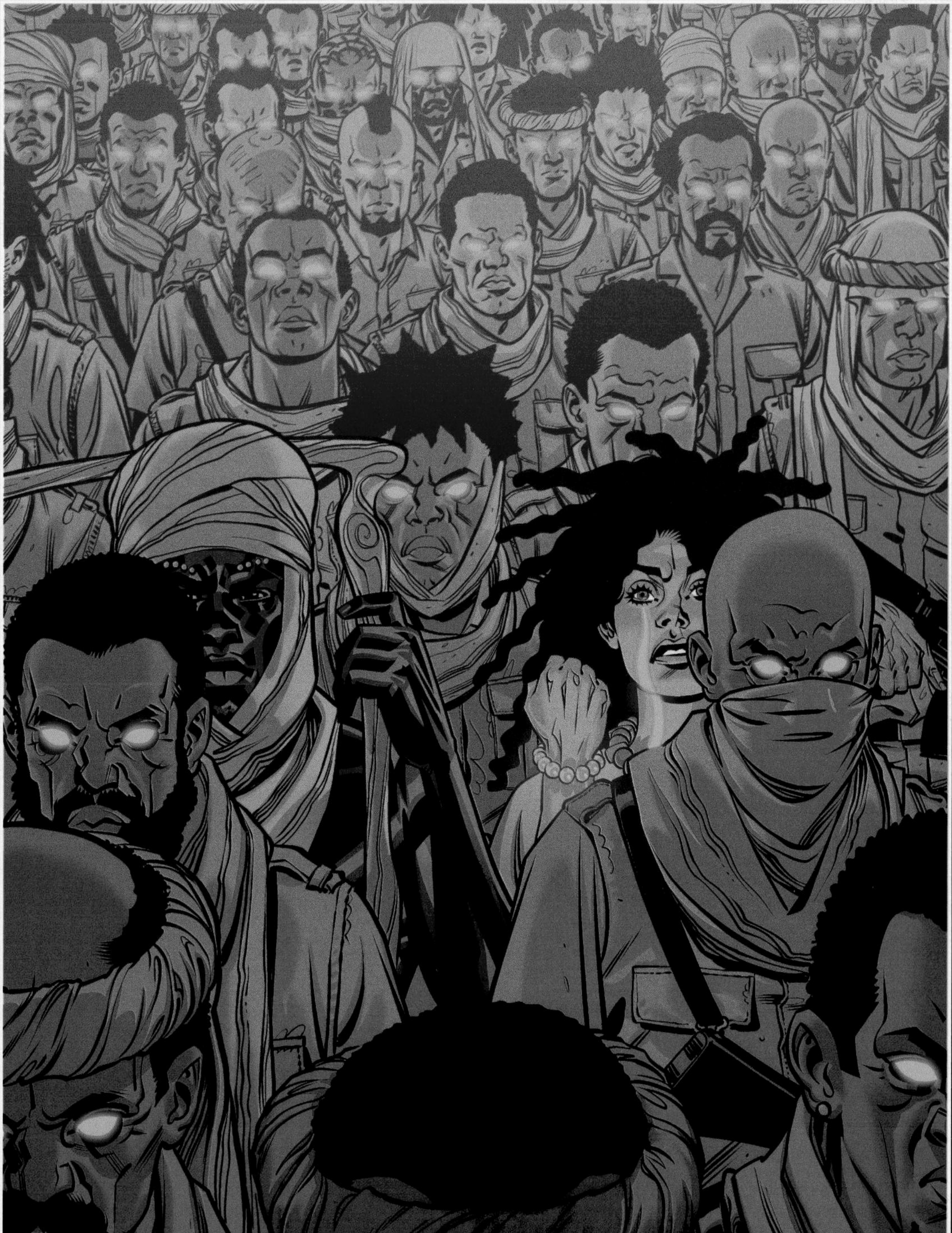

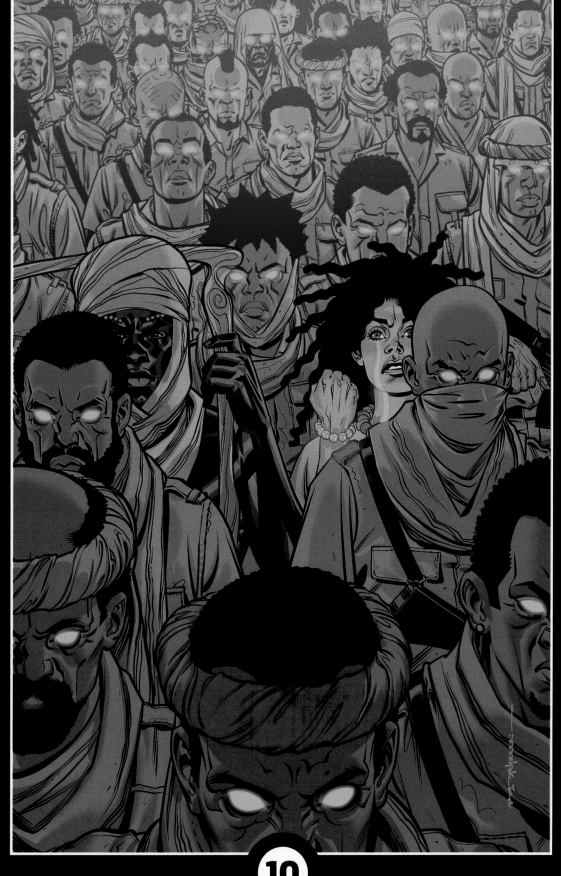

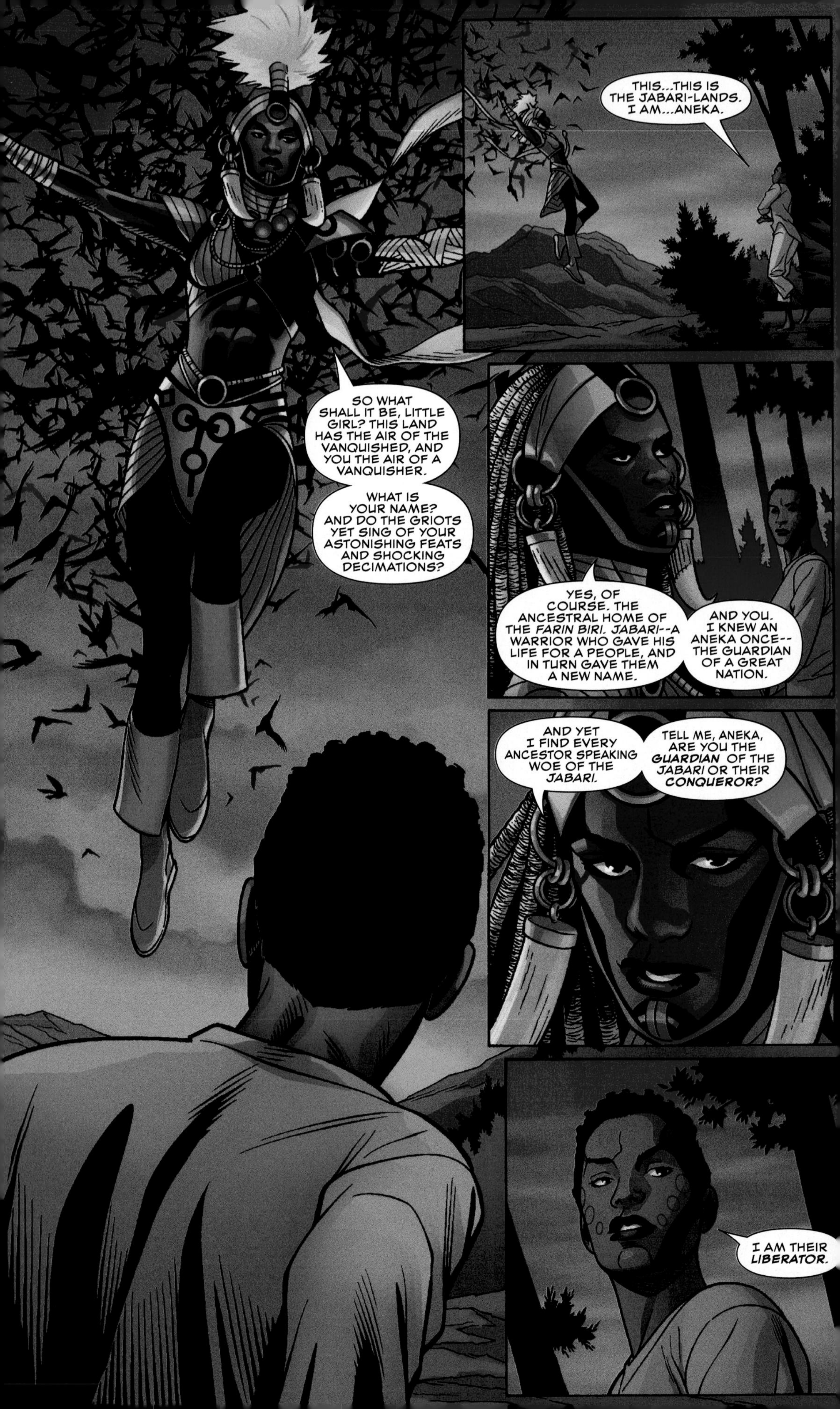
THIS...THIS IS THE JABARI-LANDS. I AM...ANEKA.
SO WHAT SHALL IT BE, LITTLE GIRL? THIS LAND HAS THE AIR OF THE VANQUISHED, AND YOU THE AIR OF A VANQUISHER.
WHAT IS YOUR NAME? AND DO THE GRIOTS YET SING OF YOUR ASTONISHING FEATS AND SHOCKING DECIMATIONS?
YES, OF COURSE. THE ANCESTRAL HOME OF THE *FARIN BIRI. JABARI*--A WARRIOR WHO GAVE HIS LIFE FOR A PEOPLE, AND IN TURN GAVE THEM A NEW NAME.
AND YOU. I KNEW AN ANEKA ONCE--THE GUARDIAN OF A GREAT NATION.
AND YET I FIND EVERY ANCESTOR SPEAKING WOE OF THE *JABARI.*
TELL ME, ANEKA, ARE YOU THE ***GUARDIAN*** OF THE *JABARI* OR THEIR ***CONQUEROR?***
I AM THEIR ***LIBERATOR.***

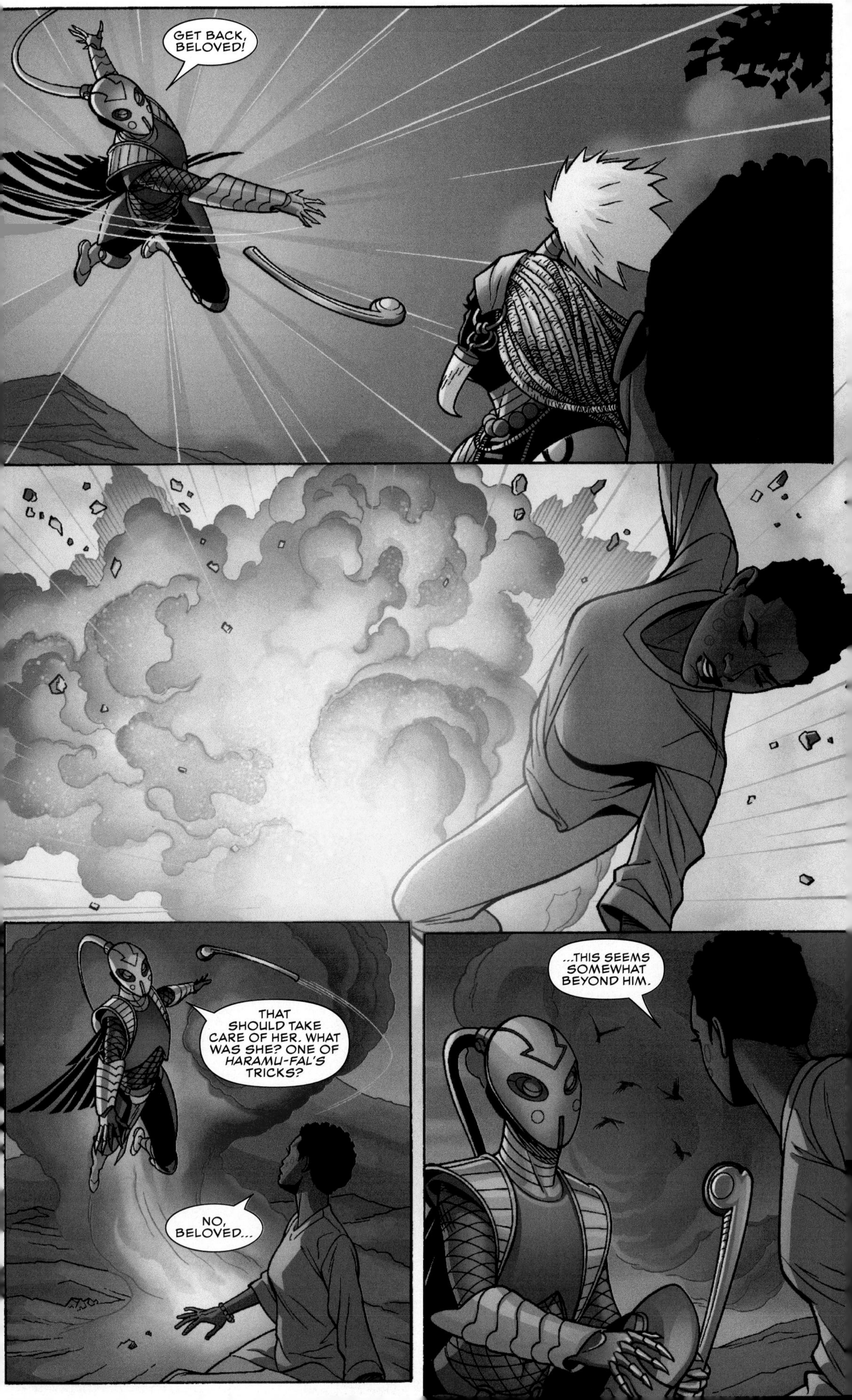
GET BACK, BELOVED!
THAT SHOULD TAKE CARE OF HER. WHAT WAS SHE? ONE OF *HARAMU-FAL'S* TRICKS?
NO, BELOVED...
...THIS SEEMS SOMEWHAT BEYOND HIM.

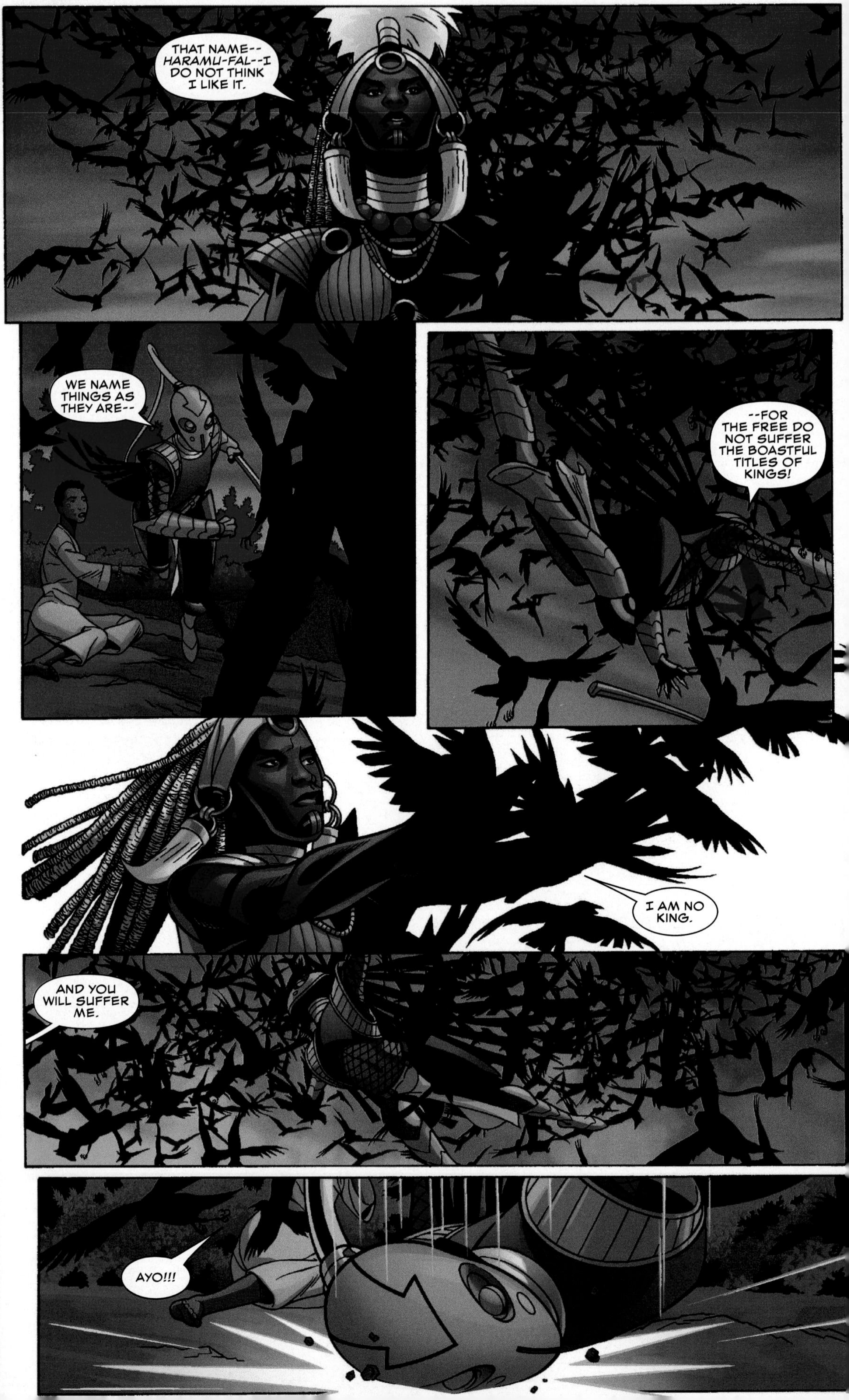
THAT NAME--
HARAMU-FAL--I DO NOT THINK I LIKE IT.
WE NAME THINGS AS THEY ARE--
--FOR THE FREE DO NOT SUFFER THE BOASTFUL TITLES OF KINGS!
I AM NO KING.
AND YOU WILL SUFFER ME.
AYO!!!

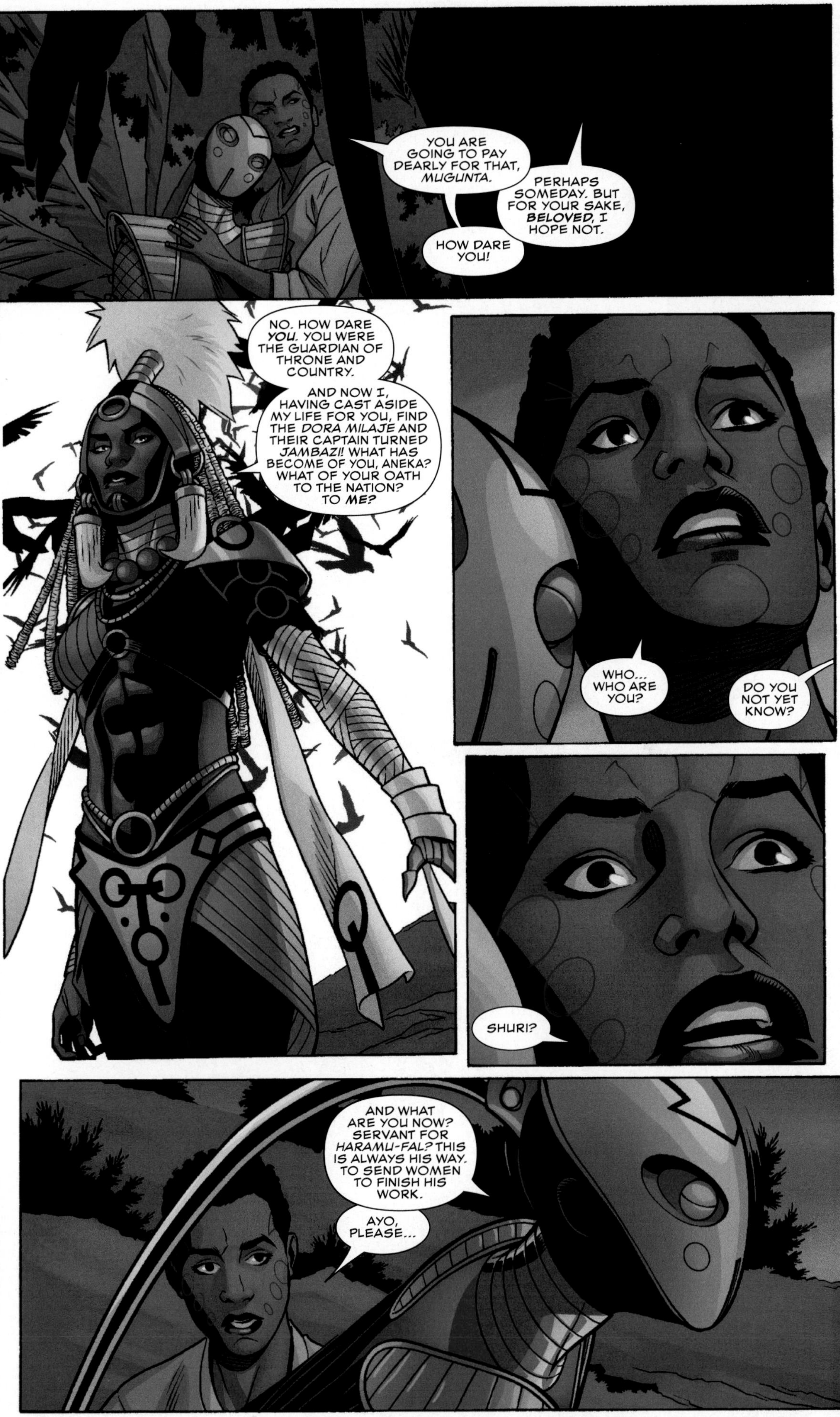
YOU ARE GOING TO PAY DEARLY FOR THAT, MUGUNTA.
HOW DARE YOU!
PERHAPS SOMEDAY. BUT FOR YOUR SAKE, BELOVED, I HOPE NOT.
NO. HOW DARE YOU. YOU WERE THE GUARDIAN OF THRONE AND COUNTRY.
AND NOW I, HAVING CAST ASIDE MY LIFE FOR YOU, FIND THE DORA MILAJE AND THEIR CAPTAIN TURNED JAMBAZI! WHAT HAS BECOME OF YOU, ANEKA? WHAT OF YOUR OATH TO THE NATION? TO ME?
WHO... WHO ARE YOU?
DO YOU NOT YET KNOW?
SHURI?
AND WHAT ARE YOU NOW? SERVANT FOR HARAMU-FAL? THIS IS ALWAYS HIS WAY. TO SEND WOMEN TO FINISH HIS WORK.
AYO, PLEASE...

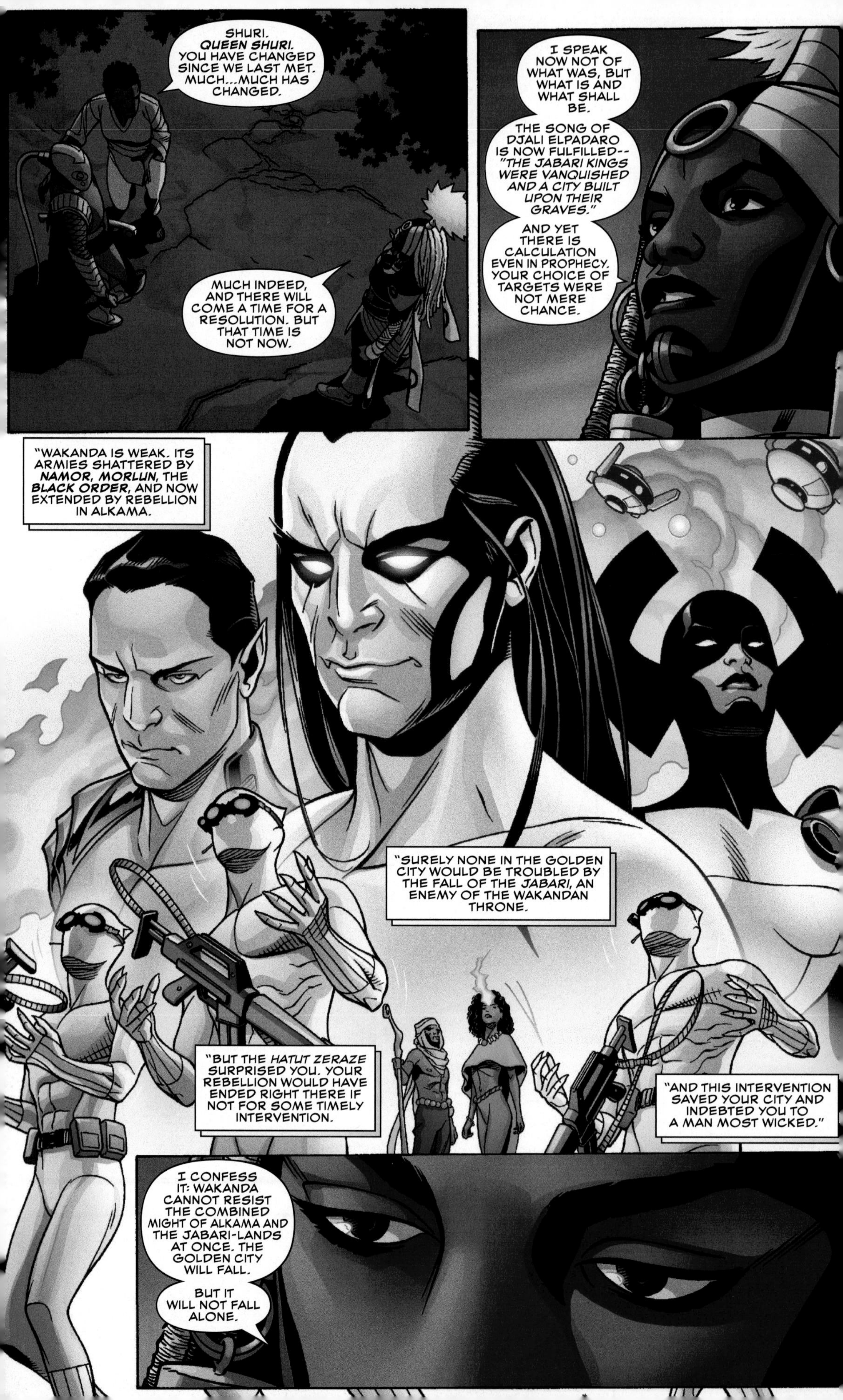
SHURI. QUEEN SHURI. YOU HAVE CHANGED SINCE WE LAST MET. MUCH...MUCH HAS CHANGED.
MUCH INDEED, AND THERE WILL COME A TIME FOR A RESOLUTION. BUT THAT TIME IS NOT NOW.
I SPEAK NOW NOT OF WHAT WAS, BUT WHAT IS AND WHAT SHALL BE.
THE SONG OF DJALI ELPADARO IS NOW FULFILLED-- "THE JABARI KINGS WERE VANQUISHED AND A CITY BUILT UPON THEIR GRAVES."
AND YET THERE IS CALCULATION EVEN IN PROPHECY. YOUR CHOICE OF TARGETS WERE NOT MERE CHANCE.
"WAKANDA IS WEAK. ITS ARMIES SHATTERED BY NAMOR, MORLUN, THE BLACK ORDER, AND NOW EXTENDED BY REBELLION IN ALKAMA.
"SURELY NONE IN THE GOLDEN CITY WOULD BE TROUBLED BY THE FALL OF THE JABARI, AN ENEMY OF THE WAKANDAN THRONE.
"BUT THE HATUT ZERAZE SURPRISED YOU. YOUR REBELLION WOULD HAVE ENDED RIGHT THERE IF NOT FOR SOME TIMELY INTERVENTION.
"AND THIS INTERVENTION SAVED YOUR CITY AND INDEBTED YOU TO A MAN MOST WICKED."
I CONFESS IT: WAKANDA CANNOT RESIST THE COMBINED MIGHT OF ALKAMA AND THE JABARI-LANDS AT ONCE. THE GOLDEN CITY WILL FALL.
BUT IT WILL NOT FALL ALONE.

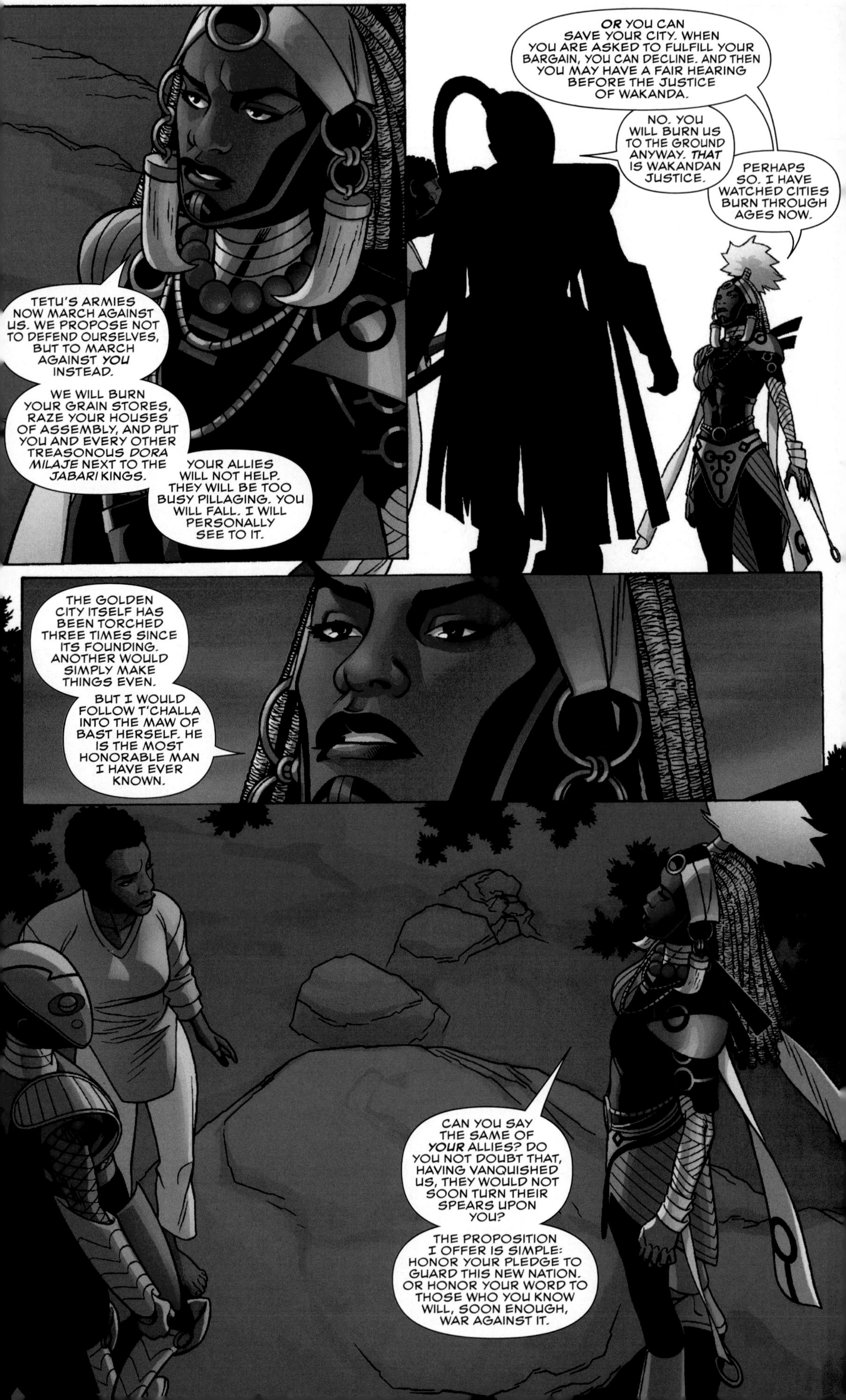
TETU'S ARMIES NOW MARCH AGAINST US. WE PROPOSE NOT TO DEFEND OURSELVES, BUT TO MARCH AGAINST *YOU* INSTEAD.
WE WILL BURN YOUR GRAIN STORES, RAZE YOUR HOUSES OF ASSEMBLY, AND PUT YOU AND EVERY OTHER TREASONOUS *DORA MILAJE* NEXT TO THE *JABARI* KINGS.
YOUR ALLIES WILL NOT HELP. THEY WILL BE TOO BUSY PILLAGING. YOU WILL FALL. I WILL PERSONALLY SEE TO IT.
OR YOU CAN SAVE YOUR CITY. WHEN YOU ARE ASKED TO FULFILL YOUR BARGAIN, YOU CAN DECLINE. AND THEN YOU MAY HAVE A FAIR HEARING BEFORE THE JUSTICE OF WAKANDA.
NO. YOU WILL BURN US TO THE GROUND ANYWAY. *THAT* IS WAKANDAN JUSTICE.
PERHAPS SO. I HAVE WATCHED CITIES BURN THROUGH AGES NOW.
THE GOLDEN CITY ITSELF HAS BEEN TORCHED THREE TIMES SINCE ITS FOUNDING. ANOTHER WOULD SIMPLY MAKE THINGS EVEN.
BUT I WOULD FOLLOW T'CHALLA INTO THE MAW OF BAST HERSELF. HE IS THE MOST HONORABLE MAN I HAVE EVER KNOWN.
CAN YOU SAY THE SAME OF *YOUR* ALLIES? DO YOU NOT DOUBT THAT, HAVING VANQUISHED US, THEY WOULD NOT SOON TURN THEIR SPEARS UPON YOU?
THE PROPOSITION I OFFER IS SIMPLE: HONOR YOUR PLEDGE TO GUARD THIS NEW NATION. OR HONOR YOUR WORD TO THOSE WHO YOU KNOW WILL, SOON ENOUGH, WAR AGAINST IT.

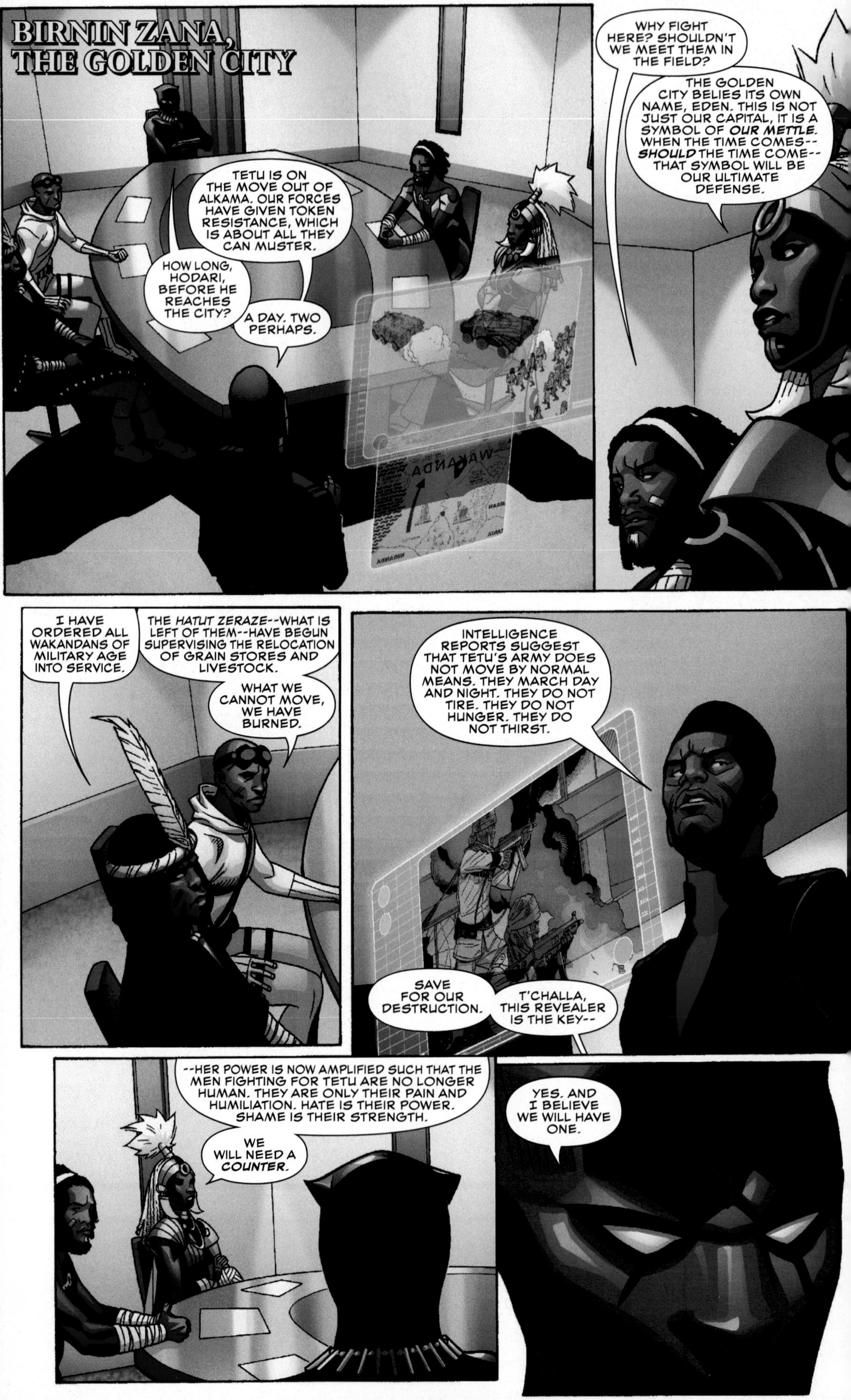
BIRNIN ZANA, THE GOLDEN CITY
TETU IS ON THE MOVE OUT OF ALKAMA. OUR FORCES HAVE GIVEN TOKEN RESISTANCE, WHICH IS ABOUT ALL THEY CAN MUSTER.
HOW LONG, HODARI, BEFORE HE REACHES THE CITY?
A DAY. TWO PERHAPS.
WHY FIGHT HERE? SHOULDN'T WE MEET THEM IN THE FIELD?
THE GOLDEN CITY BELIES ITS OWN NAME, EDEN. THIS IS NOT JUST OUR CAPITAL, IT IS A SYMBOL OF *OUR METTLE*. WHEN THE TIME COMES-- *SHOULD* THE TIME COME-- THAT SYMBOL WILL BE OUR ULTIMATE DEFENSE.
I HAVE ORDERED ALL WAKANDANS OF MILITARY AGE INTO SERVICE.
THE *HATUT ZERAZE*--WHAT IS LEFT OF THEM--HAVE BEGUN SUPERVISING THE RELOCATION OF GRAIN STORES AND LIVESTOCK.
WHAT WE CANNOT MOVE, WE HAVE BURNED.
INTELLIGENCE REPORTS SUGGEST THAT TETU'S ARMY DOES NOT MOVE BY NORMAL MEANS. THEY MARCH DAY AND NIGHT. THEY DO NOT TIRE. THEY DO NOT HUNGER. THEY DO NOT THIRST.
SAVE FOR OUR DESTRUCTION.
T'CHALLA, THIS REVEALER IS THE KEY--
--HER POWER IS NOW AMPLIFIED SUCH THAT THE MEN FIGHTING FOR TETU ARE NO LONGER HUMAN. THEY ARE ONLY THEIR PAIN AND HUMILIATION. HATE IS THEIR POWER. SHAME IS THEIR STRENGTH.
WE WILL NEED A *COUNTER.*
YES. AND I BELIEVE WE WILL HAVE ONE.

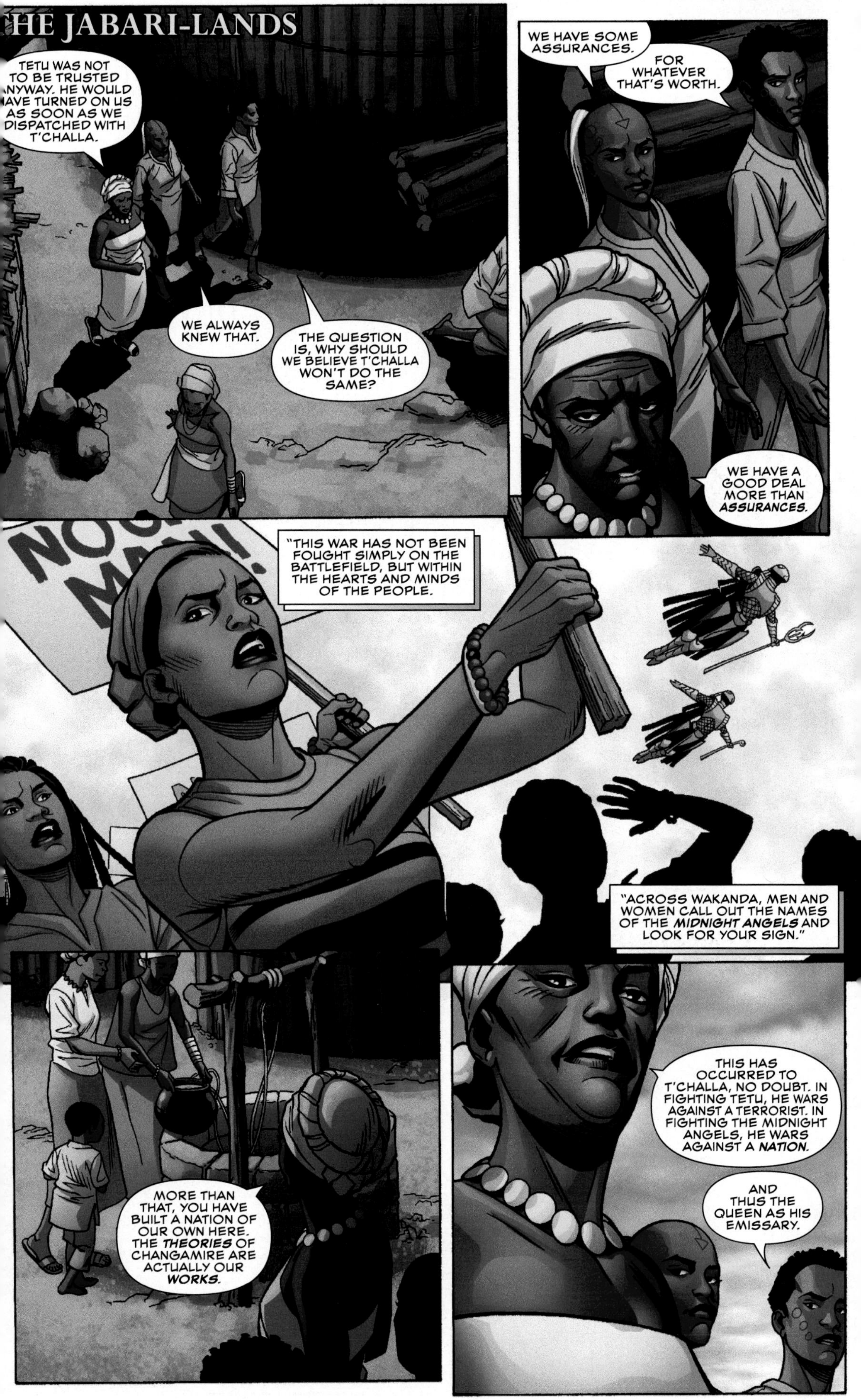

HE JABARI-LANDS
TETU WAS NOT TO BE TRUSTED NYWAY. HE WOULD AVE TURNED ON US AS SOON AS WE DISPATCHED WITH T'CHALLA.
WE ALWAYS KNEW THAT.
THE QUESTION IS, WHY SHOULD WE BELIEVE T'CHALLA WON'T DO THE SAME?
WE HAVE SOME ASSURANCES.
FOR WHATEVER THAT'S WORTH.
WE HAVE A GOOD DEAL MORE THAN *ASSURANCES*.
"THIS WAR HAS NOT BEEN FOUGHT SIMPLY ON THE BATTLEFIELD, BUT WITHIN THE HEARTS AND MINDS OF THE PEOPLE.
"ACROSS WAKANDA, MEN AND WOMEN CALL OUT THE NAMES OF THE *MIDNIGHT ANGELS* AND LOOK FOR YOUR SIGN."
MORE THAN THAT, YOU HAVE BUILT A NATION OF OUR OWN HERE. THE *THEORIES* OF CHANGAMIRE ARE ACTUALLY OUR *WORKS*.
THIS HAS OCCURRED TO T'CHALLA, NO DOUBT. IN FIGHTING TETU, HE WARS AGAINST A TERRORIST. IN FIGHTING THE MIDNIGHT ANGELS, HE WARS AGAINST A *NATION*.
AND THUS THE QUEEN AS HIS EMISSARY.

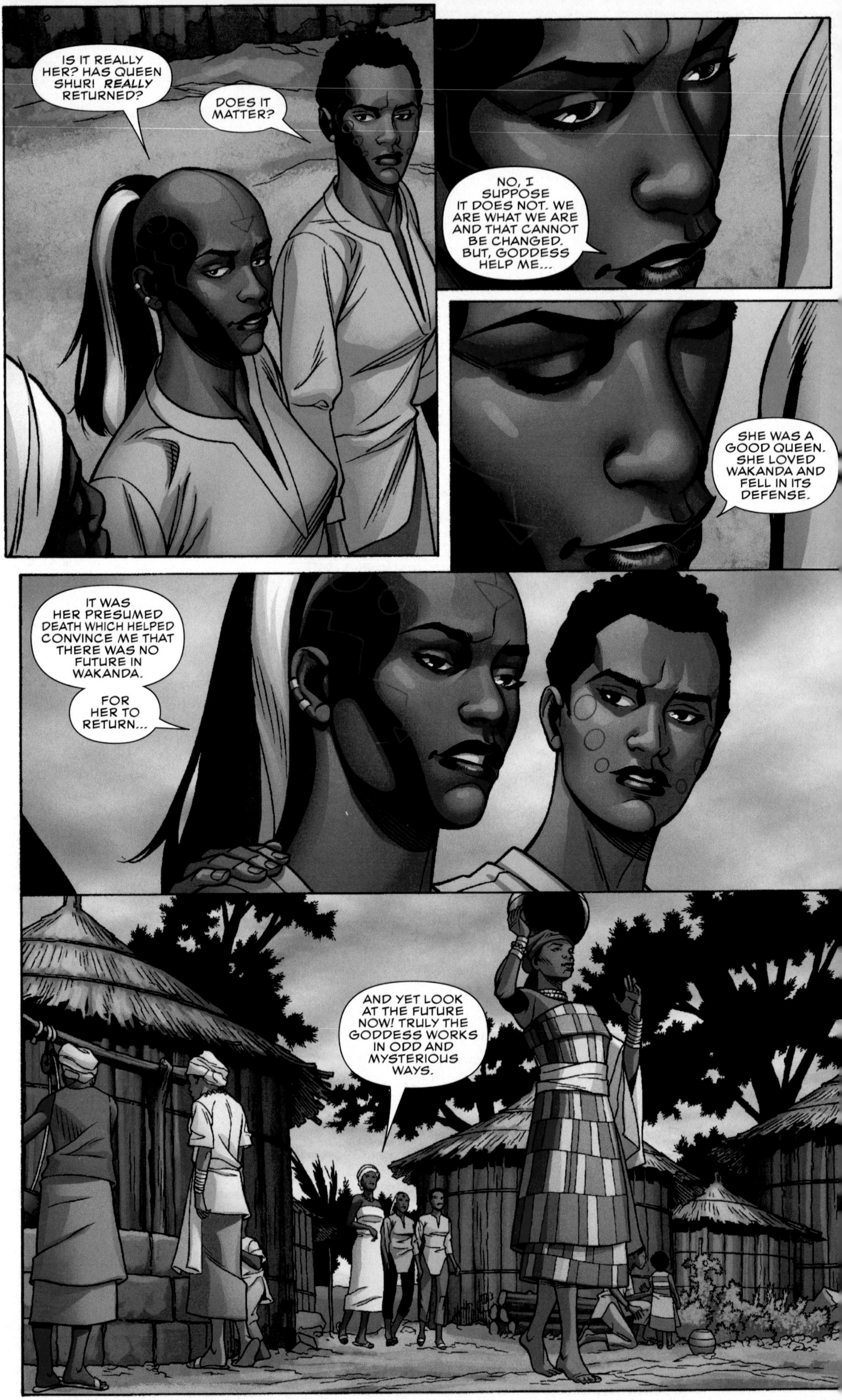
IS IT REALLY HER? HAS QUEEN SHURI *REALLY* RETURNED?
DOES IT MATTER?
NO, I SUPPOSE IT DOES NOT. WE ARE WHAT WE ARE AND THAT CANNOT BE CHANGED. BUT, GODDESS HELP ME...
SHE WAS A GOOD QUEEN. SHE LOVED WAKANDA AND FELL IN ITS DEFENSE.
IT WAS HER PRESUMED DEATH WHICH HELPED CONVINCE ME THAT THERE WAS NO FUTURE IN WAKANDA.
FOR HER TO RETURN...
AND YET LOOK AT THE FUTURE NOW! TRULY THE GODDESS WORKS IN ODD AND MYSTERIOUS WAYS.

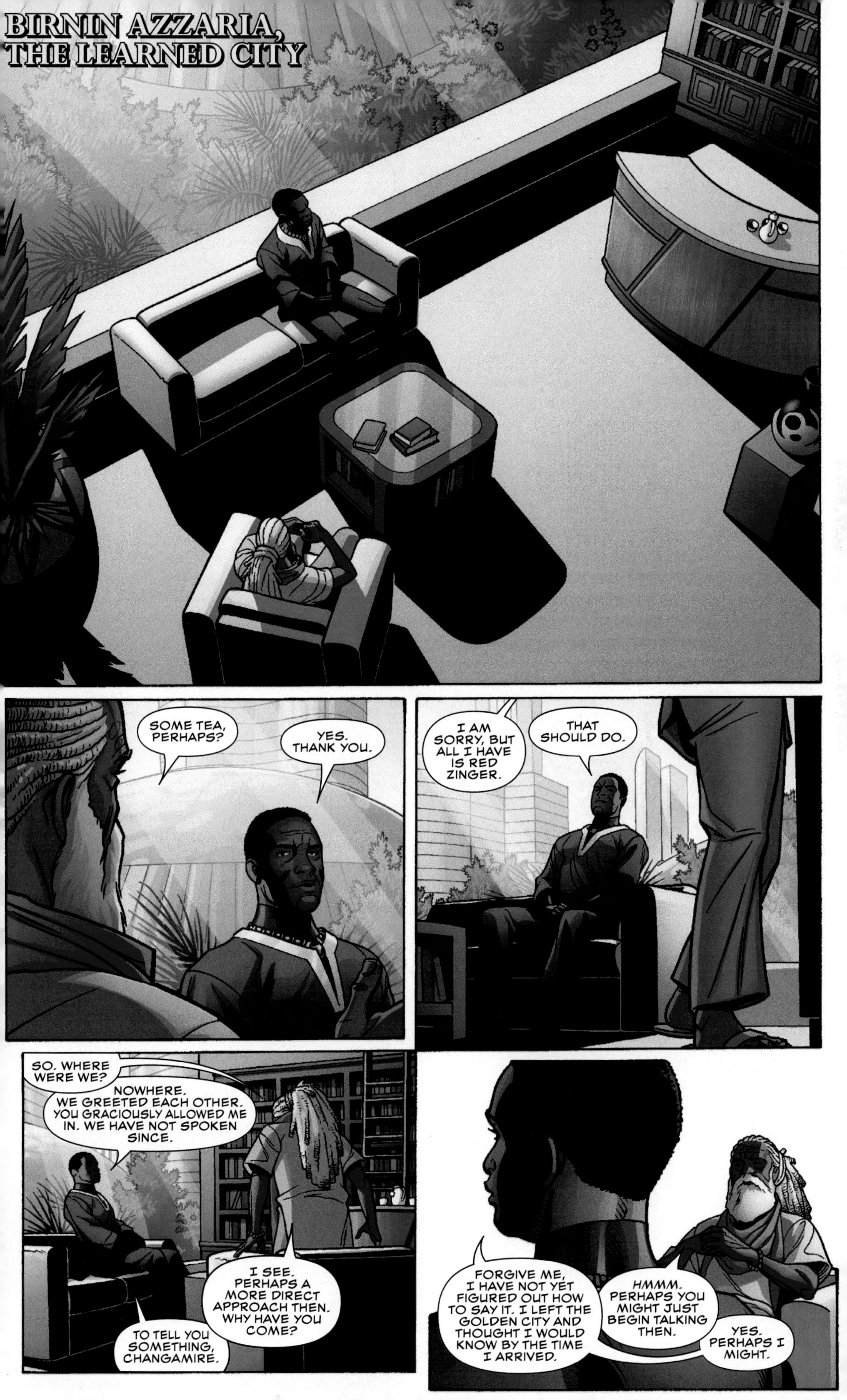
BIRNIN AZZARIA, THE LEARNED CITY
SOME TEA, PERHAPS?
YES. THANK YOU.
I AM SORRY, BUT ALL I HAVE IS RED ZINGER.
THAT SHOULD DO.
SO. WHERE WERE WE?
NOWHERE. WE GREETED EACH OTHER. YOU GRACIOUSLY ALLOWED ME IN. WE HAVE NOT SPOKEN SINCE.
I SEE. PERHAPS A MORE DIRECT APPROACH THEN. WHY HAVE YOU COME?
TO TELL YOU SOMETHING, CHANGAMIRE.
FORGIVE ME, I HAVE NOT YET FIGURED OUT HOW TO SAY IT. I LEFT THE GOLDEN CITY AND THOUGHT I WOULD KNOW BY THE TIME I ARRIVED.
HMMM. PERHAPS YOU MIGHT JUST BEGIN TALKING THEN.
YES. PERHAPS I MIGHT.

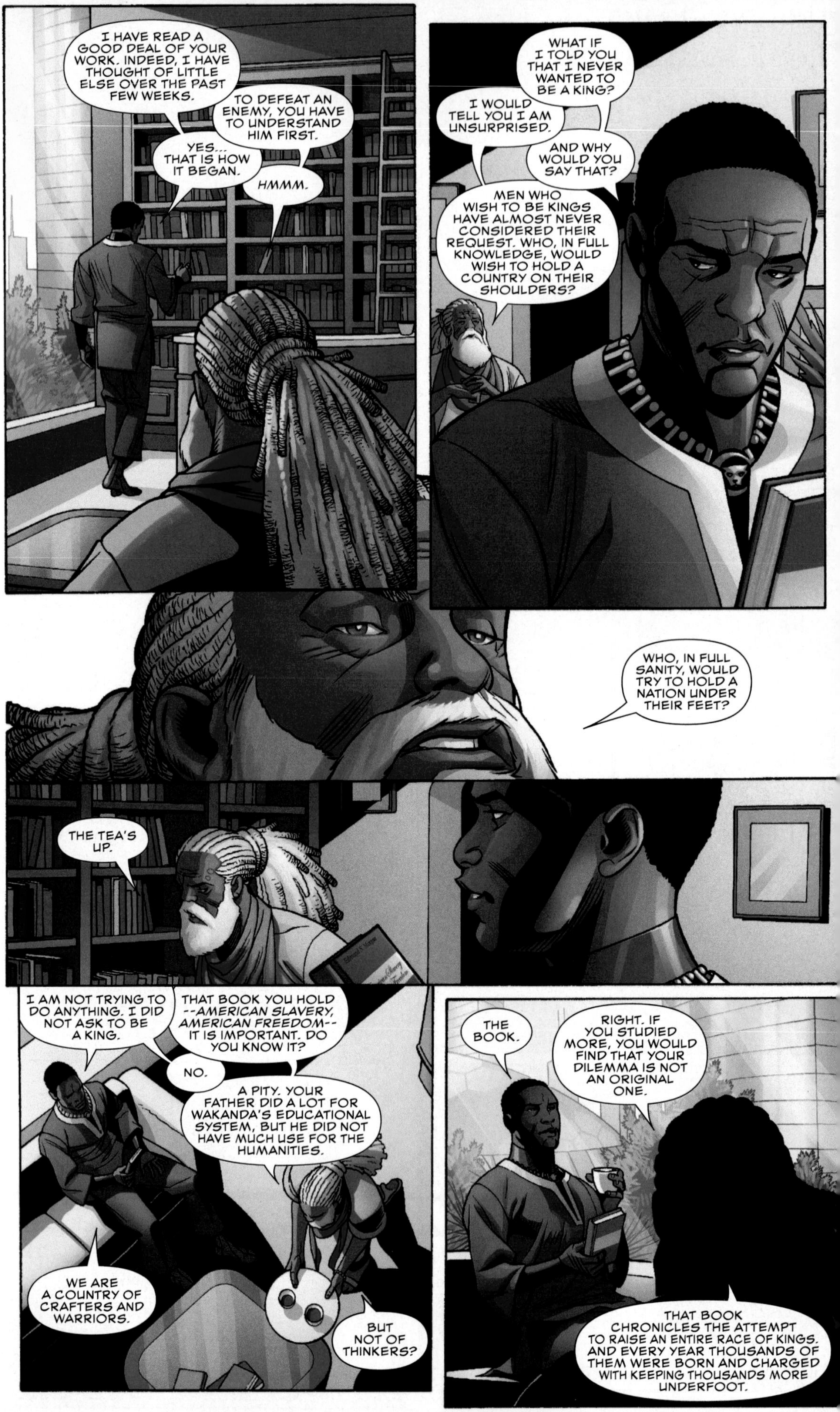
I HAVE READ A GOOD DEAL OF YOUR WORK. INDEED, I HAVE THOUGHT OF LITTLE ELSE OVER THE PAST FEW WEEKS.
TO DEFEAT AN ENEMY, YOU HAVE TO UNDERSTAND HIM FIRST.
YES... THAT IS HOW IT BEGAN.
HMMM.
WHAT IF I TOLD YOU THAT I NEVER WANTED TO BE A KING?
I WOULD TELL YOU I AM UNSURPRISED.
AND WHY WOULD YOU SAY THAT?
MEN WHO WISH TO BE KINGS HAVE ALMOST NEVER CONSIDERED THEIR REQUEST. WHO, IN FULL KNOWLEDGE, WOULD WISH TO HOLD A COUNTRY ON THEIR SHOULDERS?
WHO, IN FULL SANITY, WOULD TRY TO HOLD A NATION UNDER THEIR FEET?
THE TEA'S UP.
I AM NOT TRYING TO DO ANYTHING. I DID NOT ASK TO BE A KING.
THAT BOOK YOU HOLD --AMERICAN SLAVERY, AMERICAN FREEDOM-- IT IS IMPORTANT. DO YOU KNOW IT?
NO.
A PITY. YOUR FATHER DID A LOT FOR WAKANDA'S EDUCATIONAL SYSTEM, BUT HE DID NOT HAVE MUCH USE FOR THE HUMANITIES.
WE ARE A COUNTRY OF CRAFTERS AND WARRIORS.
BUT NOT OF THINKERS?
THE BOOK.
RIGHT. IF YOU STUDIED MORE, YOU WOULD FIND THAT YOUR DILEMMA IS NOT AN ORIGINAL ONE.
THAT BOOK CHRONICLES THE ATTEMPT TO RAISE AN ENTIRE RACE OF KINGS. AND EVERY YEAR THOUSANDS OF THEM WERE BORN AND CHARGED WITH KEEPING THOUSANDS MORE UNDERFOOT.

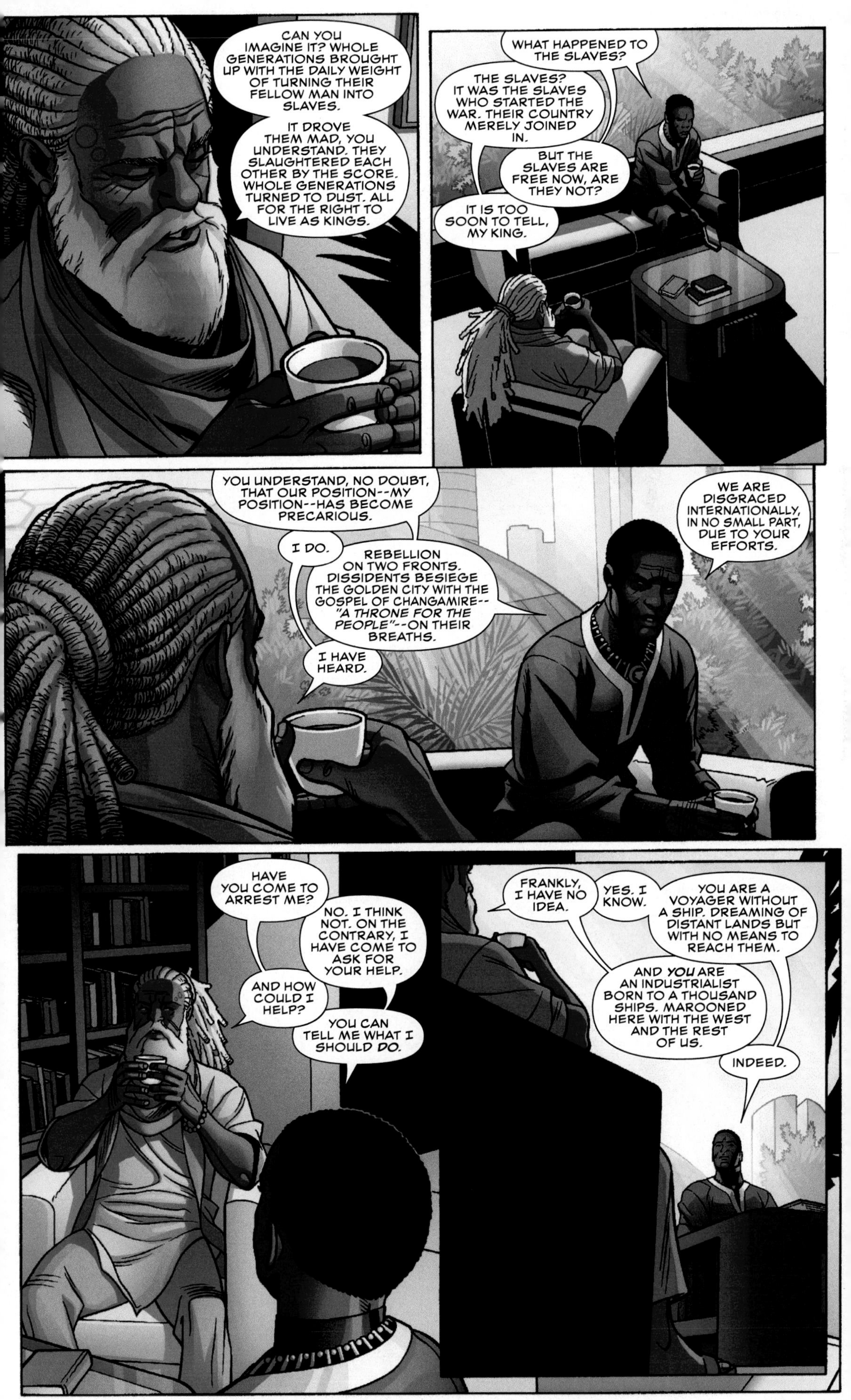
CAN YOU IMAGINE IT? WHOLE GENERATIONS BROUGHT UP WITH THE DAILY WEIGHT OF TURNING THEIR FELLOW MAN INTO SLAVES.
IT DROVE THEM MAD, YOU UNDERSTAND. THEY SLAUGHTERED EACH OTHER BY THE SCORE. WHOLE GENERATIONS TURNED TO DUST. ALL FOR THE RIGHT TO LIVE AS KINGS.
WHAT HAPPENED TO THE SLAVES?
THE SLAVES? IT WAS THE SLAVES WHO STARTED THE WAR. THEIR COUNTRY MERELY JOINED IN.
BUT THE SLAVES ARE FREE NOW, ARE THEY NOT?
IT IS TOO SOON TO TELL, MY KING.
YOU UNDERSTAND, NO DOUBT, THAT OUR POSITION--MY POSITION--HAS BECOME PRECARIOUS.
I DO.
REBELLION ON TWO FRONTS. DISSIDENTS BESIEGE THE GOLDEN CITY WITH THE GOSPEL OF CHANGAMIRE--"A THRONE FOR THE PEOPLE"--ON THEIR BREATHS.
I HAVE HEARD.
WE ARE DISGRACED INTERNATIONALLY, IN NO SMALL PART, DUE TO YOUR EFFORTS.
HAVE YOU COME TO ARREST ME?
NO. I THINK NOT. ON THE CONTRARY, I HAVE COME TO ASK FOR YOUR HELP.
AND HOW COULD I HELP?
YOU CAN TELL ME WHAT I SHOULD DO.
FRANKLY, I HAVE NO IDEA.
YES. I KNOW.
YOU ARE A VOYAGER WITHOUT A SHIP. DREAMING OF DISTANT LANDS BUT WITH NO MEANS TO REACH THEM.
AND YOU ARE AN INDUSTRIALIST BORN TO A THOUSAND SHIPS. MAROONED HERE WITH THE WEST AND THE REST OF US.
INDEED.

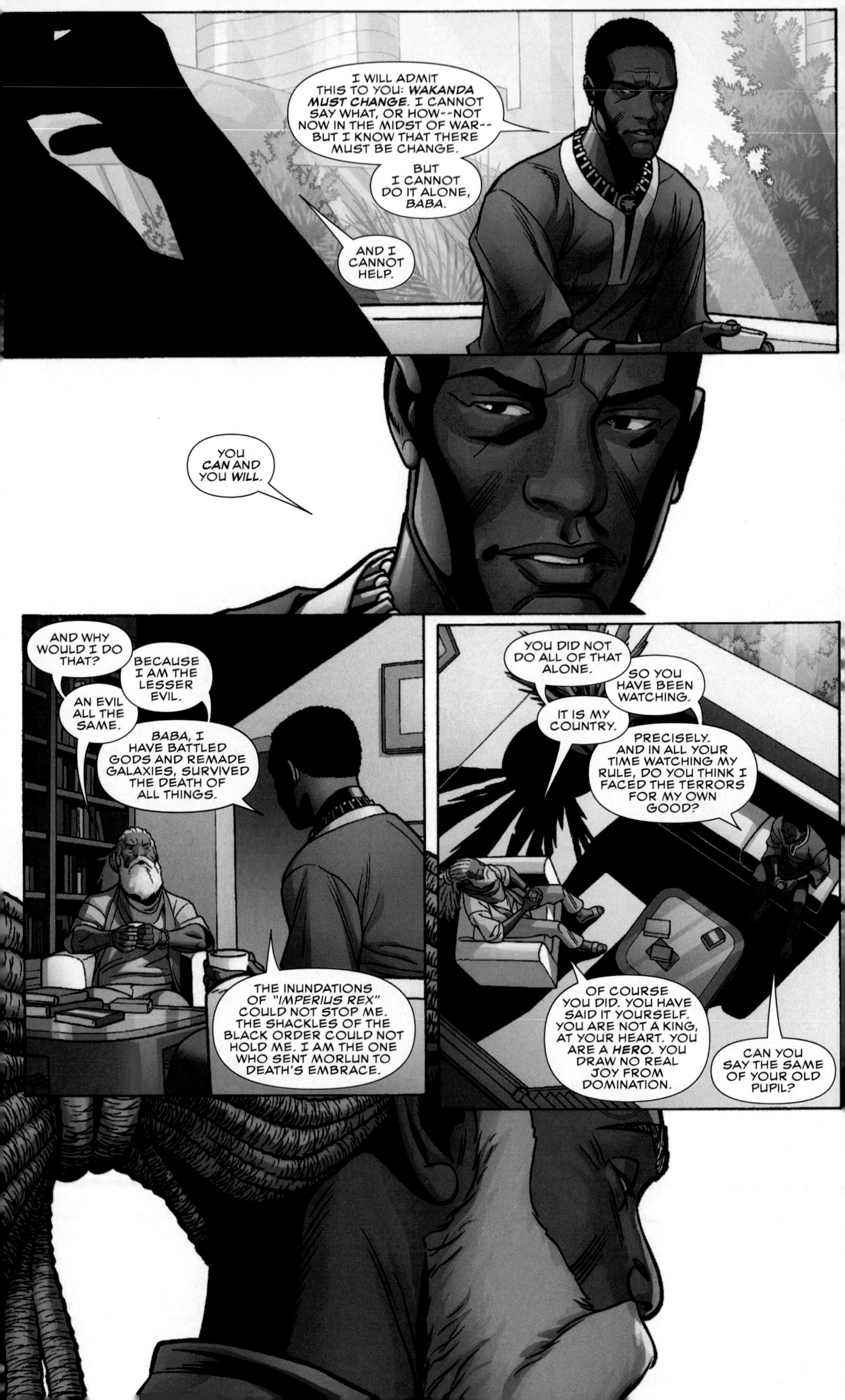
I WILL ADMIT THIS TO YOU: WAKANDA MUST CHANGE. I CANNOT SAY WHAT, OR HOW--NOT NOW IN THE MIDST OF WAR--BUT I KNOW THAT THERE MUST BE CHANGE.
BUT I CANNOT DO IT ALONE, BABA.
AND I CANNOT HELP.
YOU CAN AND YOU WILL.
AND WHY WOULD I DO THAT?
BECAUSE I AM THE LESSER EVIL.
AN EVIL ALL THE SAME.
BABA, I HAVE BATTLED GODS AND REMADE GALAXIES, SURVIVED THE DEATH OF ALL THINGS.
THE INUNDATIONS OF "IMPERIUS REX" COULD NOT STOP ME. THE SHACKLES OF THE BLACK ORDER COULD NOT HOLD ME. I AM THE ONE WHO SENT MORLUN TO DEATH'S EMBRACE.
YOU DID NOT DO ALL OF THAT ALONE.
SO YOU HAVE BEEN WATCHING.
IT IS MY COUNTRY.
PRECISELY. AND IN ALL YOUR TIME WATCHING MY RULE, DO YOU THINK I FACED THE TERRORS FOR MY OWN GOOD?
OF COURSE YOU DID. YOU HAVE SAID IT YOURSELF. YOU ARE NOT A KING, AT YOUR HEART. YOU ARE A HERO. YOU DRAW NO REAL JOY FROM DOMINATION.
CAN YOU SAY THE SAME OF YOUR OLD PUPIL?

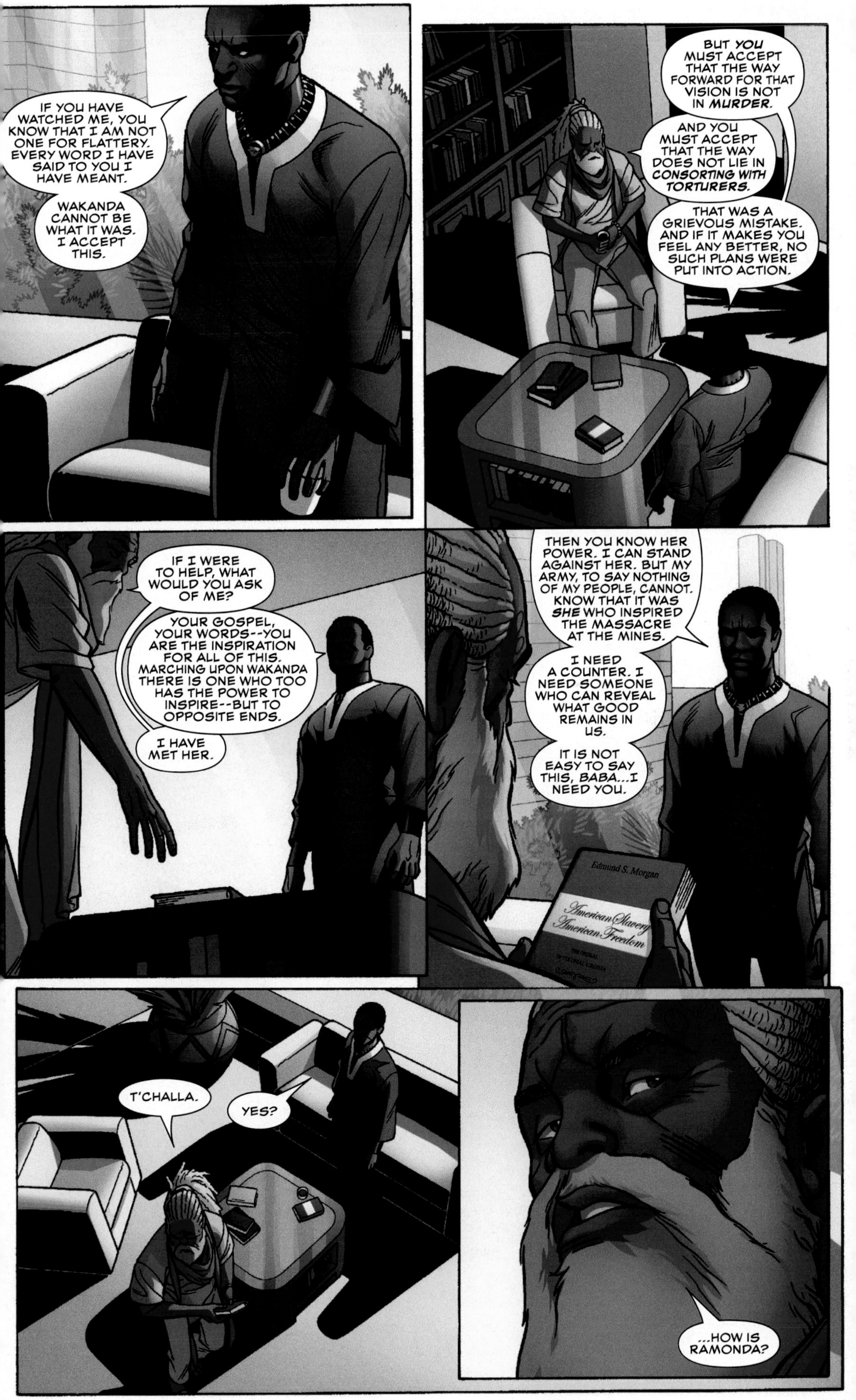
IF YOU HAVE WATCHED ME, YOU KNOW THAT I AM NOT ONE FOR FLATTERY. EVERY WORD I HAVE SAID TO YOU I HAVE MEANT.
WAKANDA CANNOT BE WHAT IT WAS. I ACCEPT THIS.
BUT *YOU* MUST ACCEPT THAT THE WAY FORWARD FOR THAT VISION IS NOT IN *MURDER*.
AND YOU MUST ACCEPT THAT THE WAY DOES NOT LIE IN *CONSORTING WITH TORTURERS*.
THAT WAS A GRIEVOUS MISTAKE. AND IF IT MAKES YOU FEEL ANY BETTER, NO SUCH PLANS WERE PUT INTO ACTION.
IF I WERE TO HELP, WHAT WOULD YOU ASK OF ME?
YOUR GOSPEL, YOUR WORDS--YOU ARE THE INSPIRATION FOR ALL OF THIS. MARCHING UPON WAKANDA THERE IS ONE WHO TOO HAS THE POWER TO INSPIRE--BUT TO OPPOSITE ENDS.
I HAVE MET HER.
THEN YOU KNOW HER POWER. I CAN STAND AGAINST HER. BUT MY ARMY, TO SAY NOTHING OF MY PEOPLE, CANNOT. KNOW THAT IT WAS *SHE* WHO INSPIRED THE MASSACRE AT THE MINES.
I NEED A COUNTER. I NEED SOMEONE WHO CAN REVEAL WHAT GOOD REMAINS IN US.
IT IS NOT EASY TO SAY THIS, BABA...I NEED YOU.
Edmund S. Morgan
American Slavery American Freedom
T'CHALLA.
YES?
...HOW IS RAMONDA?

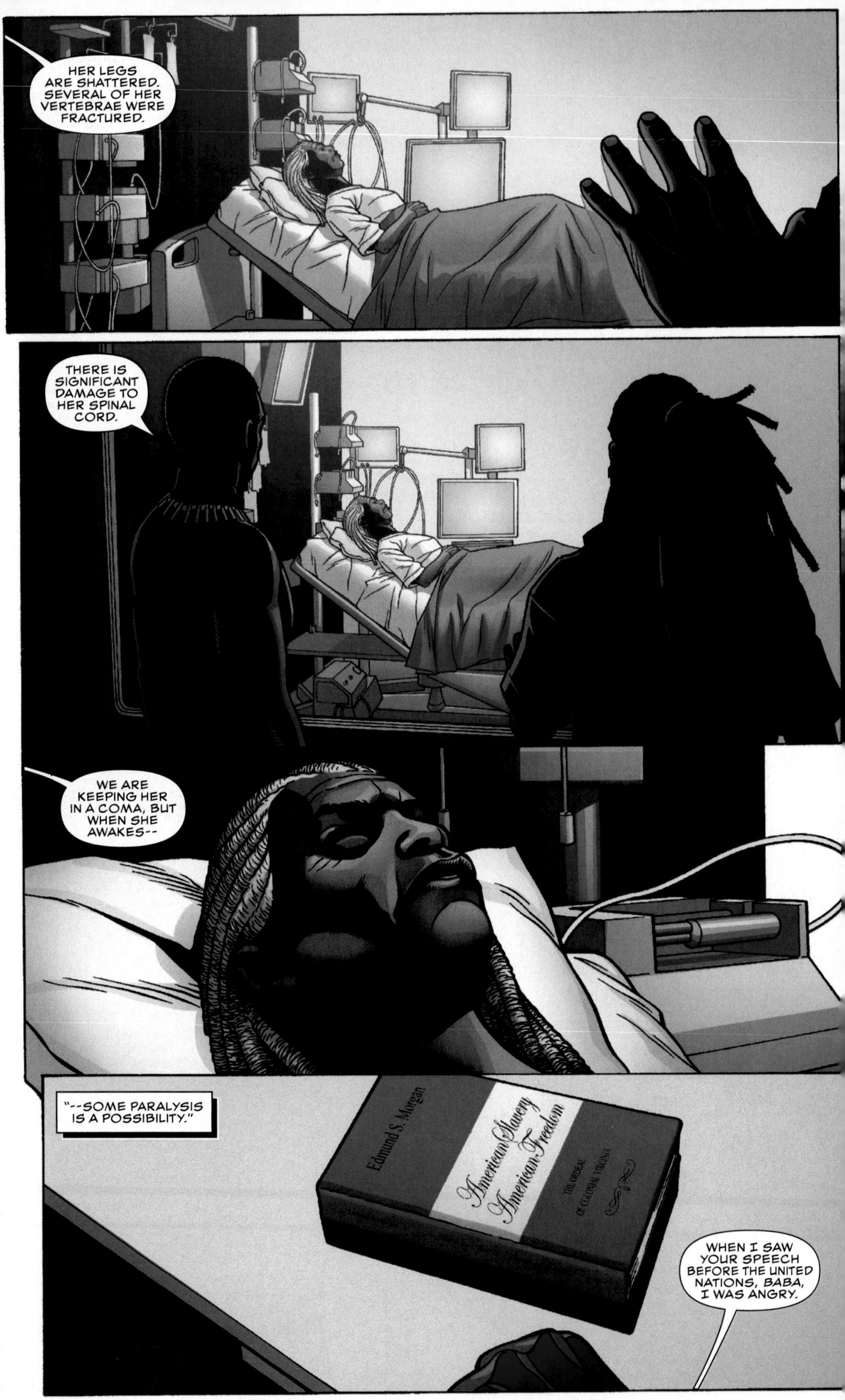
HER LEGS ARE SHATTERED. SEVERAL OF HER VERTEBRAE WERE FRACTURED.
THERE IS SIGNIFICANT DAMAGE TO HER SPINAL CORD.
WE ARE KEEPING HER IN A COMA, BUT WHEN SHE AWAKES--
"--SOME PARALYSIS IS A POSSIBILITY."
Edmund S. Morgan
American Slavery American Freedom
THE ORDEAL OF COLONIAL VIRGINIA
WHEN I SAW YOUR SPEECH BEFORE THE UNITED NATIONS, BABA, I WAS ANGRY.

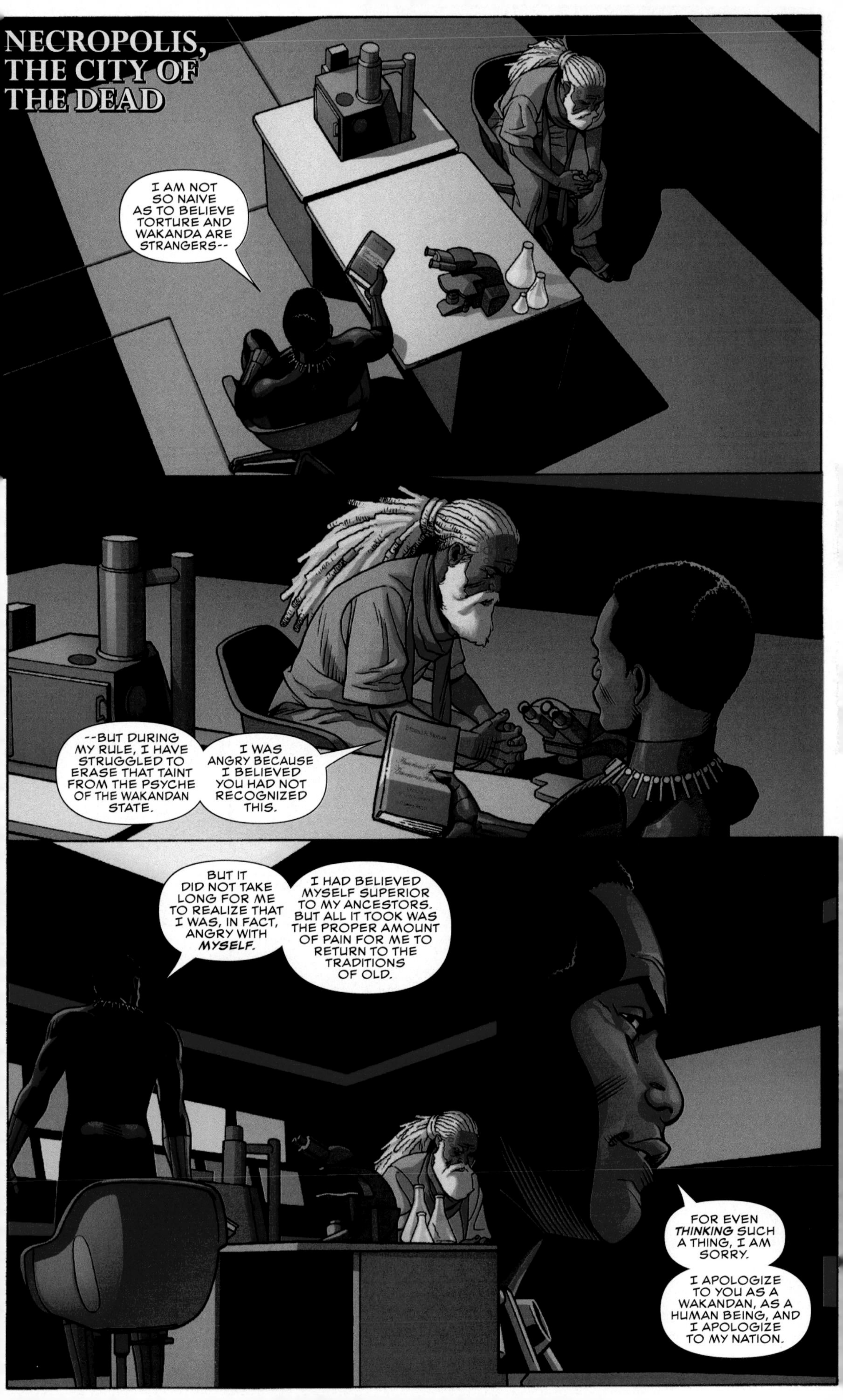
NECROPOLIS, THE CITY OF THE DEAD
I AM NOT SO NAIVE AS TO BELIEVE TORTURE AND WAKANDA ARE STRANGERS--
--BUT DURING MY RULE, I HAVE STRUGGLED TO ERASE THAT TAINT FROM THE PSYCHE OF THE WAKANDAN STATE.
I WAS ANGRY BECAUSE I BELIEVED YOU HAD NOT RECOGNIZED THIS.
BUT IT DID NOT TAKE LONG FOR ME TO REALIZE THAT I WAS, IN FACT, ANGRY WITH *MYSELF*.
I HAD BELIEVED MYSELF SUPERIOR TO MY ANCESTORS. BUT ALL IT TOOK WAS THE PROPER AMOUNT OF PAIN FOR ME TO RETURN TO THE TRADITIONS OF OLD.
FOR EVEN *THINKING* SUCH A THING, I AM SORRY.
I APOLOGIZE TO YOU AS A WAKANDAN, AS A HUMAN BEING, AND I APOLOGIZE TO MY NATION.

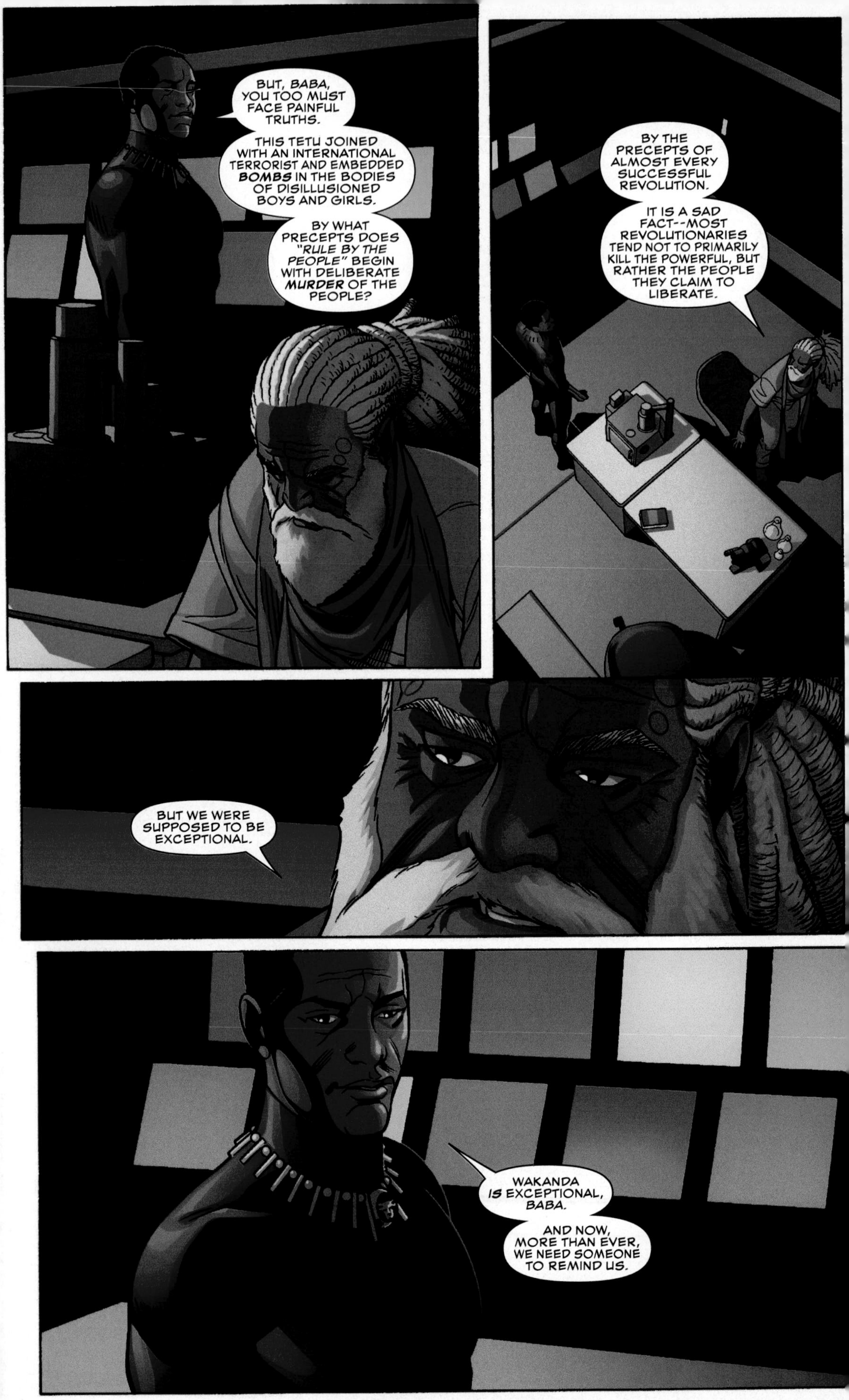

BUT, BABA, YOU TOO MUST FACE PAINFUL TRUTHS.
THIS TETU JOINED WITH AN INTERNATIONAL TERRORIST AND EMBEDDED BOMBS IN THE BODIES OF DISILLUSIONED BOYS AND GIRLS.
BY WHAT PRECEPTS DOES "RULE BY THE PEOPLE" BEGIN WITH DELIBERATE MURDER OF THE PEOPLE?
BY THE PRECEPTS OF ALMOST EVERY SUCCESSFUL REVOLUTION.
IT IS A SAD FACT--MOST REVOLUTIONARIES TEND NOT TO PRIMARILY KILL THE POWERFUL, BUT RATHER THE PEOPLE THEY CLAIM TO LIBERATE.
BUT WE WERE SUPPOSED TO BE EXCEPTIONAL.
WAKANDA IS EXCEPTIONAL, BABA.
AND NOW, MORE THAN EVER, WE NEED SOMEONE TO REMIND US.

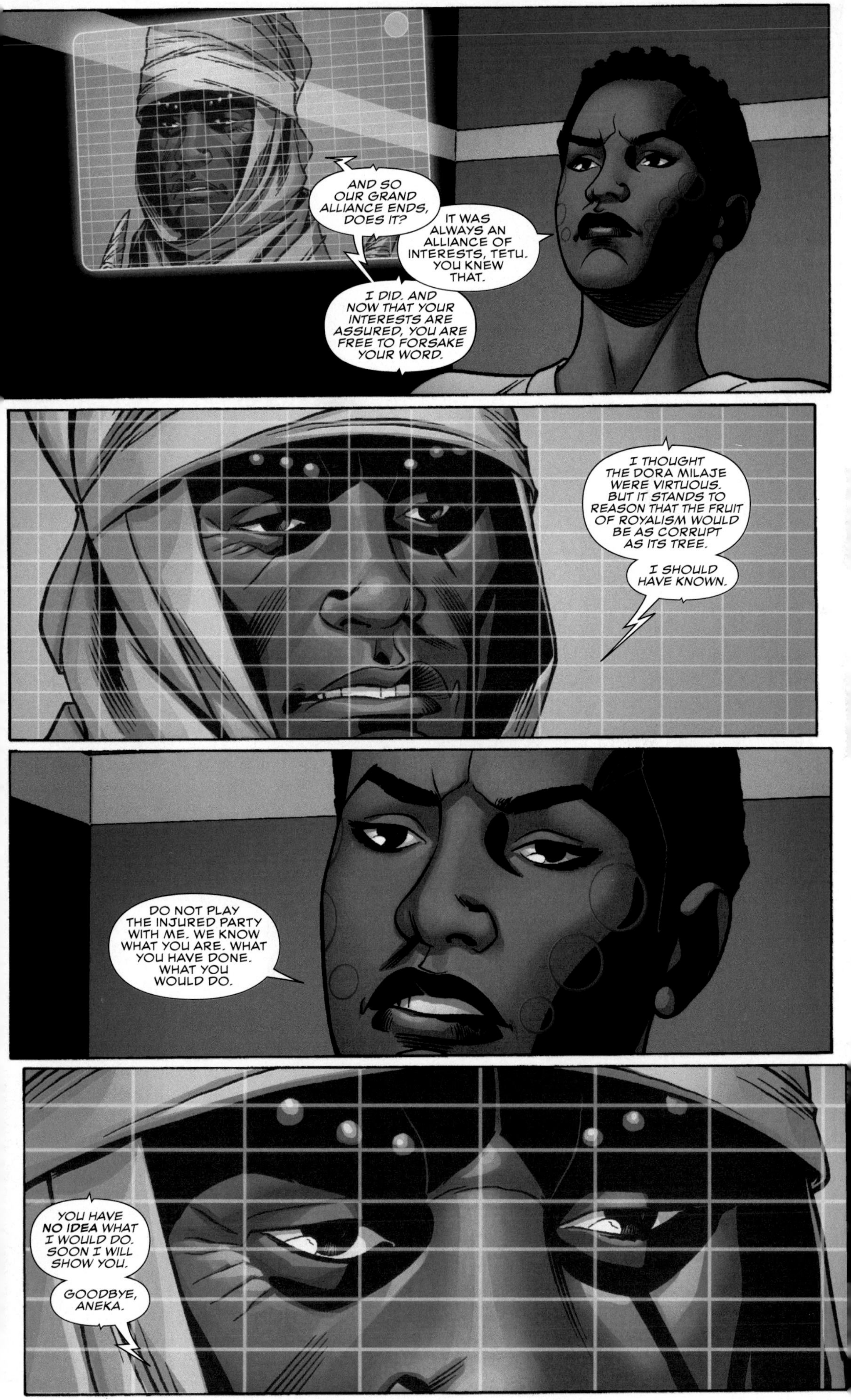
AND SO OUR GRAND ALLIANCE ENDS, DOES IT?
IT WAS ALWAYS AN ALLIANCE OF INTERESTS, TETU. YOU KNEW THAT.
I DID. AND NOW THAT YOUR INTERESTS ARE ASSURED, YOU ARE FREE TO FORSAKE YOUR WORD.
I THOUGHT THE DORA MILAJE WERE VIRTUOUS. BUT IT STANDS TO REASON THAT THE FRUIT OF ROYALISM WOULD BE AS CORRUPT AS ITS TREE.
I SHOULD HAVE KNOWN.
DO NOT PLAY THE INJURED PARTY WITH ME. WE KNOW WHAT YOU ARE. WHAT YOU HAVE DONE. WHAT YOU WOULD DO.
YOU HAVE **NO IDEA** WHAT I WOULD DO. SOON I WILL SHOW YOU.
GOODBYE, ANEKA.

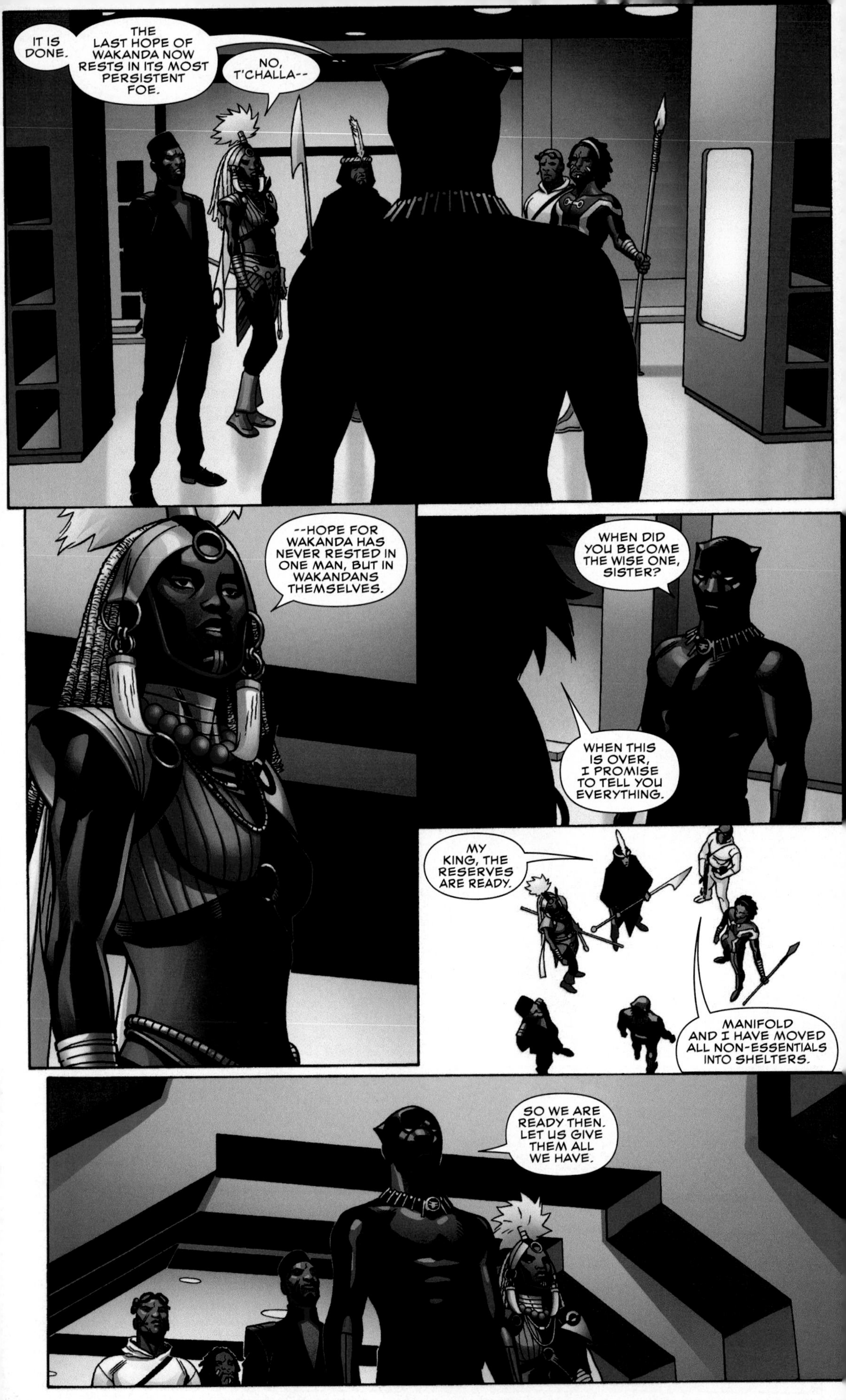
IT IS DONE.
THE LAST HOPE OF WAKANDA NOW RESTS IN ITS MOST PERSISTENT FOE.
NO, T'CHALLA--
--HOPE FOR WAKANDA HAS NEVER RESTED IN ONE MAN, BUT IN WAKANDANS THEMSELVES.
WHEN DID YOU BECOME THE WISE ONE, SISTER?
WHEN THIS IS OVER, I PROMISE TO TELL YOU EVERYTHING.
MY KING, THE RESERVES ARE READY.
MANIFOLD AND I HAVE MOVED ALL NON-ESSENTIALS INTO SHELTERS.
SO WE ARE READY THEN. LET US GIVE THEM ALL WE HAVE.

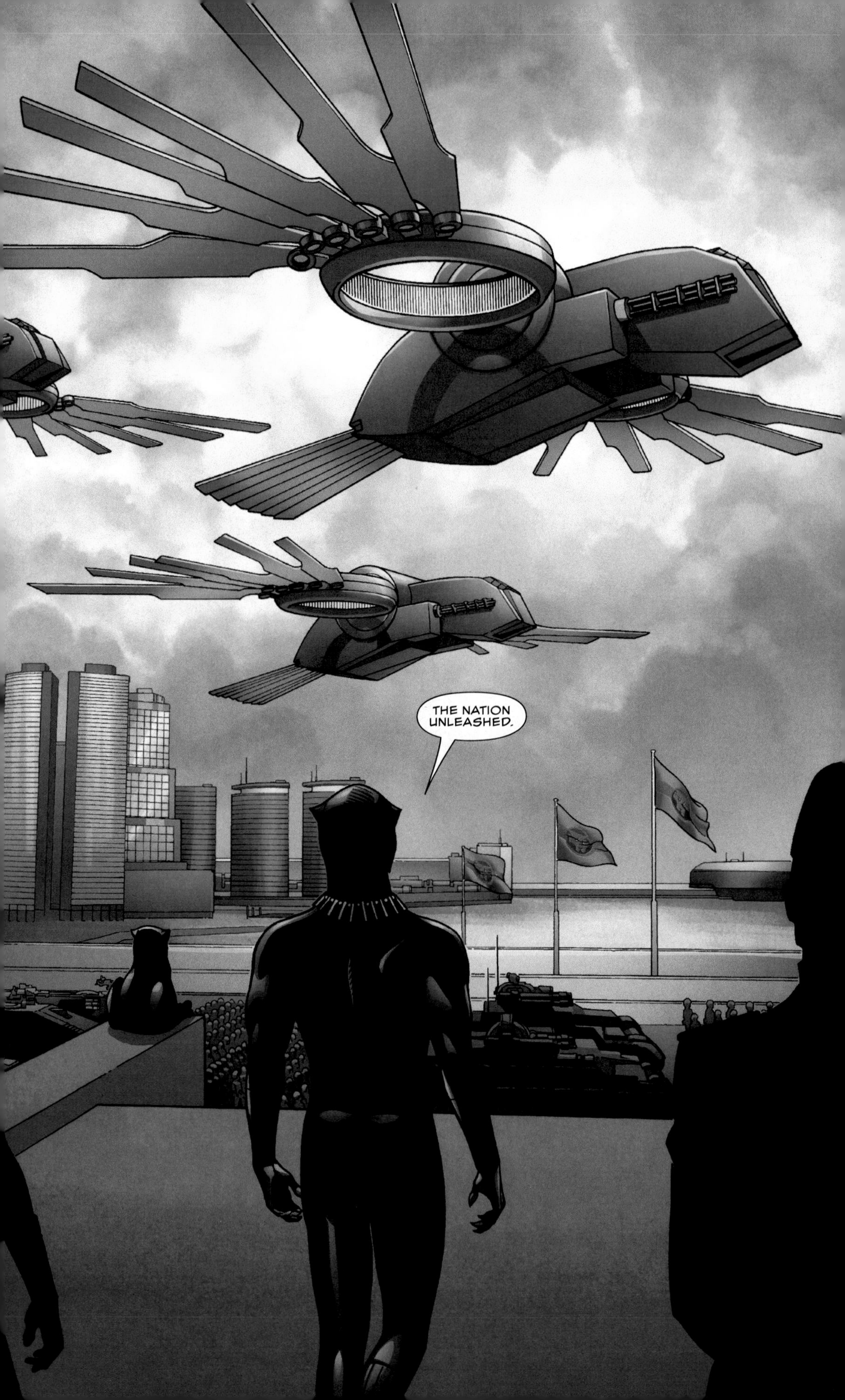
THE NATION UNLEASHED.

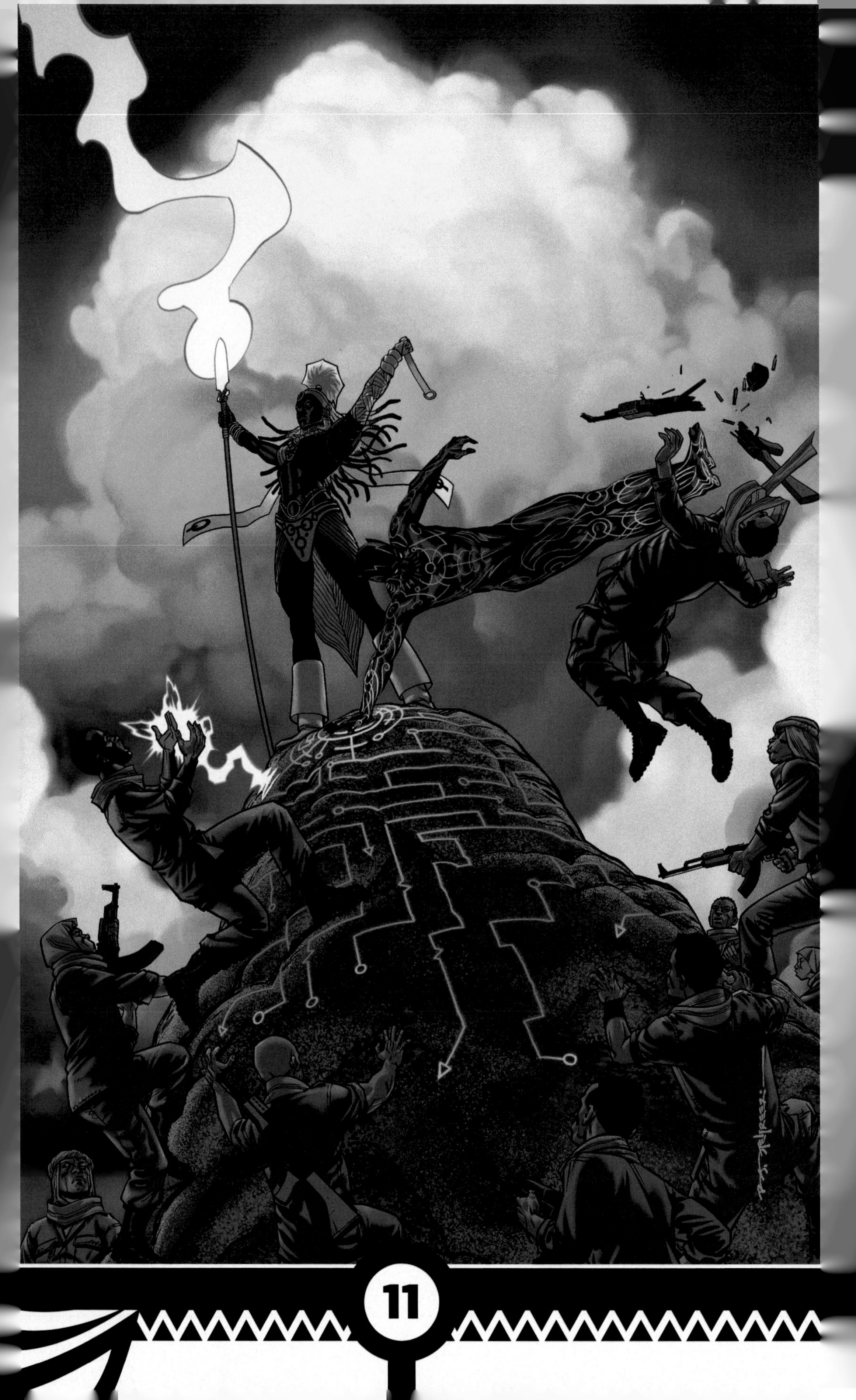

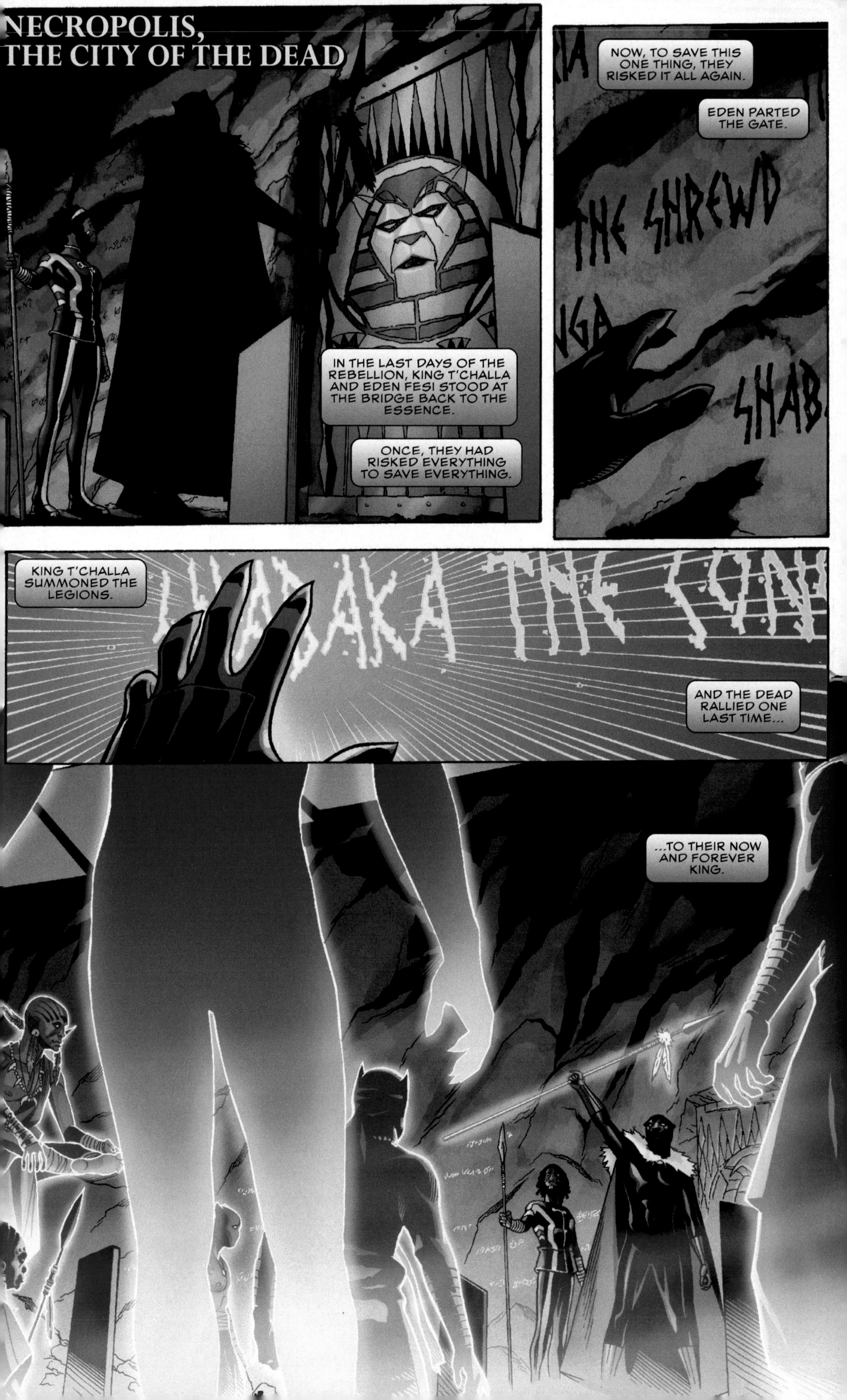
NECROPOLIS,
THE CITY OF THE DEAD
IN THE LAST DAYS OF THE REBELLION, KING T'CHALLA AND EDEN FESI STOOD AT THE BRIDGE BACK TO THE ESSENCE.
ONCE, THEY HAD RISKED EVERYTHING TO SAVE EVERYTHING.
NOW, TO SAVE THIS ONE THING, THEY RISKED IT ALL AGAIN.
EDEN PARTED THE GATE.
THE SHREWD
KING T'CHALLA SUMMONED THE LEGIONS.
AND THE DEAD RALLIED ONE LAST TIME...
...TO THEIR NOW AND FOREVER KING.

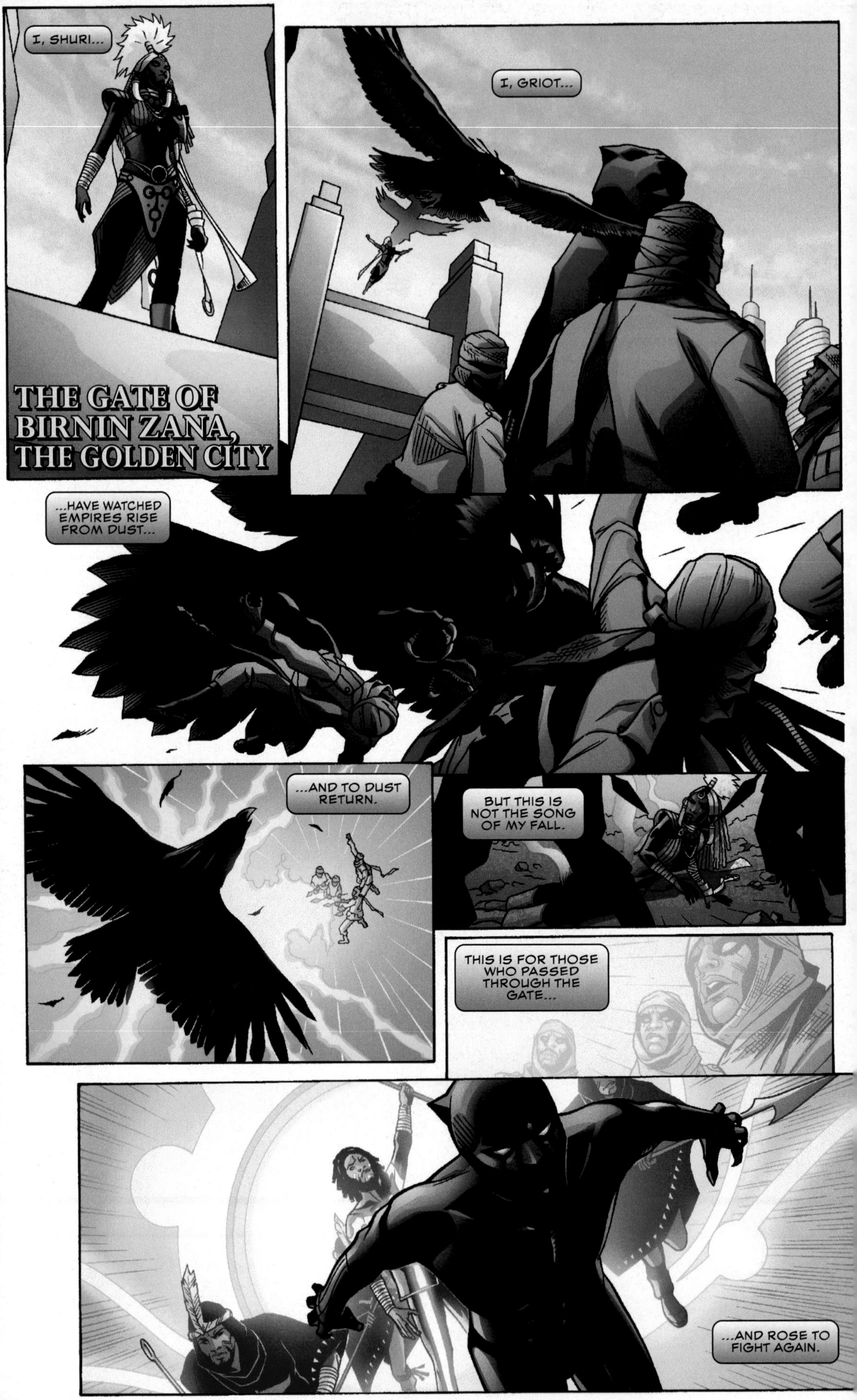
I, SHURI...
THE GATE OF BIRNIN ZANA, THE GOLDEN CITY
I, GRIOT...
...HAVE WATCHED EMPIRES RISE FROM DUST...
...AND TO DUST RETURN.
BUT THIS IS NOT THE SONG OF MY FALL.
THIS IS FOR THOSE WHO PASSED THROUGH THE GATE...
...AND ROSE TO FIGHT AGAIN.

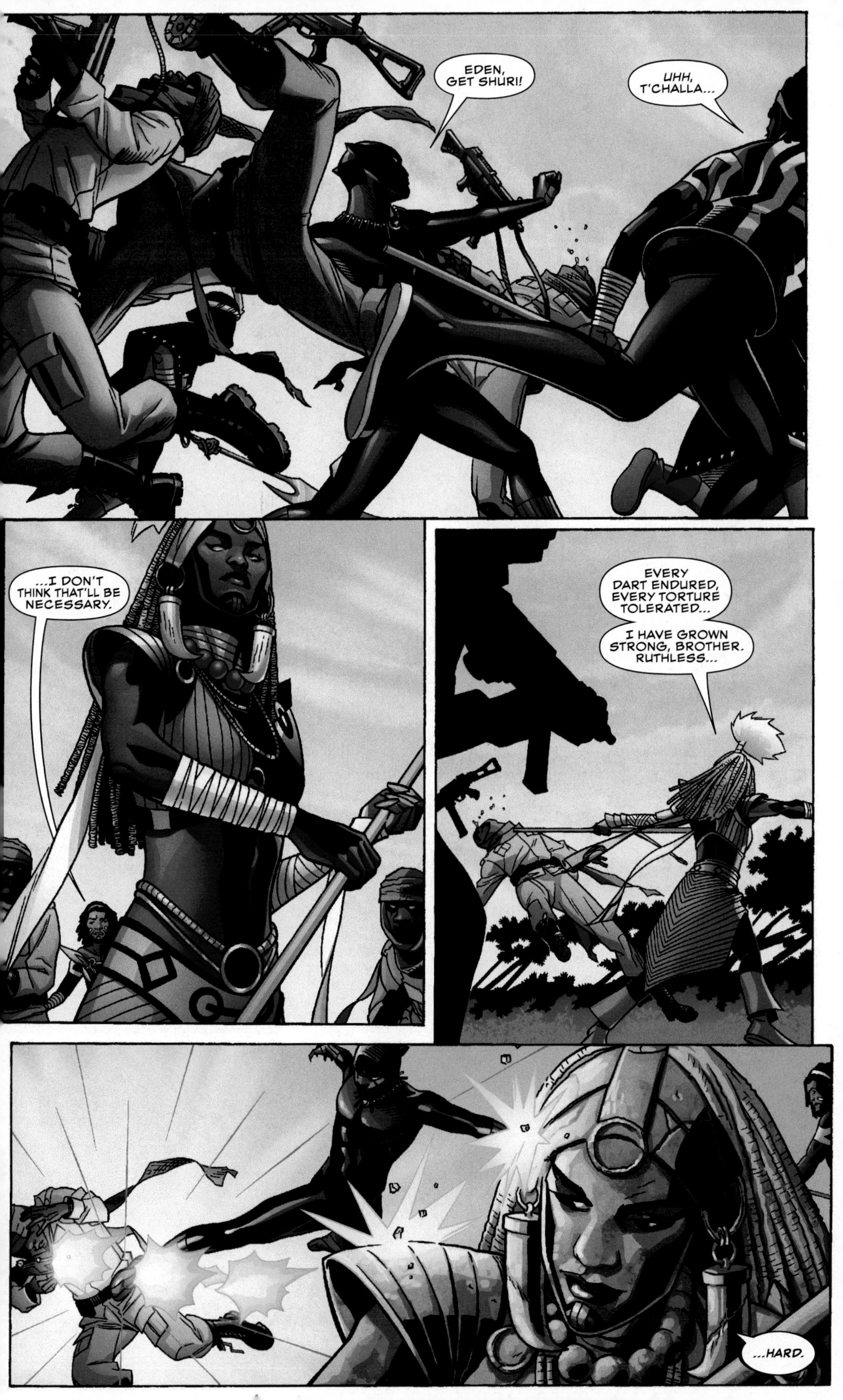
EDEN, GET SHURI!
UHH, T'CHALLA...
...I DON'T THINK THAT'LL BE NECESSARY.
EVERY DART ENDURED, EVERY TORTURE TOLERATED...
I HAVE GROWN STRONG, BROTHER. RUTHLESS...
...HARD.

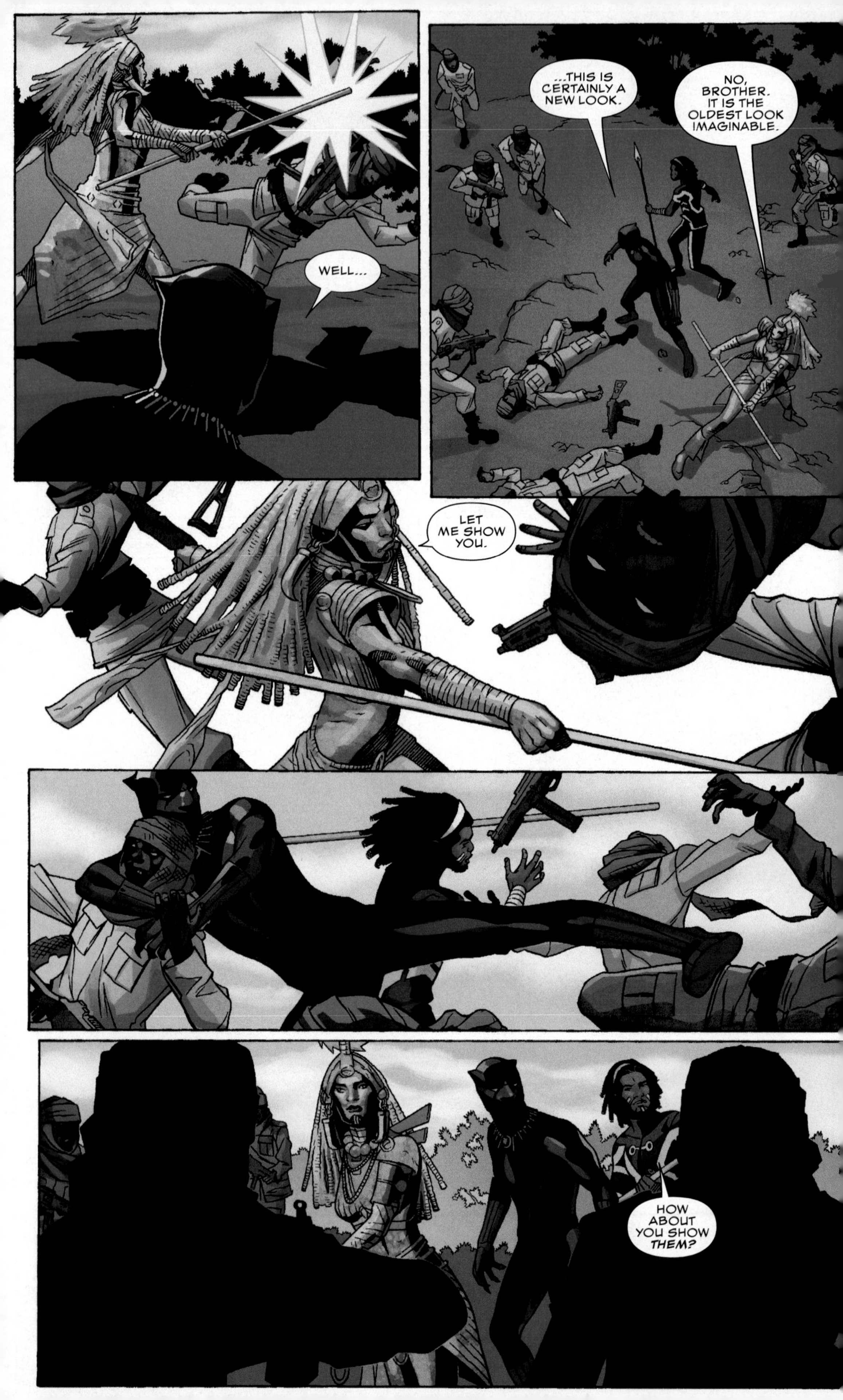
WELL...
...THIS IS CERTAINLY A NEW LOOK.
NO, BROTHER. IT IS THE OLDEST LOOK IMAGINABLE.
LET ME SHOW YOU.
HOW ABOUT YOU SHOW *THEM?*

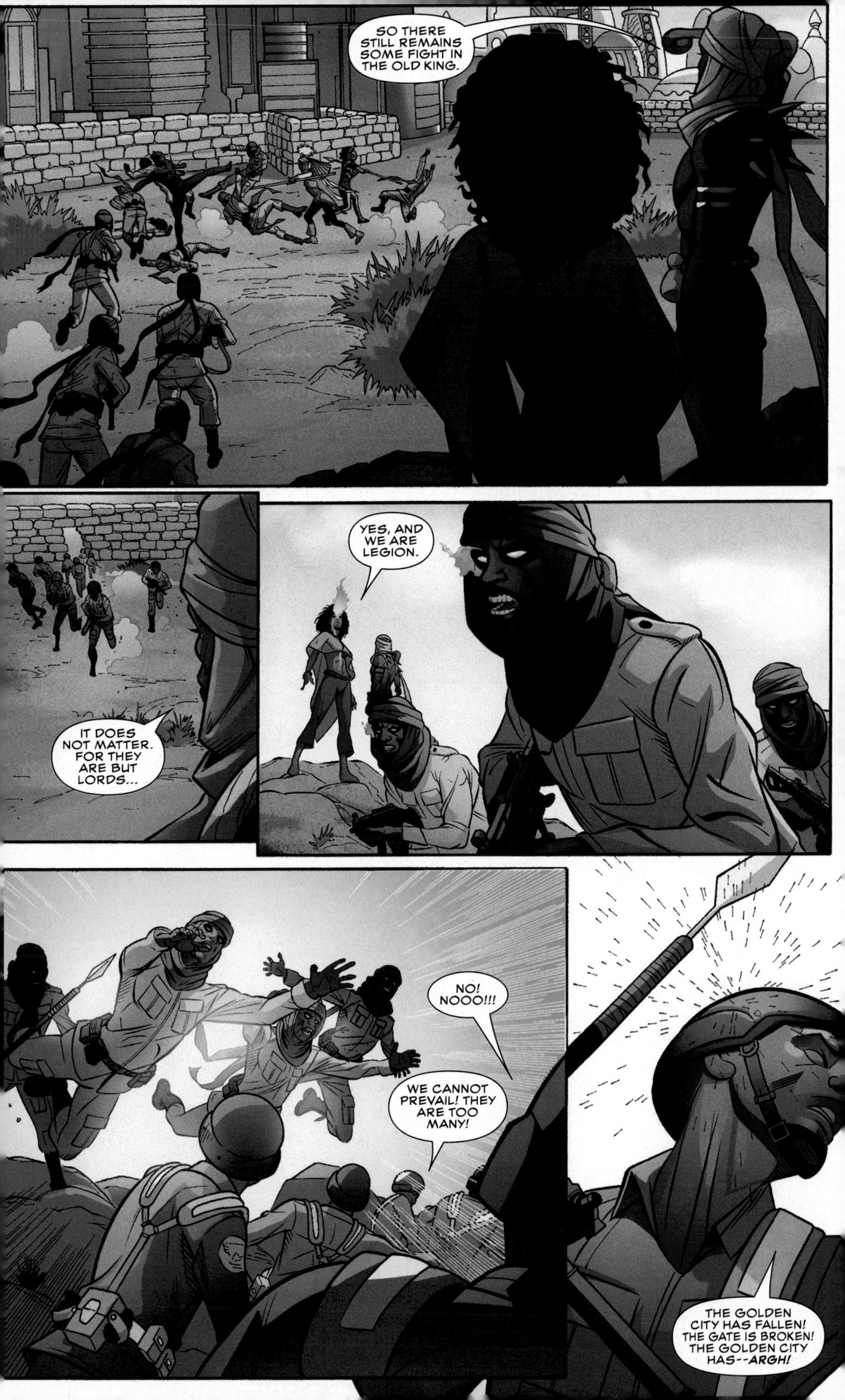
SO THERE STILL REMAINS SOME FIGHT IN THE OLD KING.
IT DOES NOT MATTER. FOR THEY ARE BUT LORDS...
YES, AND WE ARE LEGION.
NO! NOOO!!!
WE CANNOT PREVAIL! THEY ARE TOO MANY!
THE GOLDEN CITY HAS FALLEN! THE GATE IS BROKEN! THE GOLDEN CITY HAS--ARGH!

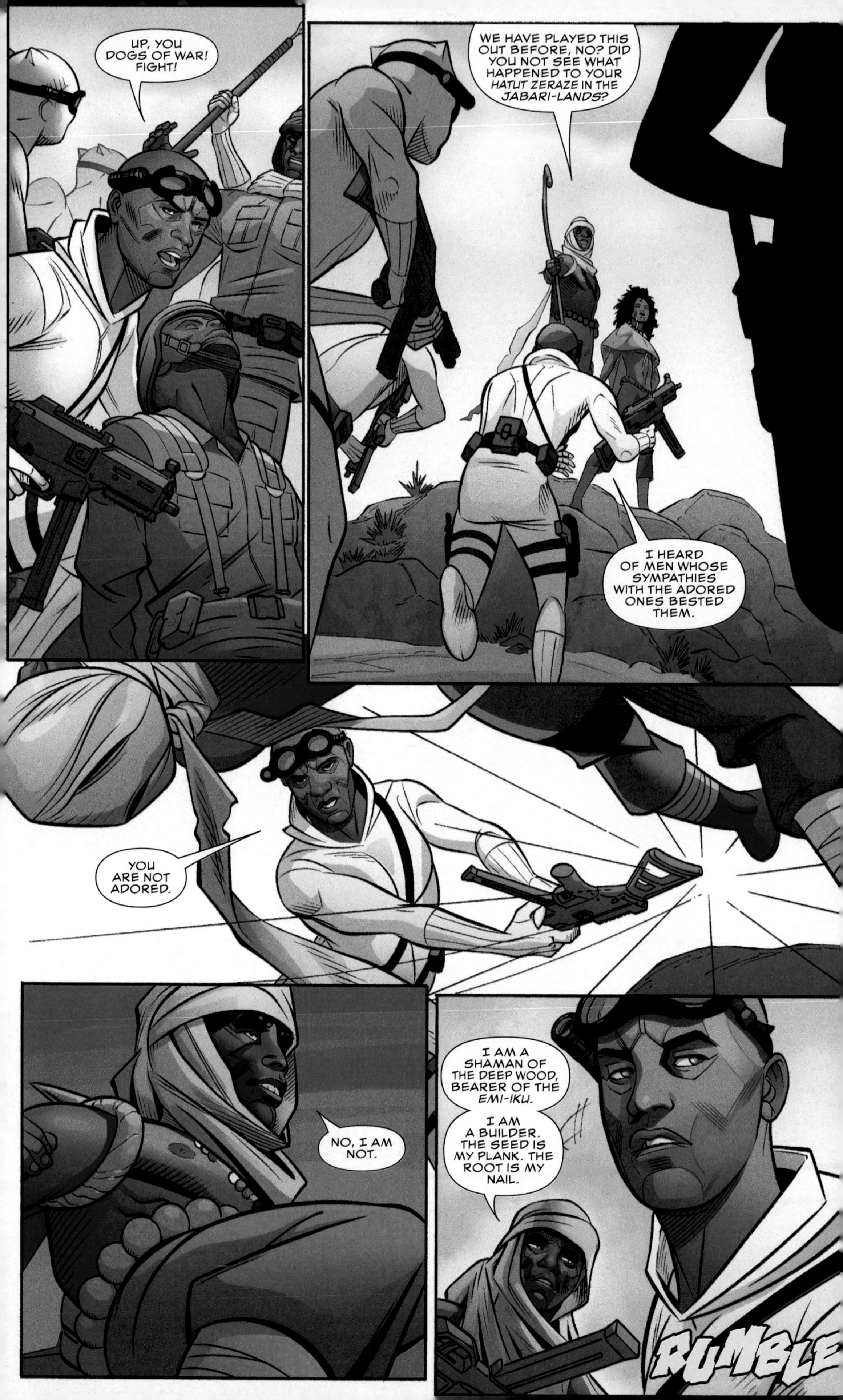
UP, YOU DOGS OF WAR! FIGHT!
WE HAVE PLAYED THIS OUT BEFORE, NO? DID YOU NOT SEE WHAT HAPPENED TO YOUR *HATUT ZERAZE* IN THE *JABARI-LANDS?*
I HEARD OF MEN WHOSE SYMPATHIES WITH THE ADORED ONES BESTED THEM.
YOU ARE NOT ADORED.
NO, I AM NOT.
I AM A SHAMAN OF THE DEEP WOOD, BEARER OF THE *EMI-IKU.*
I AM A BUILDER. THE SEED IS MY PLANK. THE ROOT IS MY NAIL.
RUMBLE

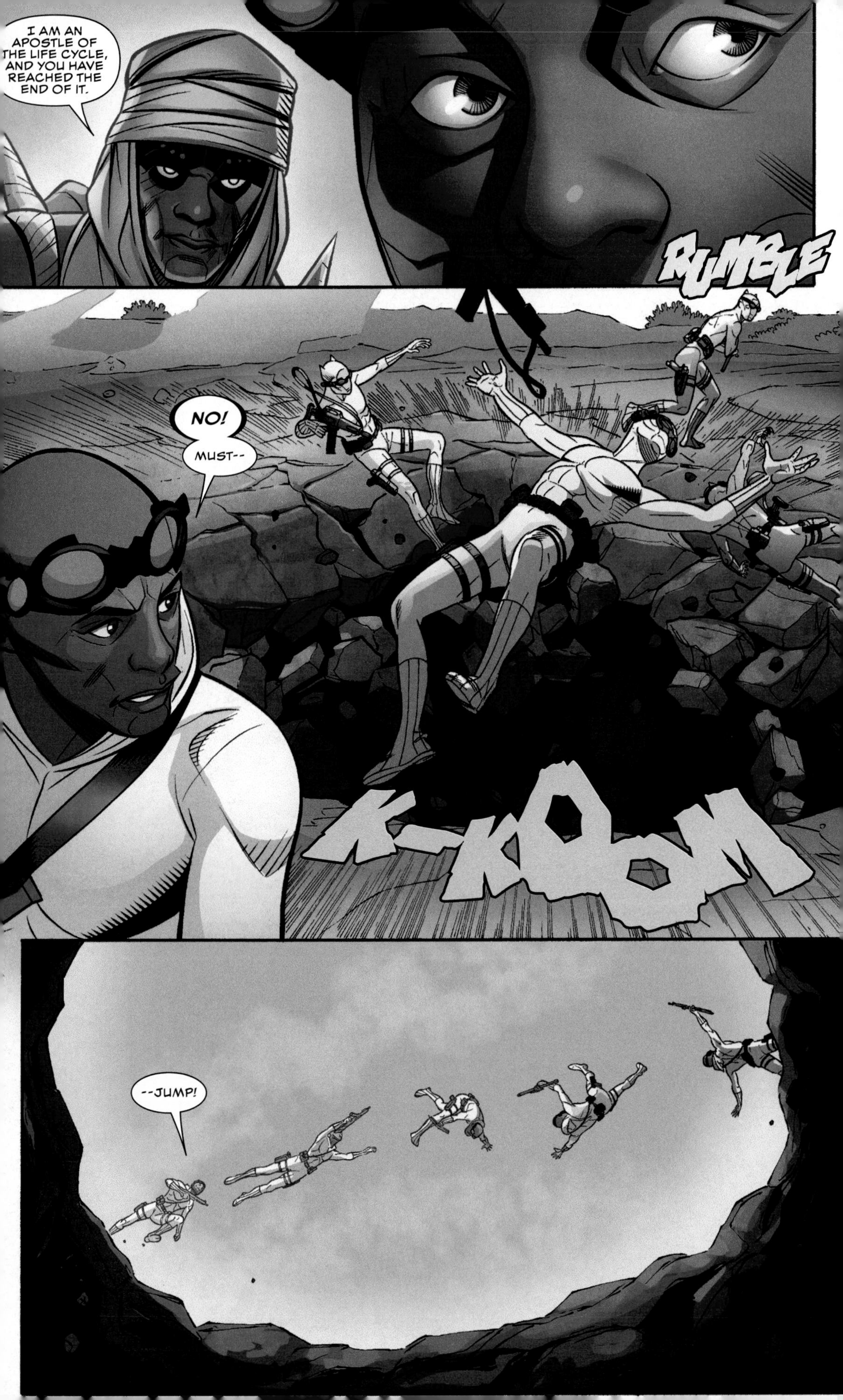
I AM AN APOSTLE OF THE LIFE CYCLE, AND YOU HAVE REACHED THE END OF IT.
RUMBLE
NO!
MUST--
K-KOOM
--JUMP!

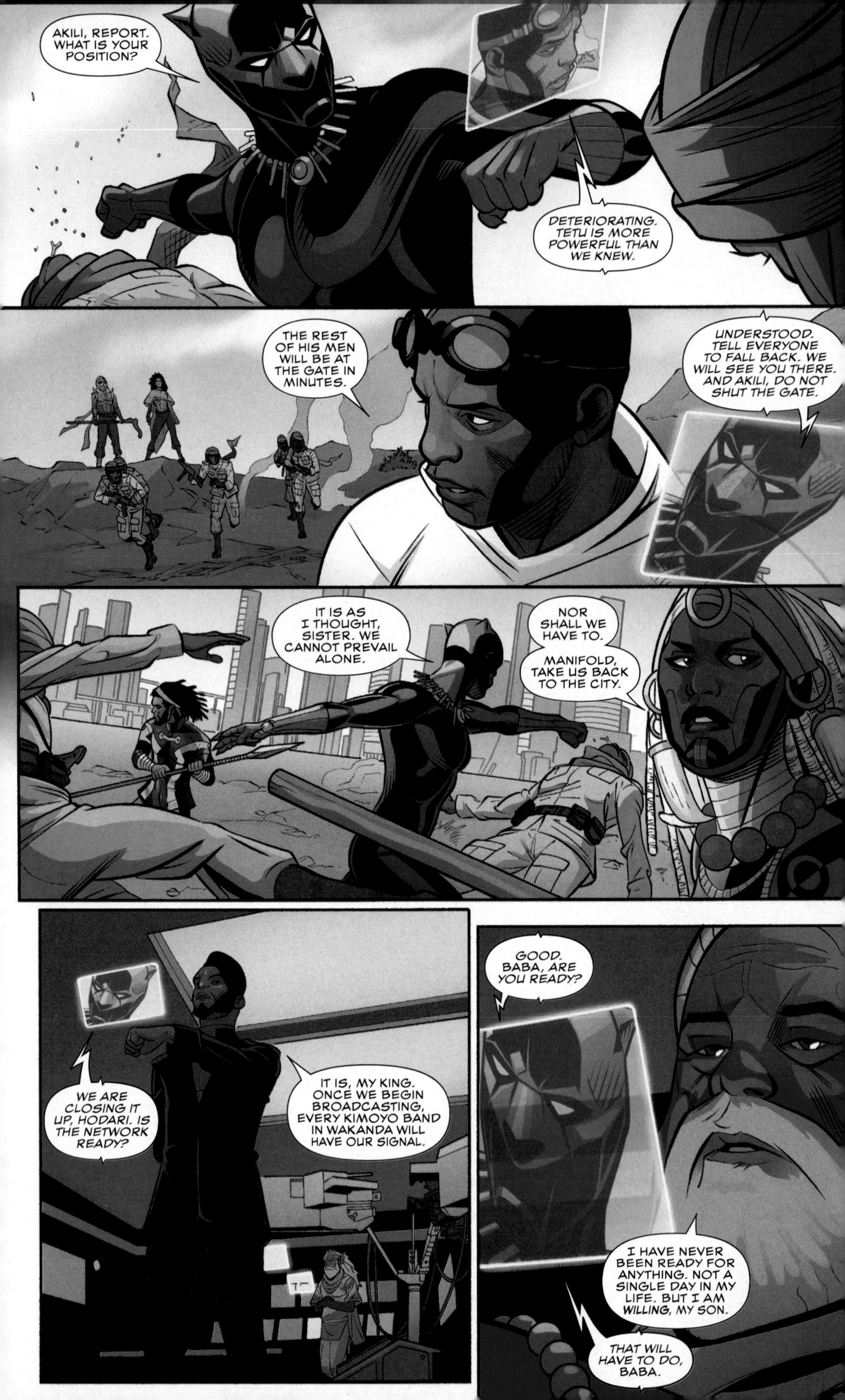
AKILI, REPORT. WHAT IS YOUR POSITION?
DETERIORATING. TETU IS MORE POWERFUL THAN WE KNEW.
THE REST OF HIS MEN WILL BE AT THE GATE IN MINUTES.
UNDERSTOOD. TELL EVERYONE TO FALL BACK. WE WILL SEE YOU THERE. AND AKILI, DO NOT SHUT THE GATE.
IT IS AS I THOUGHT, SISTER. WE CANNOT PREVAIL ALONE.
NOR SHALL WE HAVE TO.
MANIFOLD, TAKE US BACK TO THE CITY.
WE ARE CLOSING IT UP, HODARI. IS THE NETWORK READY?
IT IS, MY KING. ONCE WE BEGIN BROADCASTING, EVERY KIMOYO BAND IN WAKANDA WILL HAVE OUR SIGNAL.
GOOD. BABA, ARE YOU READY?
I HAVE NEVER BEEN READY FOR ANYTHING. NOT A SINGLE DAY IN MY LIFE. BUT I AM WILLING, MY SON.
THAT WILL HAVE TO DO, BABA.

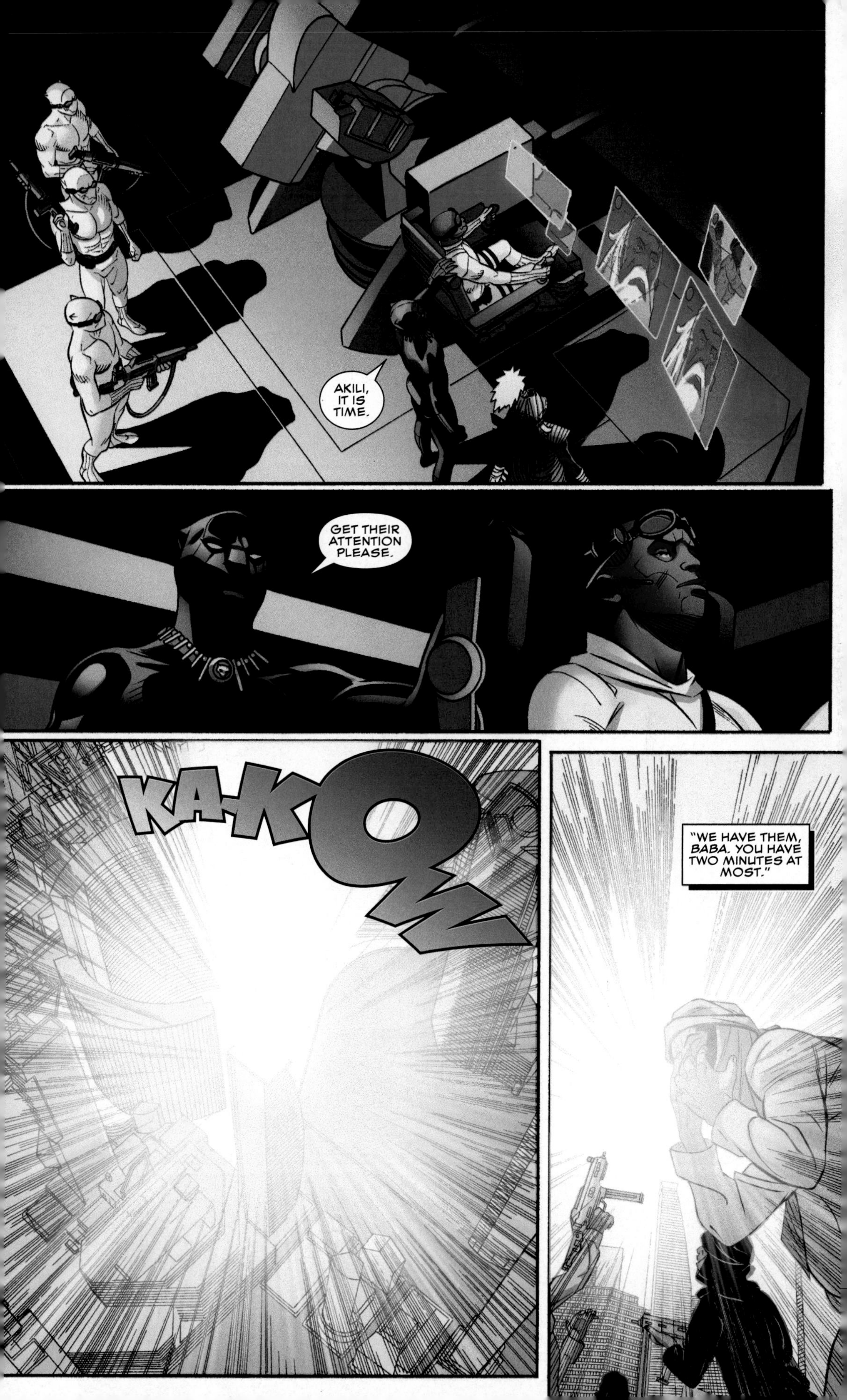
AKILI, IT IS TIME.
GET THEIR ATTENTION PLEASE.
KA-KOOM
"WE HAVE THEM, BABA. YOU HAVE TWO MINUTES AT MOST."

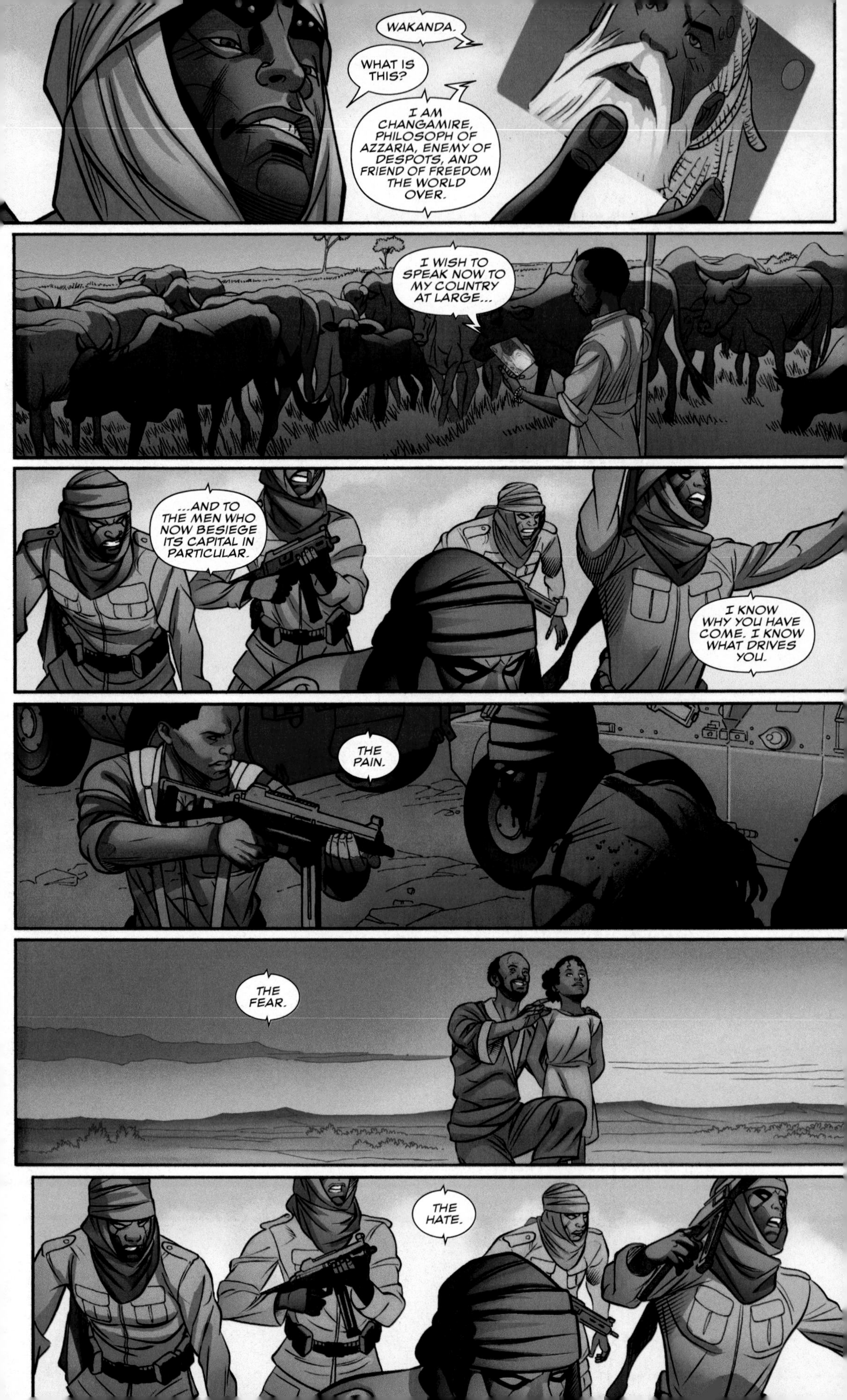
WAKANDA.
WHAT IS THIS?
I AM CHANGAMIRE, PHILOSOPH OF AZZARIA, ENEMY OF DESPOTS, AND FRIEND OF FREEDOM THE WORLD OVER.
I WISH TO SPEAK NOW TO MY COUNTRY AT LARGE...
...AND TO THE MEN WHO NOW BESIEGE ITS CAPITAL IN PARTICULAR.
I KNOW WHY YOU HAVE COME. I KNOW WHAT DRIVES YOU.
THE PAIN.
THE FEAR.
THE HATE.

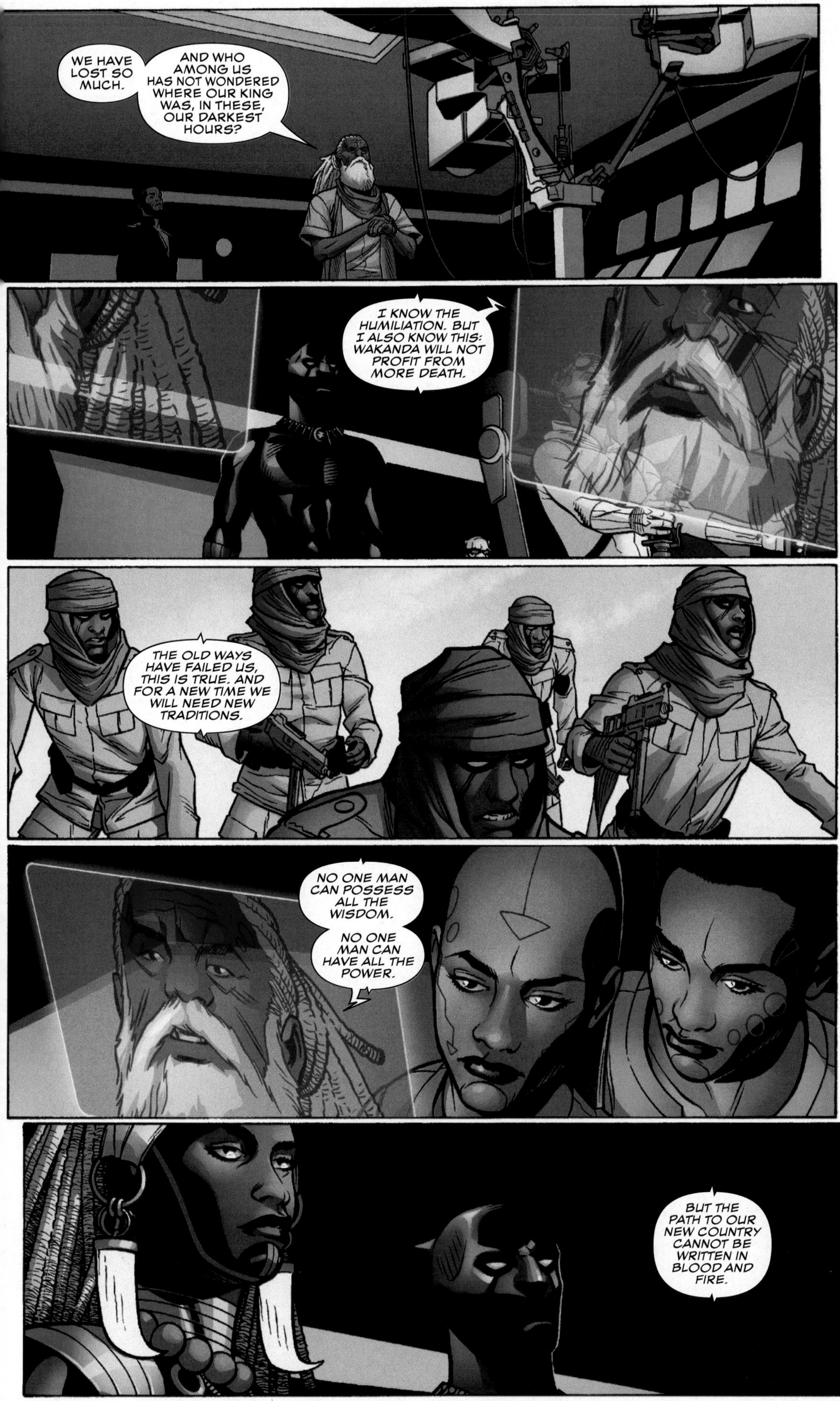
WE HAVE LOST SO MUCH.
AND WHO AMONG US HAS NOT WONDERED WHERE OUR KING WAS, IN THESE, OUR DARKEST HOURS?
I KNOW THE HUMILIATION. BUT I ALSO KNOW THIS: WAKANDA WILL NOT PROFIT FROM MORE DEATH.
THE OLD WAYS HAVE FAILED US, THIS IS TRUE. AND FOR A NEW TIME WE WILL NEED NEW TRADITIONS.
NO ONE MAN CAN POSSESS ALL THE WISDOM.
NO ONE MAN CAN HAVE ALL THE POWER.
BUT THE PATH TO OUR NEW COUNTRY CANNOT BE WRITTEN IN BLOOD AND FIRE.

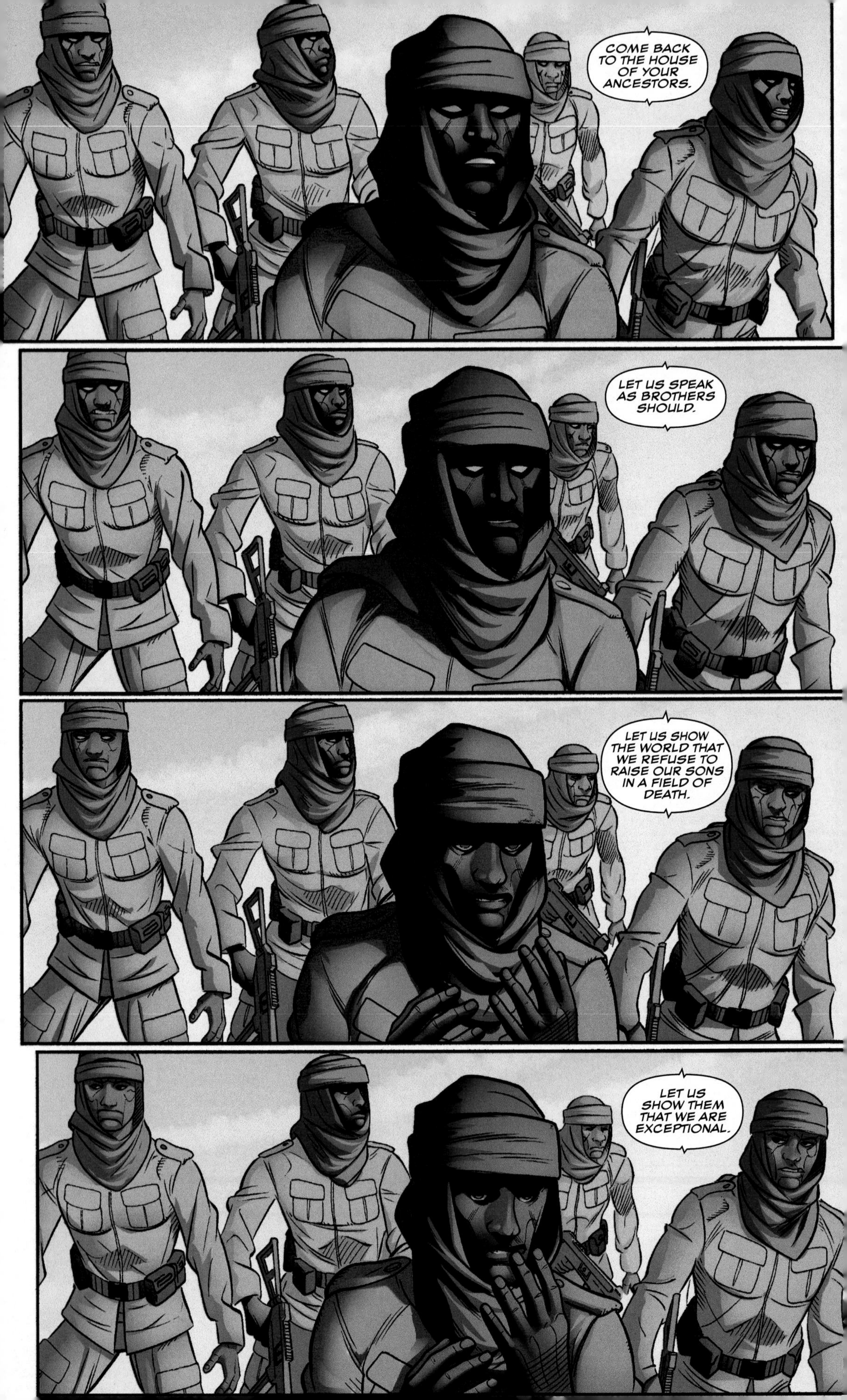
COME BACK TO THE HOUSE OF YOUR ANCESTORS.
LET US SPEAK AS BROTHERS SHOULD.
LET US SHOW THE WORLD THAT WE REFUSE TO RAISE OUR SONS IN A FIELD OF DEATH.
LET US SHOW THEM THAT WE ARE EXCEPTIONAL.

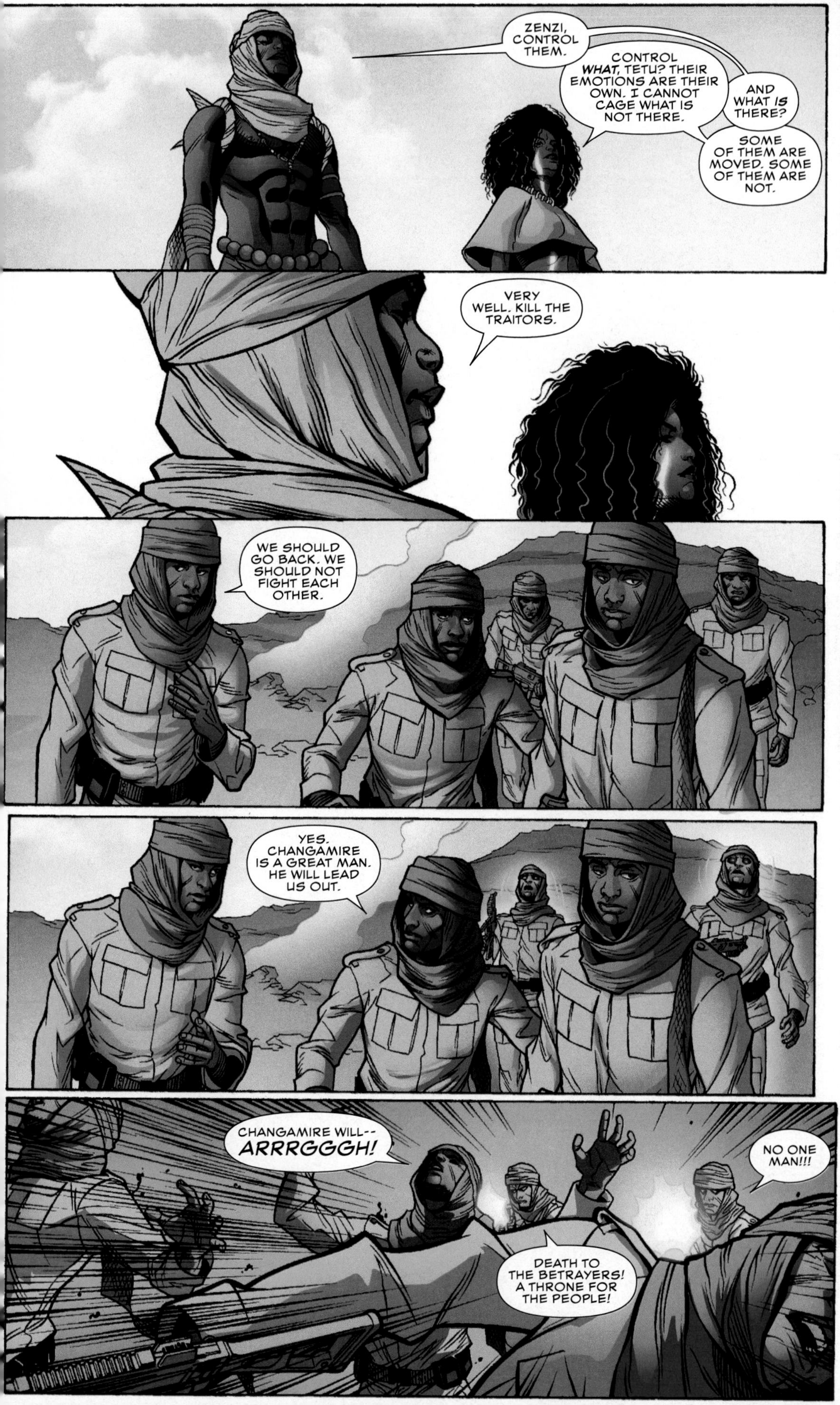
ZENZI, CONTROL THEM.
CONTROL WHAT, TETU? THEIR EMOTIONS ARE THEIR OWN. I CANNOT CAGE WHAT IS NOT THERE.
AND WHAT IS THERE?
SOME OF THEM ARE MOVED. SOME OF THEM ARE NOT.
VERY WELL. KILL THE TRAITORS.
WE SHOULD GO BACK. WE SHOULD NOT FIGHT EACH OTHER.
YES. CHANGAMIRE IS A GREAT MAN. HE WILL LEAD US OUT.
CHANGAMIRE WILL-- ARRRGGGH!
NO ONE MAN!!!
DEATH TO THE BETRAYERS! A THRONE FOR THE PEOPLE!

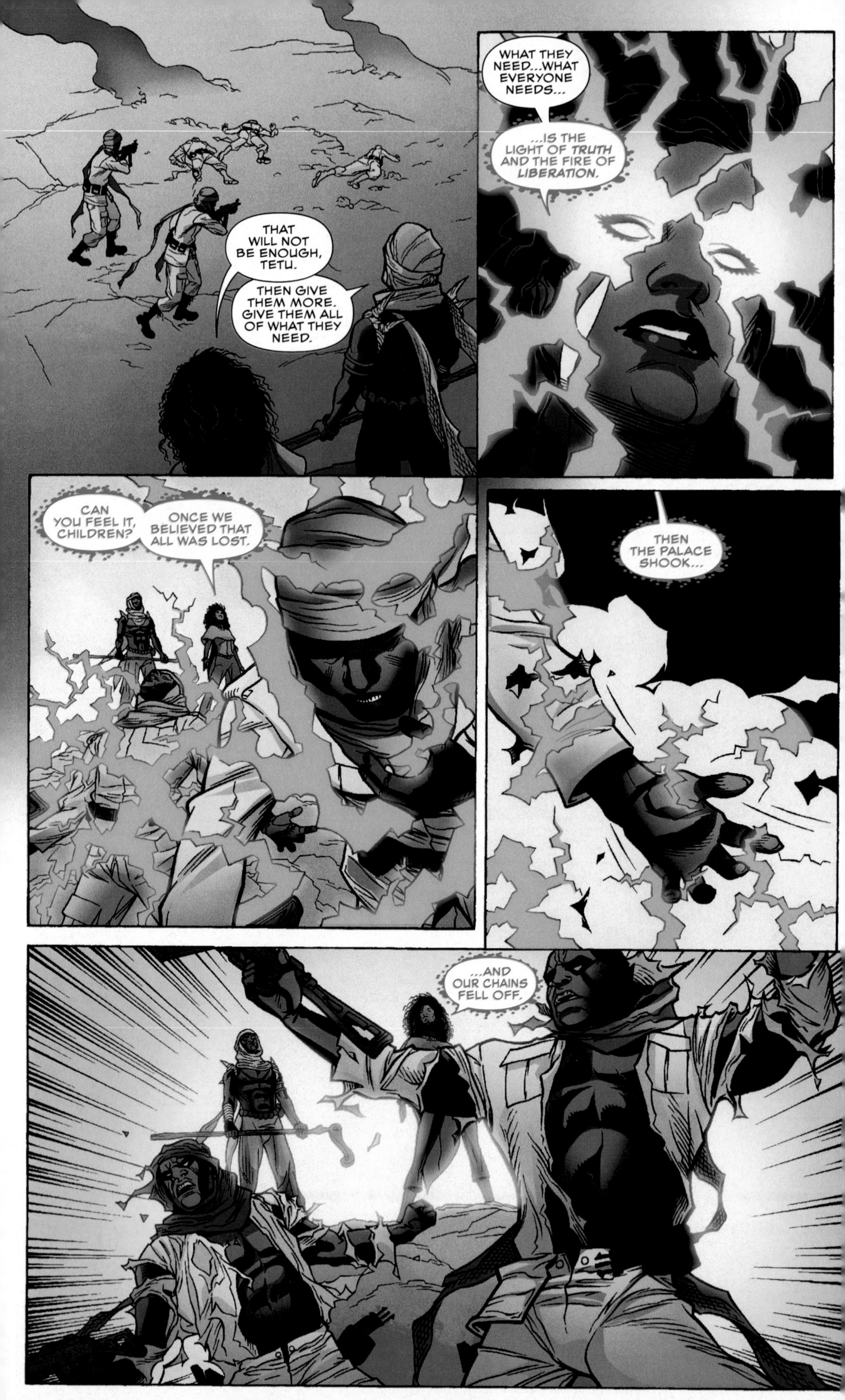
THAT WILL NOT BE ENOUGH, TETU.
THEN GIVE THEM MORE. GIVE THEM ALL OF WHAT THEY NEED.
WHAT THEY NEED...WHAT EVERYONE NEEDS...
...IS THE LIGHT OF *TRUTH* AND THE FIRE OF *LIBERATION.*
CAN YOU FEEL IT, CHILDREN?
ONCE WE BELIEVED THAT ALL WAS LOST.
THEN THE PALACE SHOOK...
...AND OUR CHAINS FELL OFF.

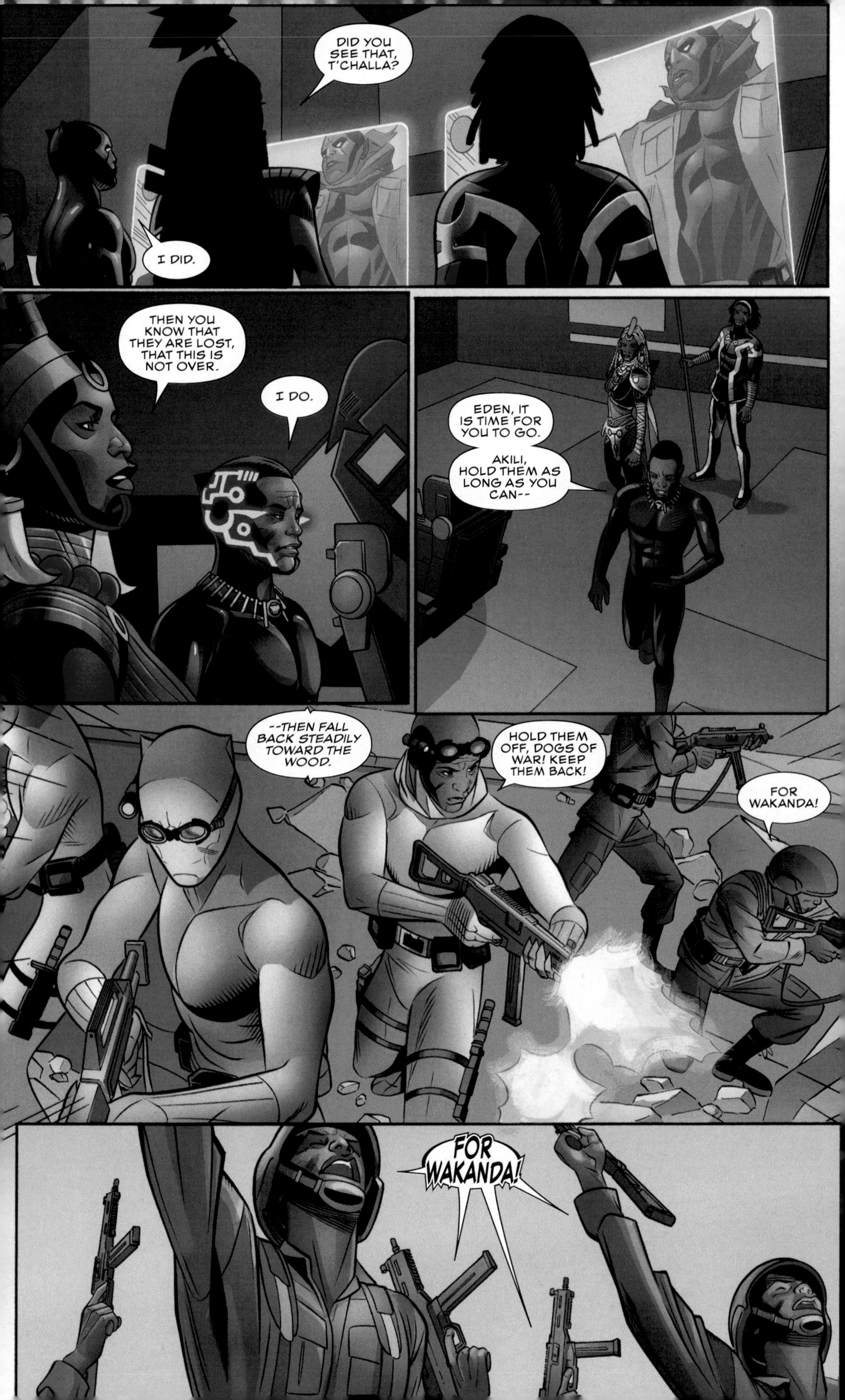
DID YOU SEE THAT, T'CHALLA?
I DID.
THEN YOU KNOW THAT THEY ARE LOST, THAT THIS IS NOT OVER.
I DO.
EDEN, IT IS TIME FOR YOU TO GO.
AKILI, HOLD THEM AS LONG AS YOU CAN--
--THEN FALL BACK STEADILY TOWARD THE WOOD.
HOLD THEM OFF, DOGS OF WAR! KEEP THEM BACK!
FOR WAKANDA!
FOR WAKANDA!

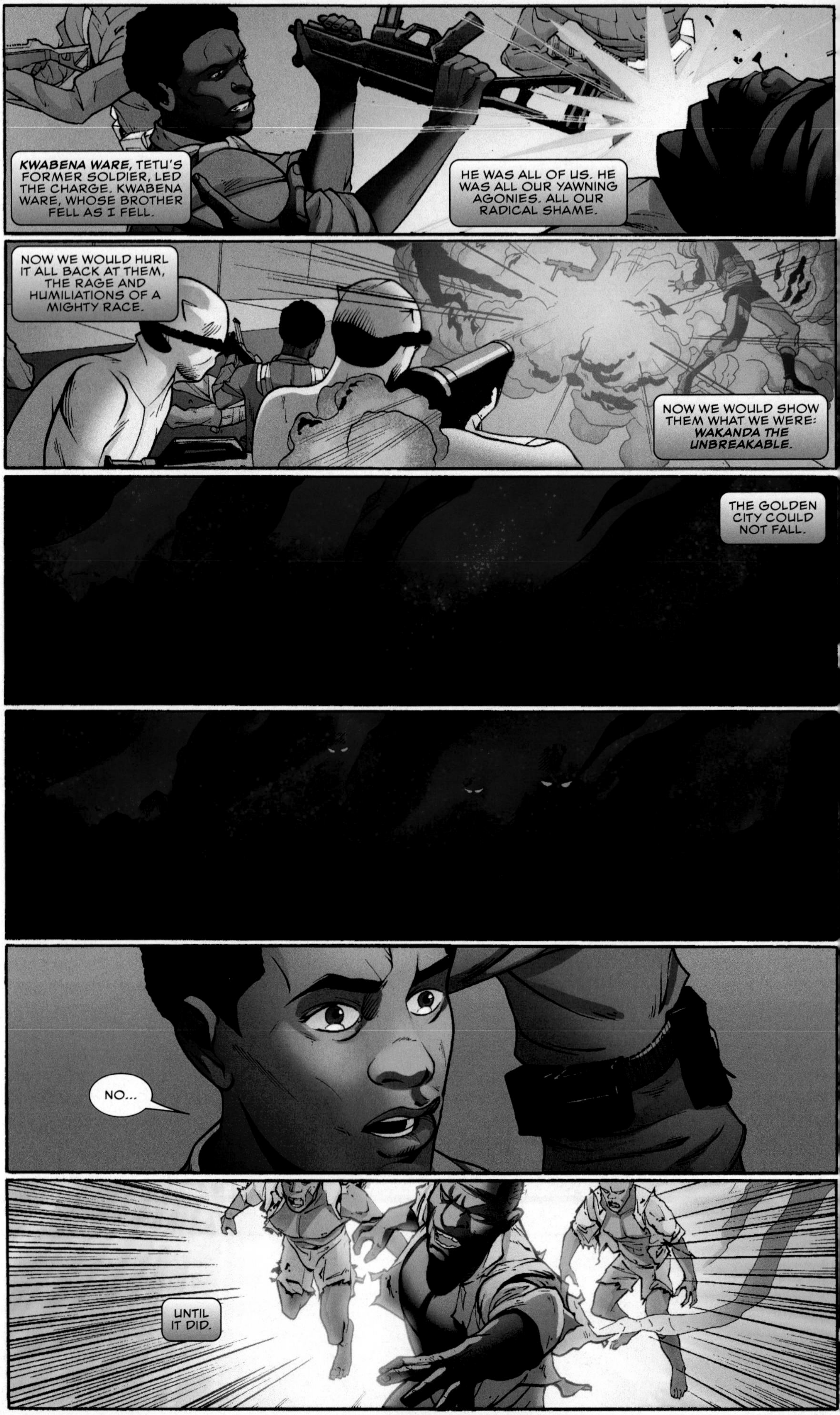
KWABENA WARE, TETU'S FORMER SOLDIER, LED THE CHARGE. KWABENA WARE, WHOSE BROTHER FELL AS I FELL.
HE WAS ALL OF US. HE WAS ALL OUR YAWNING AGONIES. ALL OUR RADICAL SHAME.
NOW WE WOULD HURL IT ALL BACK AT THEM, THE RAGE AND HUMILIATIONS OF A MIGHTY RACE.
NOW WE WOULD SHOW THEM WHAT WE WERE: WAKANDA THE UNBREAKABLE.
THE GOLDEN CITY COULD NOT FALL.
NO...
UNTIL IT DID.

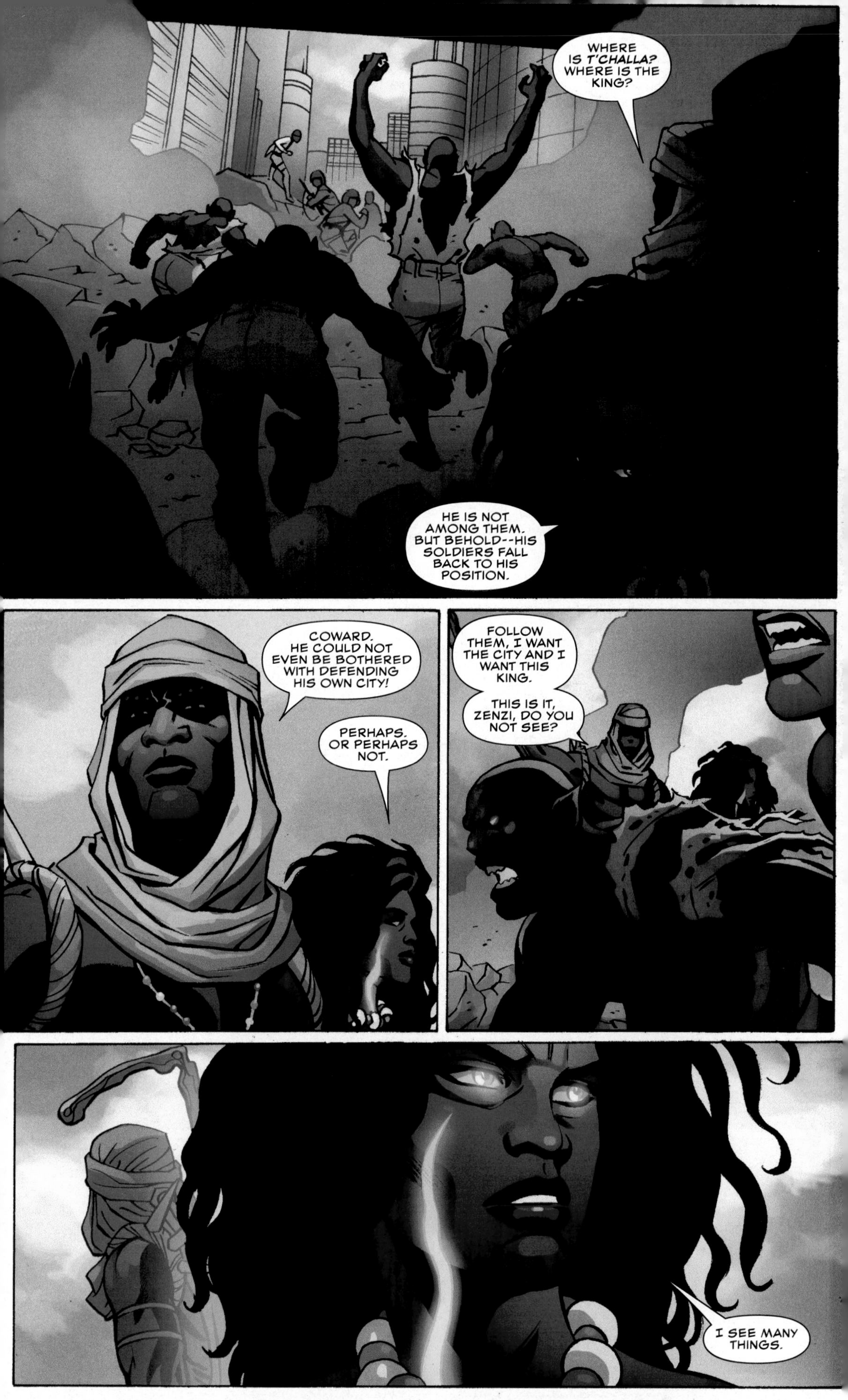
WHERE IS T'CHALLA? WHERE IS THE KING?
HE IS NOT AMONG THEM. BUT BEHOLD--HIS SOLDIERS FALL BACK TO HIS POSITION.
COWARD. HE COULD NOT EVEN BE BOTHERED WITH DEFENDING HIS OWN CITY!
PERHAPS. OR PERHAPS NOT.
FOLLOW THEM, I WANT THE CITY AND I WANT THIS KING.
THIS IS IT, ZENZI, DO YOU NOT SEE?
I SEE MANY THINGS.

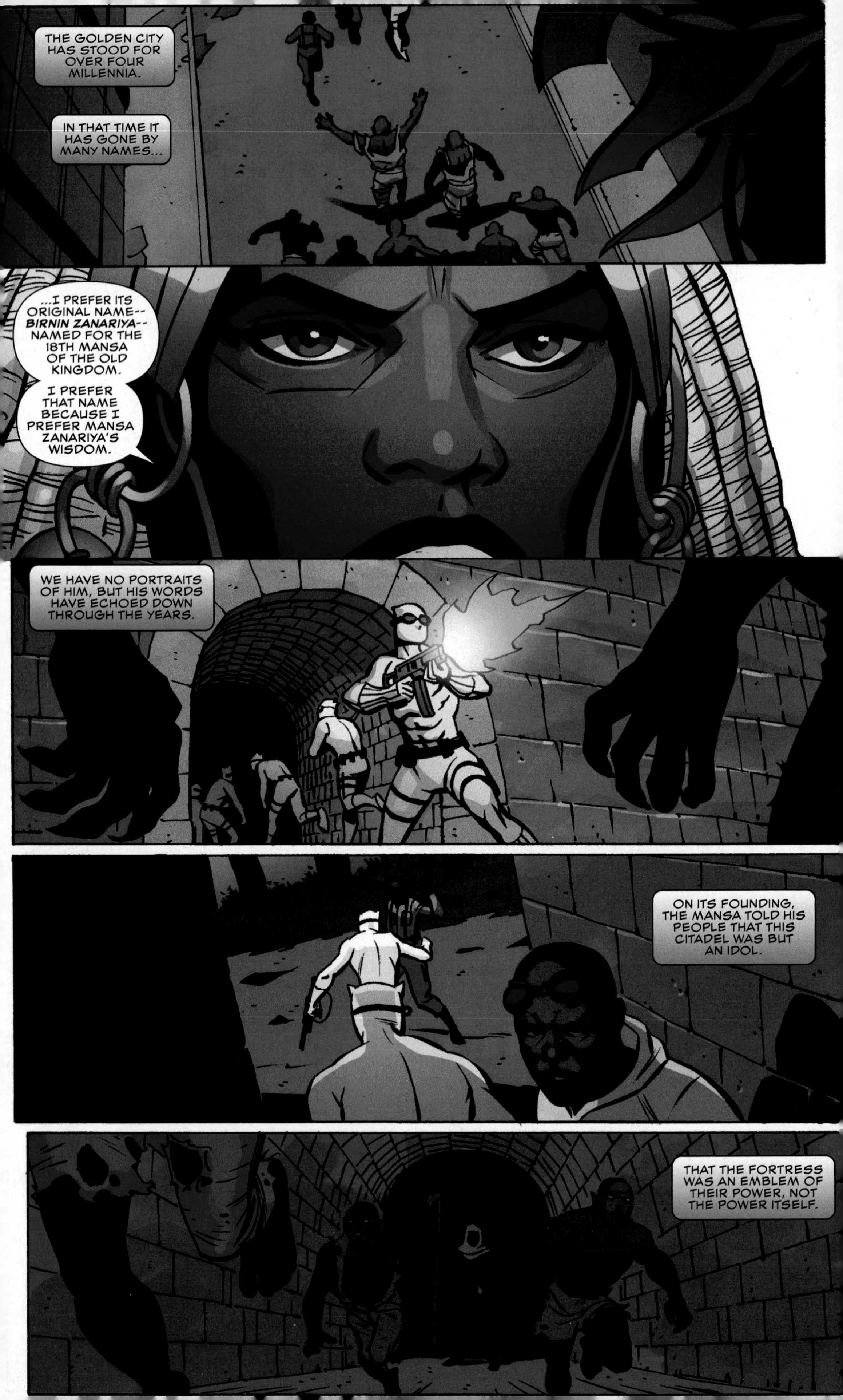
THE GOLDEN CITY HAS STOOD FOR OVER FOUR MILLENNIA.
IN THAT TIME IT HAS GONE BY MANY NAMES...
...I PREFER ITS ORIGINAL NAME-- *BIRNIN ZANARIYA*-- NAMED FOR THE 18TH MANSA OF THE OLD KINGDOM.
I PREFER THAT NAME BECAUSE I PREFER MANSA ZANARIYA'S WISDOM.
WE HAVE NO PORTRAITS OF HIM, BUT HIS WORDS HAVE ECHOED DOWN THROUGH THE YEARS.
ON ITS FOUNDING, THE MANSA TOLD HIS PEOPLE THAT THIS CITADEL WAS BUT AN IDOL.
THAT THE FORTRESS WAS AN EMBLEM OF THEIR POWER, NOT THE POWER ITSELF.

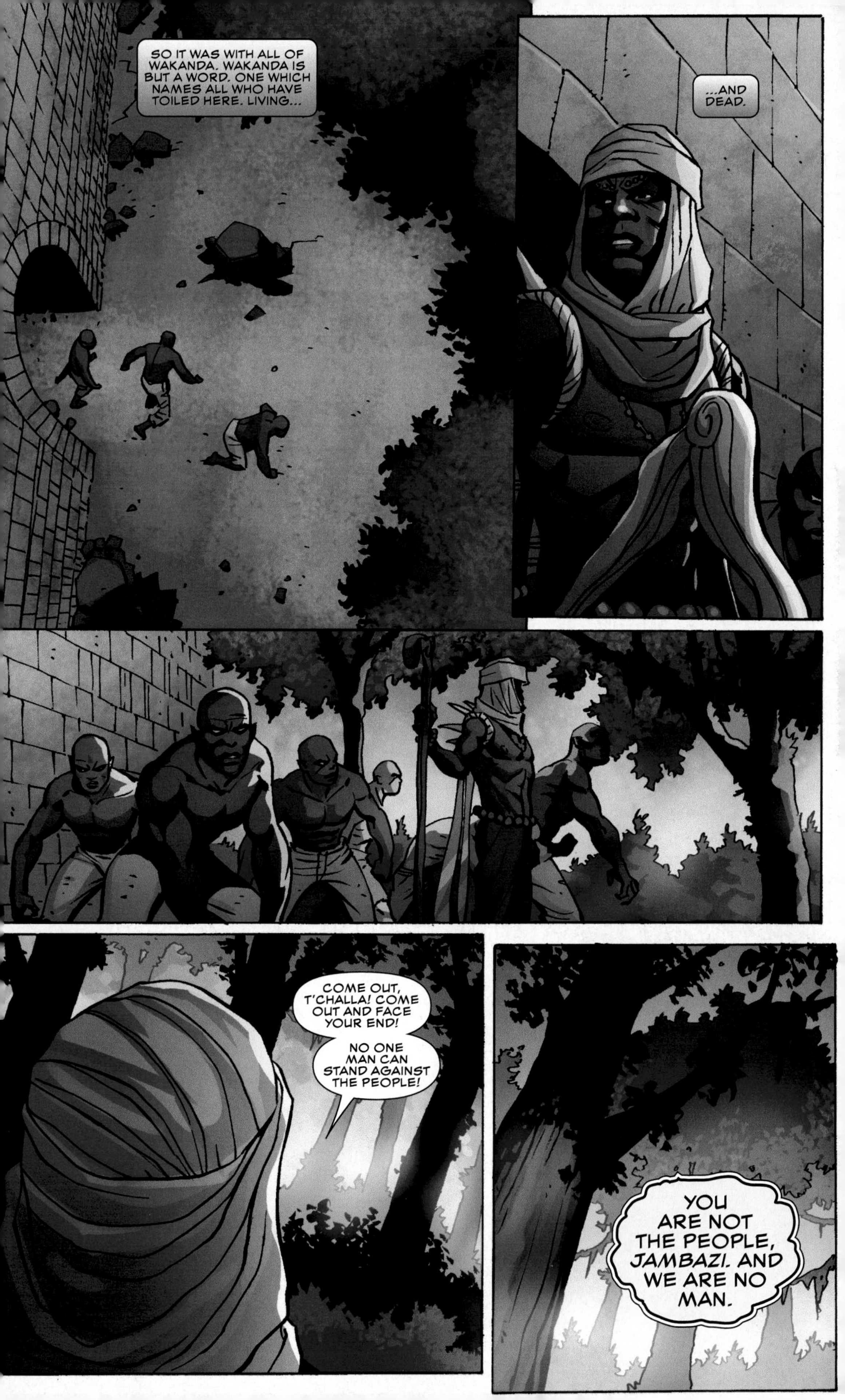
SO IT WAS WITH ALL OF WAKANDA. WAKANDA IS BUT A WORD. ONE WHICH NAMES ALL WHO HAVE TOILED HERE. LIVING...
...AND DEAD.
COME OUT, T'CHALLA! COME OUT AND FACE YOUR END!
NO ONE MAN CAN STAND AGAINST THE PEOPLE!
YOU ARE NOT THE PEOPLE, JAMBAZI. AND WE ARE NO MAN.

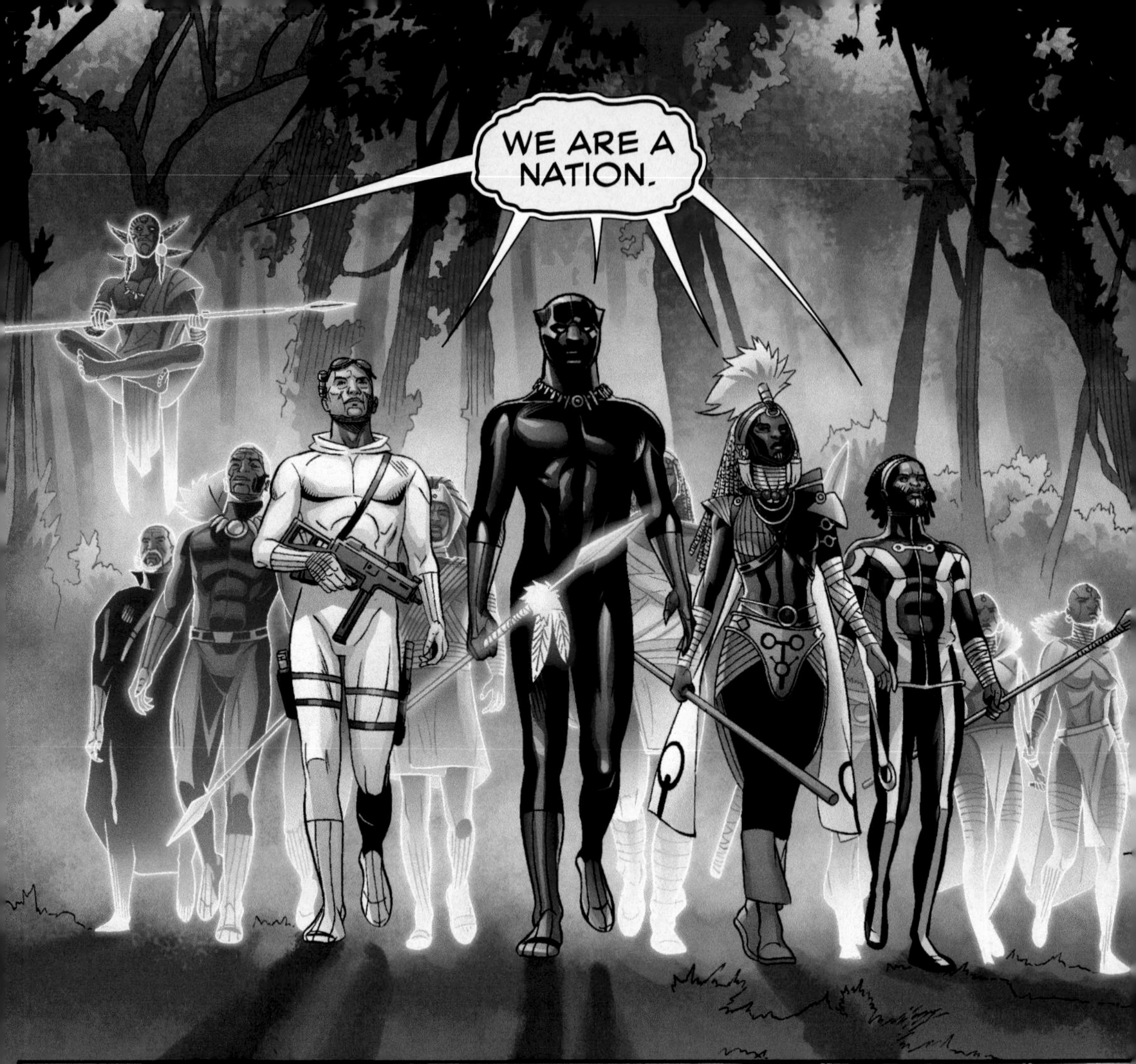
WE ARE A NATION.

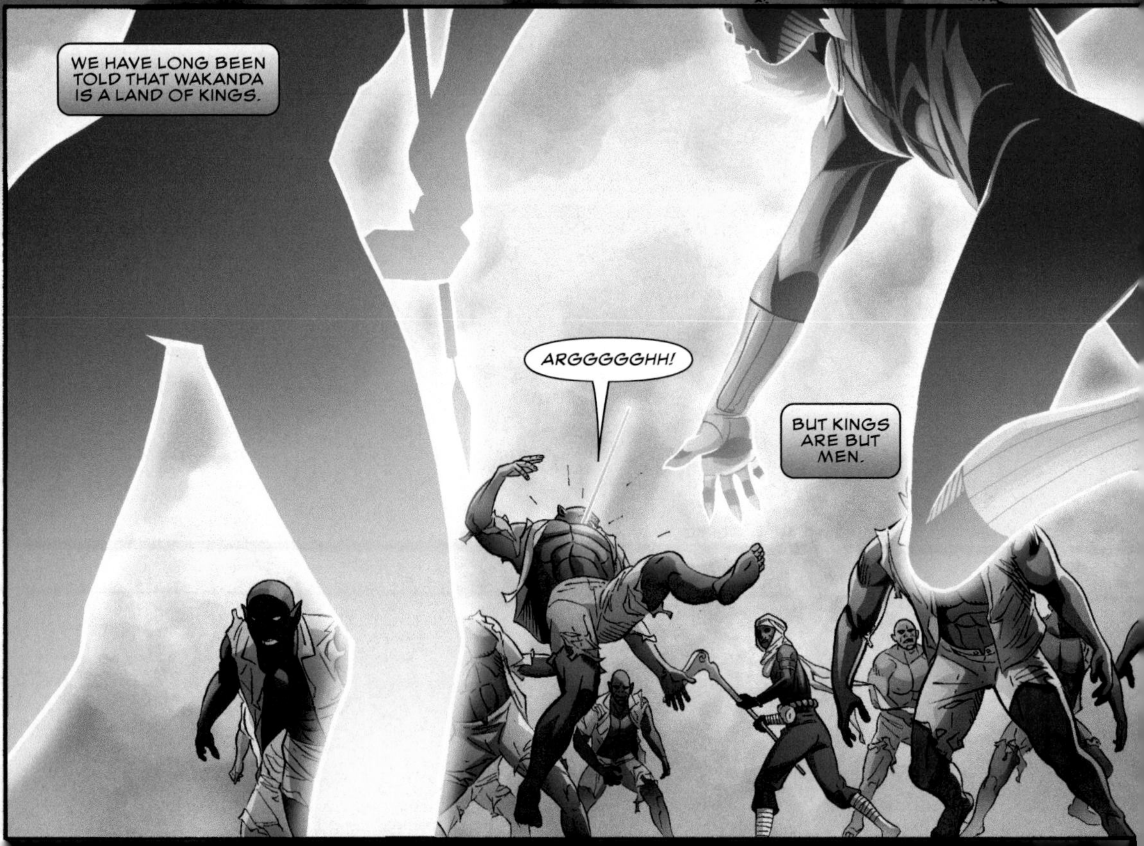
WE HAVE LONG BEEN TOLD THAT WAKANDA IS A LAND OF KINGS.
ARGGGGGHH!
BUT KINGS ARE BUT MEN.

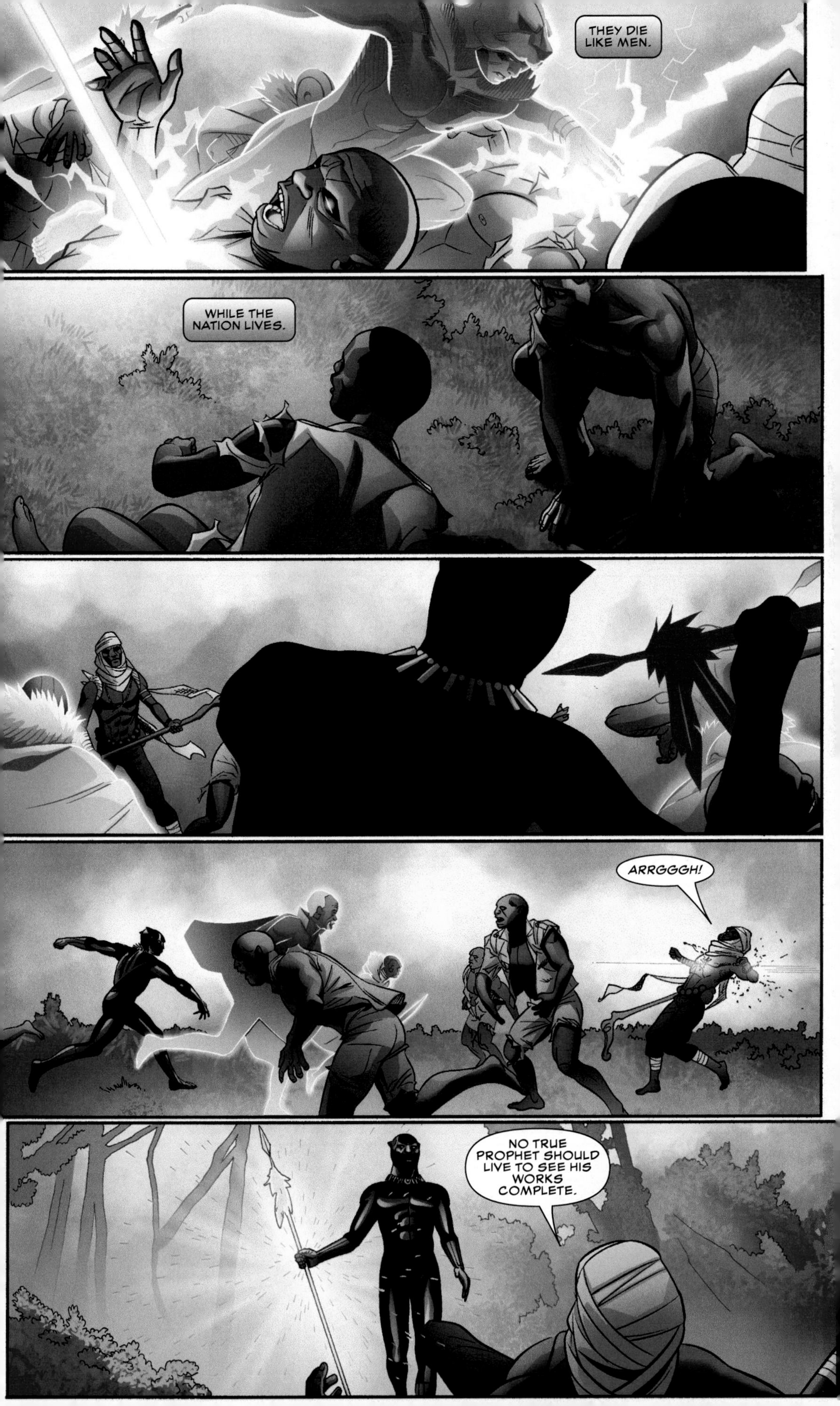
THEY DIE LIKE MEN.
WHILE THE NATION LIVES.
ARRGGGH!
NO TRUE PROPHET SHOULD LIVE TO SEE HIS WORKS COMPLETE.

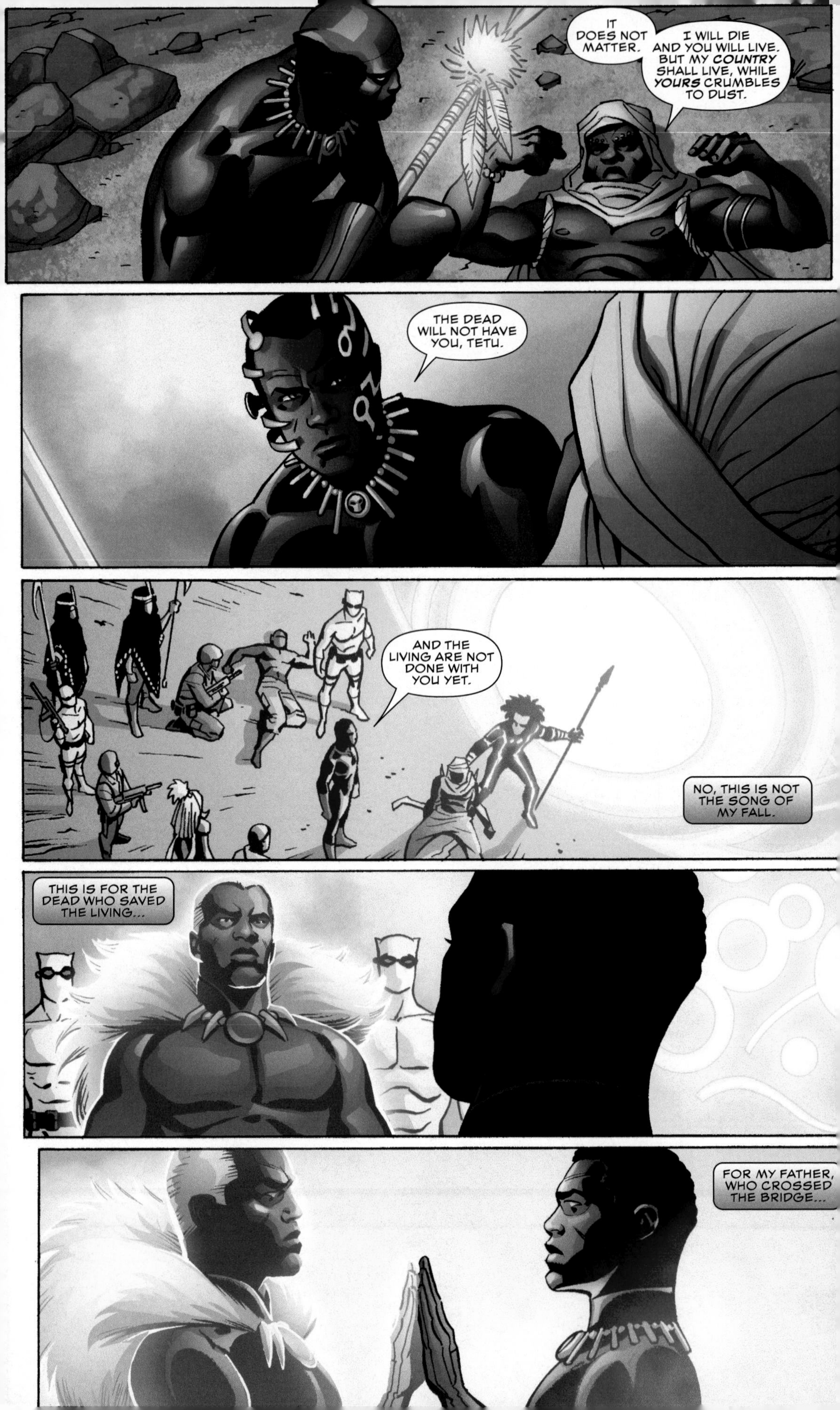
IT DOES NOT MATTER.
I WILL DIE AND YOU WILL LIVE. BUT MY COUNTRY SHALL LIVE, WHILE YOURS CRUMBLES TO DUST.
THE DEAD WILL NOT HAVE YOU, TETU.
AND THE LIVING ARE NOT DONE WITH YOU YET.
NO, THIS IS NOT THE SONG OF MY FALL.
THIS IS FOR THE DEAD WHO SAVED THE LIVING...
FOR MY FATHER, WHO CROSSED THE BRIDGE...

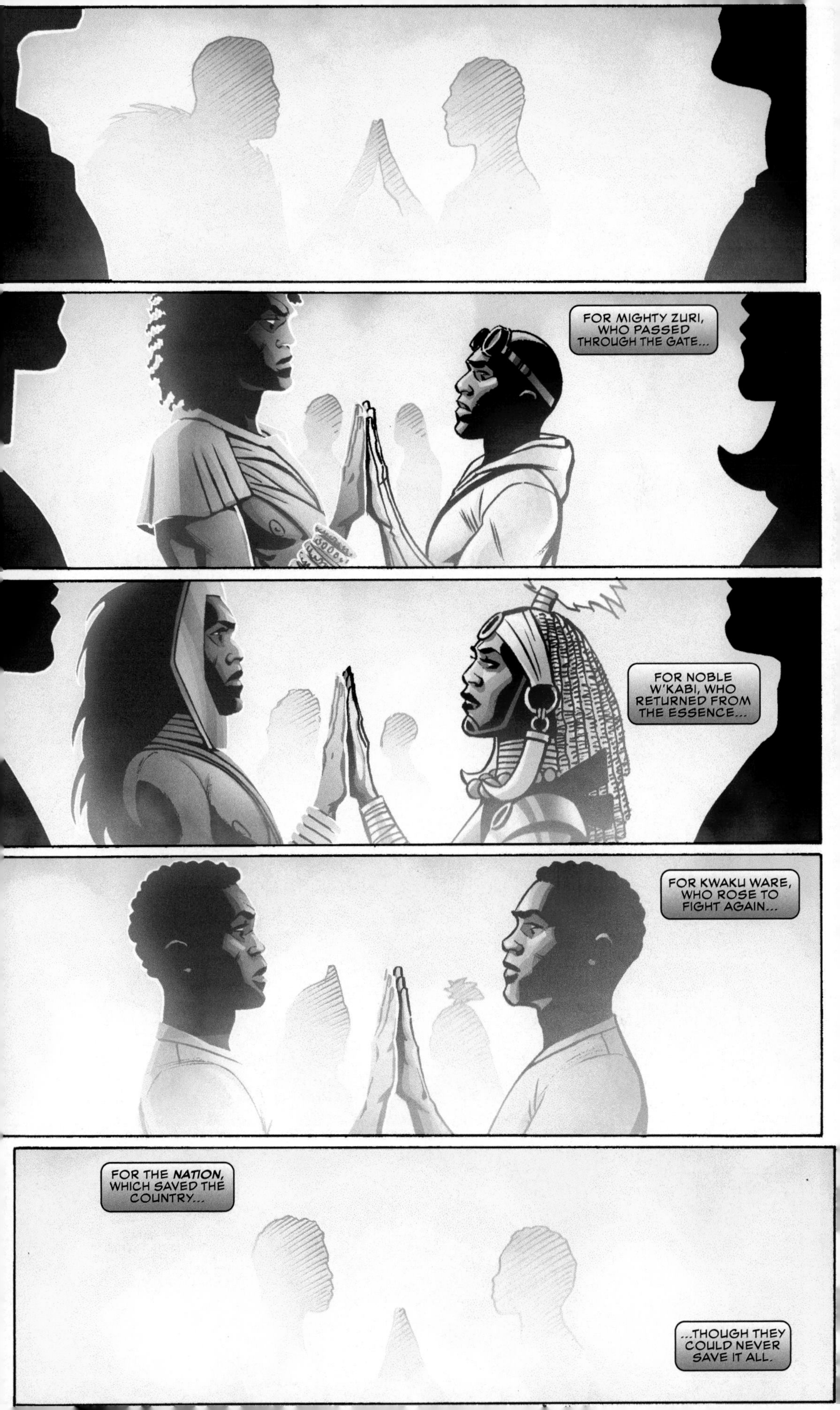
FOR MIGHTY ZURI, WHO PASSED THROUGH THE GATE...
FOR NOBLE W'KABI, WHO RETURNED FROM THE ESSENCE...
FOR KWAKU WARE, WHO ROSE TO FIGHT AGAIN...
FOR THE *NATION,* WHICH SAVED THE COUNTRY...
...THOUGH THEY COULD NEVER SAVE IT ALL.

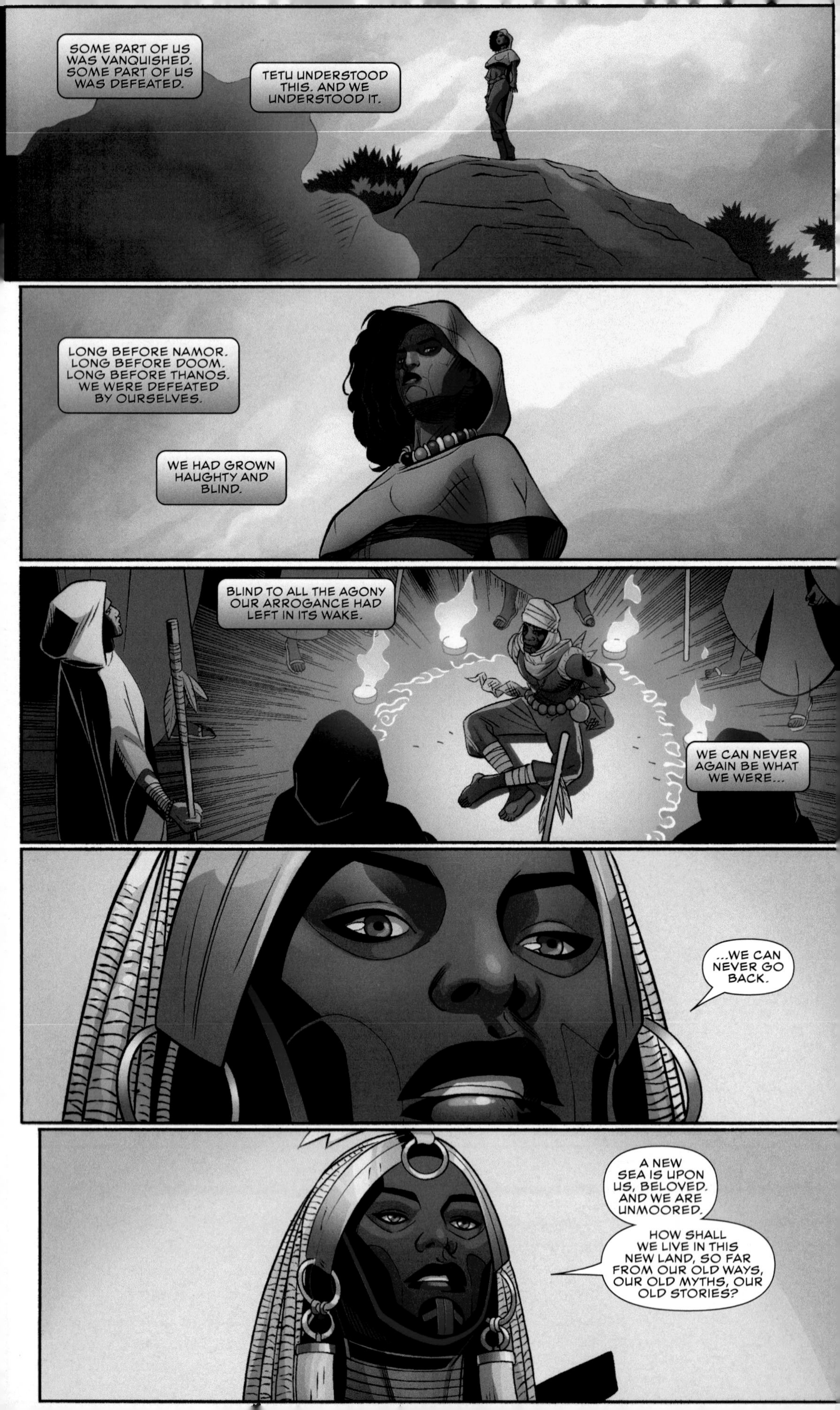
SOME PART OF US WAS VANQUISHED. SOME PART OF US WAS DEFEATED.
TETU UNDERSTOOD THIS. AND WE UNDERSTOOD IT.
LONG BEFORE NAMOR. LONG BEFORE DOOM. LONG BEFORE THANOS. WE WERE DEFEATED BY OURSELVES.
WE HAD GROWN HAUGHTY AND BLIND.
BLIND TO ALL THE AGONY OUR ARROGANCE HAD LEFT IN ITS WAKE.
WE CAN NEVER AGAIN BE WHAT WE WERE...
...WE CAN NEVER GO BACK.
A NEW SEA IS UPON US, BELOVED. AND WE ARE UNMOORED.
HOW SHALL WE LIVE IN THIS NEW LAND, SO FAR FROM OUR OLD WAYS, OUR OLD MYTHS, OUR OLD STORIES?

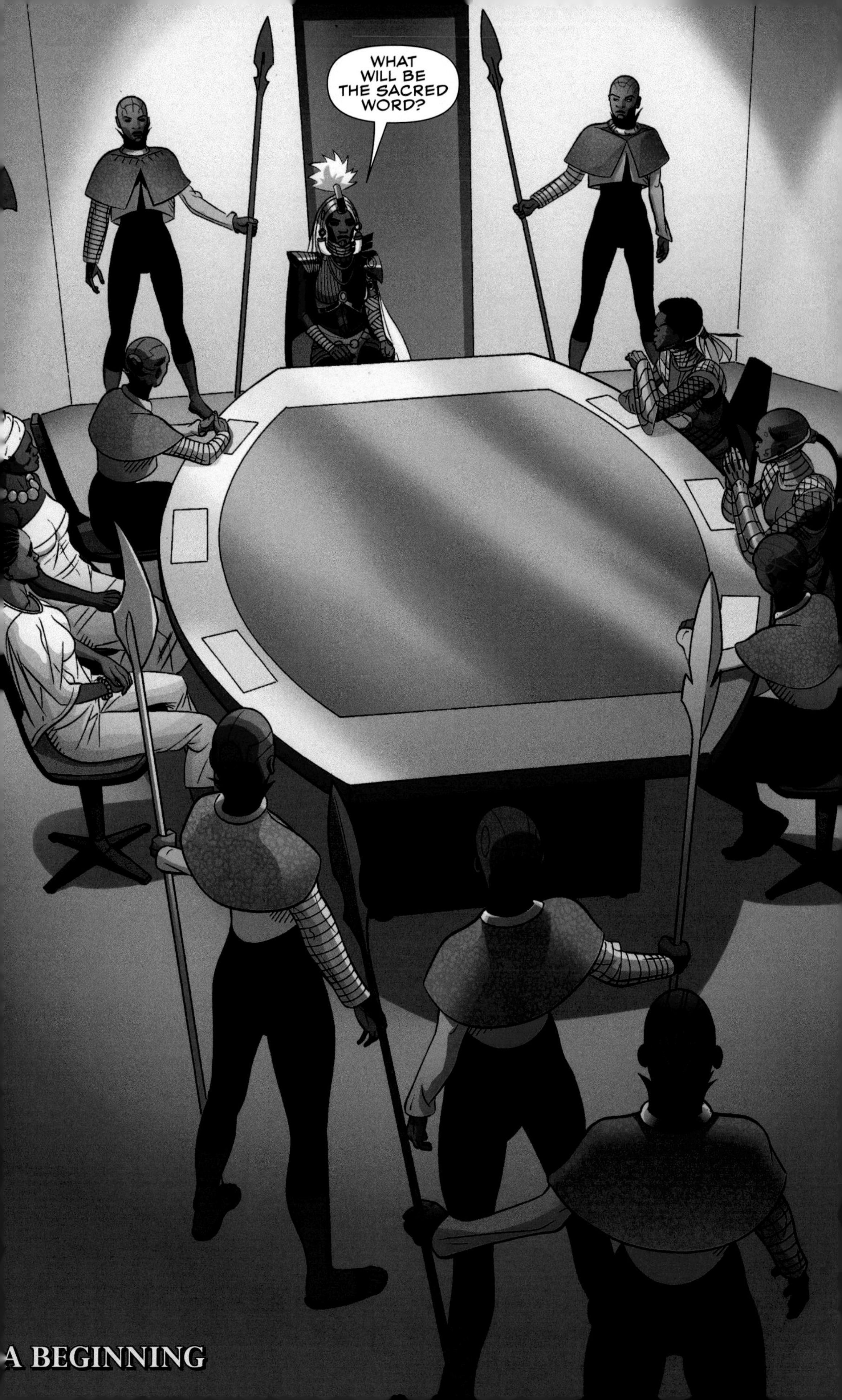
WHAT WILL BE THE SACRED WORD?
A BEGINNING

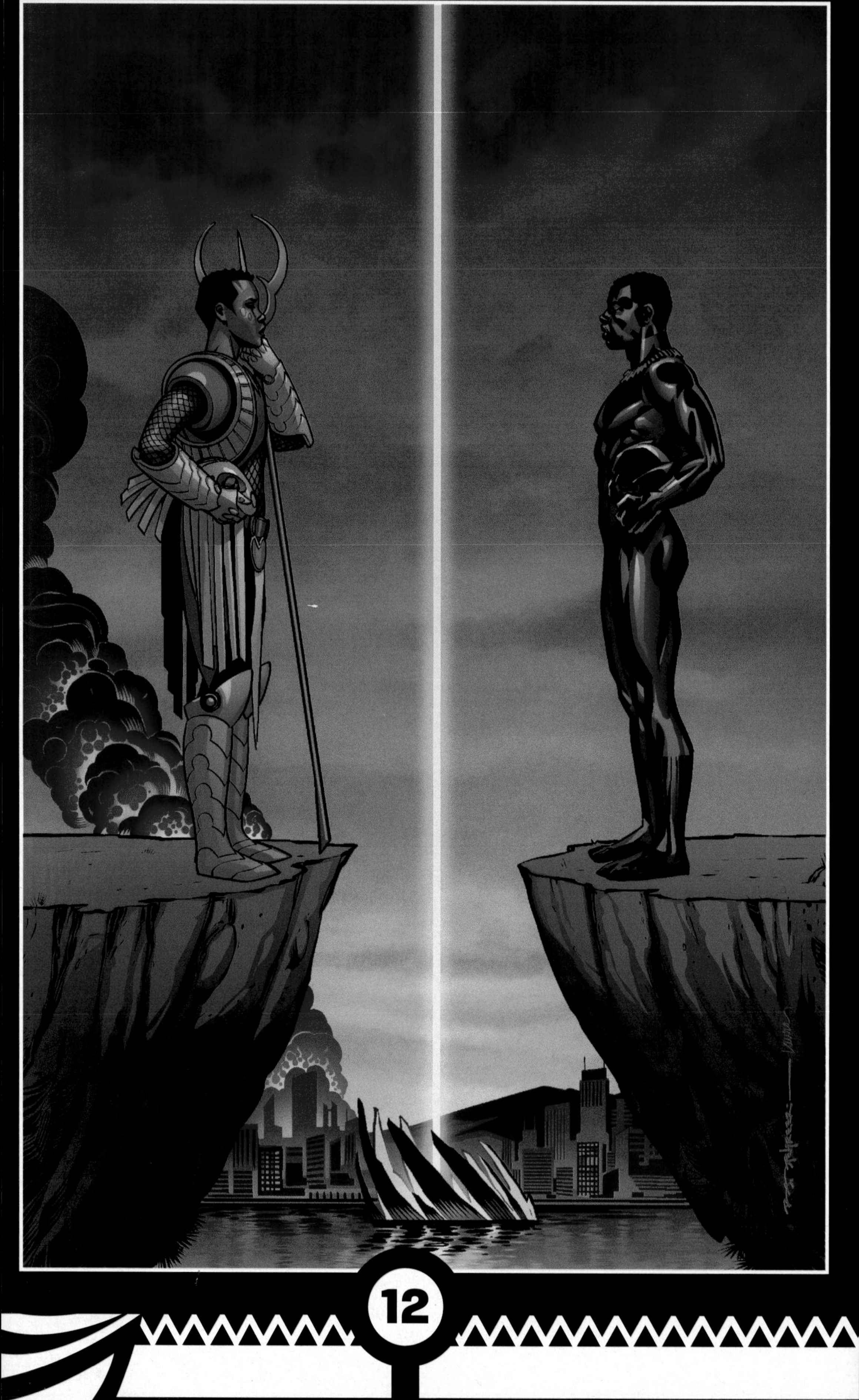

12

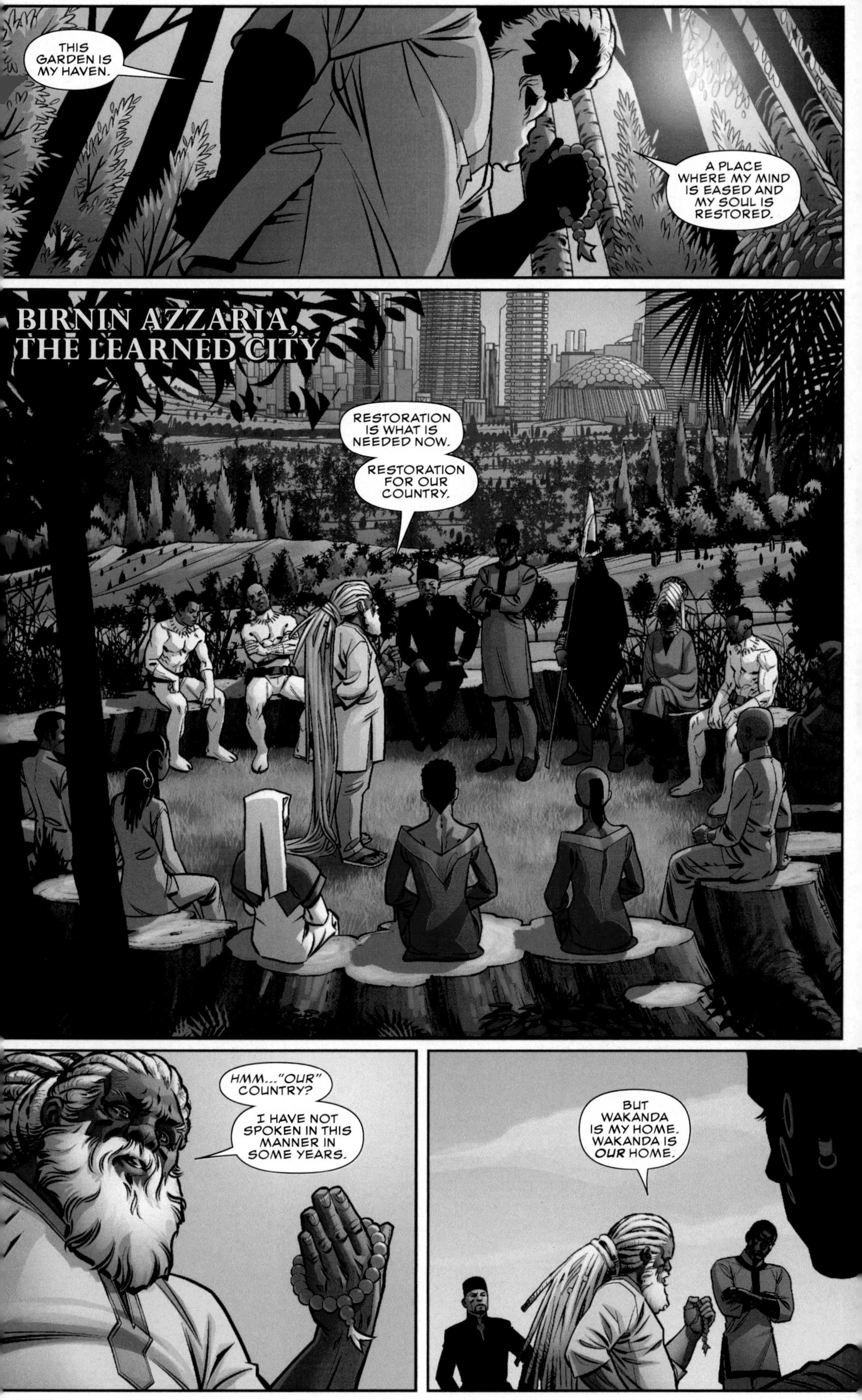
THIS GARDEN IS MY HAVEN.
A PLACE WHERE MY MIND IS EASED AND MY SOUL IS RESTORED.
BIRNIN AZZARIA, THE LEARNED CITY
RESTORATION IS WHAT IS NEEDED NOW.
RESTORATION FOR OUR COUNTRY.
HMM..."OUR" COUNTRY?
I HAVE NOT SPOKEN IN THIS MANNER IN SOME YEARS.
BUT WAKANDA IS MY HOME. WAKANDA IS *OUR* HOME.

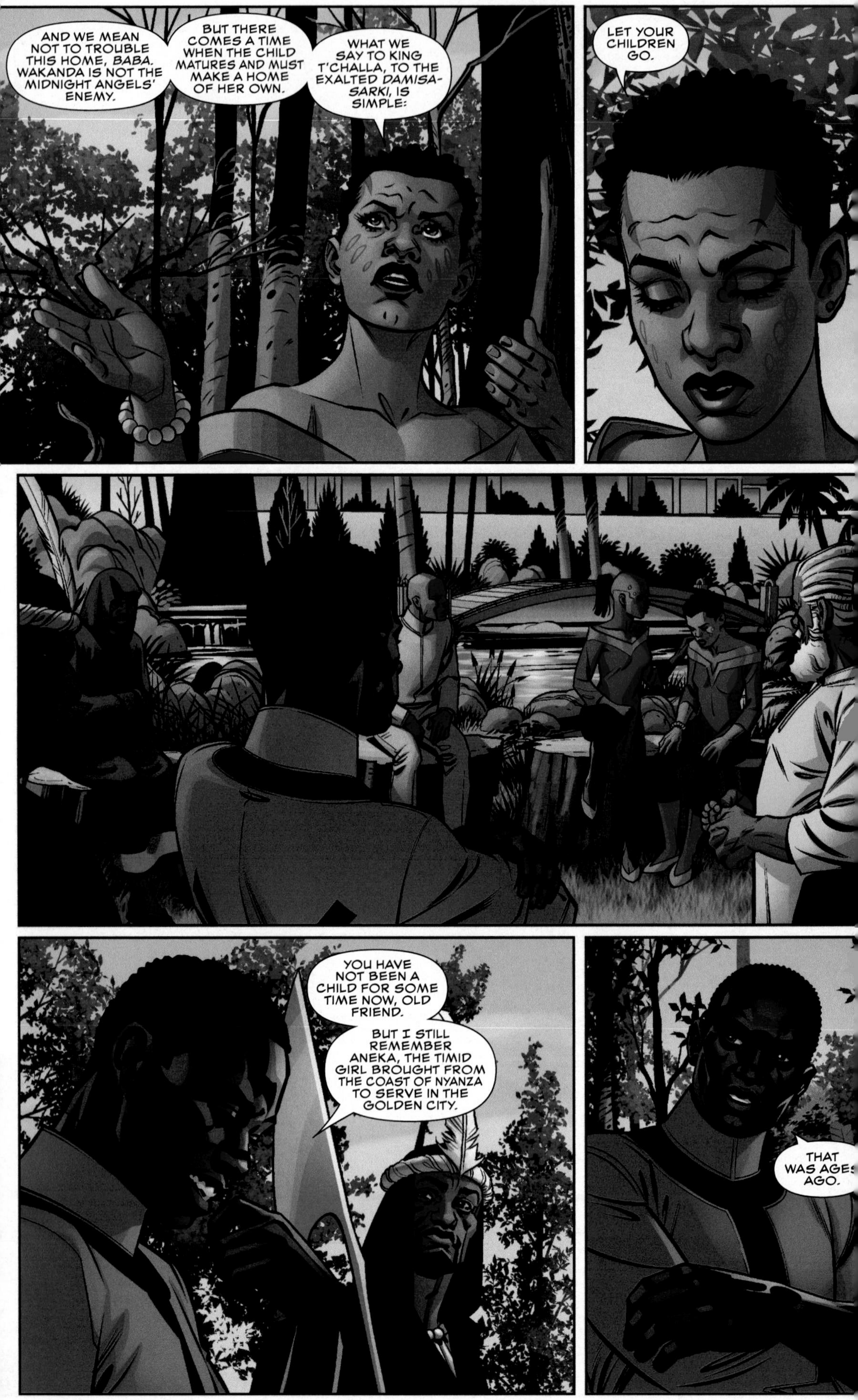

AND WE MEAN NOT TO TROUBLE THIS HOME, BABA. WAKANDA IS NOT THE MIDNIGHT ANGELS' ENEMY.
BUT THERE COMES A TIME WHEN THE CHILD MATURES AND MUST MAKE A HOME OF HER OWN.
WHAT WE SAY TO KING T'CHALLA, TO THE EXALTED DAMISA-SARKI, IS SIMPLE:
LET YOUR CHILDREN GO.
YOU HAVE NOT BEEN A CHILD FOR SOME TIME NOW, OLD FRIEND.
BUT I STILL REMEMBER ANEKA, THE TIMID GIRL BROUGHT FROM THE COAST OF NYANZA TO SERVE IN THE GOLDEN CITY.
THAT WAS AGES AGO.

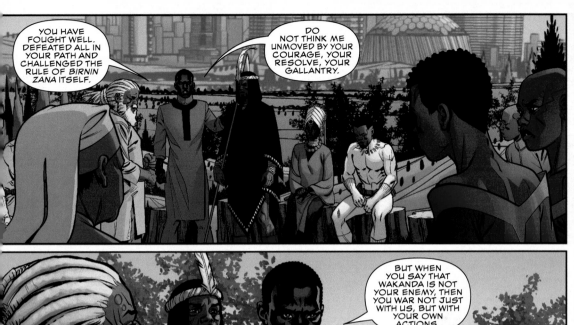

YOU HAVE FOUGHT WELL. DEFEATED ALL IN YOUR PATH AND CHALLENGED THE RULE OF *BIRNIN ZANA* ITSELF.

DO NOT THINK ME UNMOVED BY YOUR COURAGE, YOUR RESOLVE, YOUR GALLANTRY.

BUT WHEN YOU SAY THAT WAKANDA IS NOT YOUR ENEMY, THEN YOU WAR NOT JUST WITH US, BUT WITH YOUR OWN ACTIONS.

WHEN YOU MAKE YOURSELF THE LAW, WHEN YOU RESORT TO MURDER WITHIN WAKANDAN LAND, YOU WAR AGAINST US.

HAVE YOU CONSIDERED WHAT THIS HAS COST WAKANDA?

HAVE YOU CONSIDERED THE LEGIONS WHO MIGHT HAVE ENDED TETU'S CORRUPTION, BUT INSTEAD DIED FIGHTING YOU?

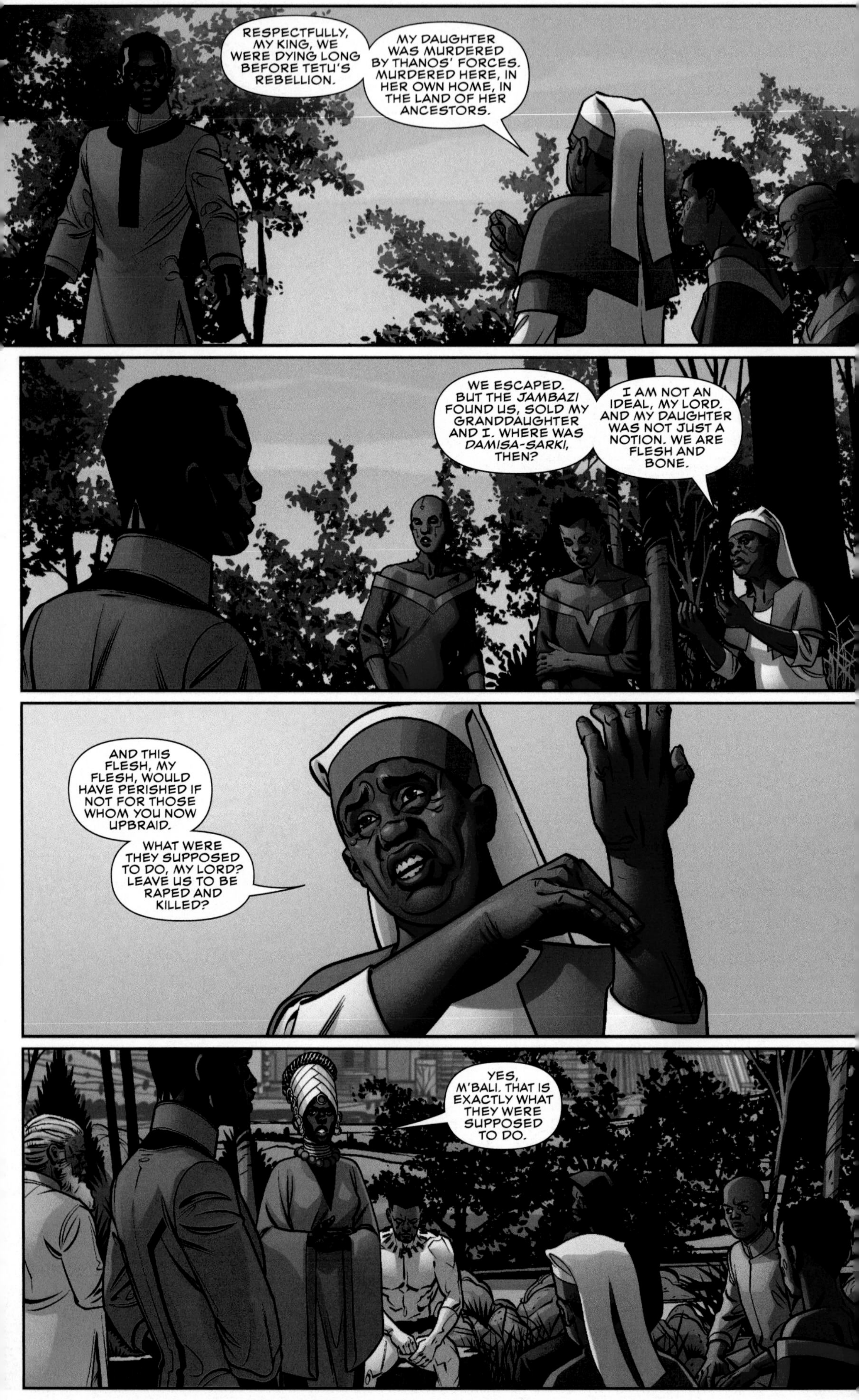
RESPECTFULLY, MY KING, WE WERE DYING LONG BEFORE TETU'S REBELLION.
MY DAUGHTER WAS MURDERED BY THANOS' FORCES. MURDERED HERE, IN HER OWN HOME, IN THE LAND OF HER ANCESTORS.
WE ESCAPED. BUT THE JAMBAZI FOUND US, SOLD MY GRANDDAUGHTER AND I. WHERE WAS DAMISA-SARKI, THEN?
I AM NOT AN IDEAL, MY LORD. AND MY DAUGHTER WAS NOT JUST A NOTION. WE ARE FLESH AND BONE.
AND THIS FLESH, MY FLESH, WOULD HAVE PERISHED IF NOT FOR THOSE WHOM YOU NOW UPBRAID.
WHAT WERE THEY SUPPOSED TO DO, MY LORD? LEAVE US TO BE RAPED AND KILLED?
YES, M'BALI. THAT IS EXACTLY WHAT THEY WERE SUPPOSED TO DO.

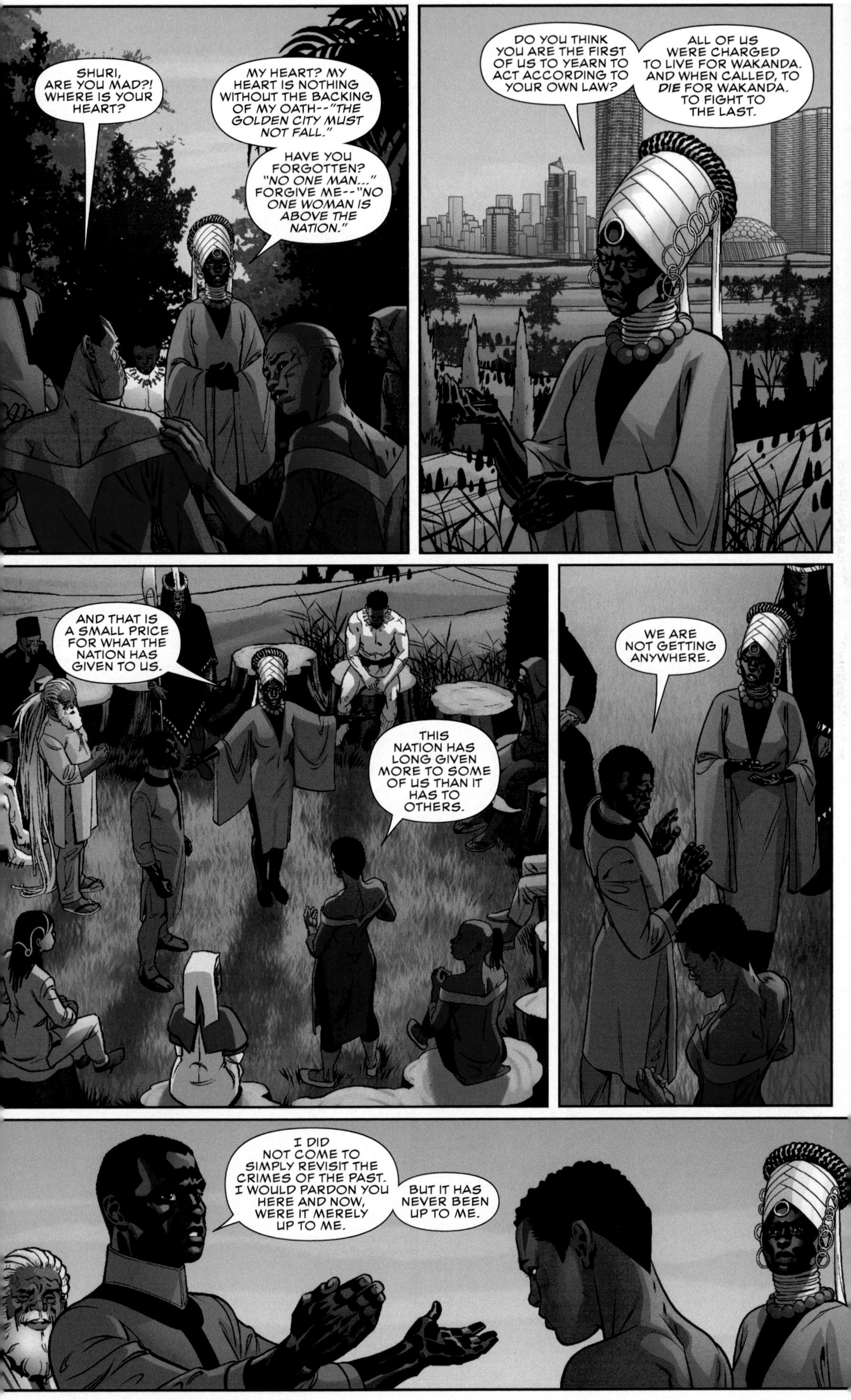
SHURI, ARE YOU MAD?! WHERE IS YOUR HEART?
MY HEART? MY HEART IS NOTHING WITHOUT THE BACKING OF MY OATH--"THE GOLDEN CITY MUST NOT FALL."
HAVE YOU FORGOTTEN? "NO ONE MAN..." FORGIVE ME--"NO ONE WOMAN IS ABOVE THE NATION."
DO YOU THINK YOU ARE THE FIRST OF US TO YEARN TO ACT ACCORDING TO YOUR OWN LAW?
ALL OF US WERE CHARGED TO LIVE FOR WAKANDA. AND WHEN CALLED, TO *DIE* FOR WAKANDA. TO FIGHT TO THE LAST.
AND THAT IS A SMALL PRICE FOR WHAT THE NATION HAS GIVEN TO US.
THIS NATION HAS LONG GIVEN MORE TO SOME OF US THAN IT HAS TO OTHERS.
WE ARE NOT GETTING ANYWHERE.
I DID NOT COME TO SIMPLY REVISIT THE CRIMES OF THE PAST. I WOULD PARDON YOU HERE AND NOW, WERE IT MERELY UP TO ME.
BUT IT HAS NEVER BEEN UP TO ME.

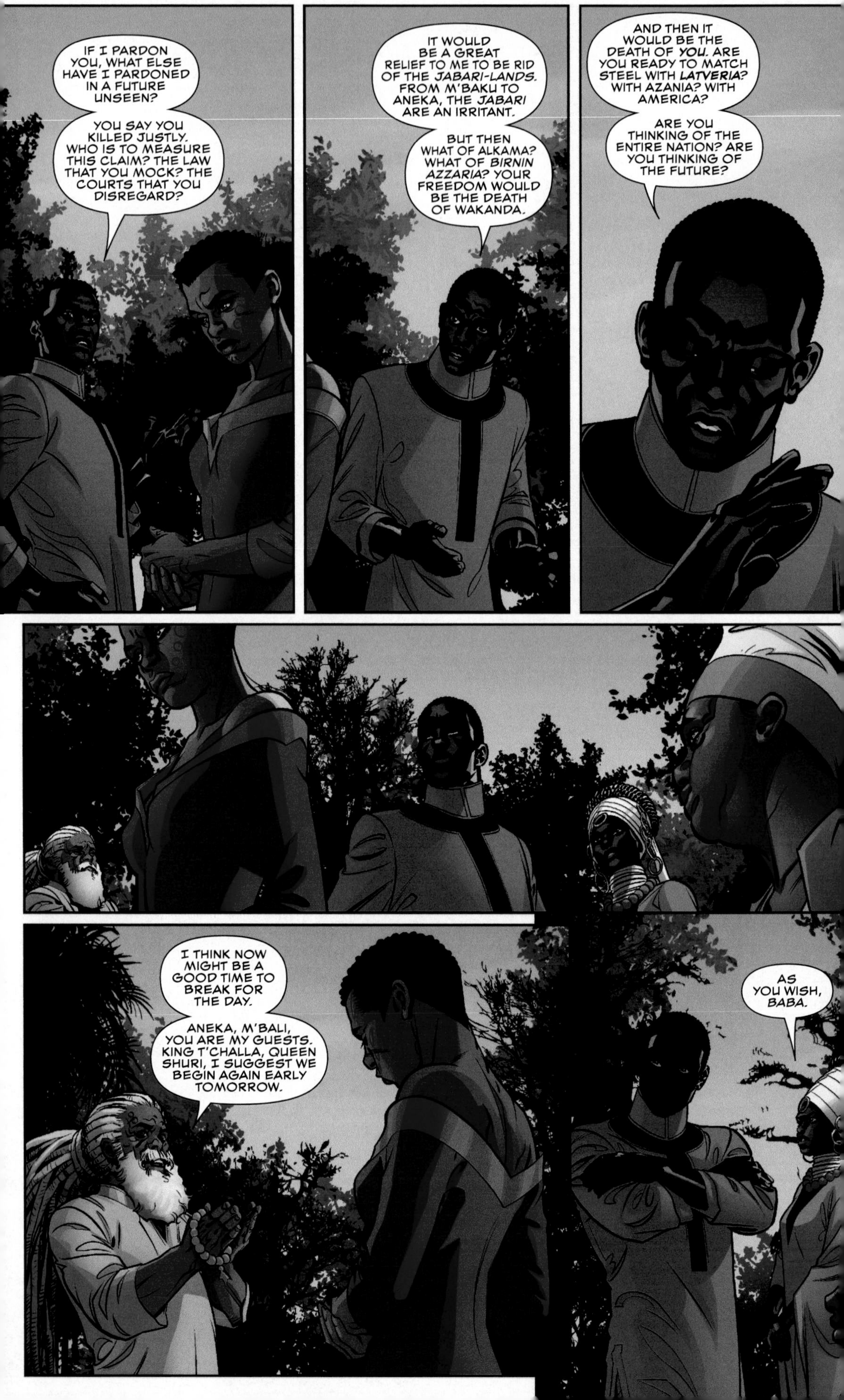

IF I PARDON YOU, WHAT ELSE HAVE I PARDONED IN A FUTURE UNSEEN?
YOU SAY YOU KILLED JUSTLY. WHO IS TO MEASURE THIS CLAIM? THE LAW THAT YOU MOCK? THE COURTS THAT YOU DISREGARD?
IT WOULD BE A GREAT RELIEF TO ME TO BE RID OF THE *JABARI-LANDS*. FROM M'BAKU TO ANEKA, THE *JABARI* ARE AN IRRITANT.
BUT THEN WHAT OF ALKAMA? WHAT OF *BIRNIN AZZARIA*? YOUR FREEDOM WOULD BE THE DEATH OF WAKANDA.
AND THEN IT WOULD BE THE DEATH OF *YOU*. ARE YOU READY TO MATCH STEEL WITH *LATVERIA*? WITH AZANIA? WITH AMERICA?
ARE YOU THINKING OF THE ENTIRE NATION? ARE YOU THINKING OF THE FUTURE?
I THINK NOW MIGHT BE A GOOD TIME TO BREAK FOR THE DAY.
ANEKA, M'BALI, YOU ARE MY GUESTS. KING T'CHALLA, QUEEN SHURI, I SUGGEST WE BEGIN AGAIN EARLY TOMORROW.
AS YOU WISH, *BABA*.

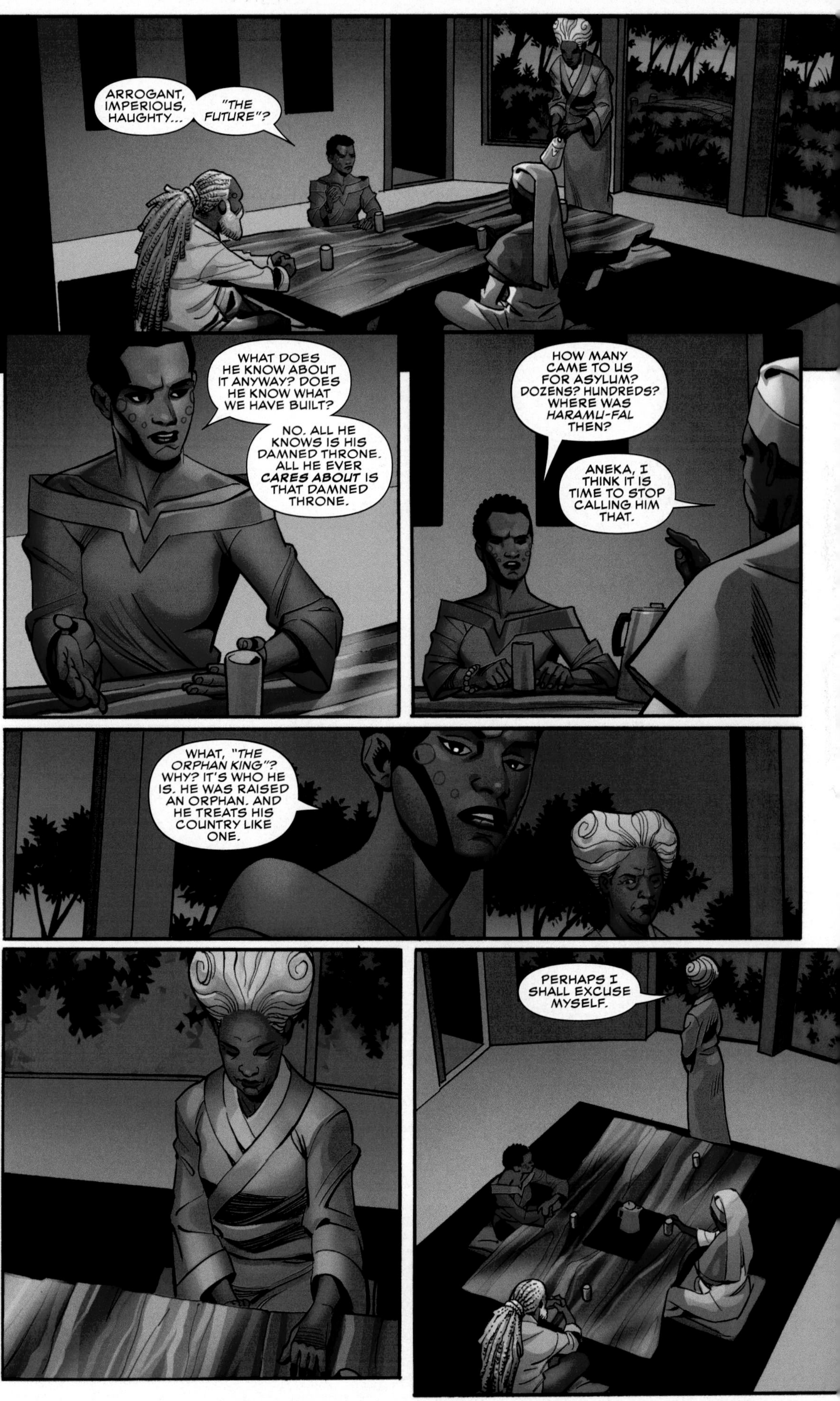
ARROGANT, IMPERIOUS, HAUGHTY...
"THE FUTURE"?
WHAT DOES HE KNOW ABOUT IT ANYWAY? DOES HE KNOW WHAT WE HAVE BUILT?
NO. ALL HE KNOWS IS HIS DAMNED THRONE. ALL HE EVER CARES ABOUT IS THAT DAMNED THRONE.
HOW MANY CAME TO US FOR ASYLUM? DOZENS? HUNDREDS? WHERE WAS HARAMU-FAL THEN?
ANEKA, I THINK IT IS TIME TO STOP CALLING HIM THAT.
WHAT, "THE ORPHAN KING"? WHY? IT'S WHO HE IS. HE WAS RAISED AN ORPHAN. AND HE TREATS HIS COUNTRY LIKE ONE.
PERHAPS I SHALL EXCUSE MYSELF.

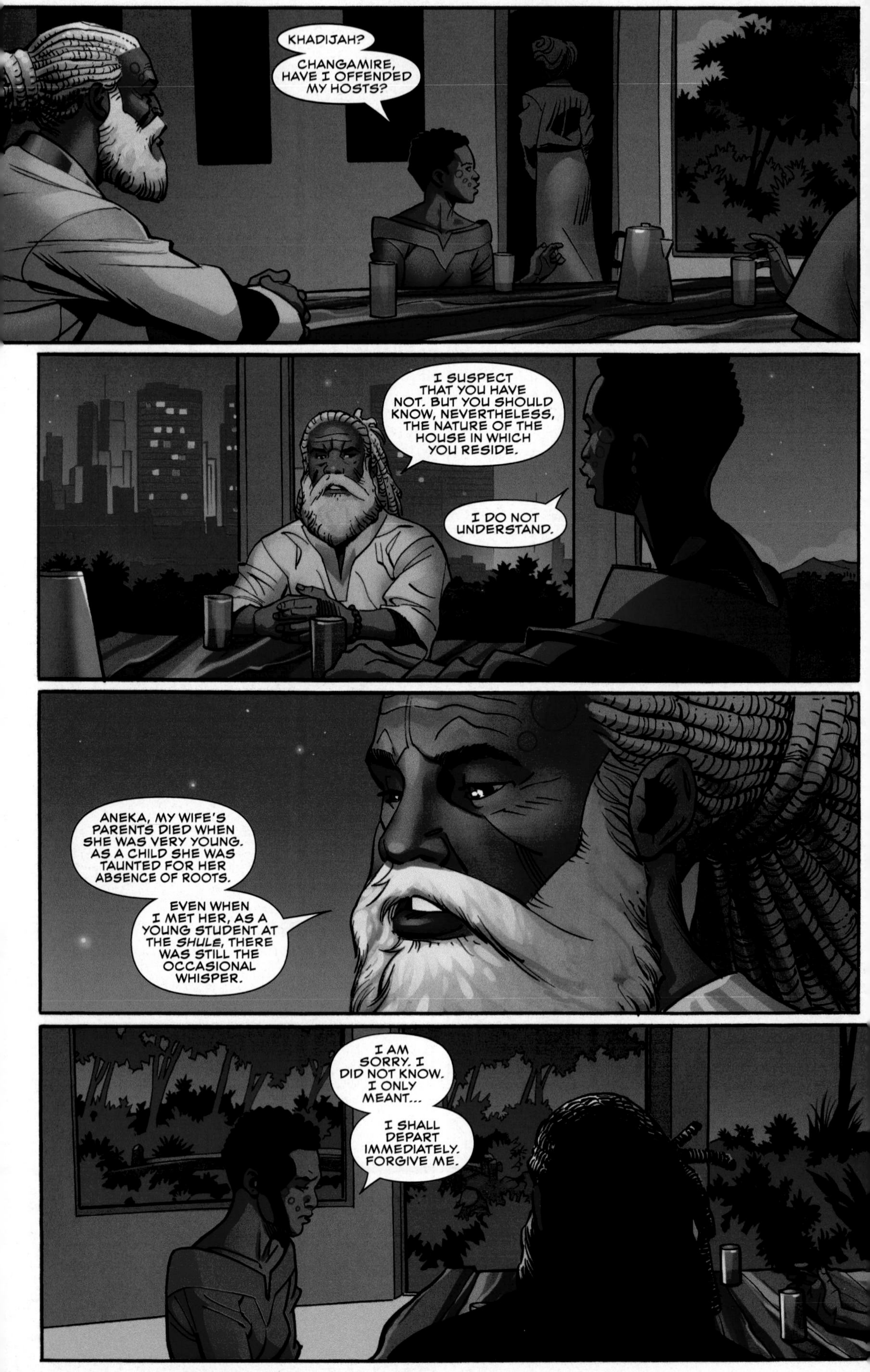
KHADIJAH?
CHANGAMIRE, HAVE I OFFENDED MY HOSTS?
I SUSPECT THAT YOU HAVE NOT. BUT YOU SHOULD KNOW, NEVERTHELESS, THE NATURE OF THE HOUSE IN WHICH YOU RESIDE.
I DO NOT UNDERSTAND.
ANEKA, MY WIFE'S PARENTS DIED WHEN SHE WAS VERY YOUNG. AS A CHILD SHE WAS TAUNTED FOR HER ABSENCE OF ROOTS.
EVEN WHEN I MET HER, AS A YOUNG STUDENT AT THE *SHULE*, THERE WAS STILL THE OCCASIONAL WHISPER.
I AM SORRY. I DID NOT KNOW. I ONLY MEANT...
I SHALL DEPART IMMEDIATELY. FORGIVE ME.

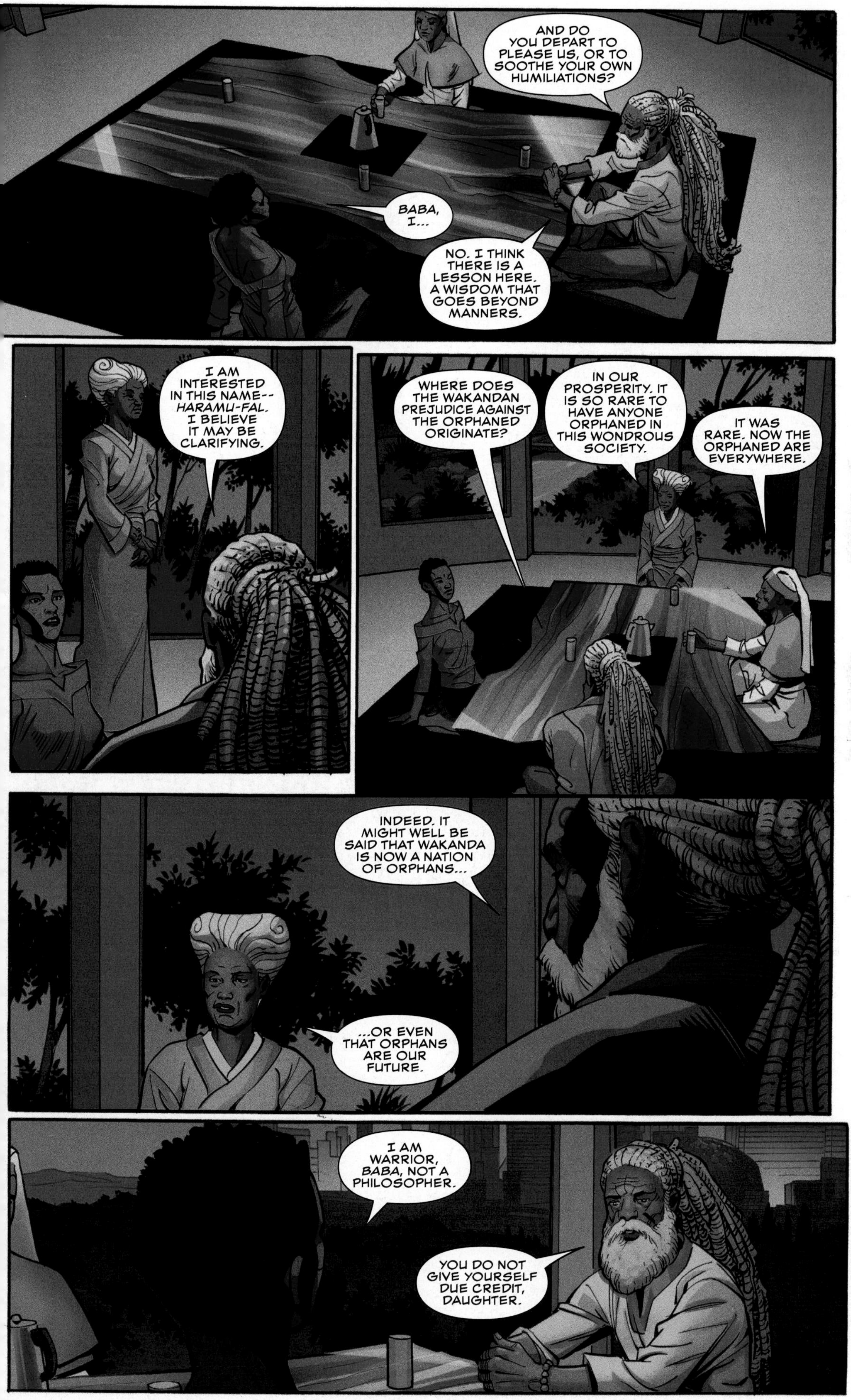

AND DO YOU DEPART TO PLEASE US, OR TO SOOTHE YOUR OWN HUMILIATIONS?
BABA, I...
NO. I THINK THERE IS A LESSON HERE. A WISDOM THAT GOES BEYOND MANNERS.
I AM INTERESTED IN THIS NAME--HARAMU-FAL. I BELIEVE IT MAY BE CLARIFYING.
WHERE DOES THE WAKANDAN PREJUDICE AGAINST THE ORPHANED ORIGINATE?
IN OUR PROSPERITY. IT IS SO RARE TO HAVE ANYONE ORPHANED IN THIS WONDROUS SOCIETY.
IT WAS RARE. NOW THE ORPHANED ARE EVERYWHERE.
INDEED. IT MIGHT WELL BE SAID THAT WAKANDA IS NOW A NATION OF ORPHANS...
...OR EVEN THAT ORPHANS ARE OUR FUTURE.
I AM WARRIOR, BABA, NOT A PHILOSOPHER.
YOU DO NOT GIVE YOURSELF DUE CREDIT, DAUGHTER.

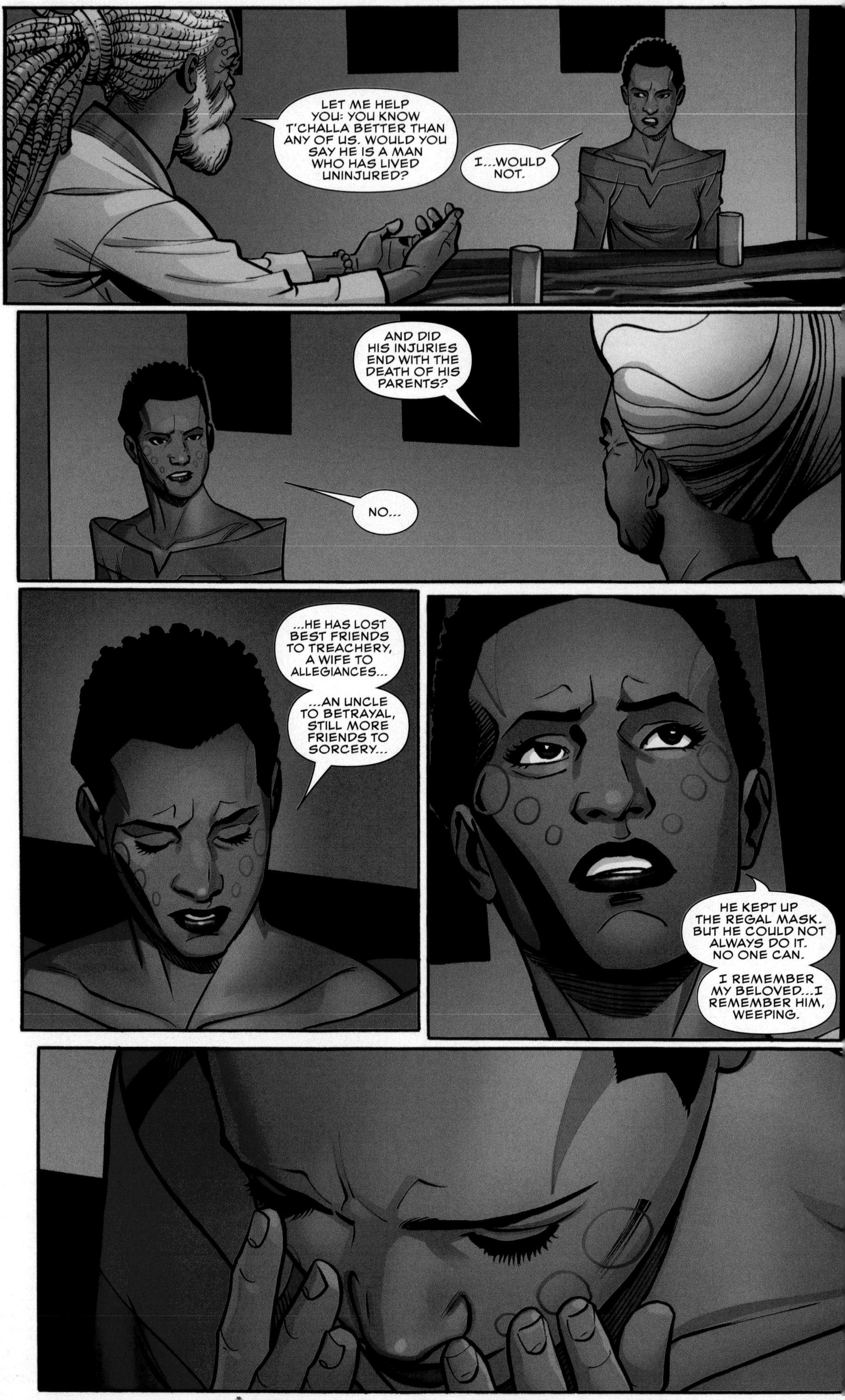
LET ME HELP YOU: YOU KNOW T'CHALLA BETTER THAN ANY OF US. WOULD YOU SAY HE IS A MAN WHO HAS LIVED UNINJURED?
I...WOULD NOT.
AND DID HIS INJURIES END WITH THE DEATH OF HIS PARENTS?
NO...
...HE HAS LOST BEST FRIENDS TO TREACHERY, A WIFE TO ALLEGIANCES...
...AN UNCLE TO BETRAYAL, STILL MORE FRIENDS TO SORCERY...
HE KEPT UP THE REGAL MASK. BUT HE COULD NOT ALWAYS DO IT. NO ONE CAN.
I REMEMBER MY BELOVED...I REMEMBER HIM, WEEPING.

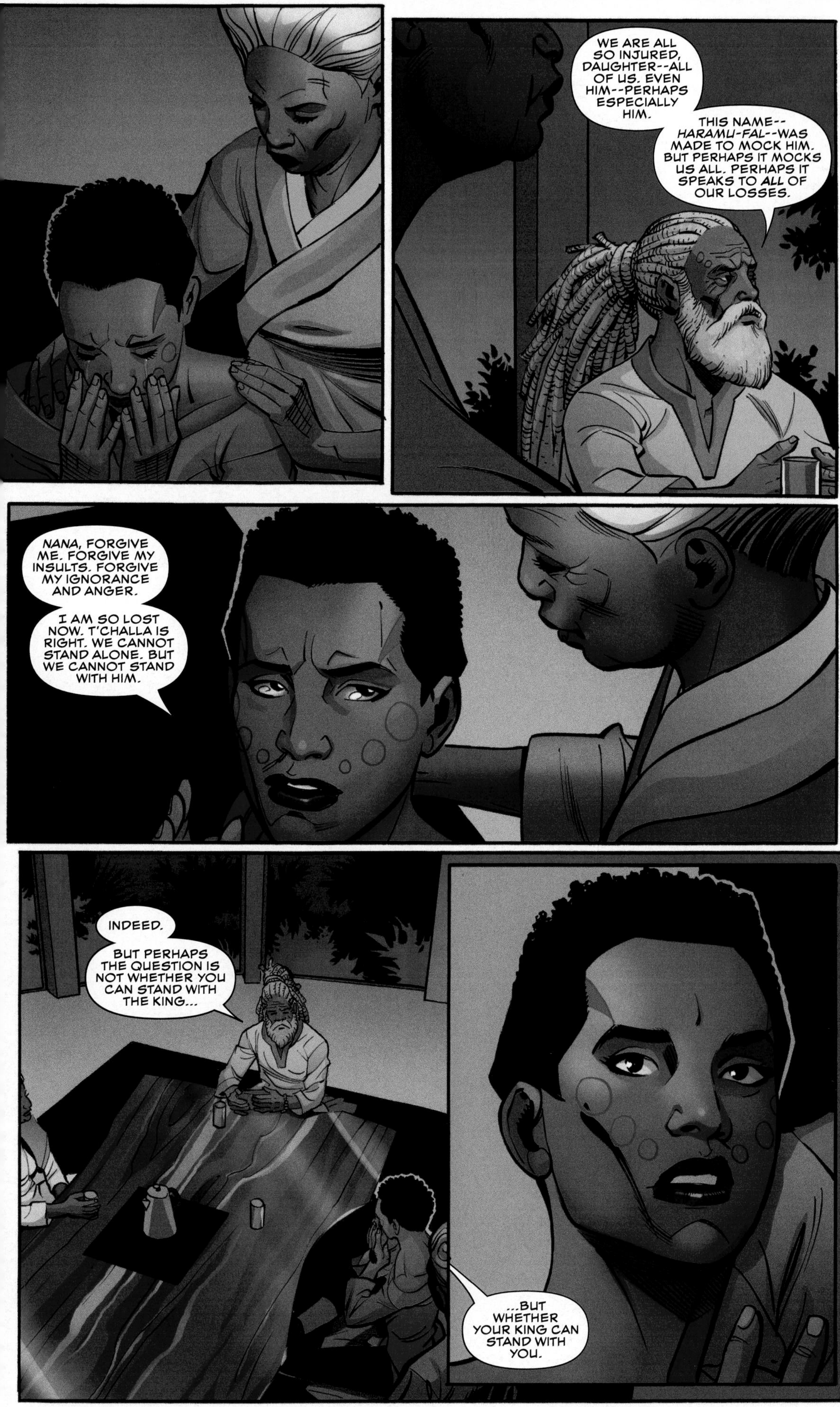
WE ARE ALL SO INJURED, DAUGHTER--ALL OF US. EVEN HIM--PERHAPS ESPECIALLY HIM.
THIS NAME--*HARAMU-FAL*--WAS MADE TO MOCK HIM. BUT PERHAPS IT MOCKS US ALL. PERHAPS IT SPEAKS TO *ALL* OF OUR LOSSES.
NANA, FORGIVE ME. FORGIVE MY INSULTS. FORGIVE MY IGNORANCE AND ANGER.
I AM SO LOST NOW. T'CHALLA IS RIGHT. WE CANNOT STAND ALONE. BUT WE CANNOT STAND WITH HIM.
INDEED.
BUT PERHAPS THE QUESTION IS NOT WHETHER YOU CAN STAND WITH THE KING...
...BUT WHETHER YOUR KING CAN STAND WITH YOU.

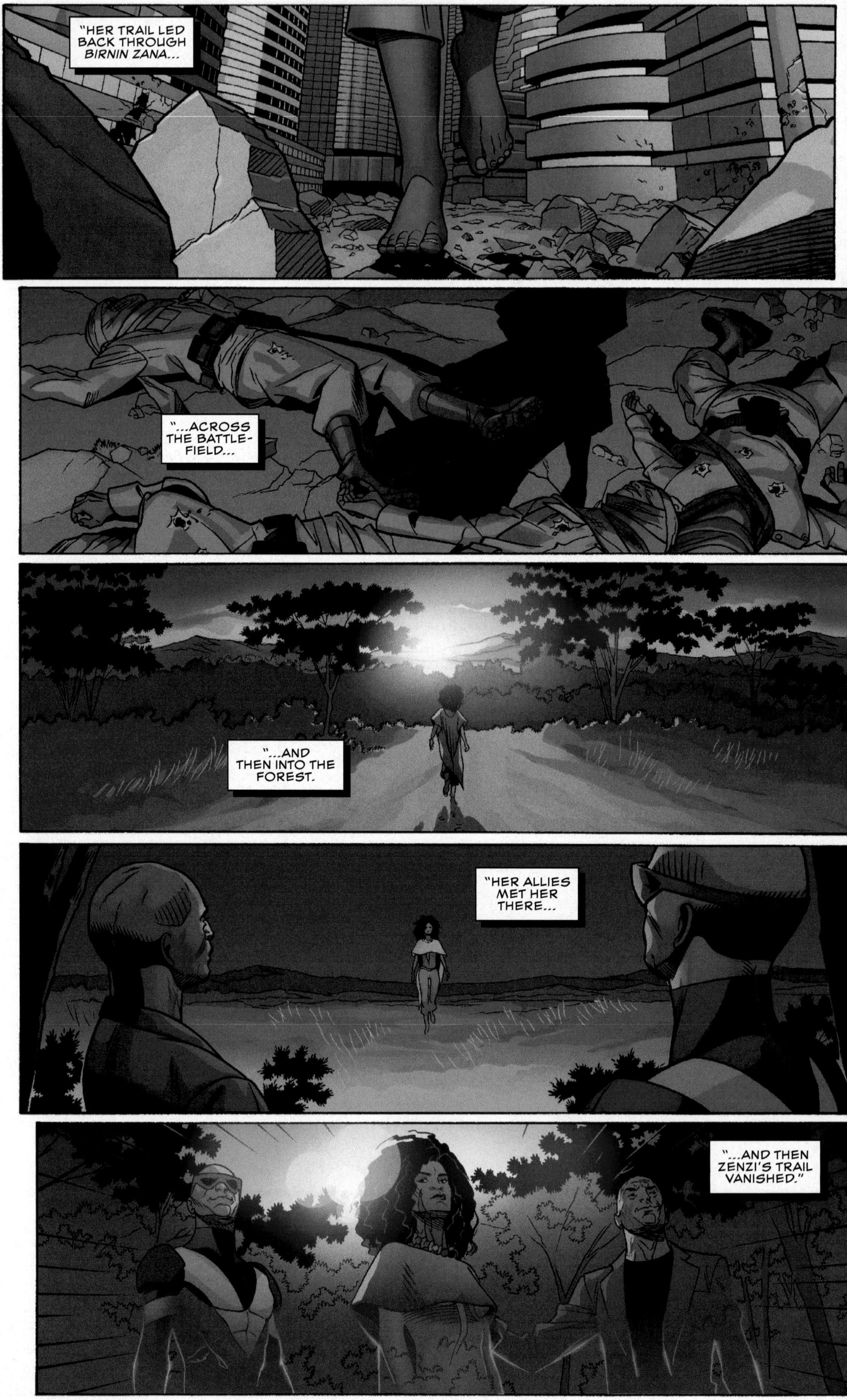
"HER TRAIL LED BACK THROUGH *BIRNIN ZANA*...
"...ACROSS THE BATTLE-FIELD...
"...AND THEN INTO THE FOREST.
"HER ALLIES MET HER THERE...
"...AND THEN ZENZI'S TRAIL VANISHED."

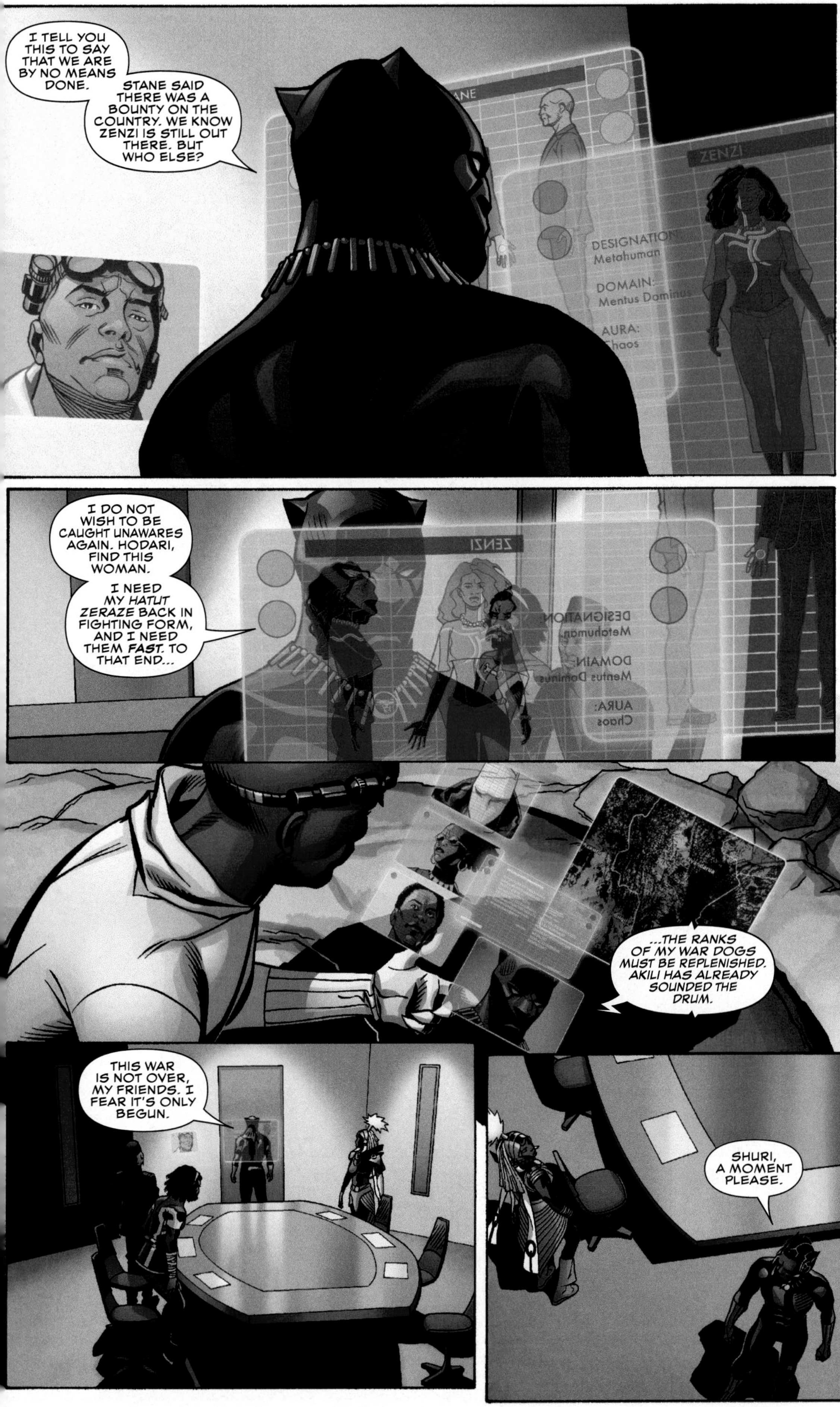
I TELL YOU THIS TO SAY THAT WE ARE BY NO MEANS DONE.
STANE SAID THERE WAS A BOUNTY ON THE COUNTRY. WE KNOW ZENZI IS STILL OUT THERE. BUT WHO ELSE?
ZENZI
DESIGNATION
Metahuman
DOMAIN:
Mentus Dominus
AURA:
Chaos
I DO NOT WISH TO BE CAUGHT UNAWARES AGAIN. HODARI, FIND THIS WOMAN.
I NEED MY *HATUT ZERAZE* BACK IN FIGHTING FORM, AND I NEED THEM ***FAST.*** TO THAT END...
...THE RANKS OF MY WAR DOGS MUST BE REPLENISHED. AKILI HAS ALREADY SOUNDED THE DRUM.
THIS WAR IS NOT OVER, MY FRIENDS. I FEAR IT'S ONLY BEGUN.
SHURI, A MOMENT PLEASE.

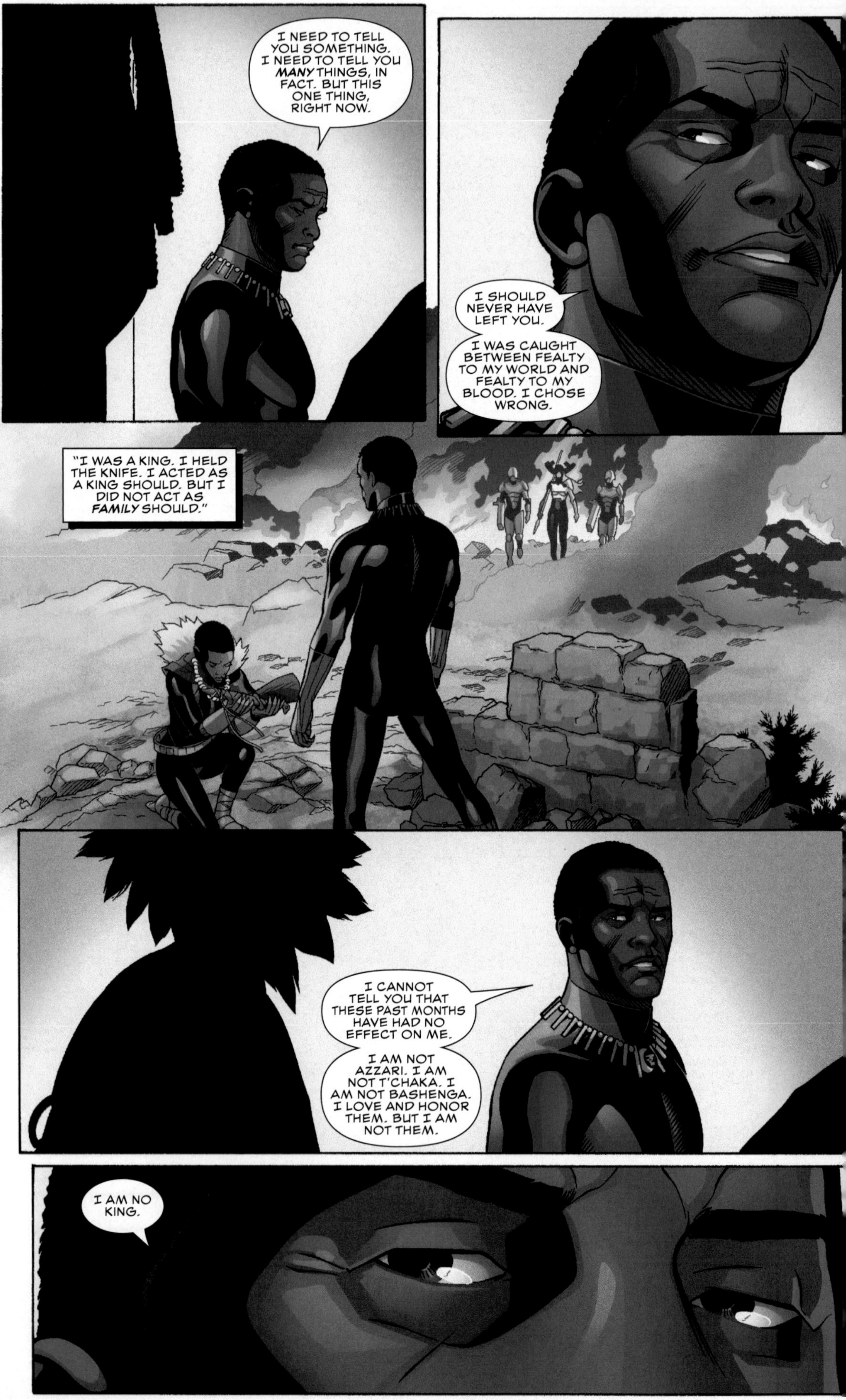
I NEED TO TELL YOU SOMETHING. I NEED TO TELL YOU *MANY* THINGS, IN FACT. BUT THIS ONE THING, RIGHT NOW.
I SHOULD NEVER HAVE LEFT YOU.
I WAS CAUGHT BETWEEN FEALTY TO MY WORLD AND FEALTY TO MY BLOOD. I CHOSE WRONG.
"I WAS A KING. I HELD THE KNIFE. I ACTED AS A KING SHOULD. BUT I DID NOT ACT AS *FAMILY* SHOULD."
I CANNOT TELL YOU THAT THESE PAST MONTHS HAVE HAD NO EFFECT ON ME.
I AM NOT AZZARI. I AM NOT T'CHAKA. I AM NOT BASHENGA. I LOVE AND HONOR THEM. BUT I AM NOT THEM.
I AM NO KING.

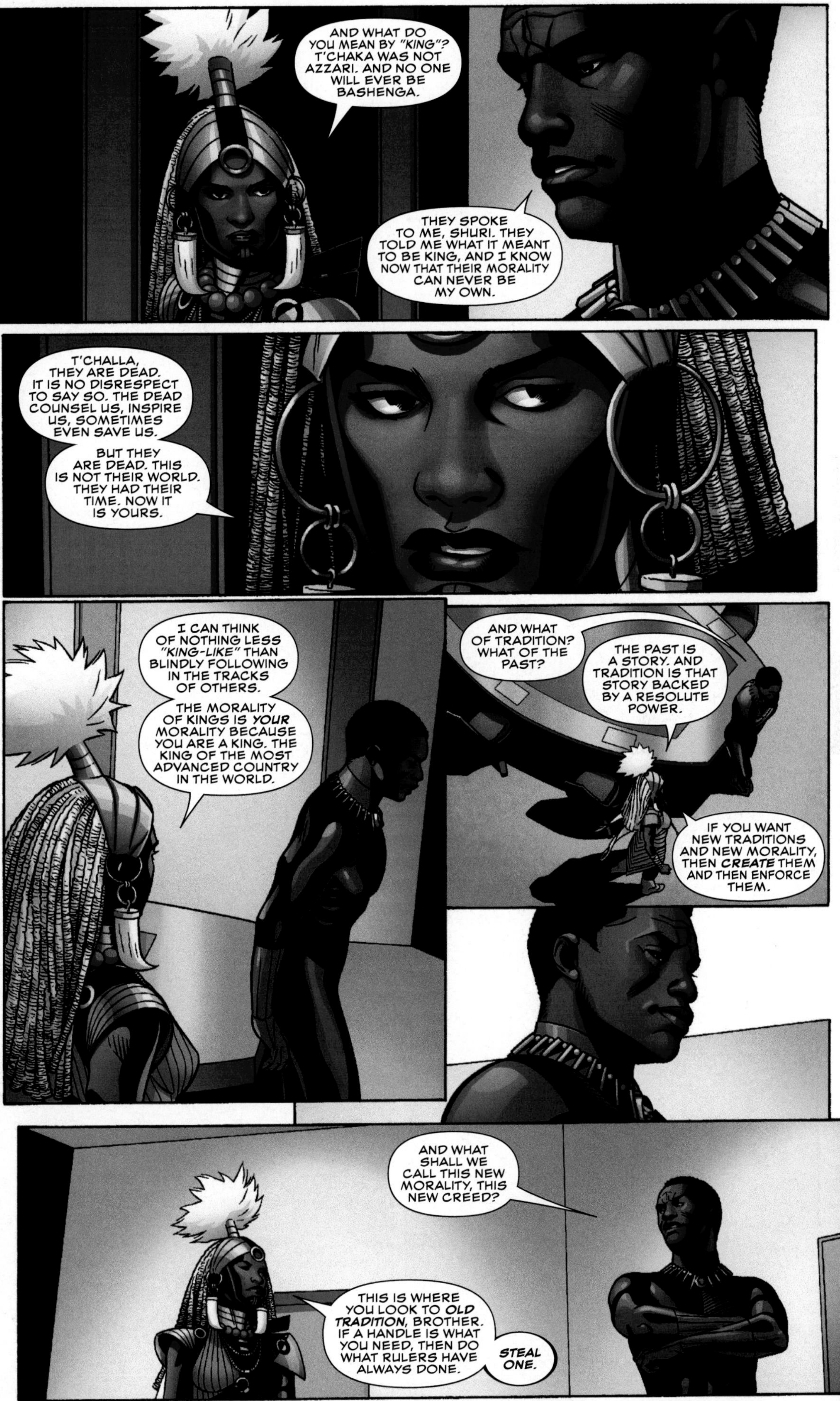
AND WHAT DO YOU MEAN BY "KING"? T'CHAKA WAS NOT AZZARI. AND NO ONE WILL EVER BE BASHENGA.
THEY SPOKE TO ME, SHURI. THEY TOLD ME WHAT IT MEANT TO BE KING, AND I KNOW NOW THAT THEIR MORALITY CAN NEVER BE MY OWN.
T'CHALLA, THEY ARE DEAD. IT IS NO DISRESPECT TO SAY SO. THE DEAD COUNSEL US, INSPIRE US, SOMETIMES EVEN SAVE US.
BUT THEY ARE DEAD. THIS IS NOT THEIR WORLD. THEY HAD THEIR TIME. NOW IT IS YOURS.
I CAN THINK OF NOTHING LESS "KING-LIKE" THAN BLINDLY FOLLOWING IN THE TRACKS OF OTHERS.
THE MORALITY OF KINGS IS YOUR MORALITY BECAUSE YOU ARE A KING. THE KING OF THE MOST ADVANCED COUNTRY IN THE WORLD.
AND WHAT OF TRADITION? WHAT OF THE PAST?
THE PAST IS A STORY. AND TRADITION IS THAT STORY BACKED BY A RESOLUTE POWER.
IF YOU WANT NEW TRADITIONS AND NEW MORALITY, THEN CREATE THEM AND THEN ENFORCE THEM.
AND WHAT SHALL WE CALL THIS NEW MORALITY, THIS NEW CREED?
THIS IS WHERE YOU LOOK TO OLD TRADITION, BROTHER. IF A HANDLE IS WHAT YOU NEED, THEN DO WHAT RULERS HAVE ALWAYS DONE.
STEAL ONE.

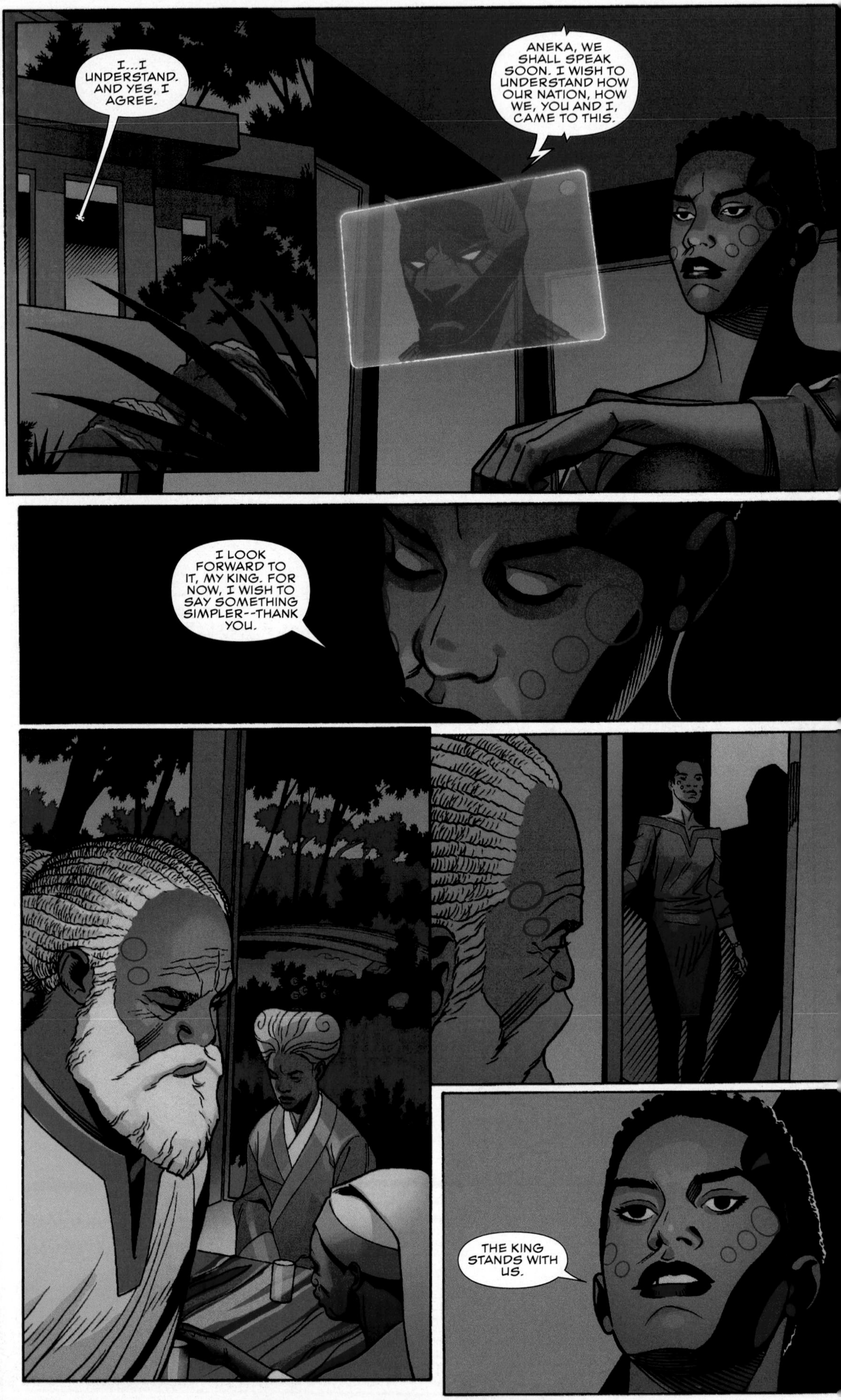

I...I UNDERSTAND. AND YES, I AGREE.
ANEKA, WE SHALL SPEAK SOON. I WISH TO UNDERSTAND HOW OUR NATION, HOW WE, YOU AND I, CAME TO THIS.
I LOOK FORWARD TO IT, MY KING. FOR NOW, I WISH TO SAY SOMETHING SIMPLER--THANK YOU.
THE KING STANDS WITH US.

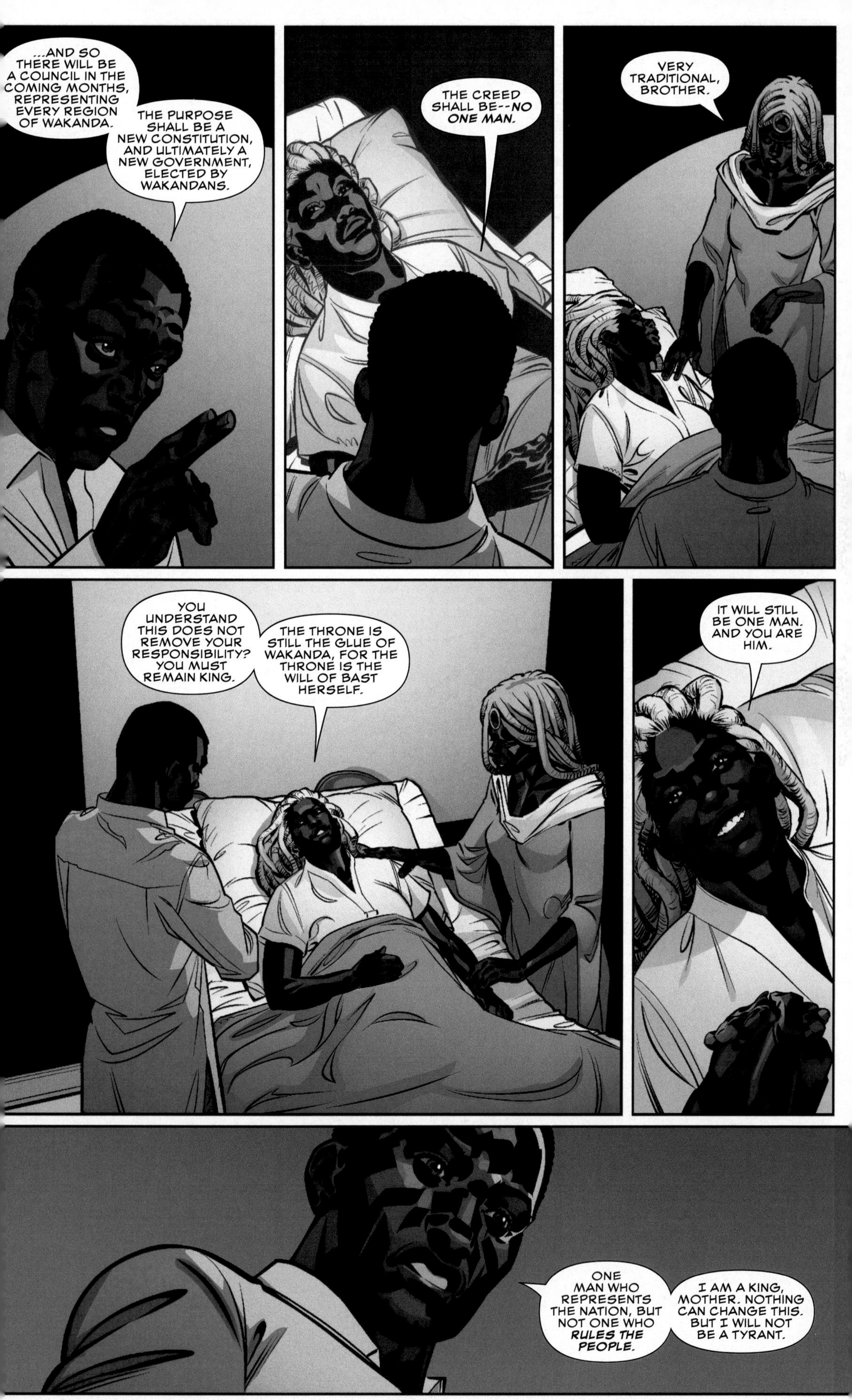
...AND SO THERE WILL BE A COUNCIL IN THE COMING MONTHS, REPRESENTING EVERY REGION OF WAKANDA.
THE PURPOSE SHALL BE A NEW CONSTITUTION, AND ULTIMATELY A NEW GOVERNMENT, ELECTED BY WAKANDANS.
THE CREED SHALL BE--*NO ONE MAN.*
VERY TRADITIONAL, BROTHER.
YOU UNDERSTAND THIS DOES NOT REMOVE YOUR RESPONSIBILITY? YOU MUST REMAIN KING.
THE THRONE IS STILL THE GLUE OF WAKANDA, FOR THE THRONE IS THE WILL OF BAST HERSELF.
IT WILL STILL BE ONE MAN. AND YOU ARE HIM.
ONE MAN WHO REPRESENTS THE NATION, BUT NOT ONE WHO *RULES THE PEOPLE.*
I AM A KING, MOTHER. NOTHING CAN CHANGE THIS. BUT I WILL NOT BE A TYRANT.

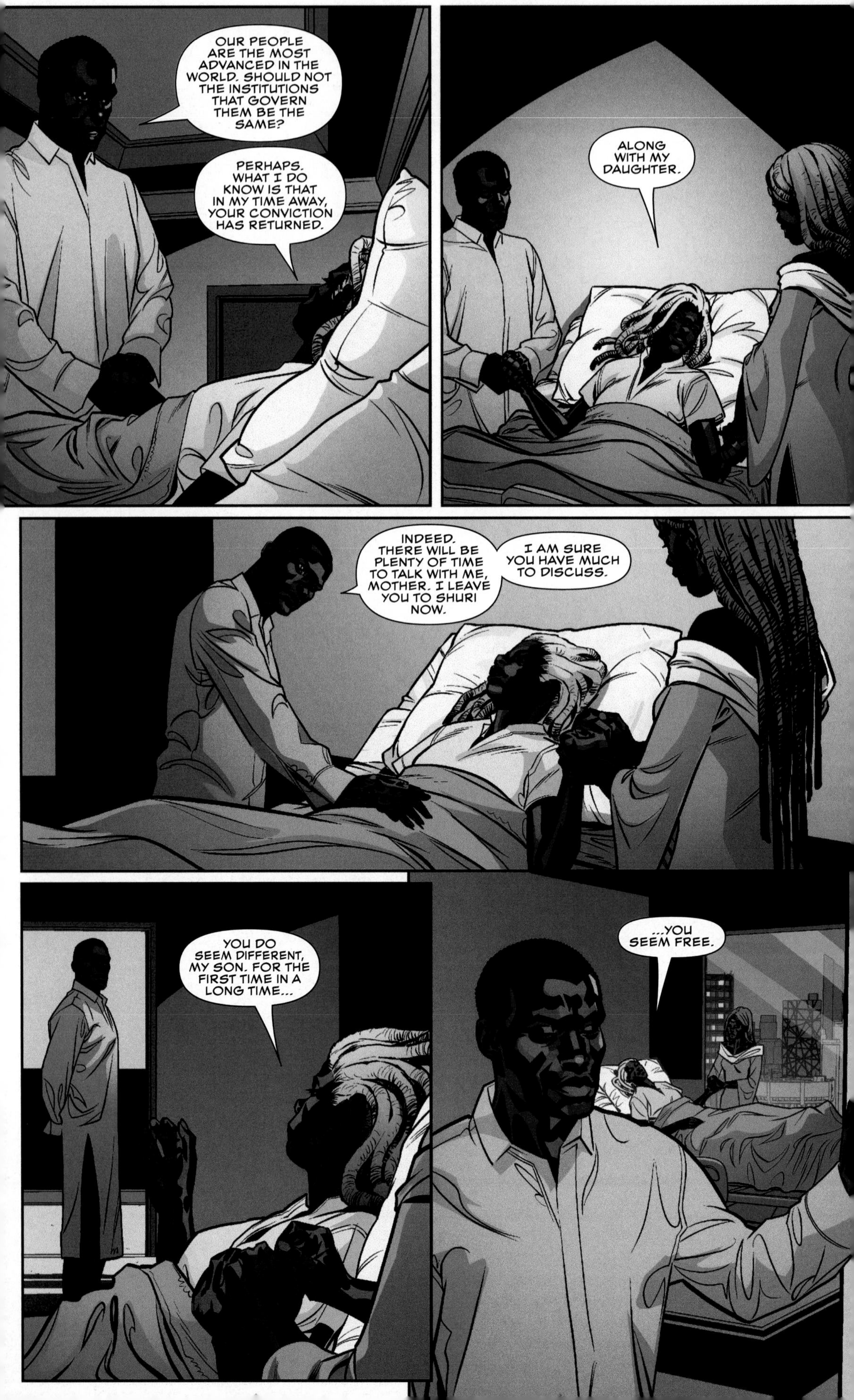
OUR PEOPLE ARE THE MOST ADVANCED IN THE WORLD. SHOULD NOT THE INSTITUTIONS THAT GOVERN THEM BE THE SAME?
PERHAPS. WHAT I DO KNOW IS THAT IN MY TIME AWAY, YOUR CONVICTION HAS RETURNED.
ALONG WITH MY DAUGHTER.
INDEED. THERE WILL BE PLENTY OF TIME TO TALK WITH ME, MOTHER. I LEAVE YOU TO SHURI NOW.
I AM SURE YOU HAVE MUCH TO DISCUSS.
YOU DO SEEM DIFFERENT, MY SON. FOR THE FIRST TIME IN A LONG TIME...
...YOU SEEM FREE.

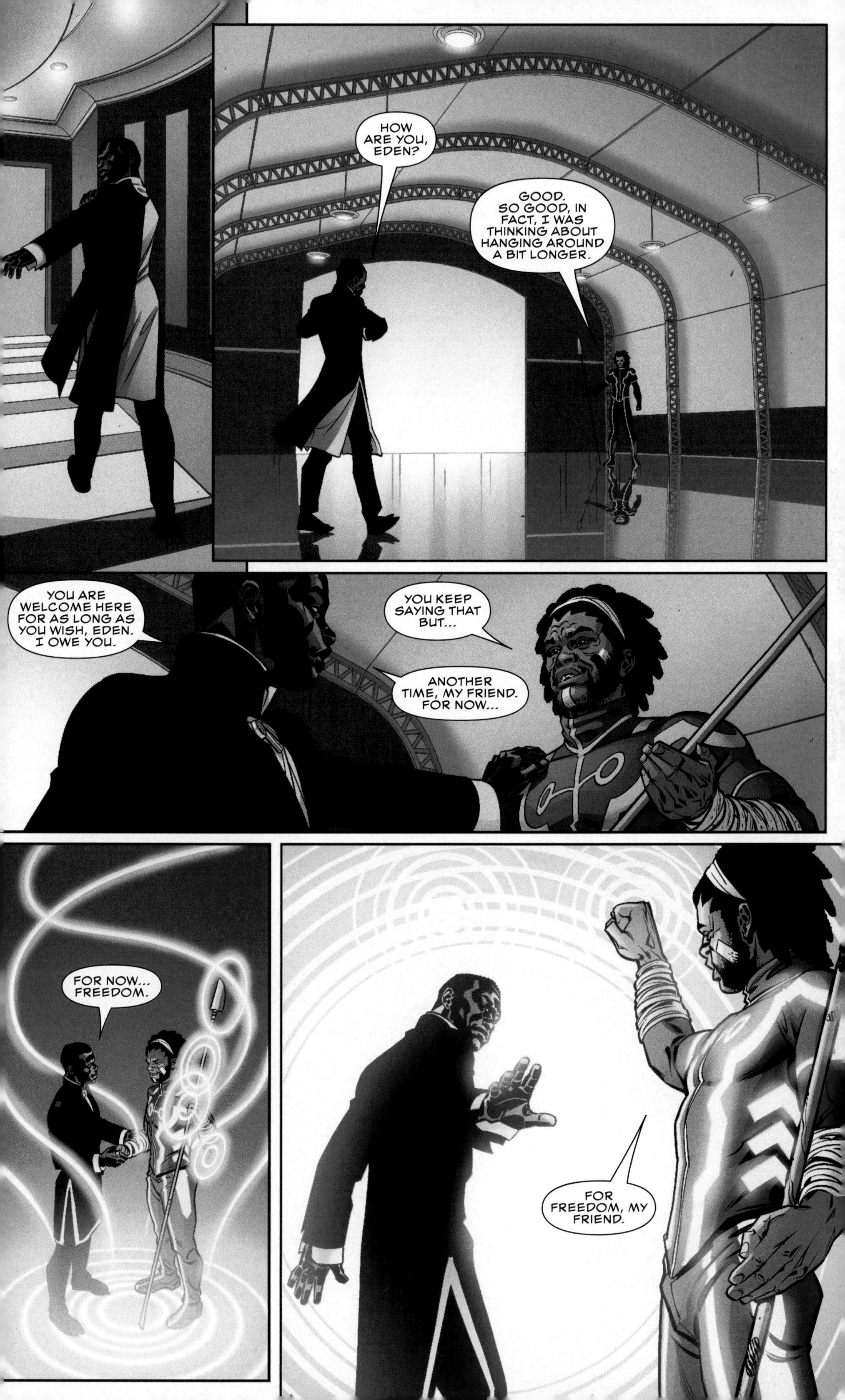
HOW ARE YOU, EDEN?
GOOD. SO GOOD, IN FACT, I WAS THINKING ABOUT HANGING AROUND A BIT LONGER.
YOU ARE WELCOME HERE FOR AS LONG AS YOU WISH, EDEN. I OWE YOU.
YOU KEEP SAYING THAT BUT...
ANOTHER TIME, MY FRIEND. FOR NOW...
FOR NOW... FREEDOM.
FOR FREEDOM, MY FRIEND.

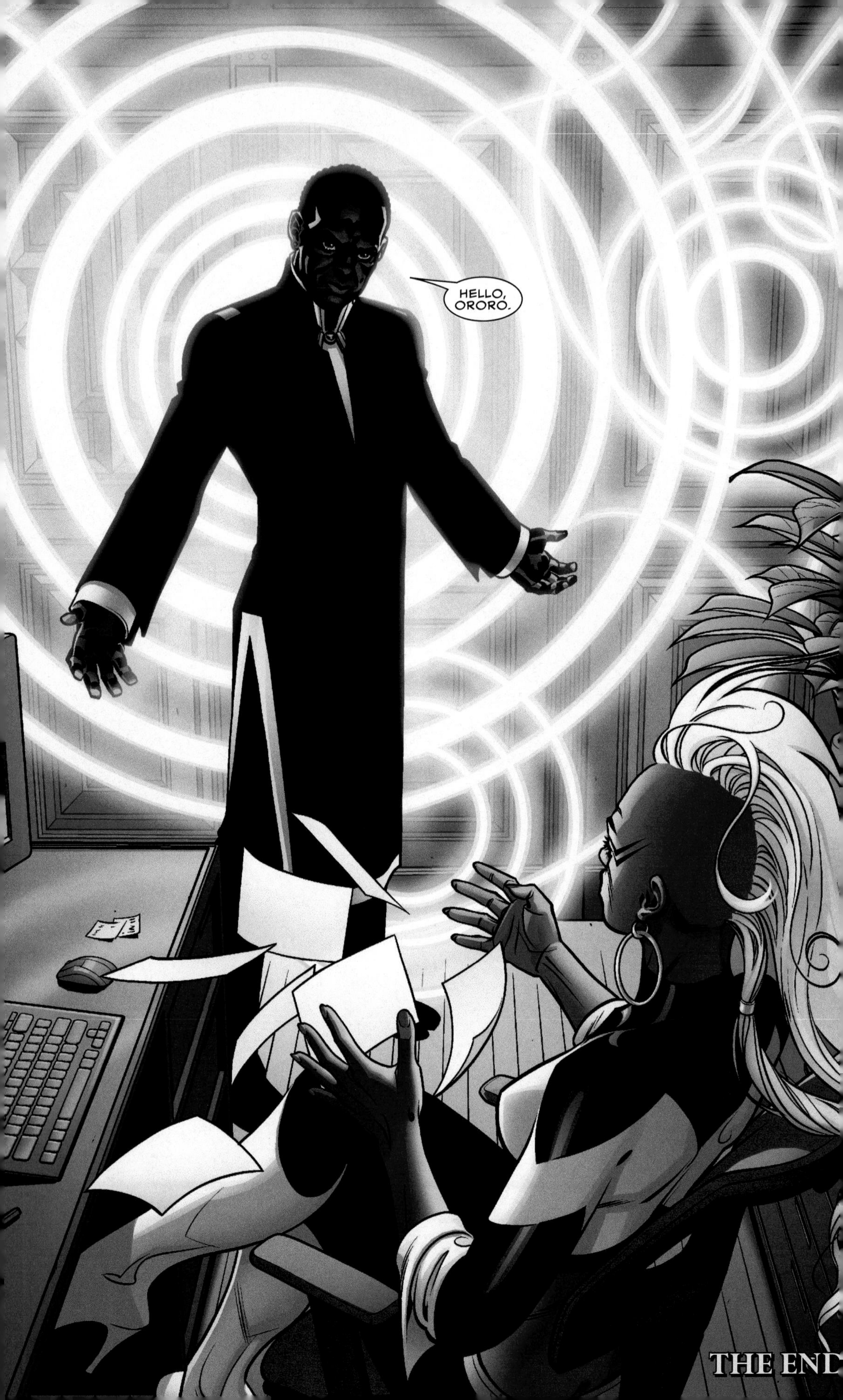
HELLO, ORORO.
THE END

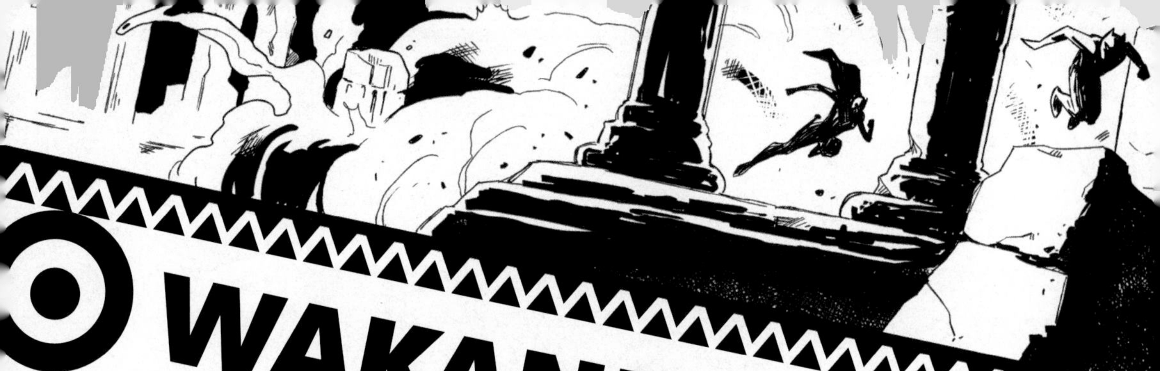

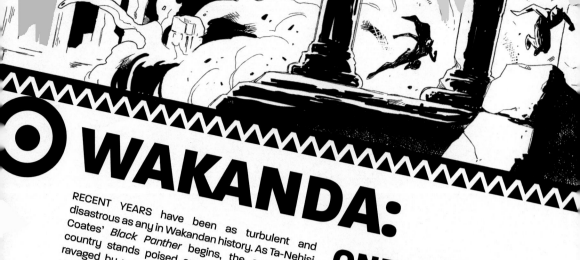

WAKANDA:

ONE NATION UNDER ATTACK

RECENT YEARS have been as turbulent and disastrous as any in Wakandan history. As Ta-Nehisi Coates' *Black Panther* begins, the once proud country stands poised on the brink of collapse, ravaged by war with **Atlantis**, the dark forces of would-be conqueror **Thanos** and the **Incursion crisis** that came close to destroying Earth.

The Golden City's fall unfolded in the pages of Jonathan Hickman's epic *New Avengers*. The following excerpts from *New Avengers #18*, *#21* and *#24* depict some of the momentous actions taken by T'Challa and his sister, Queen **Shuri**, in their desperate fight to prevent Wakanda from becoming a city of the dead.

When Earth was faced with a threat more devastating than ever before — the gradual, inevitable collapse of the **Multiverse** in a series of cataclysmic Incursions — T'Challa felt compelled to join **the Illuminati**, a group of the world's most powerful and influential super heroes including **Reed Richards, Tony Stark, Bruce Banner, Hank McCoy, Doctor Strange, Black Bolt** and **Namor**. The group worked in secret to make the hard decisions and change the fate of the planet.

But Wakanda was embroiled in an escalating conflict with Atlantis, following an attack perpetrated by Namor. Black Panther was forced to set aside his desire for revenge in favor of a hidden, and very uneasy, alliance with the Sub-Mariner.

With each Incursion, two Earths came close to collision — and the Illuminati became increasingly desperate in their efforts to save their own world without sacrificing another. They developed a weapon capable of doing the unthinkable — but could any of them bring themselves to use it?

In the pages that follow, T'Challa seeks the spiritual counsel of Black Panthers past — including his own father. Will he be able to do what they ask of him? Or will his hated enemy, Namor, seize the moment?

Months later, as the Sub-Mariner assembles a dark Cabal of villains to fight the Incursions — including the Inhuman **Maximus**, **Thanos** and the mad Titan's fearsome follower **Proxima Midnight** — the consequences of what unfolds will affect T'Challa, Shuri and their beleaguered homeland.

Wakanda's future begins with "A Nation Under Our Feet" — now learn how the last chapter of its history came to a close!

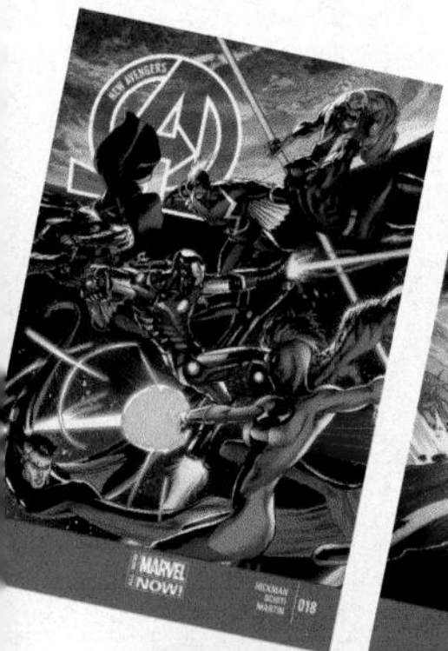

NEW AVENGERS
MARVEL NOW!
HICKMAN SCHITI MARTIN 018

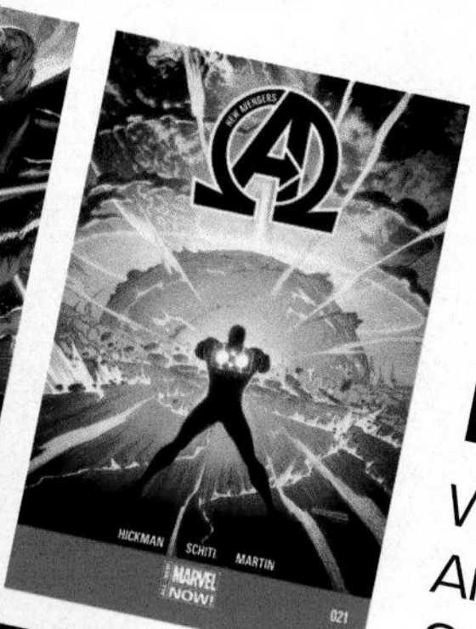

NEW AVENGERS
HICKMAN SCHITI MARTIN
MARVEL NOW!
021

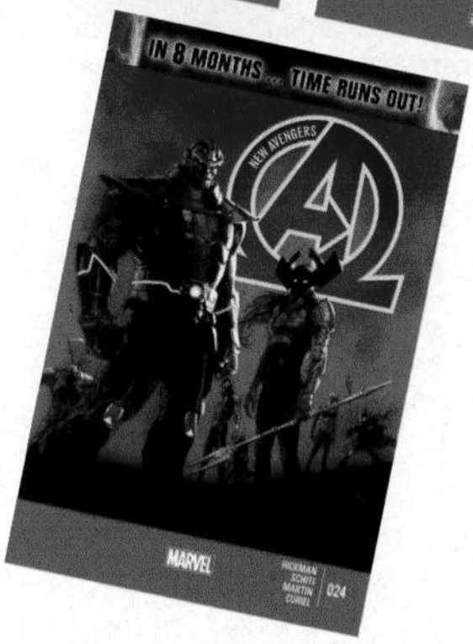

IN 8 MONTHS... TIME RUNS OUT!
NEW AVENGERS
MARVEL
HICKMAN SCHITI MARTIN CURIEL 024

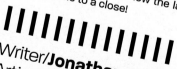

Writer/**Jonathan Hickman**
Artists/**Valerio Schiti with Salvador Larroca (#21)**
Color Artists/**Frank Martin with Paul Mounts (#21) & David Curiel (#24)**
Letterer/**VC's Joe Caramagna**
Cover Art/**Dustin Weaver & Jason Keith (#18, #21) and Gabriele Dell'Otto (#24)**
Assistant Editor/**Jake Thomas**
Editors/**Tom Brevoort with Wil Moss**

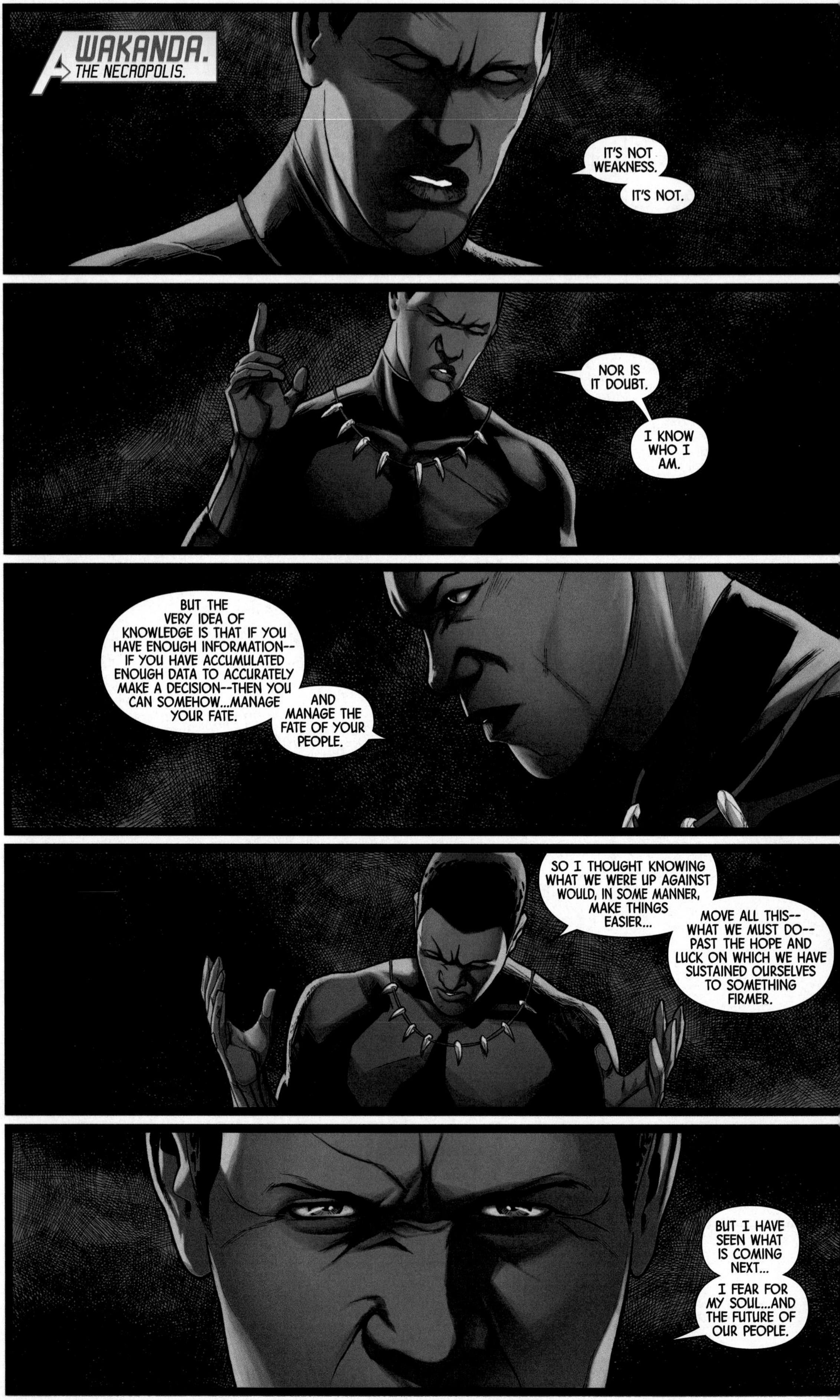
WAKANDA.
THE NECROPOLIS.
IT'S NOT WEAKNESS.
IT'S NOT.
NOR IS IT DOUBT.
I KNOW WHO I AM.
BUT THE VERY IDEA OF KNOWLEDGE IS THAT IF YOU HAVE ENOUGH INFORMATION-- IF YOU HAVE ACCUMULATED ENOUGH DATA TO ACCURATELY MAKE A DECISION--THEN YOU CAN SOMEHOW...MANAGE YOUR FATE.
AND MANAGE THE FATE OF YOUR PEOPLE.
SO I THOUGHT KNOWING WHAT WE WERE UP AGAINST WOULD, IN SOME MANNER, MAKE THINGS EASIER...
MOVE ALL THIS-- WHAT WE MUST DO-- PAST THE HOPE AND LUCK ON WHICH WE HAVE SUSTAINED OURSELVES TO SOMETHING FIRMER.
BUT I HAVE SEEN WHAT IS COMING NEXT...
I FEAR FOR MY SOUL...AND THE FUTURE OF OUR PEOPLE.

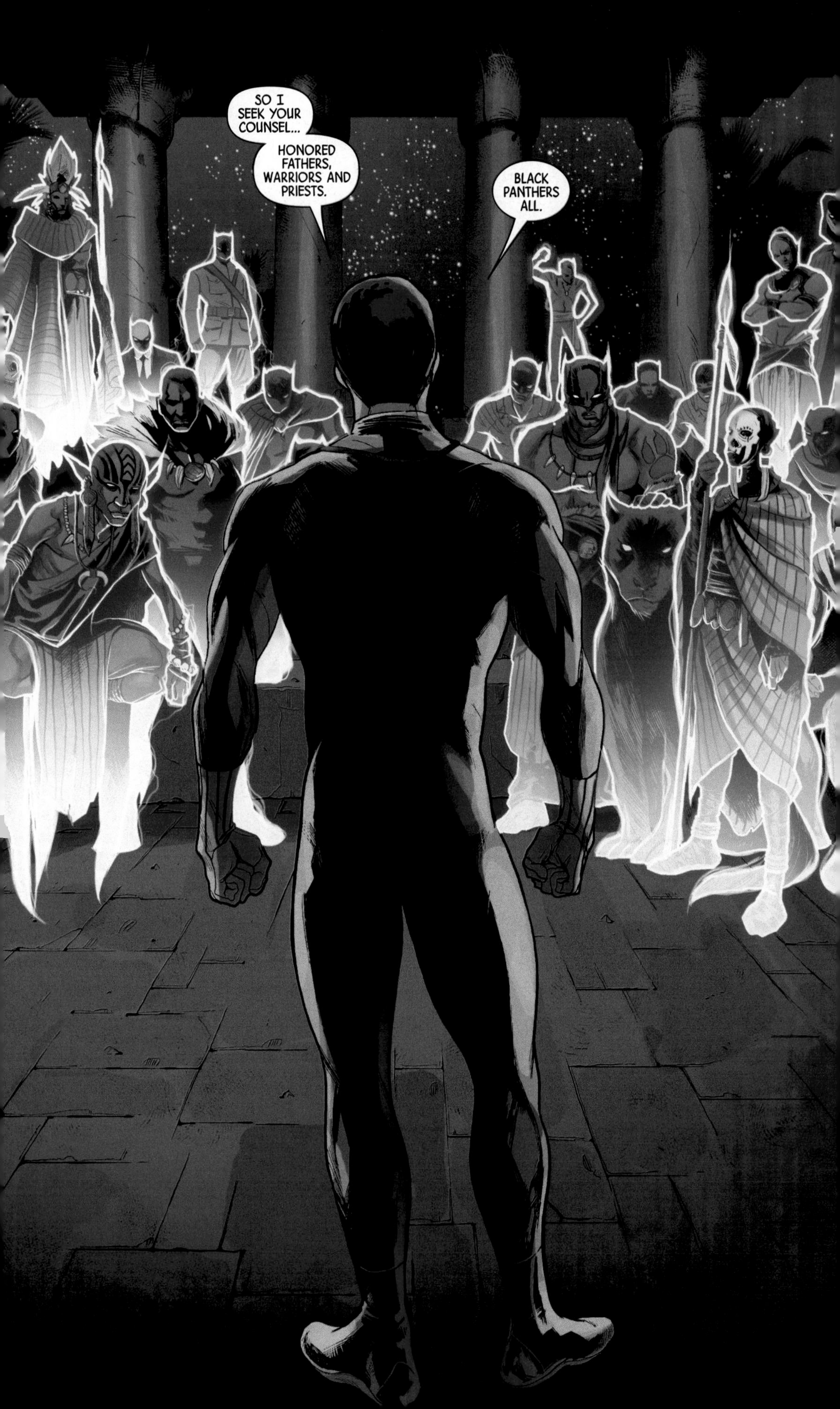
SO I SEEK YOUR COUNSEL...
HONORED FATHERS, WARRIORS AND PRIESTS.
BLACK PANTHERS ALL.

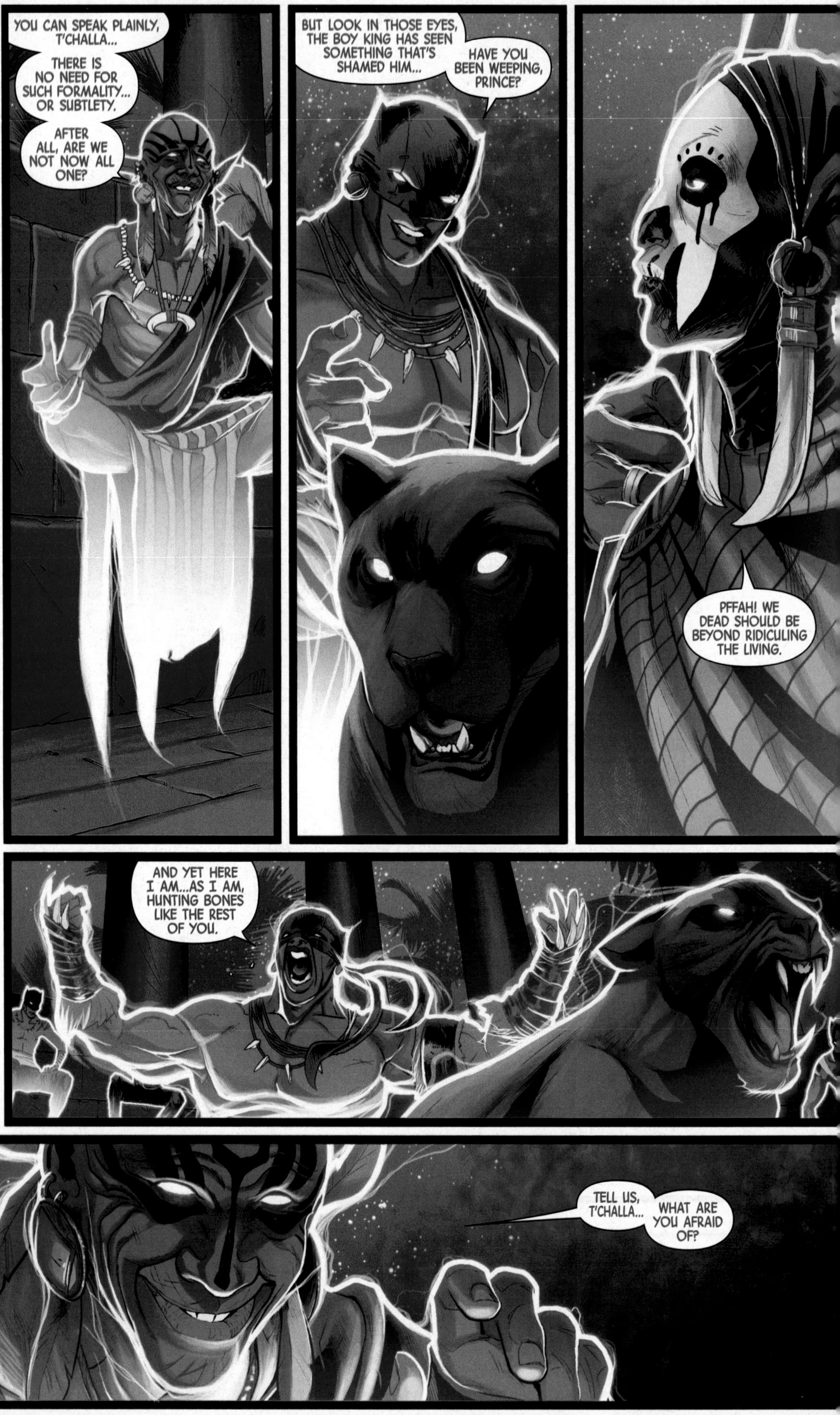
YOU CAN SPEAK PLAINLY, T'CHALLA...
THERE IS NO NEED FOR SUCH FORMALITY... OR SUBTLETY.
AFTER ALL, ARE WE NOT NOW ALL ONE?
BUT LOOK IN THOSE EYES, THE BOY KING HAS SEEN SOMETHING THAT'S SHAMED HIM...
HAVE YOU BEEN WEEPING, PRINCE?
PFFAH! WE DEAD SHOULD BE BEYOND RIDICULING THE LIVING.
AND YET HERE I AM...AS I AM, HUNTING BONES LIKE THE REST OF YOU.
TELL US, T'CHALLA...
WHAT ARE YOU AFRAID OF?

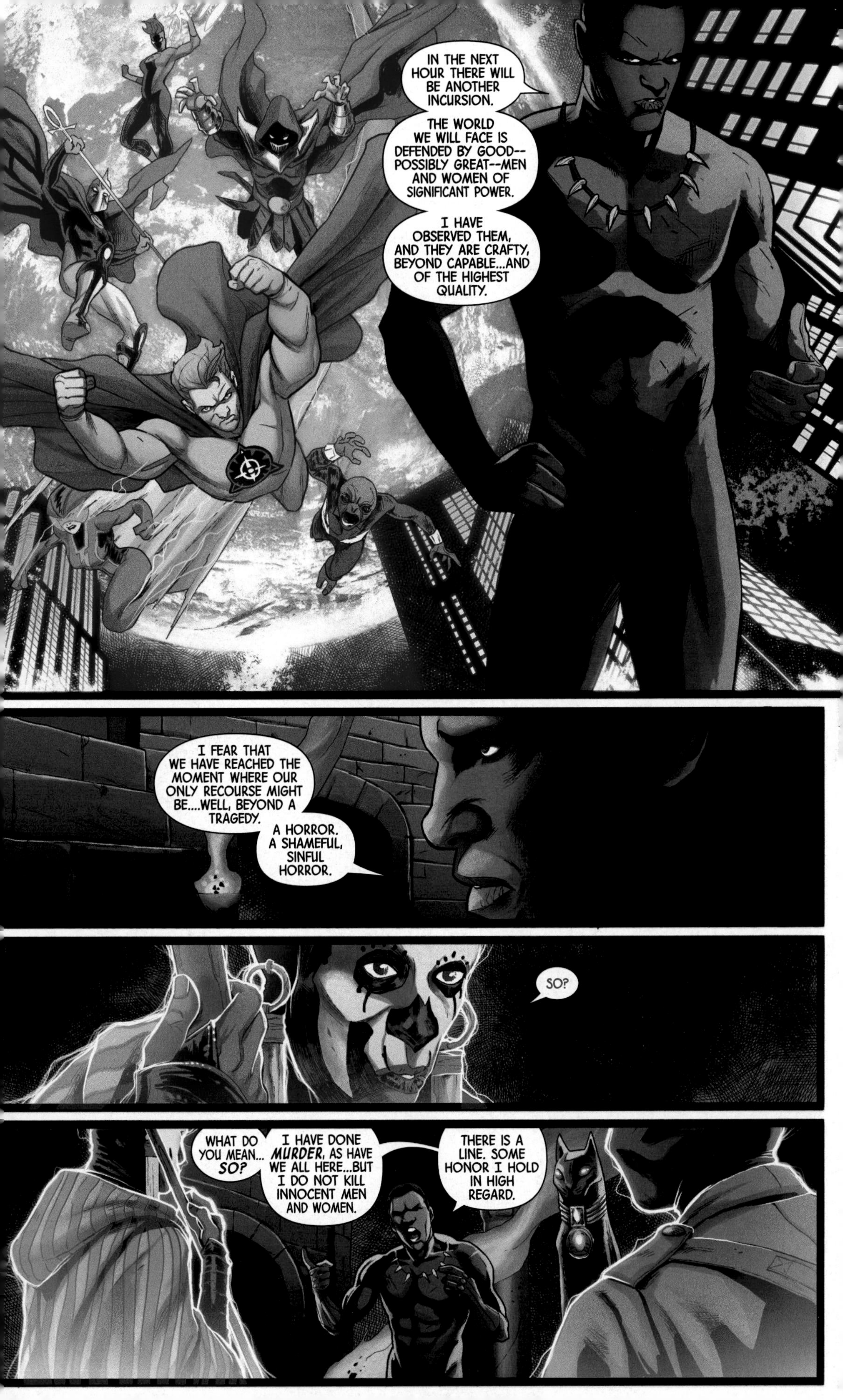
IN THE NEXT HOUR THERE WILL BE ANOTHER INCURSION.
THE WORLD WE WILL FACE IS DEFENDED BY GOOD-- POSSIBLY GREAT--MEN AND WOMEN OF SIGNIFICANT POWER.
I HAVE OBSERVED THEM, AND THEY ARE CRAFTY, BEYOND CAPABLE...AND OF THE HIGHEST QUALITY.
I FEAR THAT WE HAVE REACHED THE MOMENT WHERE OUR ONLY RECOURSE MIGHT BE....WELL, BEYOND A TRAGEDY.
A HORROR. A SHAMEFUL, SINFUL HORROR.
SO?
WHAT DO YOU MEAN... SO?
I HAVE DONE MURDER, AS HAVE WE ALL HERE...BUT I DO NOT KILL INNOCENT MEN AND WOMEN.
THERE IS A LINE. SOME HONOR I HOLD IN HIGH REGARD.

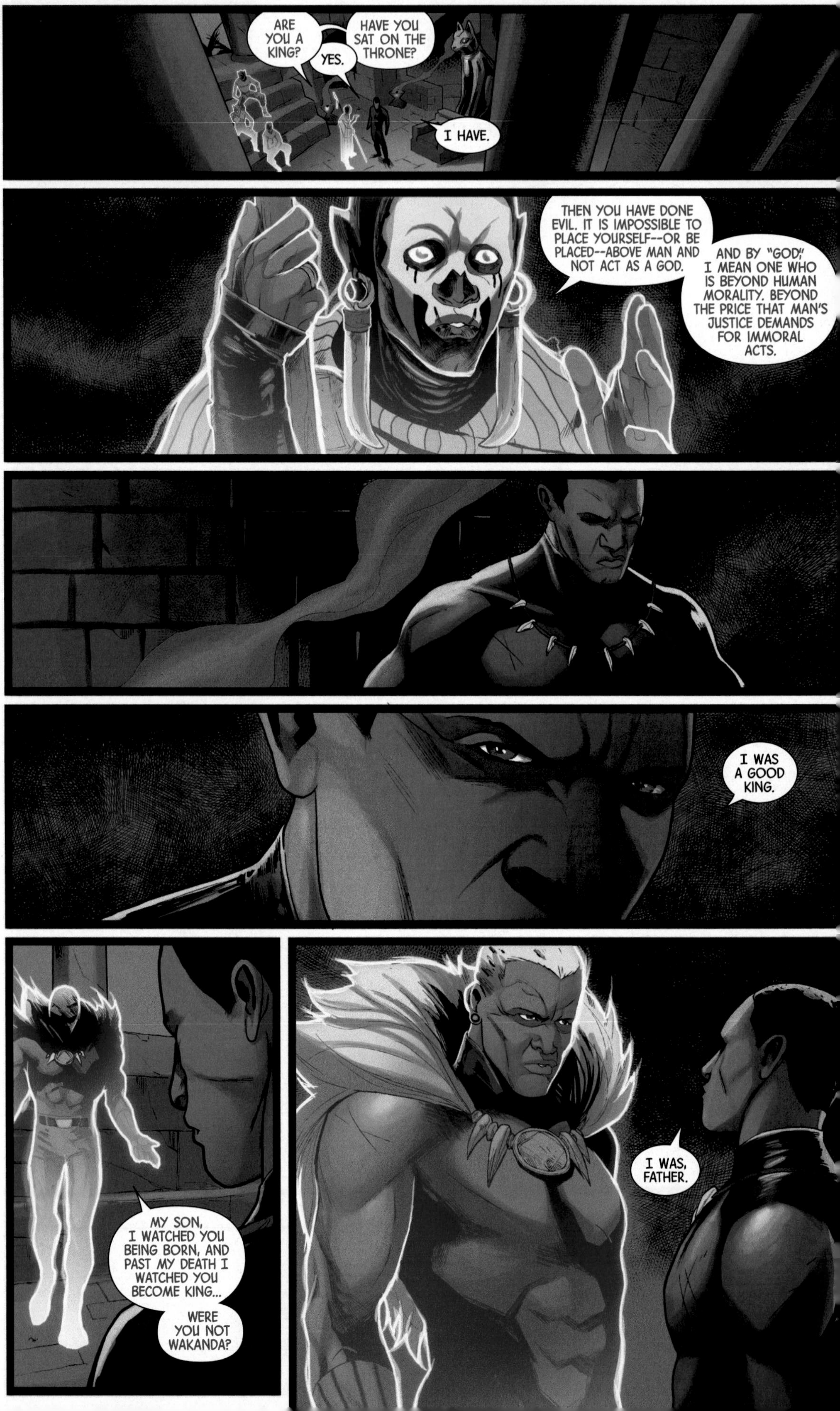

ARE YOU A KING?
YES.
HAVE YOU SAT ON THE THRONE?
I HAVE.
THEN YOU HAVE DONE EVIL. IT IS IMPOSSIBLE TO PLACE YOURSELF--OR BE PLACED--ABOVE MAN AND NOT ACT AS A GOD.
AND BY "GOD," I MEAN ONE WHO IS BEYOND HUMAN MORALITY. BEYOND THE PRICE THAT MAN'S JUSTICE DEMANDS FOR IMMORAL ACTS.
I WAS A GOOD KING.
MY SON, I WATCHED YOU BEING BORN, AND PAST MY DEATH I WATCHED YOU BECOME KING...
WERE YOU NOT WAKANDA?
I WAS, FATHER.

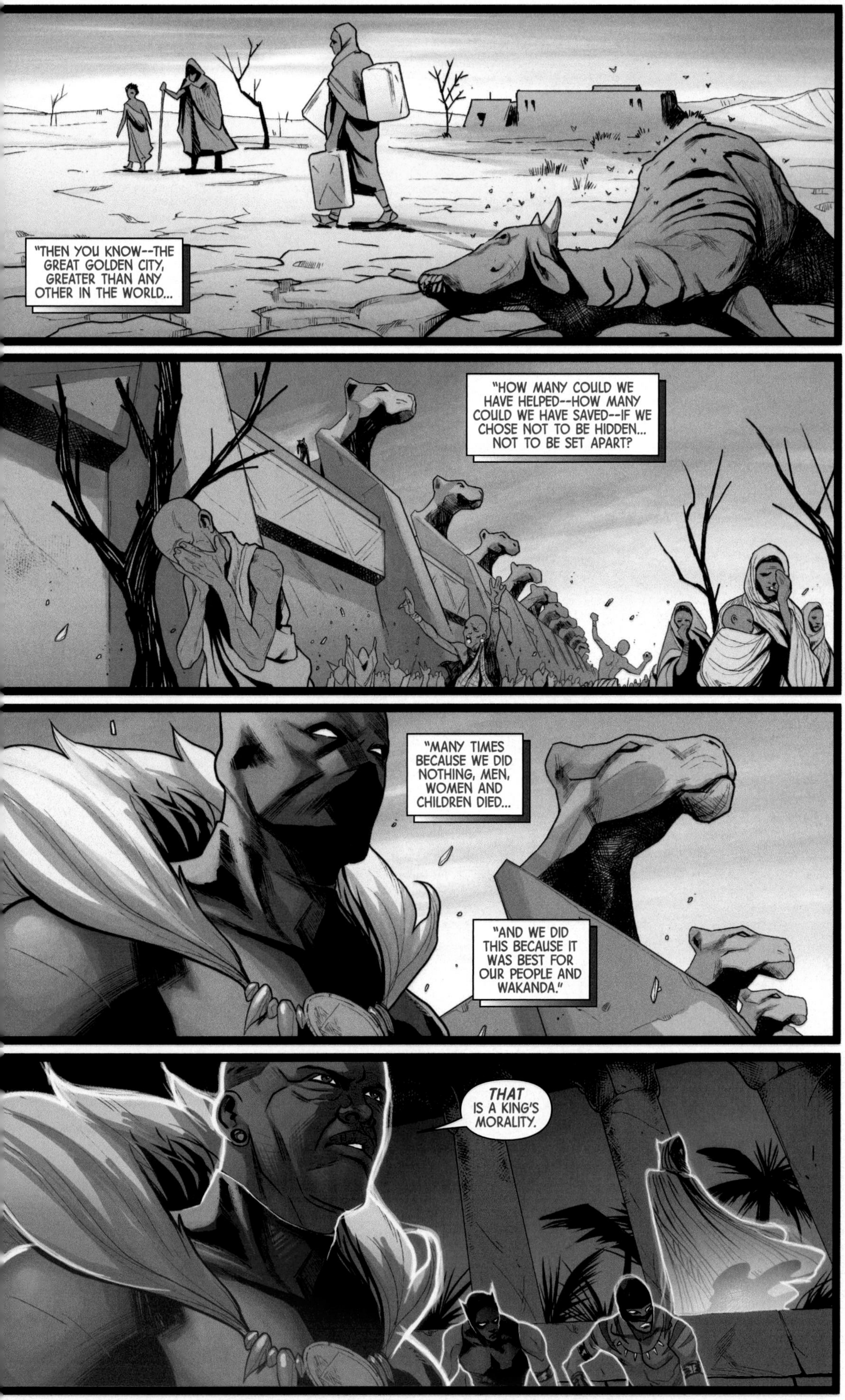
"THEN YOU KNOW--THE GREAT GOLDEN CITY, GREATER THAN ANY OTHER IN THE WORLD...
"HOW MANY COULD WE HAVE HELPED--HOW MANY COULD WE HAVE SAVED--IF WE CHOSE NOT TO BE HIDDEN... NOT TO BE SET APART?
"MANY TIMES BECAUSE WE DID NOTHING, MEN, WOMEN AND CHILDREN DIED...
"AND WE DID THIS BECAUSE IT WAS BEST FOR OUR PEOPLE AND WAKANDA."
THAT IS A KING'S MORALITY.

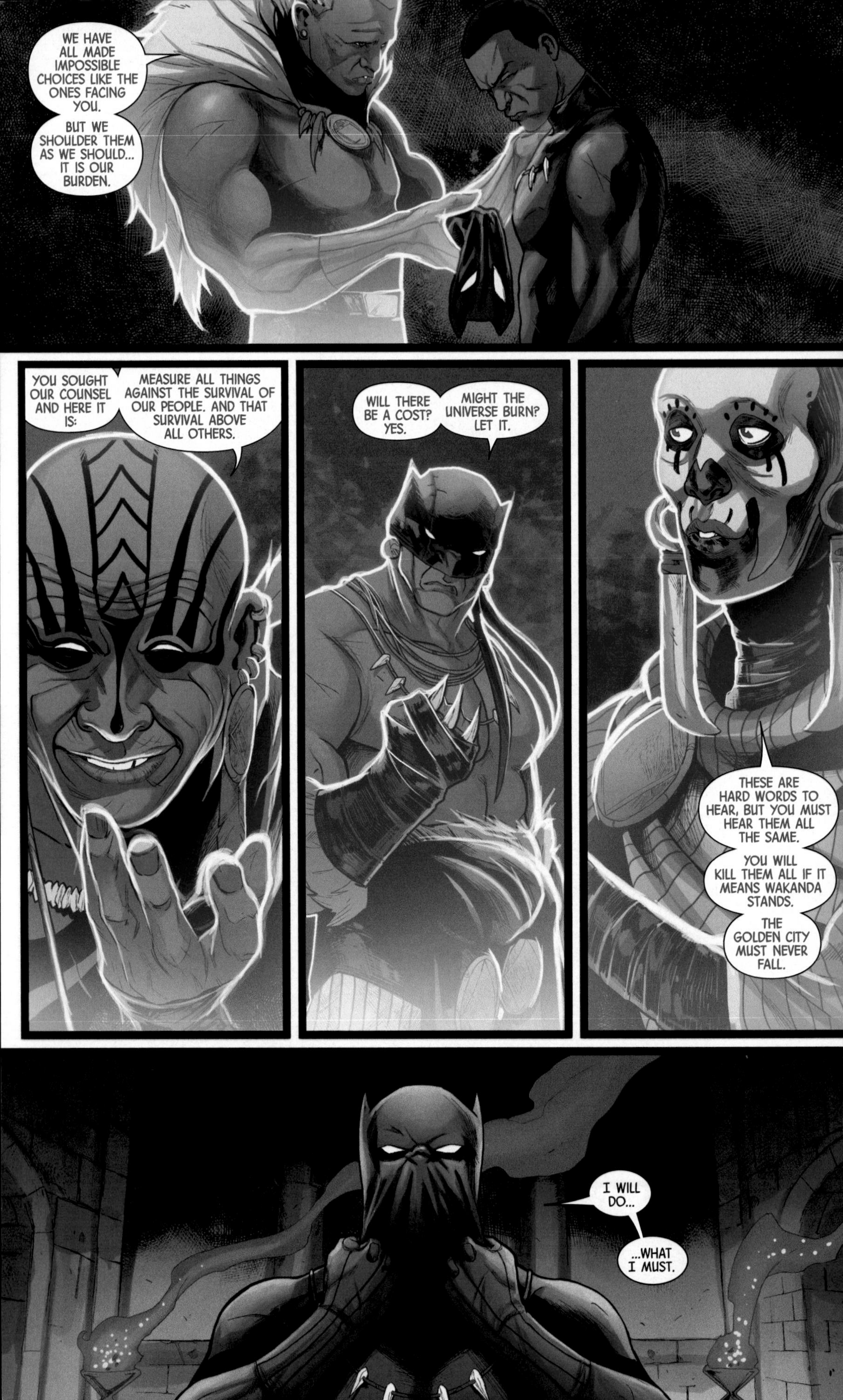
WE HAVE ALL MADE IMPOSSIBLE CHOICES LIKE THE ONES FACING YOU.
BUT WE SHOULDER THEM AS WE SHOULD... IT IS OUR BURDEN.
YOU SOUGHT OUR COUNSEL AND HERE IT IS:
MEASURE ALL THINGS AGAINST THE SURVIVAL OF OUR PEOPLE. AND THAT SURVIVAL ABOVE ALL OTHERS.
WILL THERE BE A COST? YES.
MIGHT THE UNIVERSE BURN? LET IT.
THESE ARE HARD WORDS TO HEAR, BUT YOU MUST HEAR THEM ALL THE SAME.
YOU WILL KILL THEM ALL IF IT MEANS WAKANDA STANDS.
THE GOLDEN CITY MUST NEVER FALL.
I WILL DO...
...WHAT I MUST.

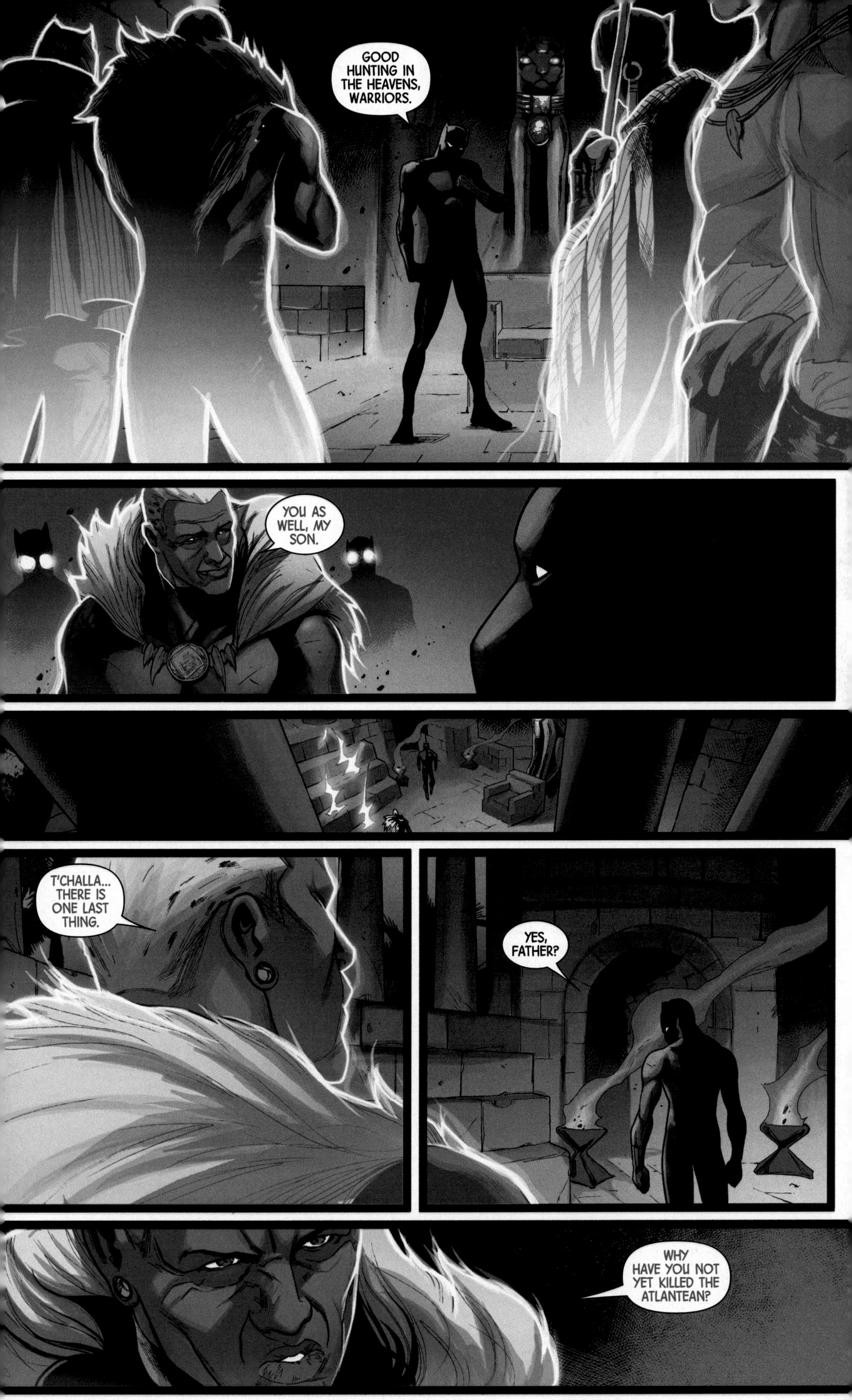
GOOD HUNTING IN THE HEAVENS, WARRIORS.
YOU AS WELL, MY SON.
T'CHALLA... THERE IS ONE LAST THING.
YES, FATHER?
WHY HAVE YOU NOT YET KILLED THE ATLANTEAN?

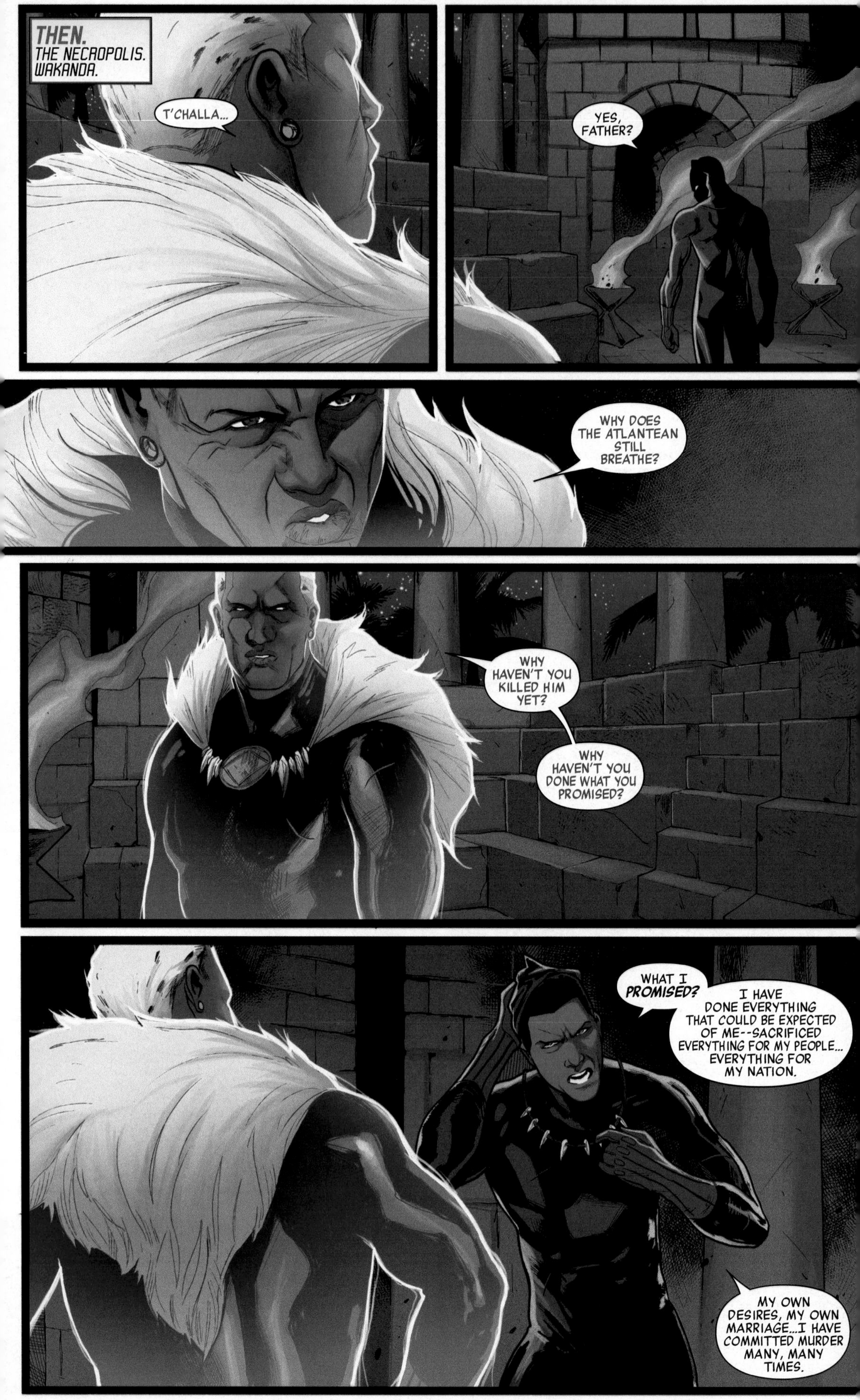
THEN.
THE NECROPOLIS.
WAKANDA.
T'CHALLA...
YES, FATHER?
WHY DOES THE ATLANTEAN STILL BREATHE?
WHY HAVEN'T YOU KILLED HIM YET?
WHY HAVEN'T YOU DONE WHAT YOU PROMISED?
WHAT I *PROMISED?*
I HAVE DONE EVERYTHING THAT COULD BE EXPECTED OF ME--SACRIFICED EVERYTHING FOR MY PEOPLE... EVERYTHING FOR MY NATION.
MY OWN DESIRES, MY OWN MARRIAGE...I HAVE COMMITTED MURDER MANY, MANY TIMES.

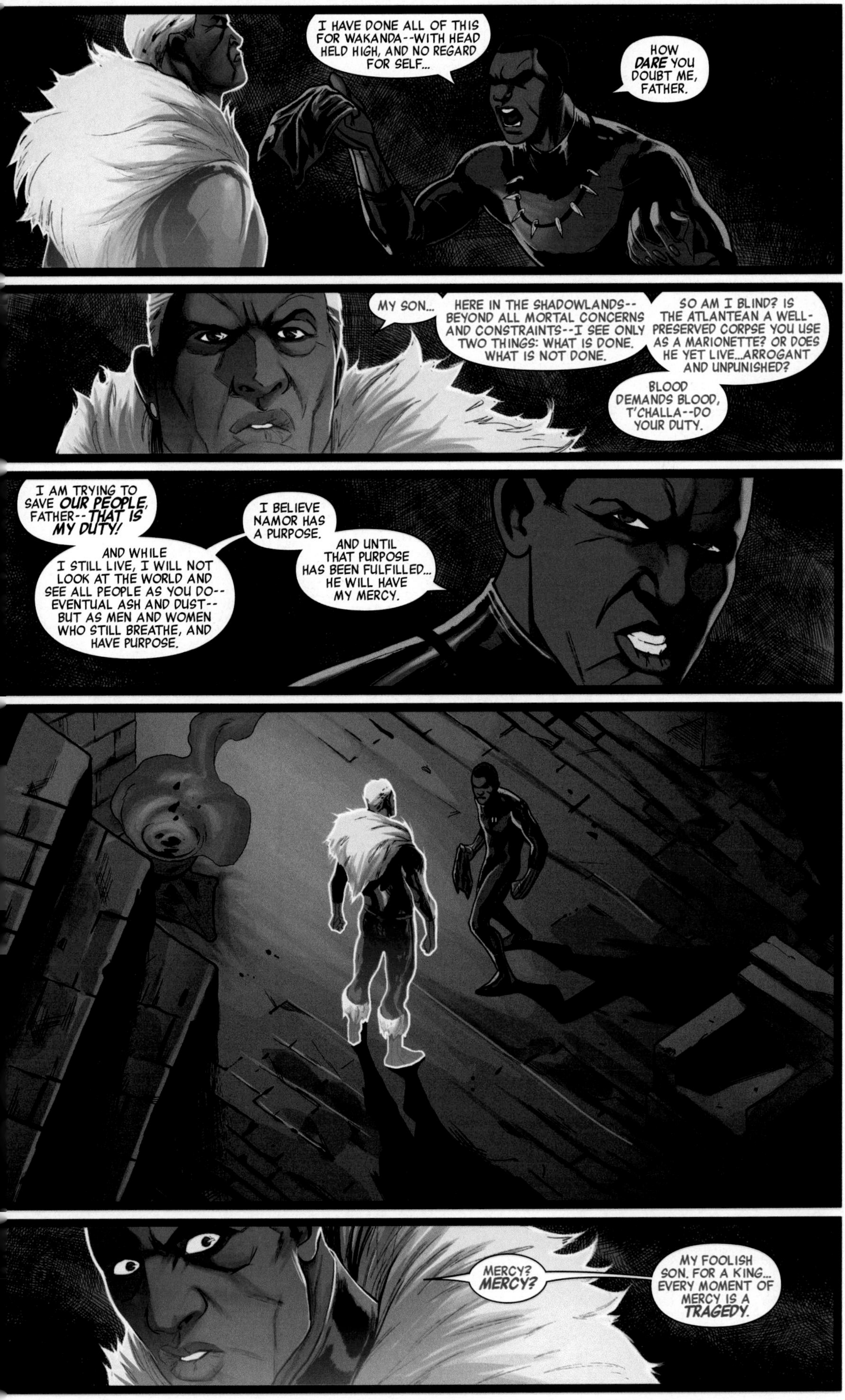
I HAVE DONE ALL OF THIS FOR WAKANDA--WITH HEAD HELD HIGH, AND NO REGARD FOR SELF...
HOW DARE YOU DOUBT ME, FATHER.
MY SON...
HERE IN THE SHADOWLANDS--BEYOND ALL MORTAL CONCERNS AND CONSTRAINTS--I SEE ONLY TWO THINGS: WHAT IS DONE. WHAT IS NOT DONE.
SO AM I BLIND? IS THE ATLANTEAN A WELL-PRESERVED CORPSE YOU USE AS A MARIONETTE? OR DOES HE YET LIVE...ARROGANT AND UNPUNISHED?
BLOOD DEMANDS BLOOD, T'CHALLA--DO YOUR DUTY.
I AM TRYING TO SAVE OUR PEOPLE, FATHER--THAT IS MY DUTY!
AND WHILE I STILL LIVE, I WILL NOT LOOK AT THE WORLD AND SEE ALL PEOPLE AS YOU DO--EVENTUAL ASH AND DUST--BUT AS MEN AND WOMEN WHO STILL BREATHE, AND HAVE PURPOSE.
I BELIEVE NAMOR HAS A PURPOSE.
AND UNTIL THAT PURPOSE HAS BEEN FULFILLED... HE WILL HAVE MY MERCY.
MERCY? MERCY?
MY FOOLISH SON. FOR A KING... EVERY MOMENT OF MERCY IS A TRAGEDY.

EARTH-616.
TEN MINUTES TO COLLISION.

TRIGGER ACTIVE.

ARE WE **REALLY** GOING TO DO THIS?

WE'RE OUT OF TIME, BRUCE... WE'RE OUT OF OPTIONS...WE HAVE TO.

BUT...I...I DON'T THINK I CAN.

I KNOW IT'S A NECESSARY EVIL. I KNOW I WOULD BE SAVING HUNDREDS OF TRILLIONS OF LIVES AT THE COST OF MERE BILLIONS. I KNOW THERE IS NO REAL SHAME IN COMING TO THAT CONCLUSION--IN MAKING THAT CHOICE.

BUT EVEN WITH ALL THINGS HANGING IN THE BALANCE... THERE IS A LINE.

AND I **CAN'T** DO THIS.

WELL, DON'T LOOK AT ME... I HELPED BUILD THE THING, I'M NOT USING IT EITHER.

BRUCE? HENRY? NO.

ABSOLUTELY NOT.

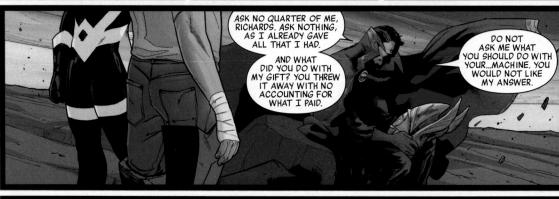

ASK NO QUARTER OF ME, RICHARDS. ASK NOTHING, AS I ALREADY GAVE ALL THAT I HAD.

AND WHAT DID YOU DO WITH MY GIFT? YOU THREW IT AWAY WITH NO ACCOUNTING FOR WHAT I PAID.

DO NOT ASK ME WHAT YOU SHOULD DO WITH YOUR...MACHINE. YOU WOULD NOT LIKE MY ANSWER.

AND YOU, BLACK BOLT? WOULD YO--

GIVE THE TRIGGER TO ME, REED.

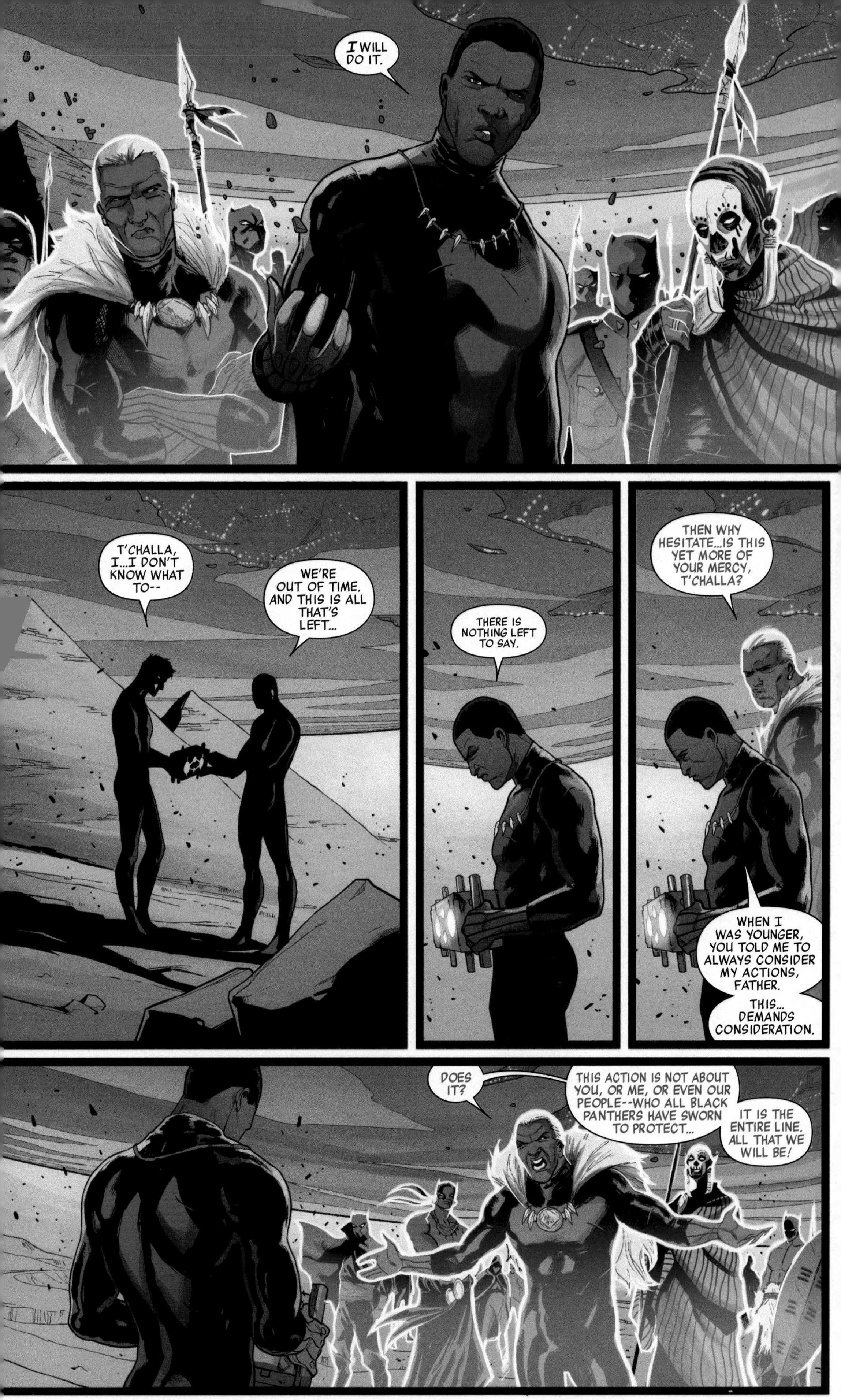

I WILL DO IT.
T'CHALLA, I...I DON'T KNOW WHAT TO--
WE'RE OUT OF TIME. AND THIS IS ALL THAT'S LEFT...
THERE IS NOTHING LEFT TO SAY.
THEN WHY HESITATE...IS THIS YET MORE OF YOUR MERCY, T'CHALLA?
WHEN I WAS YOUNGER, YOU TOLD ME TO ALWAYS CONSIDER MY ACTIONS, FATHER.
THIS... DEMANDS CONSIDERATION.
DOES IT?
THIS ACTION IS NOT ABOUT YOU, OR ME, OR EVEN OUR PEOPLE--WHO ALL BLACK PANTHERS HAVE SWORN TO PROTECT...
IT IS THE ENTIRE LINE. ALL THAT WE WILL BE!

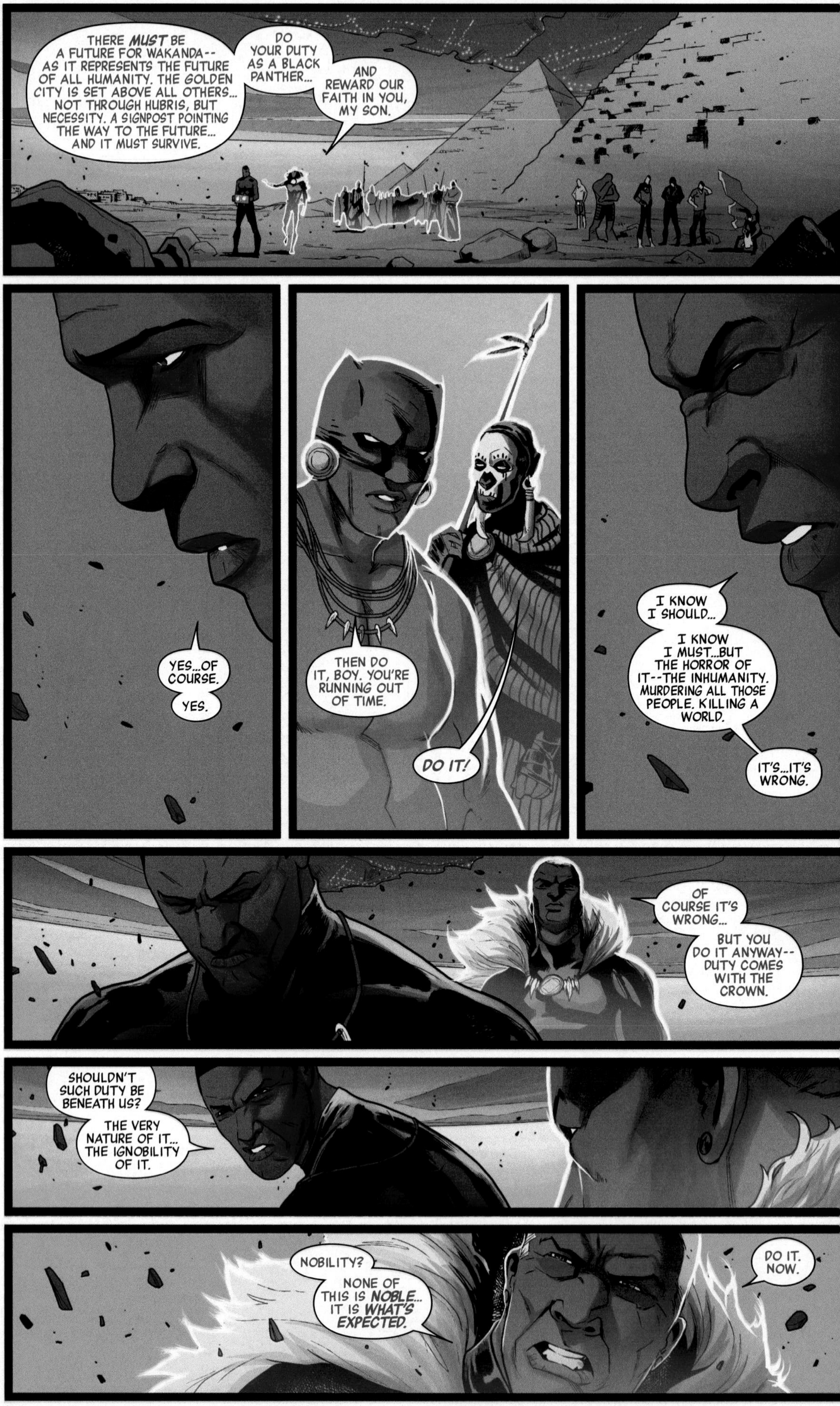

THERE MUST BE A FUTURE FOR WAKANDA-- AS IT REPRESENTS THE FUTURE OF ALL HUMANITY. THE GOLDEN CITY IS SET ABOVE ALL OTHERS... NOT THROUGH HUBRIS, BUT NECESSITY. A SIGNPOST POINTING THE WAY TO THE FUTURE... AND IT MUST SURVIVE.
DO YOUR DUTY AS A BLACK PANTHER...
AND REWARD OUR FAITH IN YOU, MY SON.
YES...OF COURSE.
YES.
THEN DO IT, BOY. YOU'RE RUNNING OUT OF TIME.
DO IT!
I KNOW I SHOULD...
I KNOW I MUST...BUT THE HORROR OF IT--THE INHUMANITY. MURDERING ALL THOSE PEOPLE. KILLING A WORLD.
IT'S...IT'S WRONG.
OF COURSE IT'S WRONG...
BUT YOU DO IT ANYWAY-- DUTY COMES WITH THE CROWN.
SHOULDN'T SUCH DUTY BE BENEATH US?
THE VERY NATURE OF IT... THE IGNOBILITY OF IT.
NOBILITY?
NONE OF THIS IS NOBLE... IT IS WHAT'S EXPECTED.
DO IT. NOW.

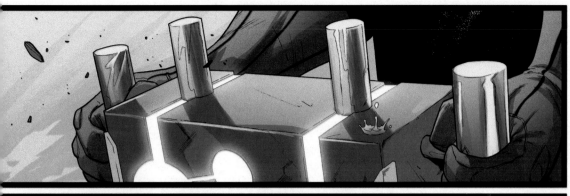

I CAN'T. I WANT TO DO THE RIGHT THING... FOR YOU, FATHER...FOR MY PEOPLE. BUT I CAN'T DO THIS.

WE WERE CURSED WHEN WE MADE THIS MACHINE...

WE WERE DAMNED THE VERY DAY WE THOUGHT IT WAS FOR MEN TO DECIDE THINGS SUCH AS THIS.

DAMNED, T'CHALLA?

PERHAPS THAT WOULD BE FITTING...

BUT YOU STILL HAVE TIME.

IT...IS WRONG...

AND I CANNOT DO IT, FATHER!

I CANNOT.

NO. YOU CHOOSE NOT TO-- IT IS *YOUR CHOICE.*

SO HERE IS MINE: THERE IS AN ETERNITY... AND IN IT, YOU ARE DEAD TO ME, AND TO US ALL.

YOU HAVE NO PEOPLE.

YOU ARE NO BLACK PANTHER.

YOU ARE NO LONGER MY SON.

I'M SORRY...I'M SORRY...

IT'S OKAY, T'CHALLA.

IT'S OKAY. I UNDERSTAND...

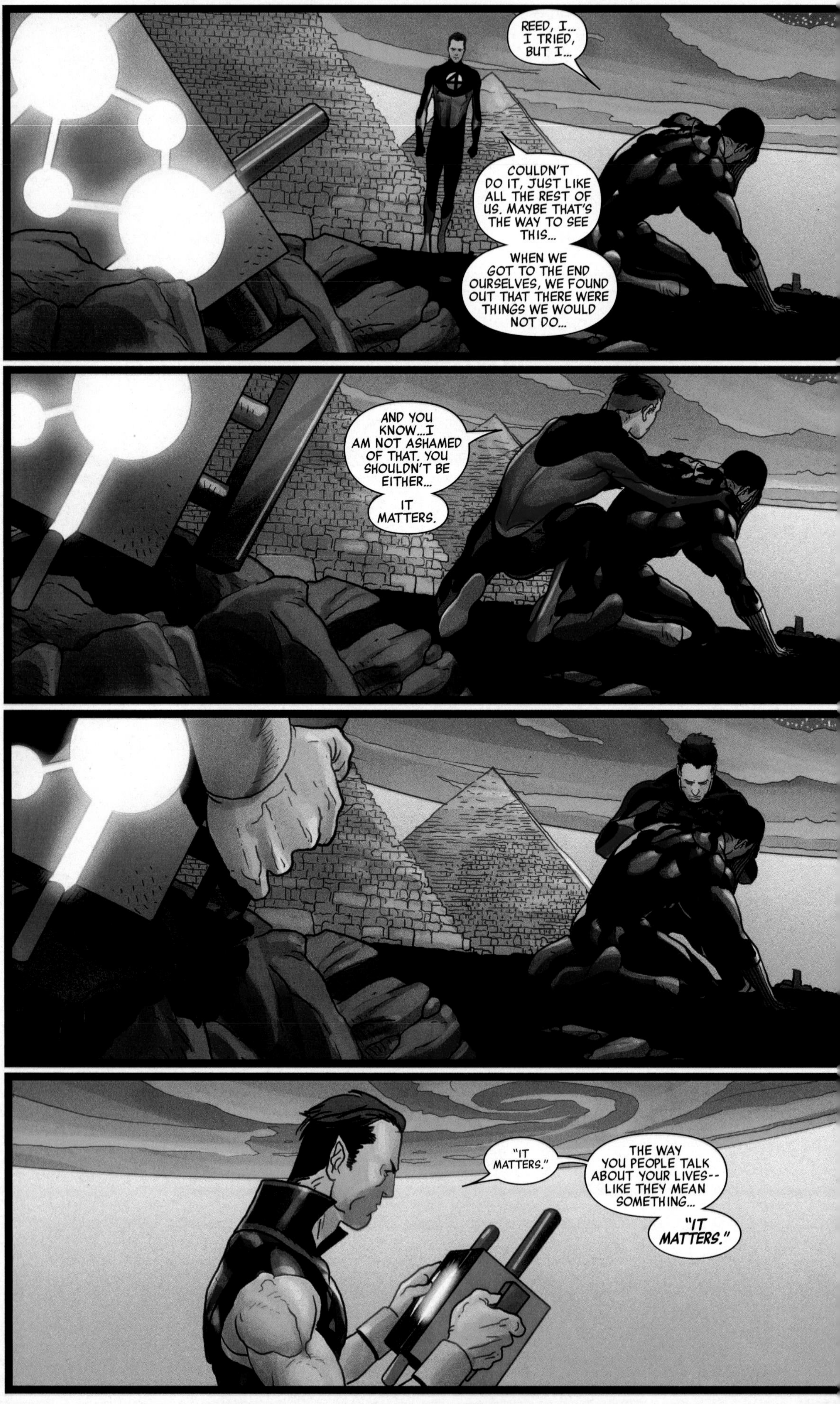
REED, I... I TRIED, BUT I...
COULDN'T DO IT, JUST LIKE ALL THE REST OF US. MAYBE THAT'S THE WAY TO SEE THIS...
WHEN WE GOT TO THE END OURSELVES, WE FOUND OUT THAT THERE WERE THINGS WE WOULD NOT DO...
AND YOU KNOW...I AM NOT ASHAMED OF THAT. YOU SHOULDN'T BE EITHER...
IT MATTERS.
"IT MATTERS."
THE WAY YOU PEOPLE TALK ABOUT YOUR LIVES-- LIKE THEY MEAN SOMETHING...
"IT MATTERS."

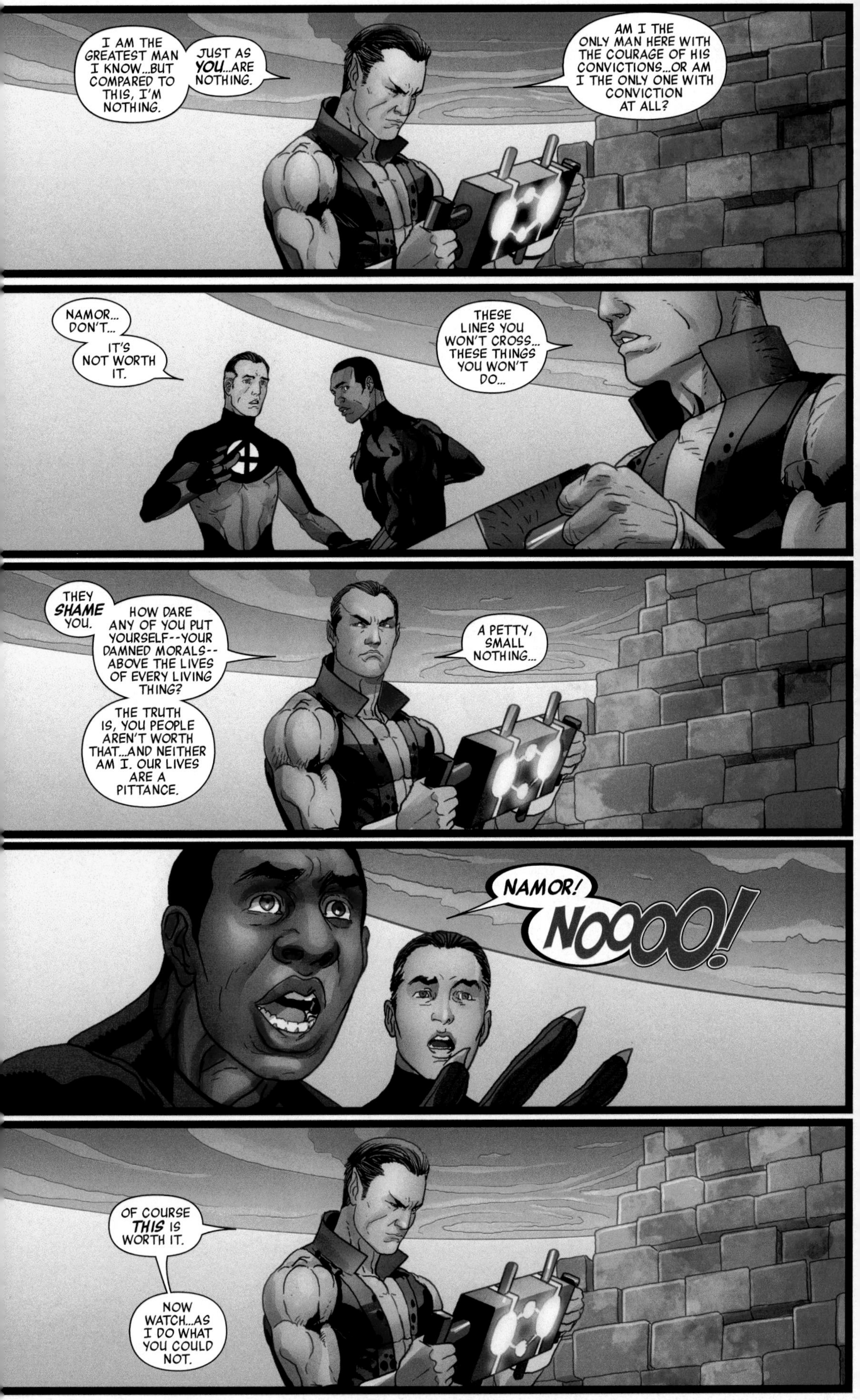
I AM THE GREATEST MAN I KNOW...BUT COMPARED TO THIS, I'M NOTHING.
JUST AS YOU...ARE NOTHING.
AM I THE ONLY MAN HERE WITH THE COURAGE OF HIS CONVICTIONS...OR AM I THE ONLY ONE WITH CONVICTION AT ALL?
NAMOR... DON'T...
IT'S NOT WORTH IT.
THESE LINES YOU WON'T CROSS... THESE THINGS YOU WON'T DO...
THEY SHAME YOU.
HOW DARE ANY OF YOU PUT YOURSELF--YOUR DAMNED MORALS--ABOVE THE LIVES OF EVERY LIVING THING?
THE TRUTH IS, YOU PEOPLE AREN'T WORTH THAT...AND NEITHER AM I. OUR LIVES ARE A PITTANCE.
A PETTY, SMALL NOTHING...
NAMOR! NOOOO!
OF COURSE THIS IS WORTH IT.
NOW WATCH...AS I DO WHAT YOU COULD NOT.

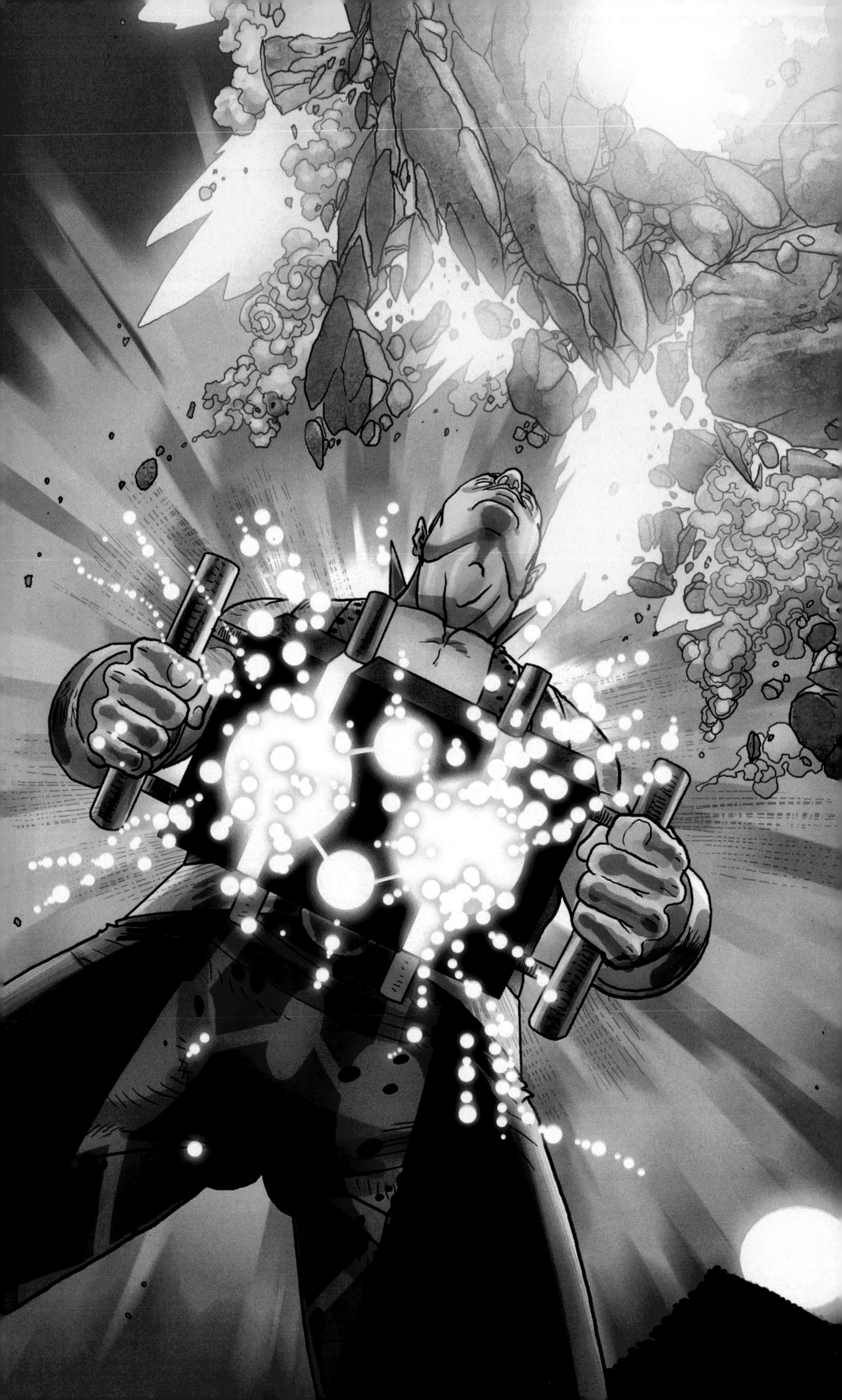

EIGHT MONTHS LATER

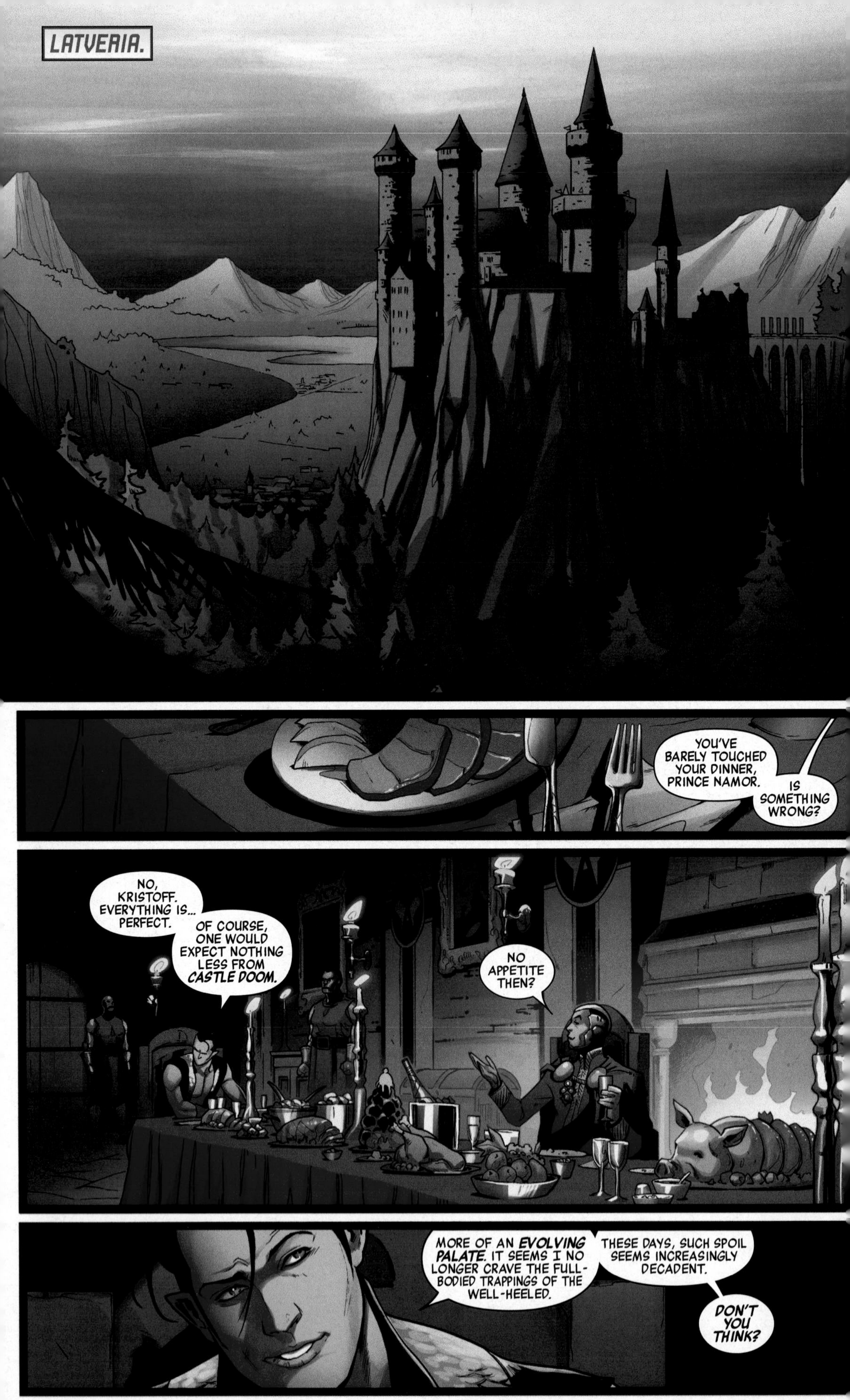
LATVERIA.
YOU'VE BARELY TOUCHED YOUR DINNER, PRINCE NAMOR.
IS SOMETHING WRONG?
NO, KRISTOFF. EVERYTHING IS... PERFECT.
OF COURSE, ONE WOULD EXPECT NOTHING LESS FROM CASTLE DOOM.
NO APPETITE THEN?
MORE OF AN EVOLVING PALATE. IT SEEMS I NO LONGER CRAVE THE FULL-BODIED TRAPPINGS OF THE WELL-HEELED.
THESE DAYS, SUCH SPOIL SEEMS INCREASINGLY DECADENT.
DON'T YOU THINK?

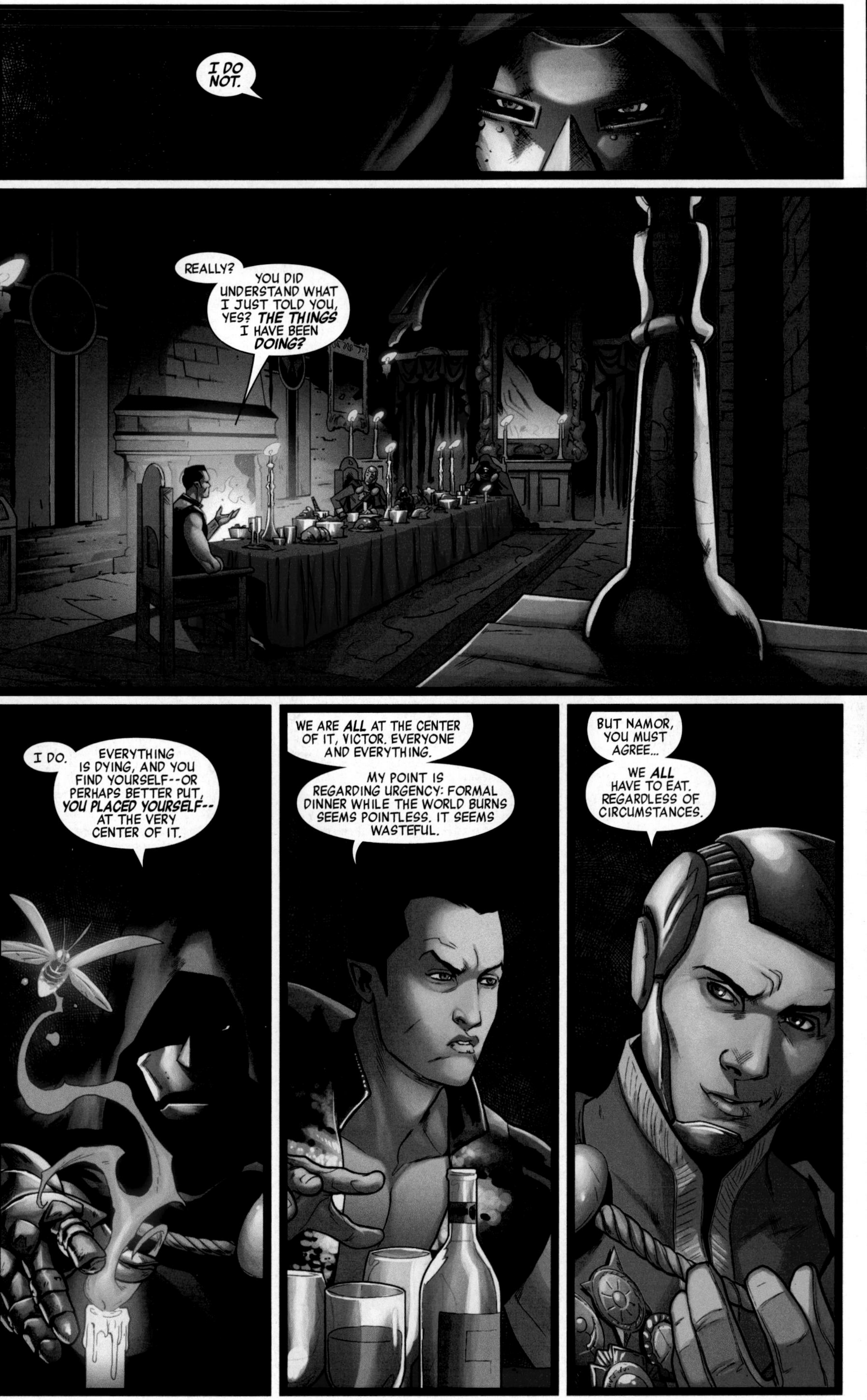
I DO NOT.
REALLY?
YOU DID UNDERSTAND WHAT I JUST TOLD YOU, YES? THE THINGS I HAVE BEEN DOING?
I DO.
EVERYTHING IS DYING, AND YOU FIND YOURSELF--OR PERHAPS BETTER PUT, YOU PLACED YOURSELF--AT THE VERY CENTER OF IT.
WE ARE ALL AT THE CENTER OF IT, VICTOR. EVERYONE AND EVERYTHING.
MY POINT IS REGARDING URGENCY: FORMAL DINNER WHILE THE WORLD BURNS SEEMS POINTLESS. IT SEEMS WASTEFUL.
BUT NAMOR, YOU MUST AGREE...
WE ALL HAVE TO EAT. REGARDLESS OF CIRCUMSTANCES.

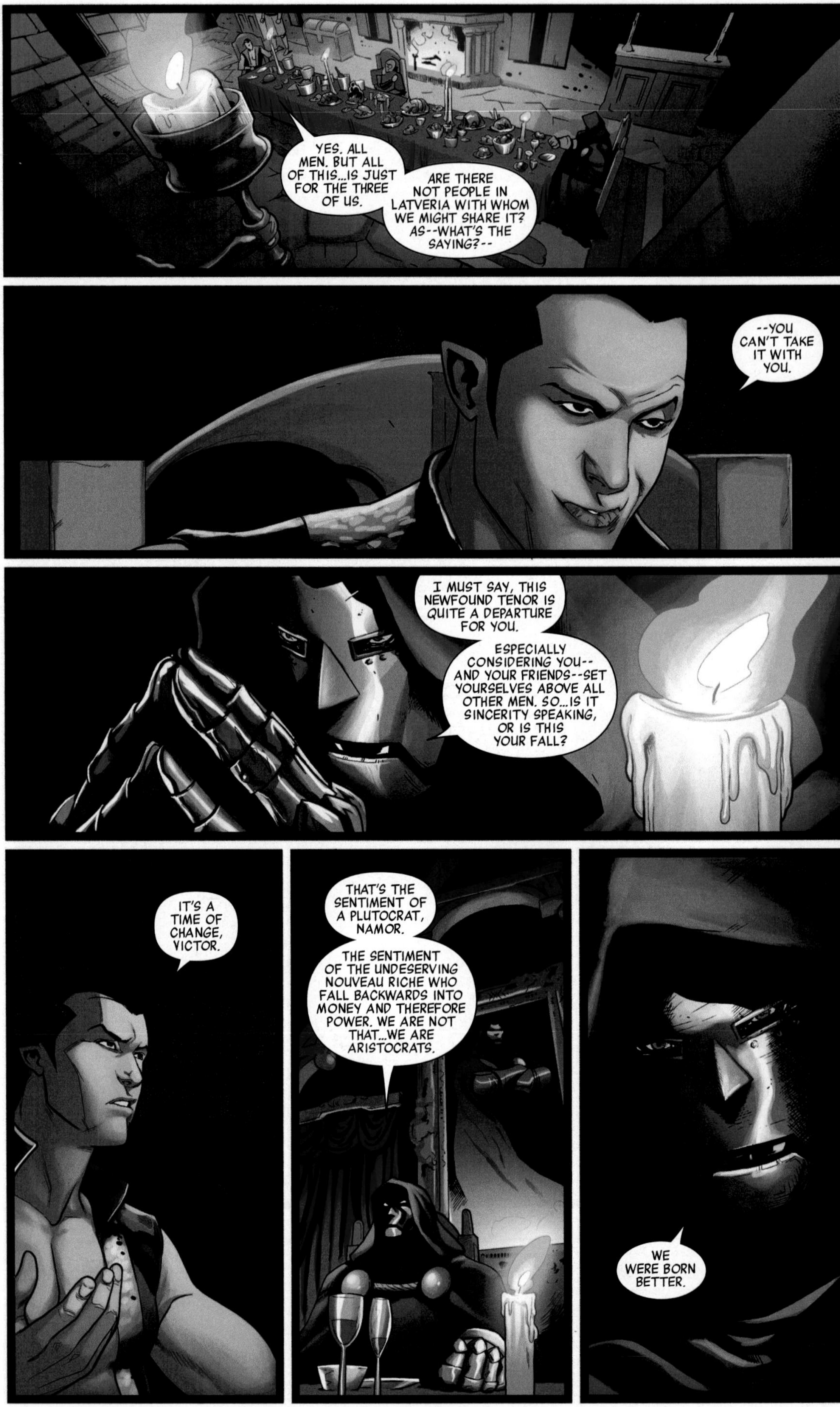
YES. ALL MEN. BUT ALL OF THIS...IS JUST FOR THE THREE OF US.
ARE THERE NOT PEOPLE IN LATVERIA WITH WHOM WE MIGHT SHARE IT? AS--WHAT'S THE SAYING?--
--YOU CAN'T TAKE IT WITH YOU.
I MUST SAY, THIS NEWFOUND TENOR IS QUITE A DEPARTURE FOR YOU.
ESPECIALLY CONSIDERING YOU--AND YOUR FRIENDS--SET YOURSELVES ABOVE ALL OTHER MEN. SO...IS IT SINCERITY SPEAKING, OR IS THIS YOUR FALL?
IT'S A TIME OF CHANGE, VICTOR.
THAT'S THE SENTIMENT OF A PLUTOCRAT, NAMOR.
THE SENTIMENT OF THE UNDESERVING NOUVEAU RICHE WHO FALL BACKWARDS INTO MONEY AND THEREFORE POWER. WE ARE NOT THAT...WE ARE ARISTOCRATS.
WE WERE BORN BETTER.

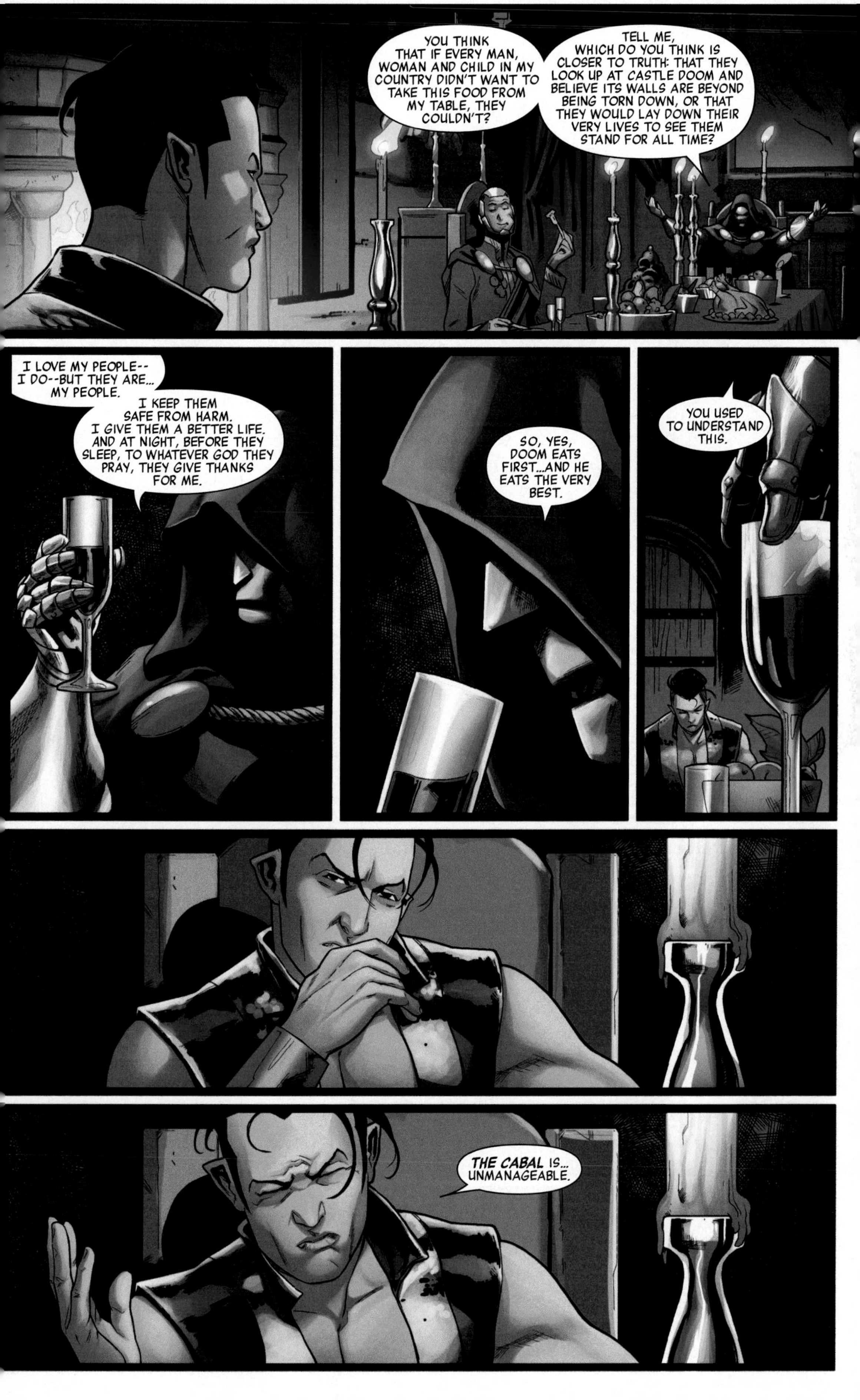
YOU THINK THAT IF EVERY MAN, WOMAN AND CHILD IN MY COUNTRY DIDN'T WANT TO TAKE THIS FOOD FROM MY TABLE, THEY COULDN'T?
TELL ME, WHICH DO YOU THINK IS CLOSER TO TRUTH: THAT THEY LOOK UP AT CASTLE DOOM AND BELIEVE ITS WALLS ARE BEYOND BEING TORN DOWN, OR THAT THEY WOULD LAY DOWN THEIR VERY LIVES TO SEE THEM STAND FOR ALL TIME?
I LOVE MY PEOPLE-- I DO--BUT THEY ARE... MY PEOPLE.
I KEEP THEM SAFE FROM HARM. I GIVE THEM A BETTER LIFE. AND AT NIGHT, BEFORE THEY SLEEP, TO WHATEVER GOD THEY PRAY, THEY GIVE THANKS FOR ME.
SO, YES, DOOM EATS FIRST...AND HE EATS THE VERY BEST.
YOU USED TO UNDERSTAND THIS.
THE CABAL IS... UNMANAGEABLE.

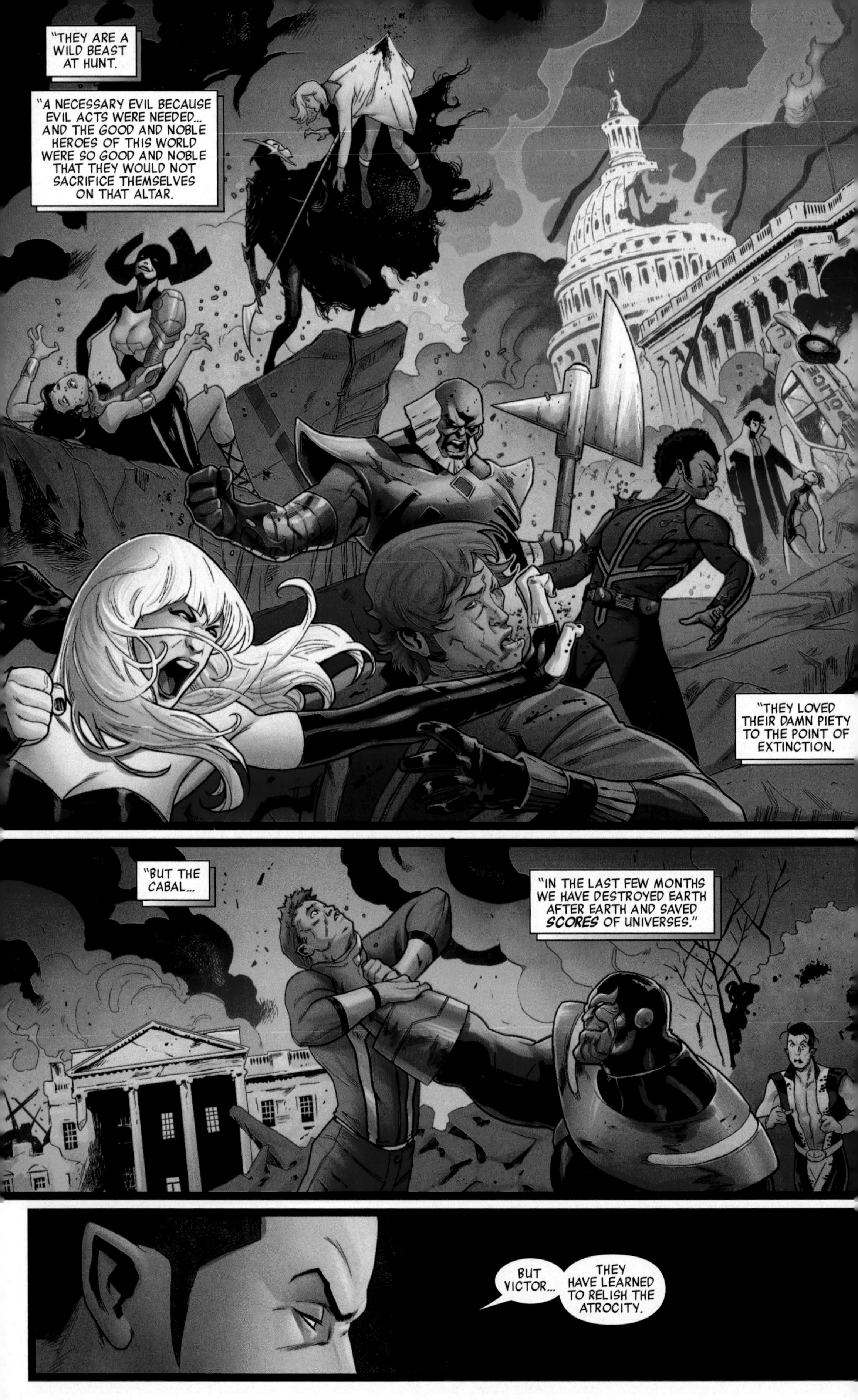
"THEY ARE A WILD BEAST AT HUNT.
"A NECESSARY EVIL BECAUSE EVIL ACTS WERE NEEDED... AND THE GOOD AND NOBLE HEROES OF THIS WORLD WERE SO GOOD AND NOBLE THAT THEY WOULD NOT SACRIFICE THEMSELVES ON THAT ALTAR.
POLICE
"THEY LOVED THEIR DAMN PIETY TO THE POINT OF EXTINCTION.
"BUT THE CABAL...
"IN THE LAST FEW MONTHS WE HAVE DESTROYED EARTH AFTER EARTH AND SAVED SCORES OF UNIVERSES."
BUT VICTOR...
THEY HAVE LEARNED TO RELISH THE ATROCITY.

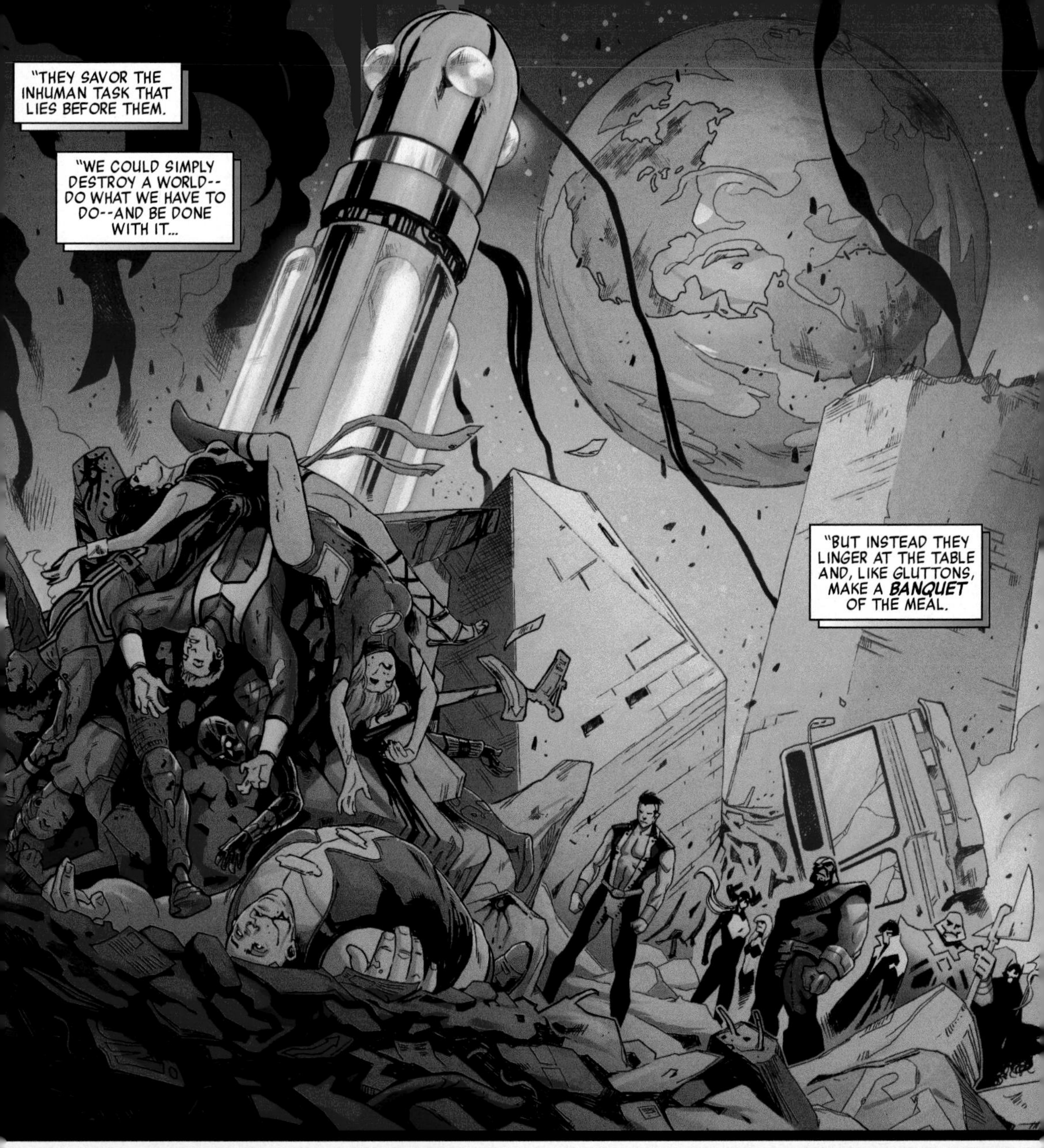
"THEY SAVOR THE INHUMAN TASK THAT LIES BEFORE THEM.
"WE COULD SIMPLY DESTROY A WORLD--DO WHAT WE HAVE TO DO--AND BE DONE WITH IT...
"BUT INSTEAD THEY LINGER AT THE TABLE AND, LIKE GLUTTONS, MAKE A BANQUET OF THE MEAL.

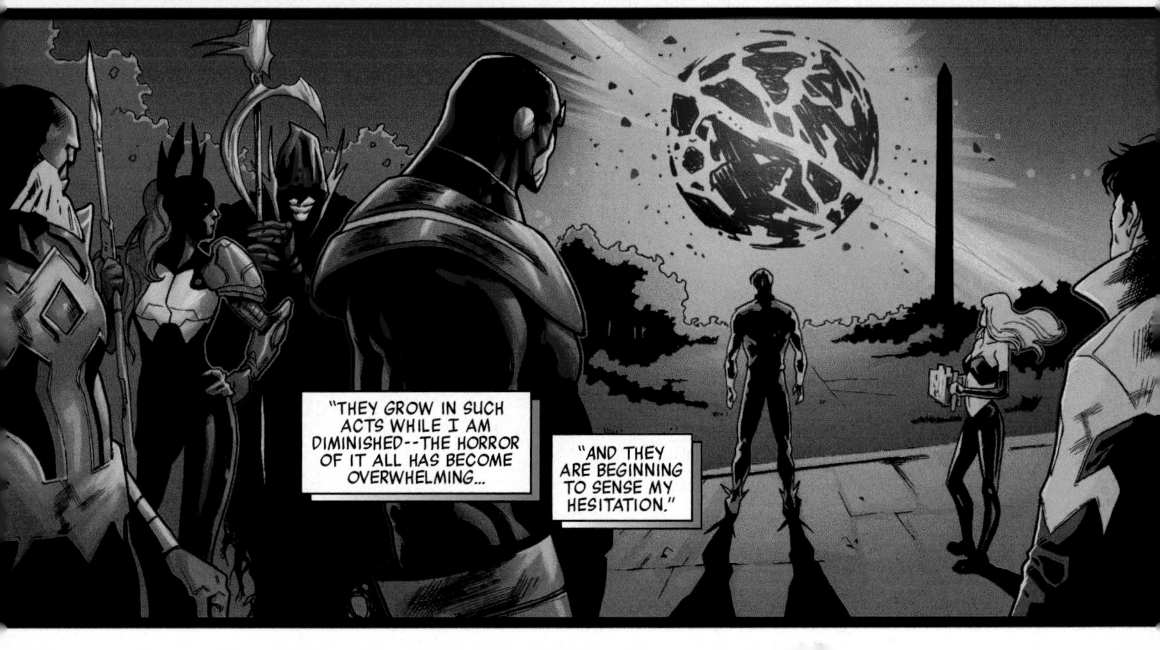
"THEY GROW IN SUCH ACTS WHILE I AM DIMINISHED--THE HORROR OF IT ALL HAS BECOME OVERWHELMING...
"AND THEY ARE BEGINNING TO SENSE MY HESITATION."

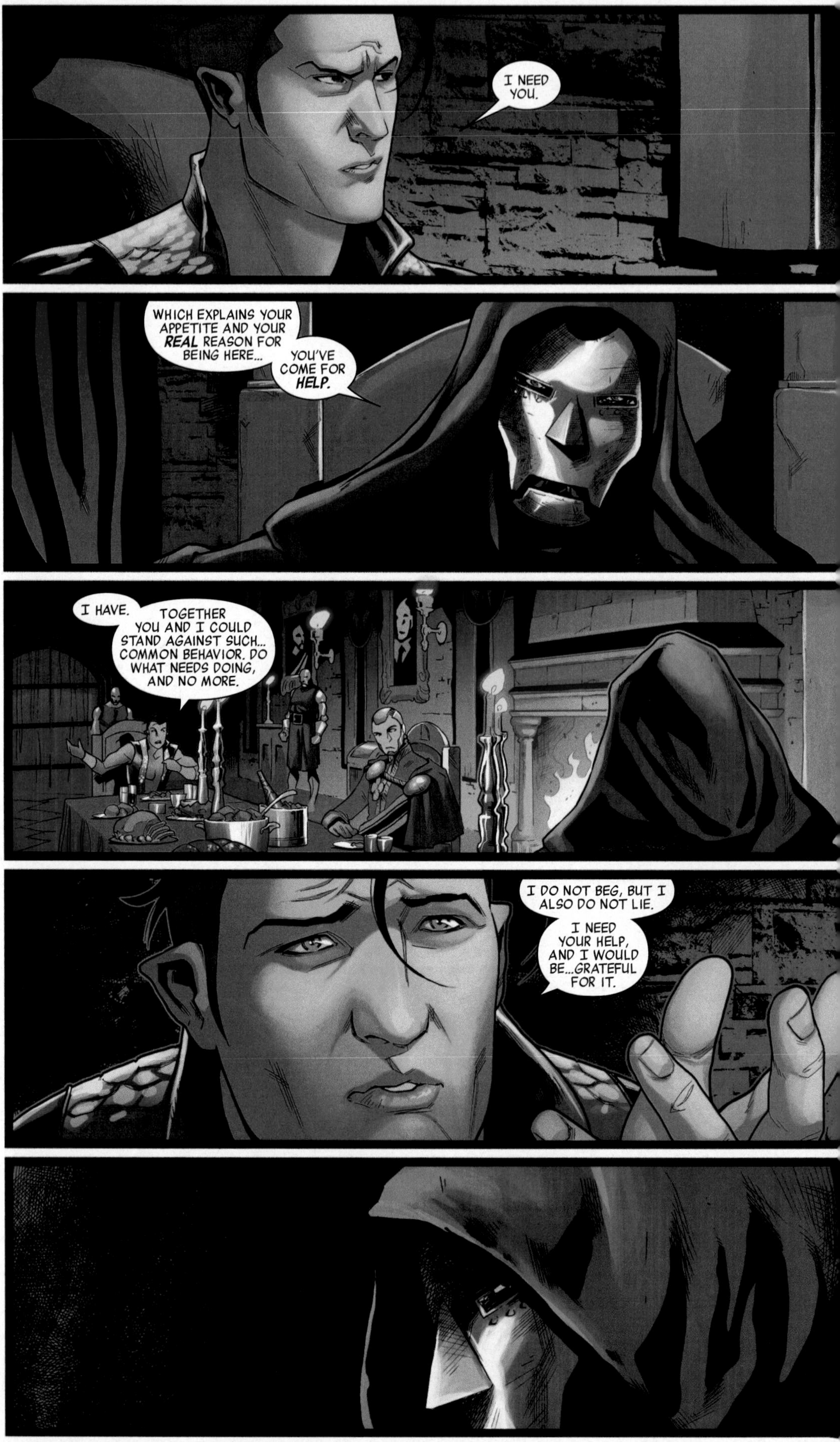
I NEED YOU.
WHICH EXPLAINS YOUR APPETITE AND YOUR REAL REASON FOR BEING HERE...
YOU'VE COME FOR HELP.
I HAVE.
TOGETHER YOU AND I COULD STAND AGAINST SUCH... COMMON BEHAVIOR. DO WHAT NEEDS DOING, AND NO MORE.
I DO NOT BEG, BUT I ALSO DO NOT LIE.
I NEED YOUR HELP, AND I WOULD BE...GRATEFUL FOR IT.

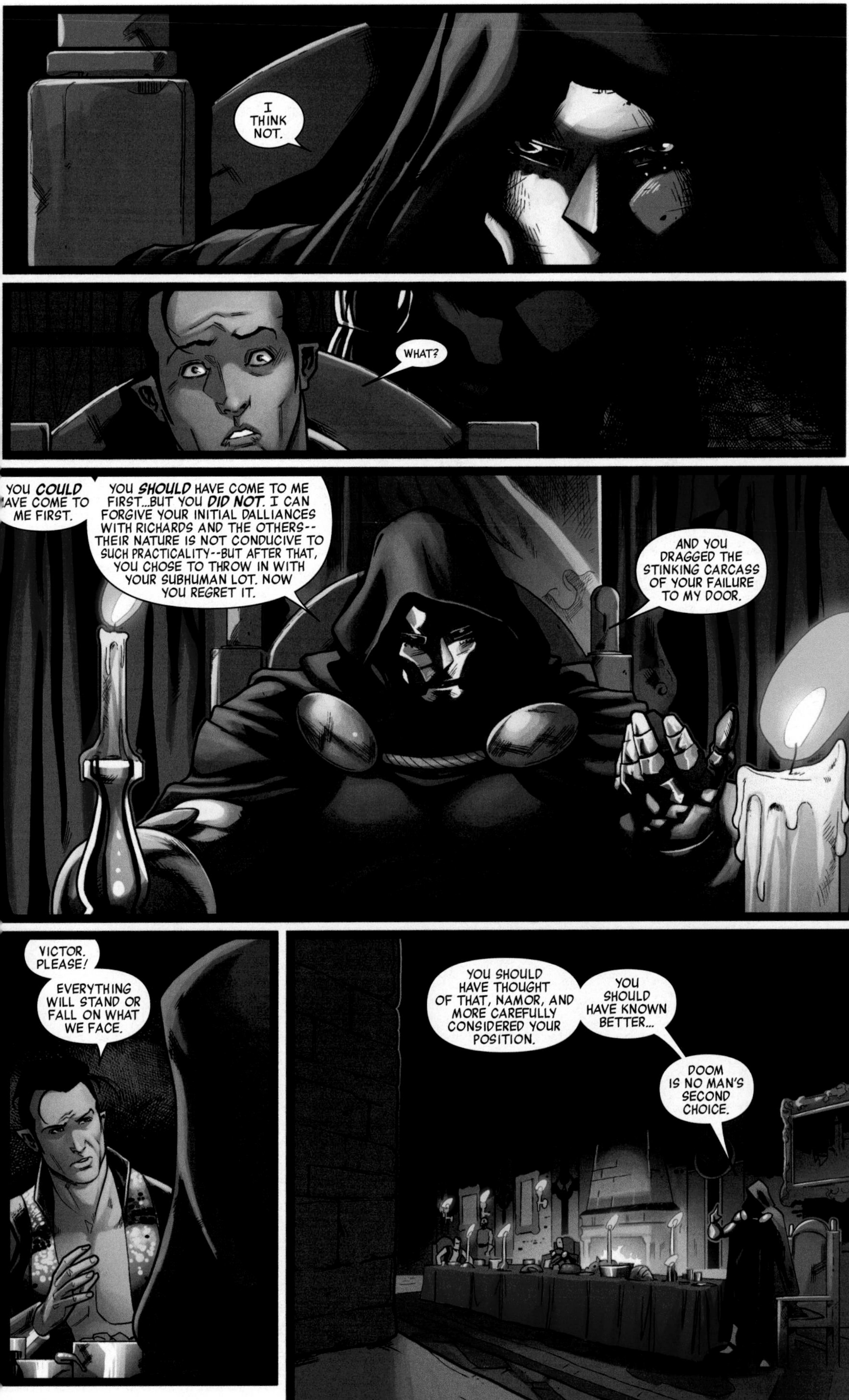
I THINK NOT.
WHAT?
YOU *COULD* HAVE COME TO ME FIRST.
YOU *SHOULD* HAVE COME TO ME FIRST...BUT YOU *DID NOT*. I CAN FORGIVE YOUR INITIAL DALLIANCES WITH RICHARDS AND THE OTHERS--THEIR NATURE IS NOT CONDUCIVE TO SUCH PRACTICALITY--BUT AFTER THAT, YOU CHOSE TO THROW IN WITH YOUR SUBHUMAN LOT. NOW YOU REGRET IT.
AND YOU DRAGGED THE STINKING CARCASS OF YOUR FAILURE TO MY DOOR.
VICTOR. PLEASE!
EVERYTHING WILL STAND OR FALL ON WHAT WE FACE.
YOU SHOULD HAVE THOUGHT OF THAT, NAMOR, AND MORE CAREFULLY CONSIDERED YOUR POSITION.
YOU SHOULD HAVE KNOWN BETTER...
DOOM IS NO MAN'S SECOND CHOICE.

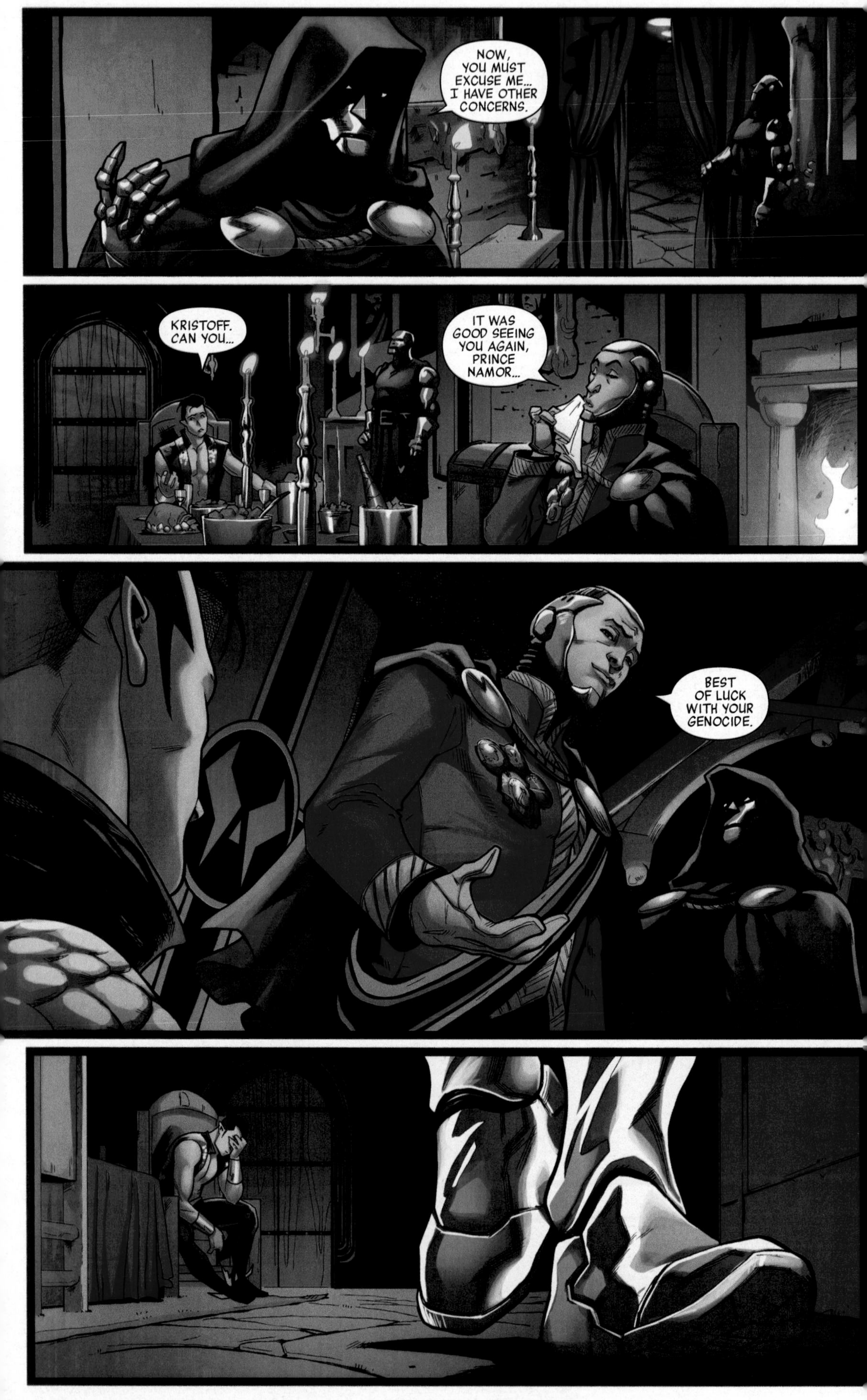
NOW, YOU MUST EXCUSE ME... I HAVE OTHER CONCERNS.
KRISTOFF. CAN YOU...
IT WAS GOOD SEEING YOU AGAIN, PRINCE NAMOR...
BEST OF LUCK WITH YOUR GENOCIDE.

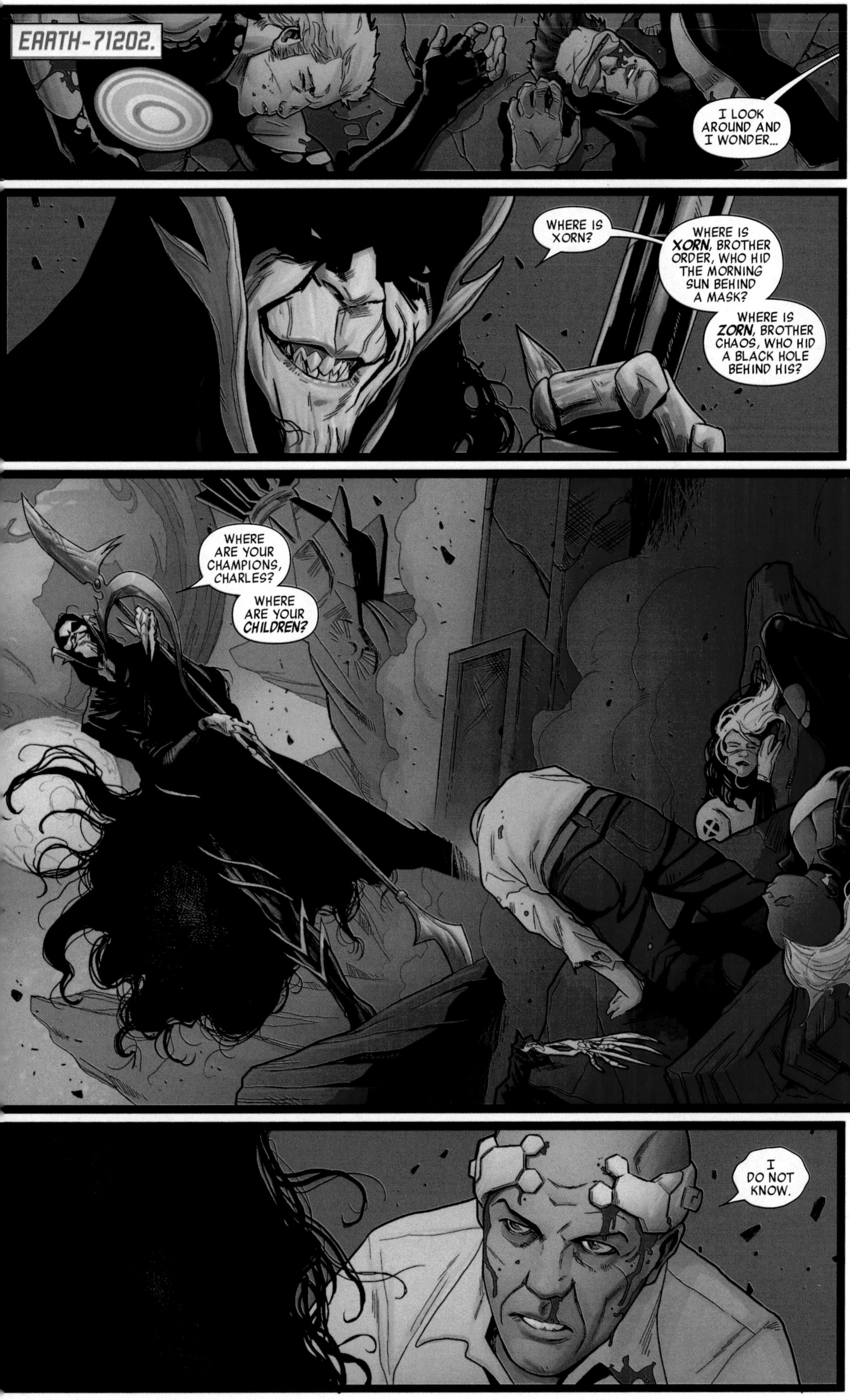
EARTH-71202.
I LOOK AROUND AND I WONDER...
WHERE IS XORN?
WHERE IS XORN, BROTHER ORDER, WHO HID THE MORNING SUN BEHIND A MASK?
WHERE IS ZORN, BROTHER CHAOS, WHO HID A BLACK HOLE BEHIND HIS?
WHERE ARE YOUR CHAMPIONS, CHARLES?
WHERE ARE YOUR CHILDREN?
I DO NOT KNOW.

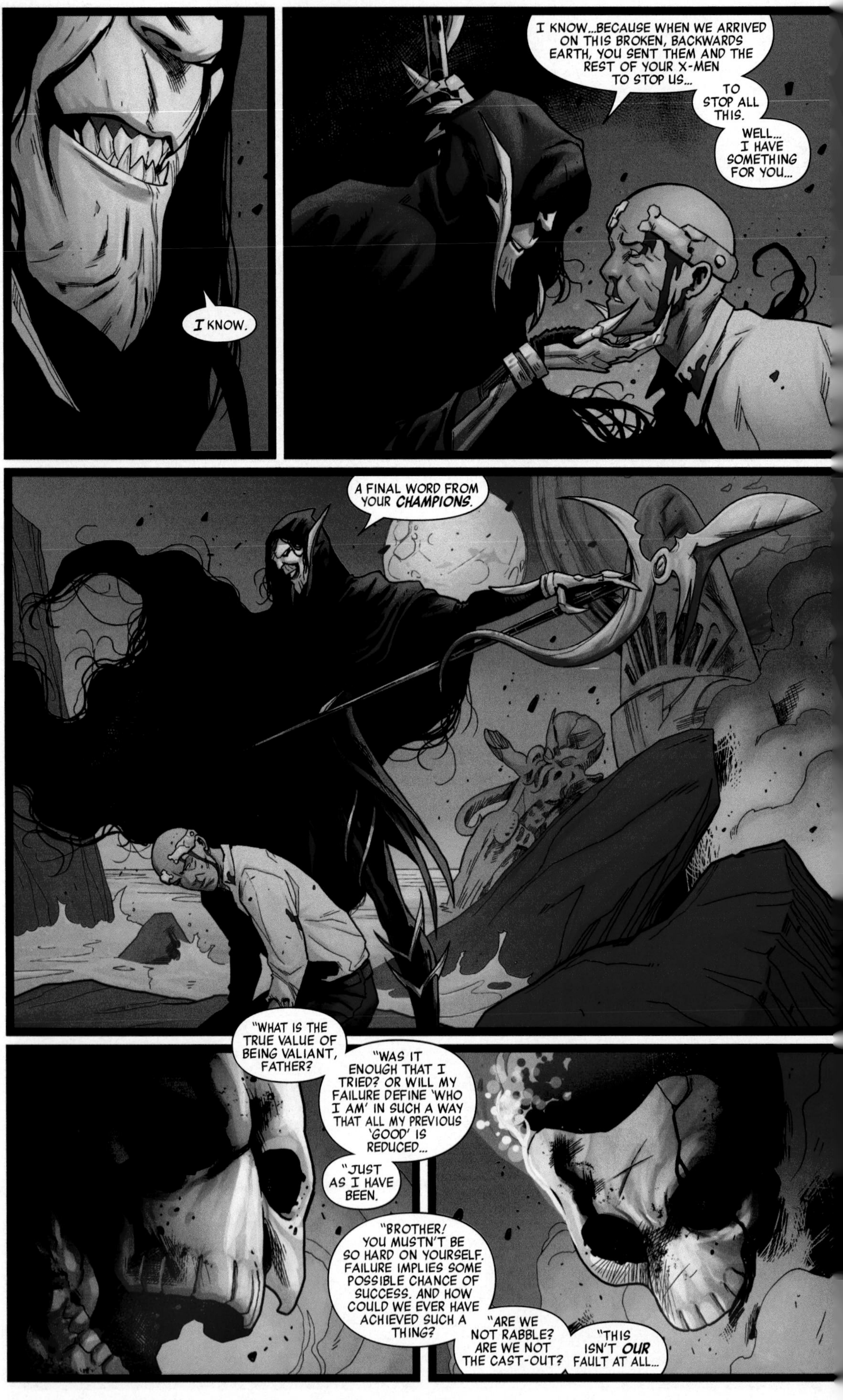
I KNOW.
I KNOW...BECAUSE WHEN WE ARRIVED ON THIS BROKEN, BACKWARDS EARTH, YOU SENT THEM AND THE REST OF YOUR X-MEN TO STOP US...
TO STOP ALL THIS.
WELL... I HAVE SOMETHING FOR YOU...
A FINAL WORD FROM YOUR CHAMPIONS.
"WHAT IS THE TRUE VALUE OF BEING VALIANT, FATHER?
"WAS IT ENOUGH THAT I TRIED? OR WILL MY FAILURE DEFINE 'WHO I AM' IN SUCH A WAY THAT ALL MY PREVIOUS 'GOOD' IS REDUCED...
"JUST AS I HAVE BEEN.
"BROTHER! YOU MUSTN'T BE SO HARD ON YOURSELF. FAILURE IMPLIES SOME POSSIBLE CHANCE OF SUCCESS. AND HOW COULD WE EVER HAVE ACHIEVED SUCH A THING?
"ARE WE NOT RABBLE? ARE WE NOT THE CAST-OUT?
"THIS ISN'T OUR FAULT AT ALL...

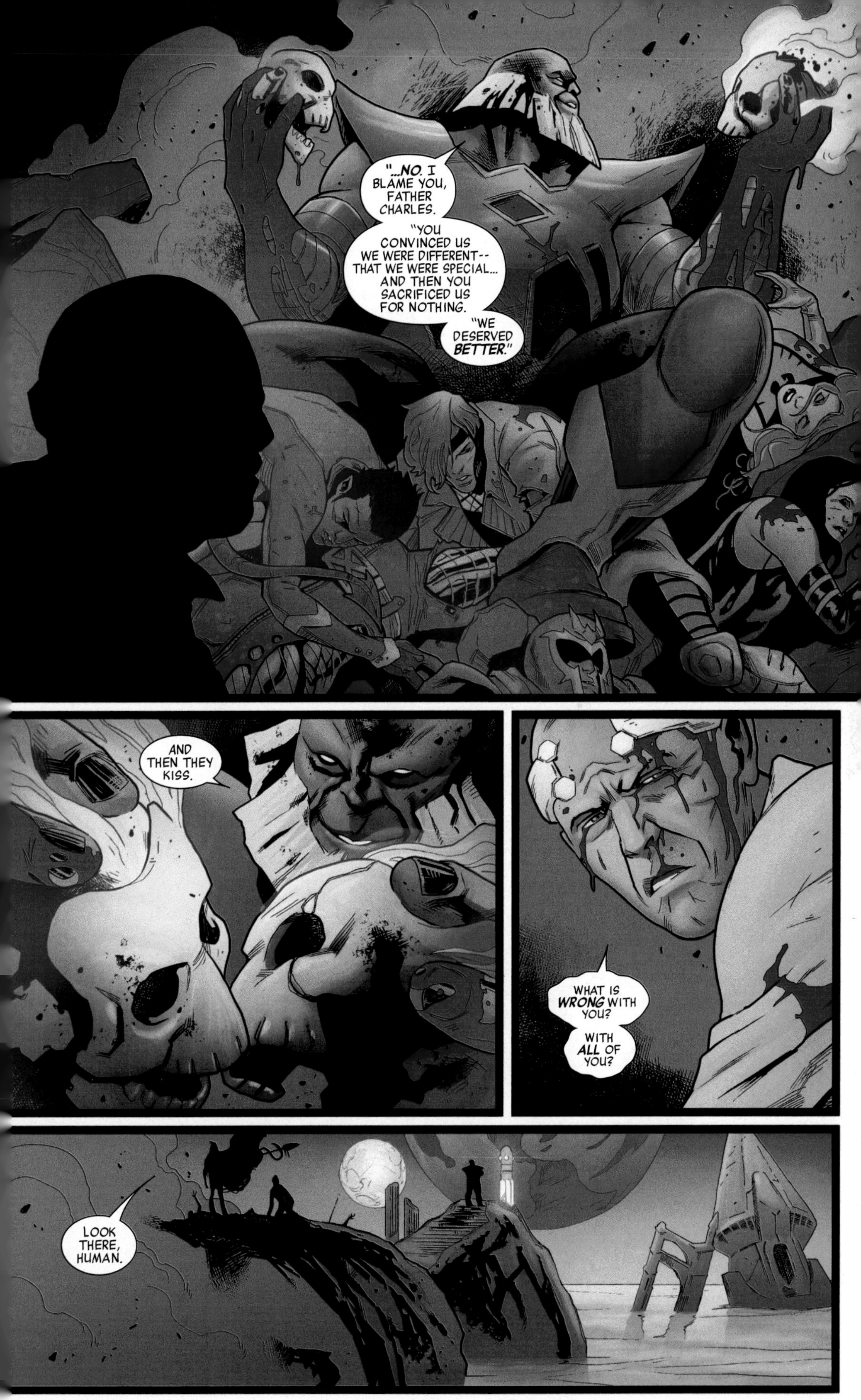
"...NO. I BLAME YOU, FATHER CHARLES.
"YOU CONVINCED US WE WERE DIFFERENT-- THAT WE WERE SPECIAL... AND THEN YOU SACRIFICED US FOR NOTHING.
"WE DESERVED BETTER."
AND THEN THEY KISS.
WHAT IS WRONG WITH YOU?
WITH ALL OF YOU?
LOOK THERE, HUMAN.

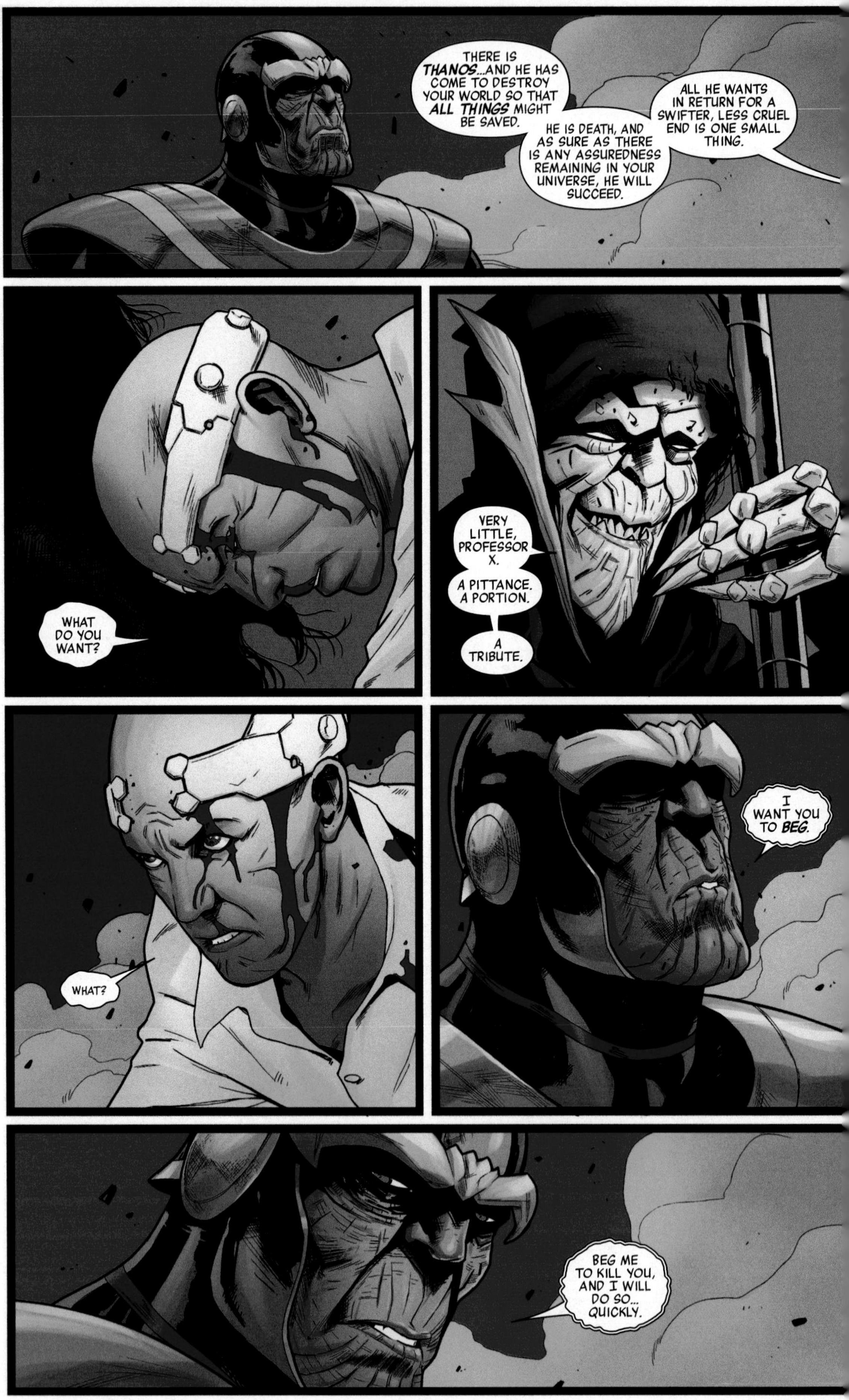
THERE IS THANOS...AND HE HAS COME TO DESTROY YOUR WORLD SO THAT ALL THINGS MIGHT BE SAVED.
HE IS DEATH, AND AS SURE AS THERE IS ANY ASSUREDNESS REMAINING IN YOUR UNIVERSE, HE WILL SUCCEED.
ALL HE WANTS IN RETURN FOR A SWIFTER, LESS CRUEL END IS ONE SMALL THING.
WHAT DO YOU WANT?
VERY LITTLE, PROFESSOR X.
A PITTANCE. A PORTION.
A TRIBUTE.
WHAT?
I WANT YOU TO BEG.
BEG ME TO KILL YOU, AND I WILL DO SO... QUICKLY.

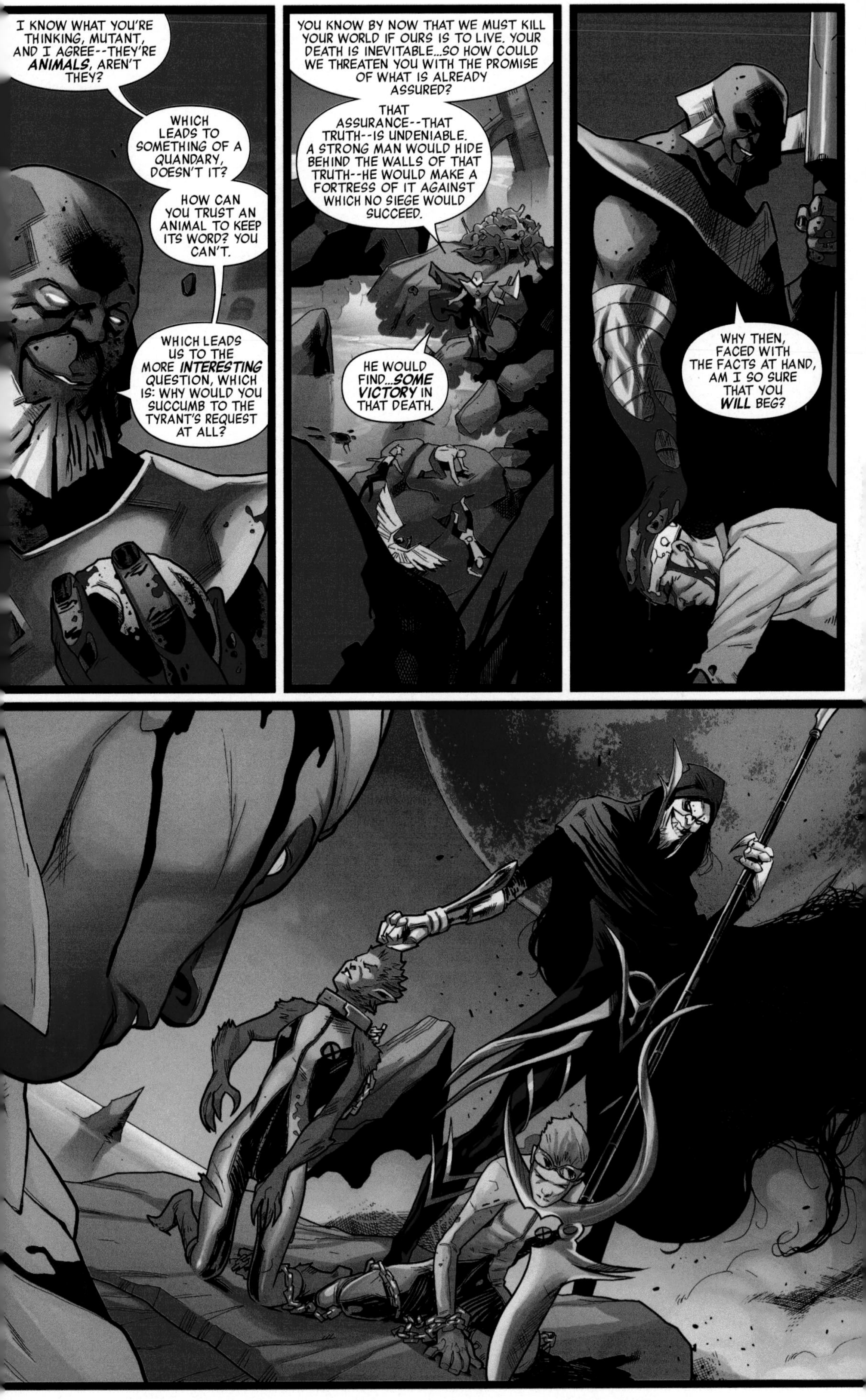
I KNOW WHAT YOU'RE THINKING, MUTANT, AND I AGREE--THEY'RE ANIMALS, AREN'T THEY?
WHICH LEADS TO SOMETHING OF A QUANDARY, DOESN'T IT?
HOW CAN YOU TRUST AN ANIMAL TO KEEP ITS WORD? YOU CAN'T.
WHICH LEADS US TO THE MORE INTERESTING QUESTION, WHICH IS: WHY WOULD YOU SUCCUMB TO THE TYRANT'S REQUEST AT ALL?
YOU KNOW BY NOW THAT WE MUST KILL YOUR WORLD IF OURS IS TO LIVE. YOUR DEATH IS INEVITABLE...SO HOW COULD WE THREATEN YOU WITH THE PROMISE OF WHAT IS ALREADY ASSURED?
THAT ASSURANCE--THAT TRUTH--IS UNDENIABLE. A STRONG MAN WOULD HIDE BEHIND THE WALLS OF THAT TRUTH--HE WOULD MAKE A FORTRESS OF IT AGAINST WHICH NO SIEGE WOULD SUCCEED.
HE WOULD FIND...SOME VICTORY IN THAT DEATH.
WHY THEN, FACED WITH THE FACTS AT HAND, AM I SO SURE THAT YOU WILL BEG?

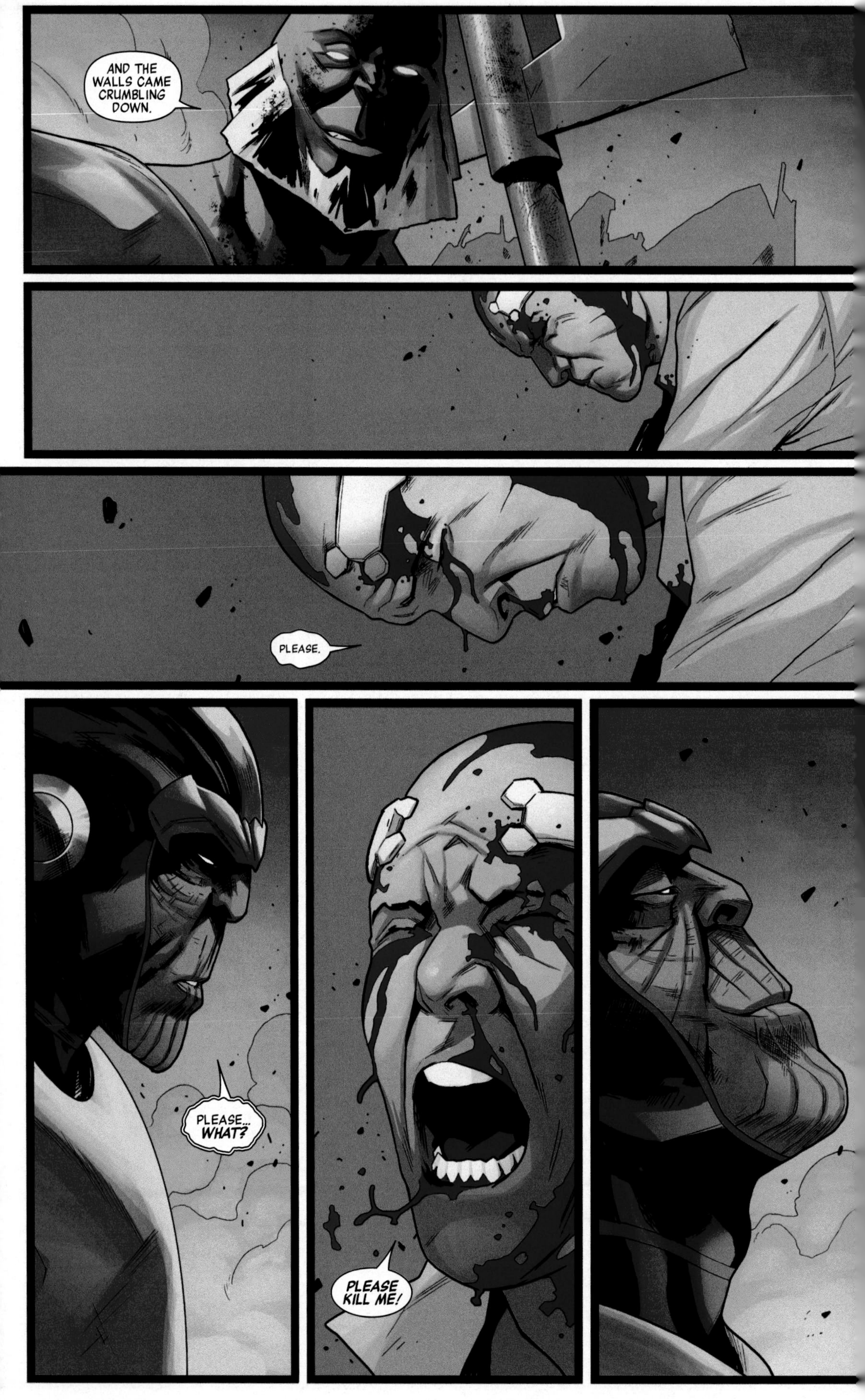
AND THE WALLS CAME CRUMBLING DOWN.
PLEASE.
PLEASE... WHAT?
PLEASE KILL ME!

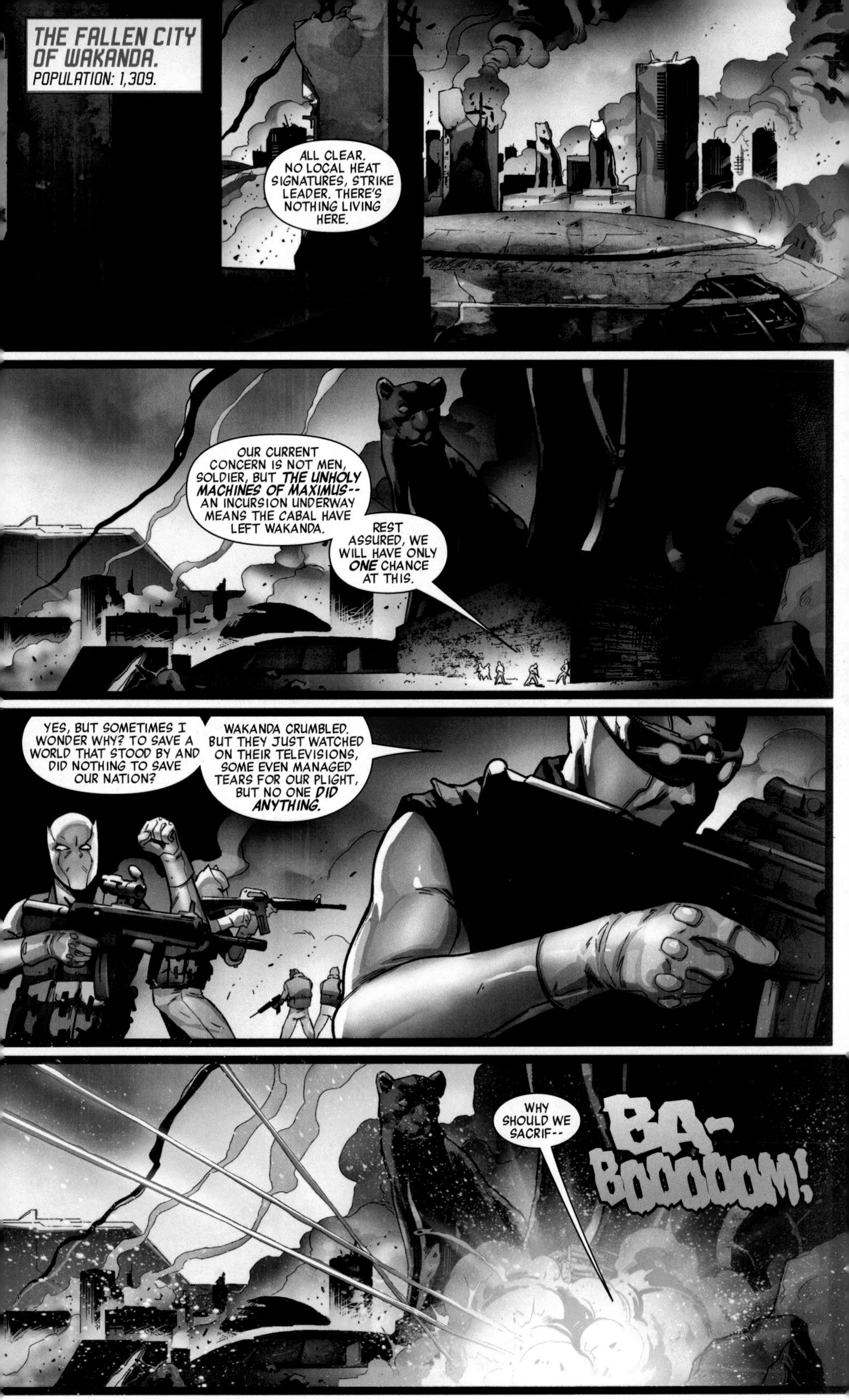
THE FALLEN CITY OF WAKANDA.
POPULATION: 1,309.
ALL CLEAR. NO LOCAL HEAT SIGNATURES, STRIKE LEADER. THERE'S NOTHING LIVING HERE.
OUR CURRENT CONCERN IS NOT MEN, SOLDIER, BUT *THE UNHOLY MACHINES OF MAXIMUS*-- AN INCURSION UNDERWAY MEANS THE CABAL HAVE LEFT WAKANDA.
REST ASSURED, WE WILL HAVE ONLY *ONE* CHANCE AT THIS.
YES, BUT SOMETIMES I WONDER WHY? TO SAVE A WORLD THAT STOOD BY AND DID NOTHING TO SAVE OUR NATION?
WAKANDA CRUMBLED. BUT THEY JUST WATCHED ON THEIR TELEVISIONS, SOME EVEN MANAGED TEARS FOR OUR PLIGHT, BUT NO ONE *DID ANYTHING.*
WHY SHOULD WE SACRIF--
BA-BOOOOOM!

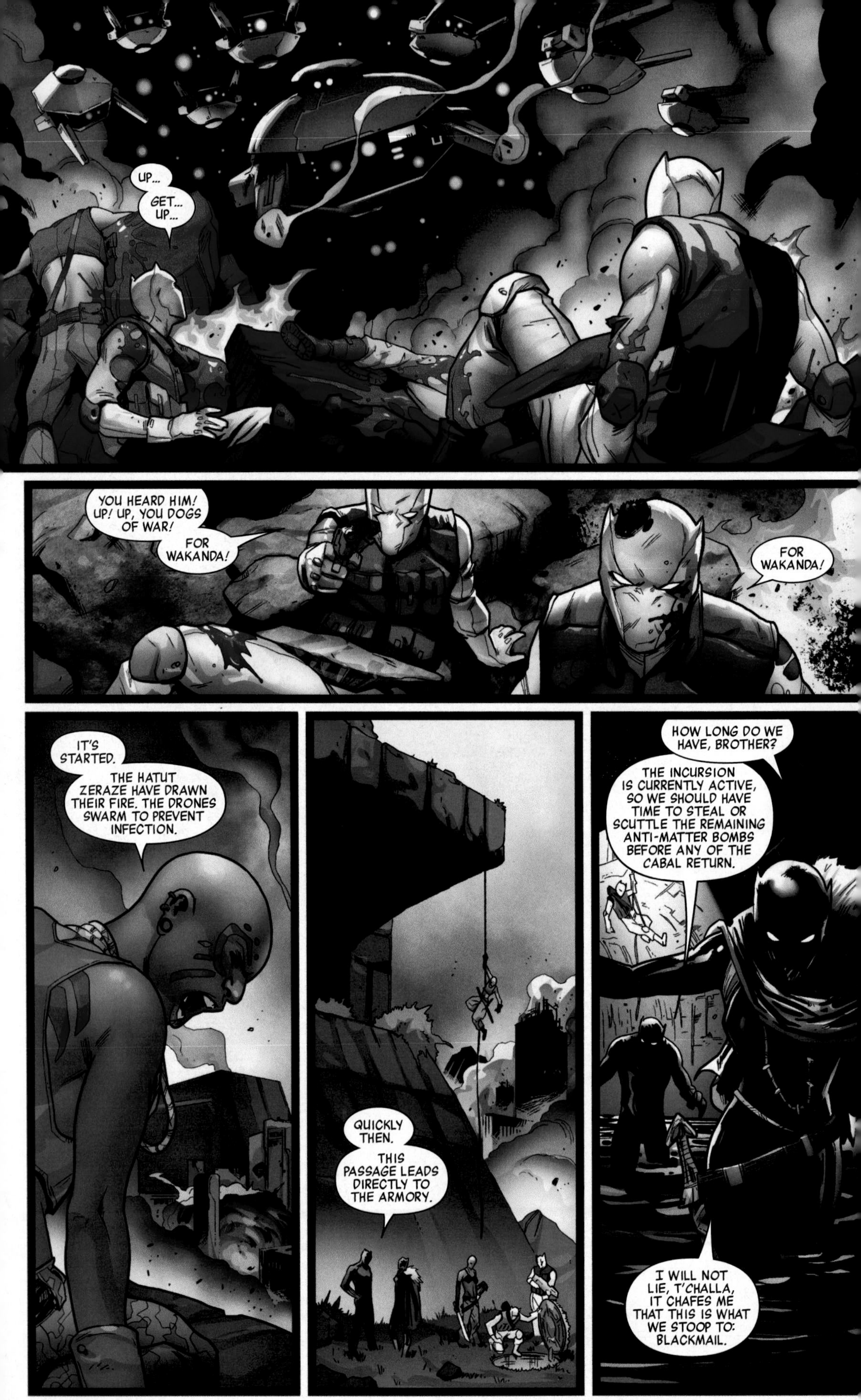
UP...
GET... UP...
YOU HEARD HIM! UP! UP, YOU DOGS OF WAR!
FOR WAKANDA!
FOR WAKANDA!
IT'S STARTED.
THE HATUT ZERAZE HAVE DRAWN THEIR FIRE. THE DRONES SWARM TO PREVENT INFECTION.
QUICKLY THEN.
THIS PASSAGE LEADS DIRECTLY TO THE ARMORY.
HOW LONG DO WE HAVE, BROTHER?
THE INCURSION IS CURRENTLY ACTIVE, SO WE SHOULD HAVE TIME TO STEAL OR SCUTTLE THE REMAINING ANTI-MATTER BOMBS BEFORE ANY OF THE CABAL RETURN.
I WILL NOT LIE, T'CHALLA, IT CHAFES ME THAT THIS IS WHAT WE STOOP TO: BLACKMAIL.

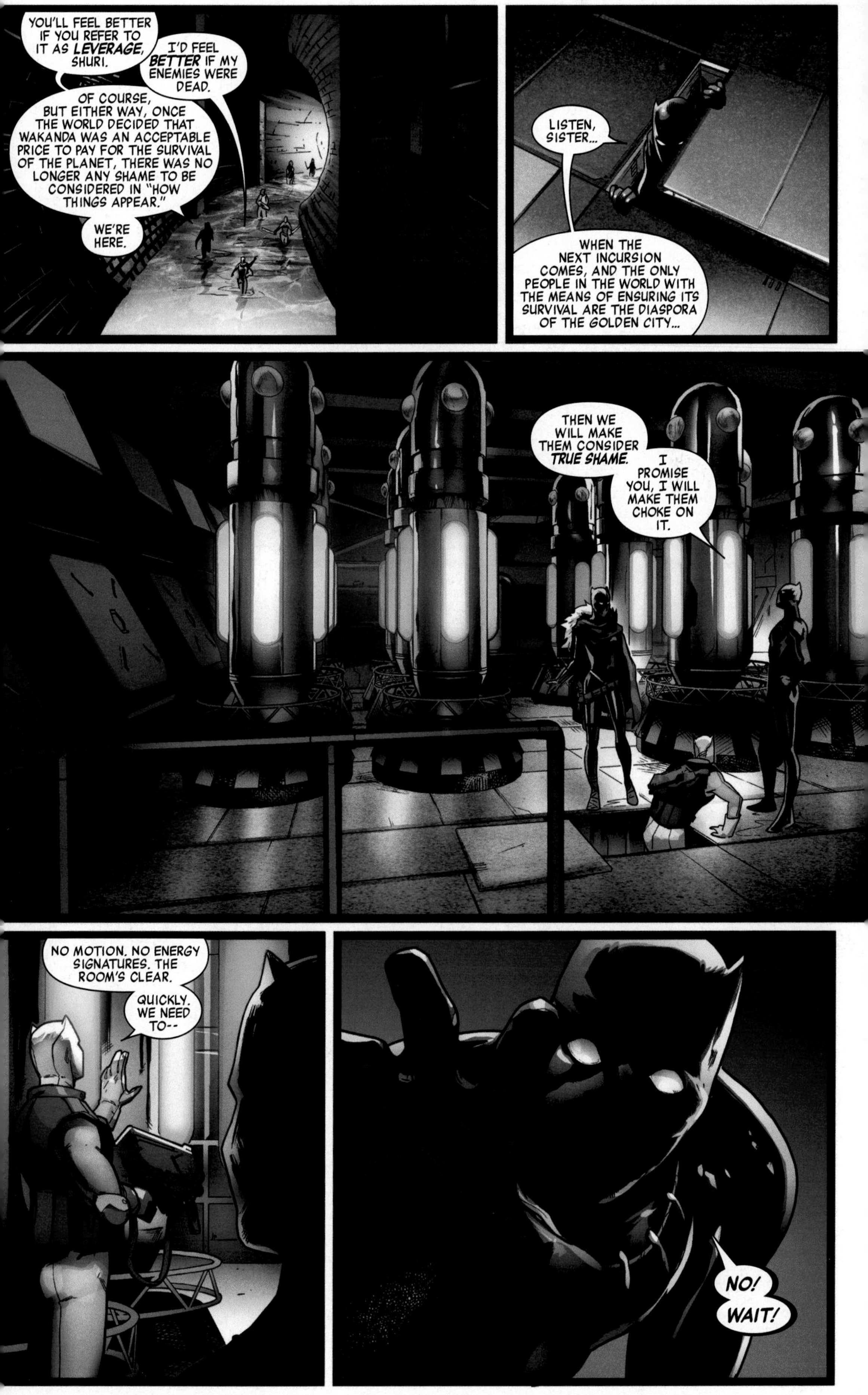
YOU'LL FEEL BETTER IF YOU REFER TO IT AS LEVERAGE, SHURI.
I'D FEEL BETTER IF MY ENEMIES WERE DEAD.
OF COURSE, BUT EITHER WAY, ONCE THE WORLD DECIDED THAT WAKANDA WAS AN ACCEPTABLE PRICE TO PAY FOR THE SURVIVAL OF THE PLANET, THERE WAS NO LONGER ANY SHAME TO BE CONSIDERED IN "HOW THINGS APPEAR."
WE'RE HERE.
LISTEN, SISTER...
WHEN THE NEXT INCURSION COMES, AND THE ONLY PEOPLE IN THE WORLD WITH THE MEANS OF ENSURING ITS SURVIVAL ARE THE DIASPORA OF THE GOLDEN CITY...
THEN WE WILL MAKE THEM CONSIDER TRUE SHAME.
I PROMISE YOU, I WILL MAKE THEM CHOKE ON IT.
NO MOTION. NO ENERGY SIGNATURES. THE ROOM'S CLEAR.
QUICKLY. WE NEED TO--
NO!
WAIT!

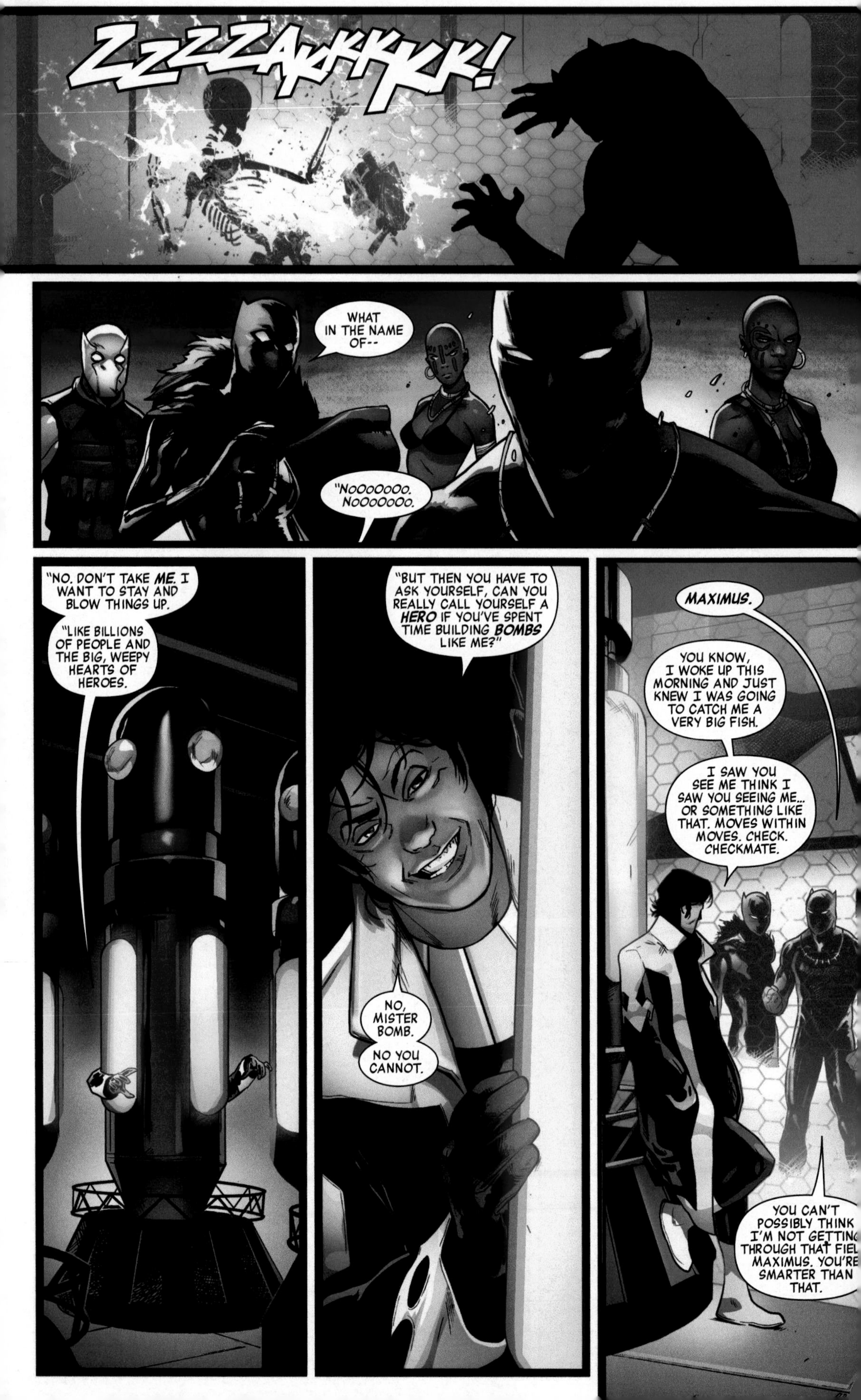
ZZZZAKKKKK!
WHAT IN THE NAME OF--
"NOOOOOOO. NOOOOOOO.
"NO. DON'T TAKE *ME*. I WANT TO STAY AND BLOW THINGS UP.
"LIKE BILLIONS OF PEOPLE AND THE BIG, WEEPY HEARTS OF HEROES.
"BUT THEN YOU HAVE TO ASK YOURSELF, CAN YOU REALLY CALL YOURSELF A *HERO* IF YOU'VE SPENT TIME BUILDING *BOMBS* LIKE ME?"
NO, MISTER BOMB.
NO YOU CANNOT.
MAXIMUS.
YOU KNOW, I WOKE UP THIS MORNING AND JUST KNEW I WAS GOING TO CATCH ME A VERY BIG FISH.
I SAW YOU SEE ME THINK I SAW YOU SEEING ME... OR SOMETHING LIKE THAT. MOVES WITHIN MOVES. CHECK. CHECKMATE.
YOU CAN'T POSSIBLY THINK I'M NOT GETTING THROUGH THAT FIEL MAXIMUS. YOU'RE SMARTER THAN THAT.

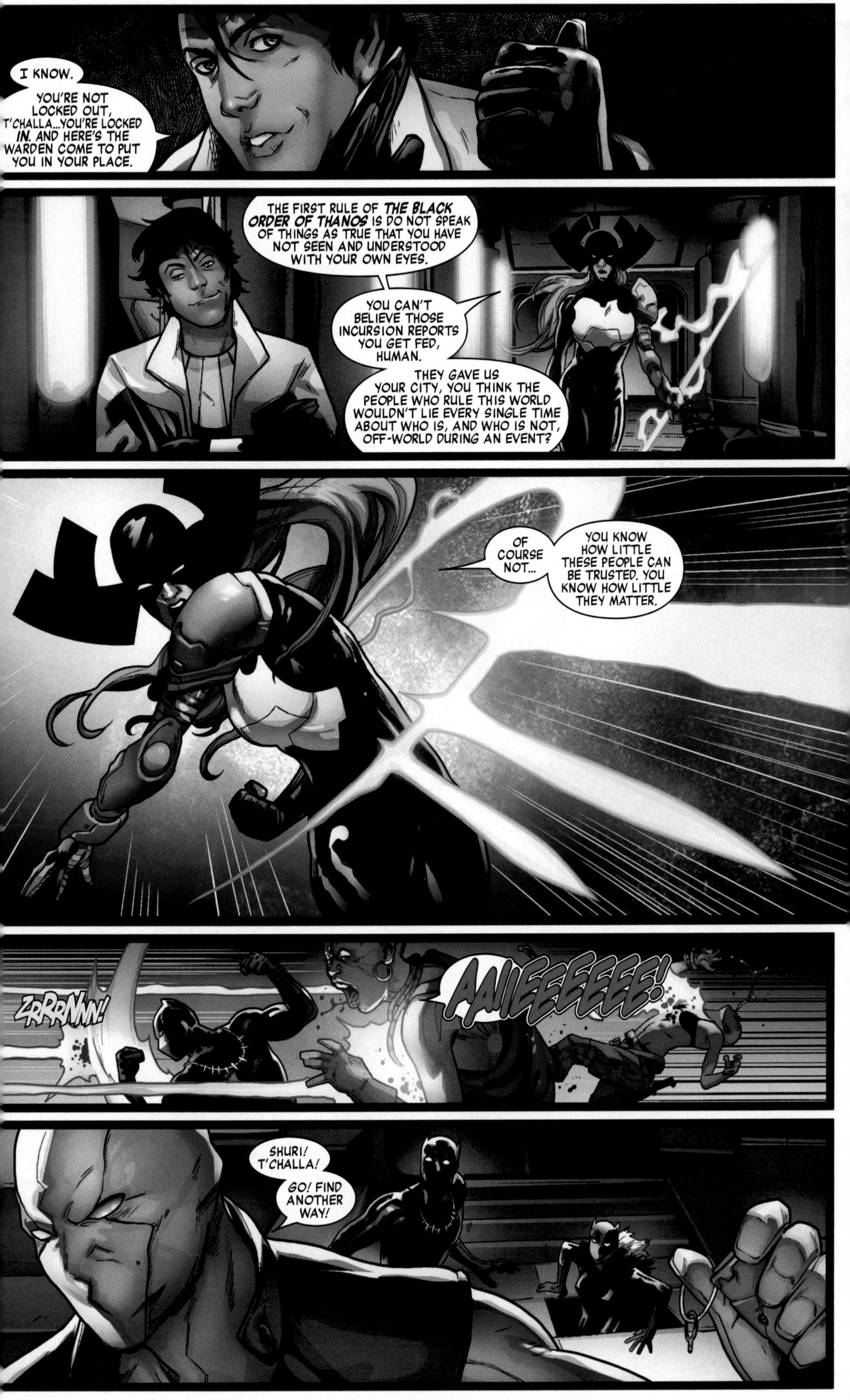

I KNOW.
YOU'RE NOT LOCKED OUT, T'CHALLA...YOU'RE LOCKED *IN.* AND HERE'S THE WARDEN COME TO PUT YOU IN YOUR PLACE.
THE FIRST RULE OF ***THE BLACK ORDER OF THANOS*** IS DO NOT SPEAK OF THINGS AS TRUE THAT YOU HAVE NOT SEEN AND UNDERSTOOD WITH YOUR OWN EYES.
YOU CAN'T BELIEVE THOSE INCURSION REPORTS YOU GET FED, HUMAN.
THEY GAVE US YOUR CITY, YOU THINK THE PEOPLE WHO RULE THIS WORLD WOULDN'T LIE EVERY SINGLE TIME ABOUT WHO IS, AND WHO IS NOT, OFF-WORLD DURING AN EVENT?
OF COURSE NOT...
YOU KNOW HOW LITTLE THESE PEOPLE CAN BE TRUSTED. YOU KNOW HOW LITTLE THEY MATTER.
ZRRRNNN!
AAIIEEEEEEE!
SHURI! T'CHALLA!
GO! FIND ANOTHER WAY!

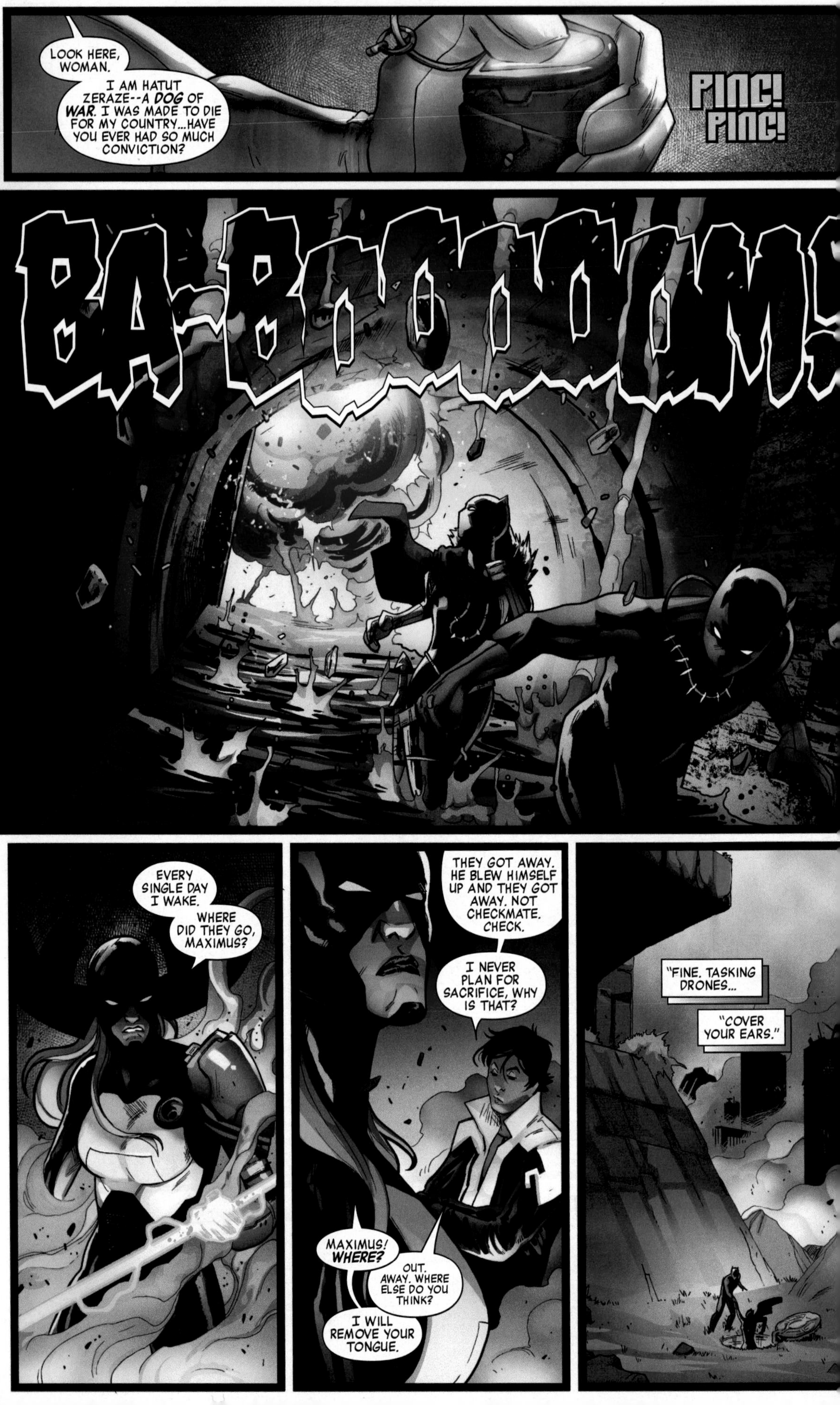
LOOK HERE, WOMAN.
I AM HATUT ZERAZE--A DOG OF WAR. I WAS MADE TO DIE FOR MY COUNTRY...HAVE YOU EVER HAD SO MUCH CONVICTION?
PING! PING!
BA-BOOOOM!
EVERY SINGLE DAY I WAKE.
WHERE DID THEY GO, MAXIMUS?
THEY GOT AWAY. HE BLEW HIMSELF UP AND THEY GOT AWAY. NOT CHECKMATE. CHECK.
I NEVER PLAN FOR SACRIFICE, WHY IS THAT?
MAXIMUS! WHERE?
OUT. AWAY. WHERE ELSE DO YOU THINK?
I WILL REMOVE YOUR TONGUE.
"FINE. TASKING DRONES...
"COVER YOUR EARS."

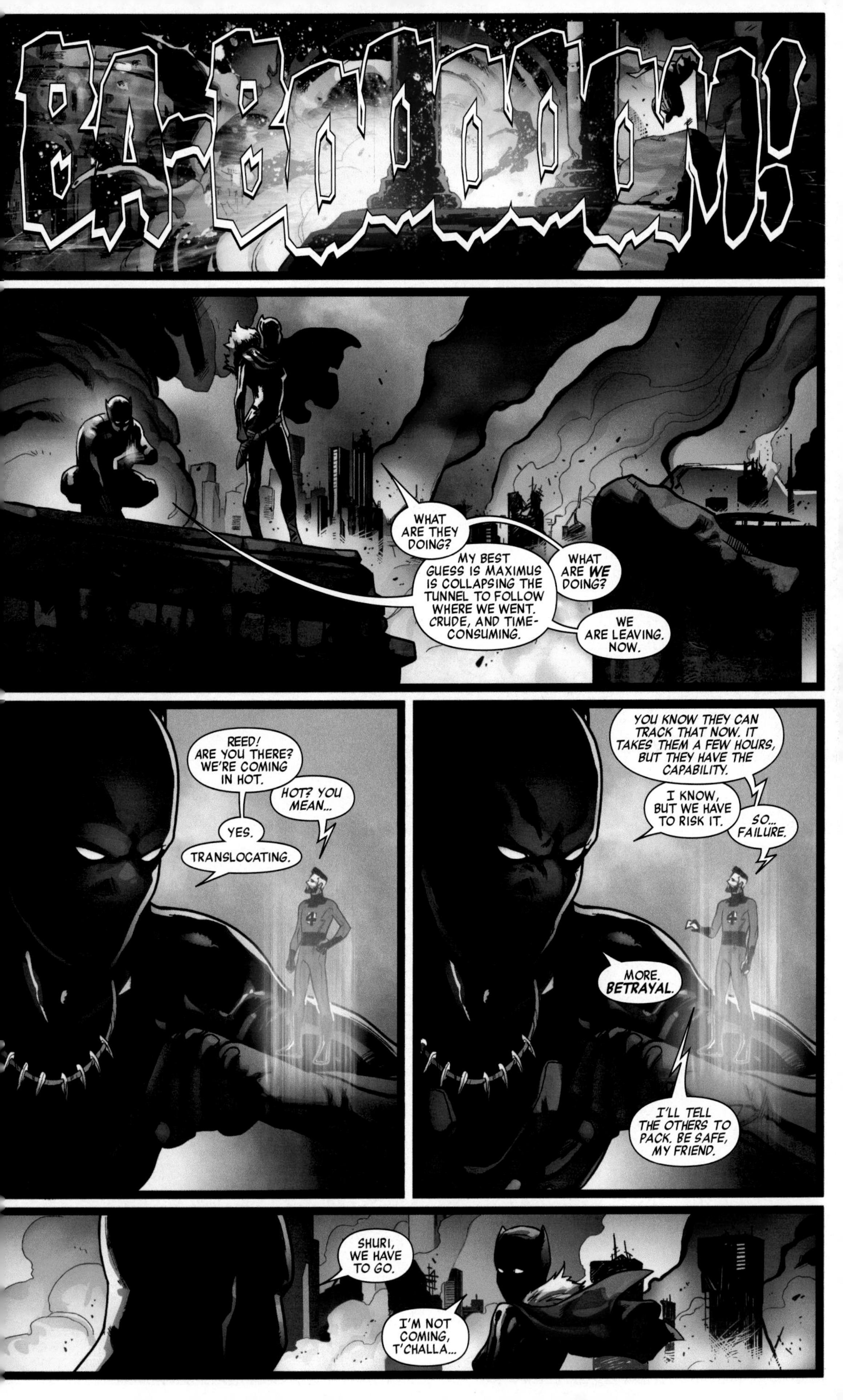
BA-BOOOOOOM!
WHAT ARE THEY DOING?
MY BEST GUESS IS MAXIMUS IS COLLAPSING THE TUNNEL TO FOLLOW WHERE WE WENT. CRUDE, AND TIME-CONSUMING.
WHAT ARE WE DOING?
WE ARE LEAVING. NOW.
REED! ARE YOU THERE? WE'RE COMING IN HOT.
HOT? YOU MEAN...
YES.
TRANSLOCATING.
YOU KNOW THEY CAN TRACK THAT NOW. IT TAKES THEM A FEW HOURS, BUT THEY HAVE THE CAPABILITY.
I KNOW, BUT WE HAVE TO RISK IT.
SO... FAILURE.
MORE. BETRAYAL.
I'LL TELL THE OTHERS TO PACK. BE SAFE, MY FRIEND.
SHURI, WE HAVE TO GO.
I'M NOT COMING, T'CHALLA...

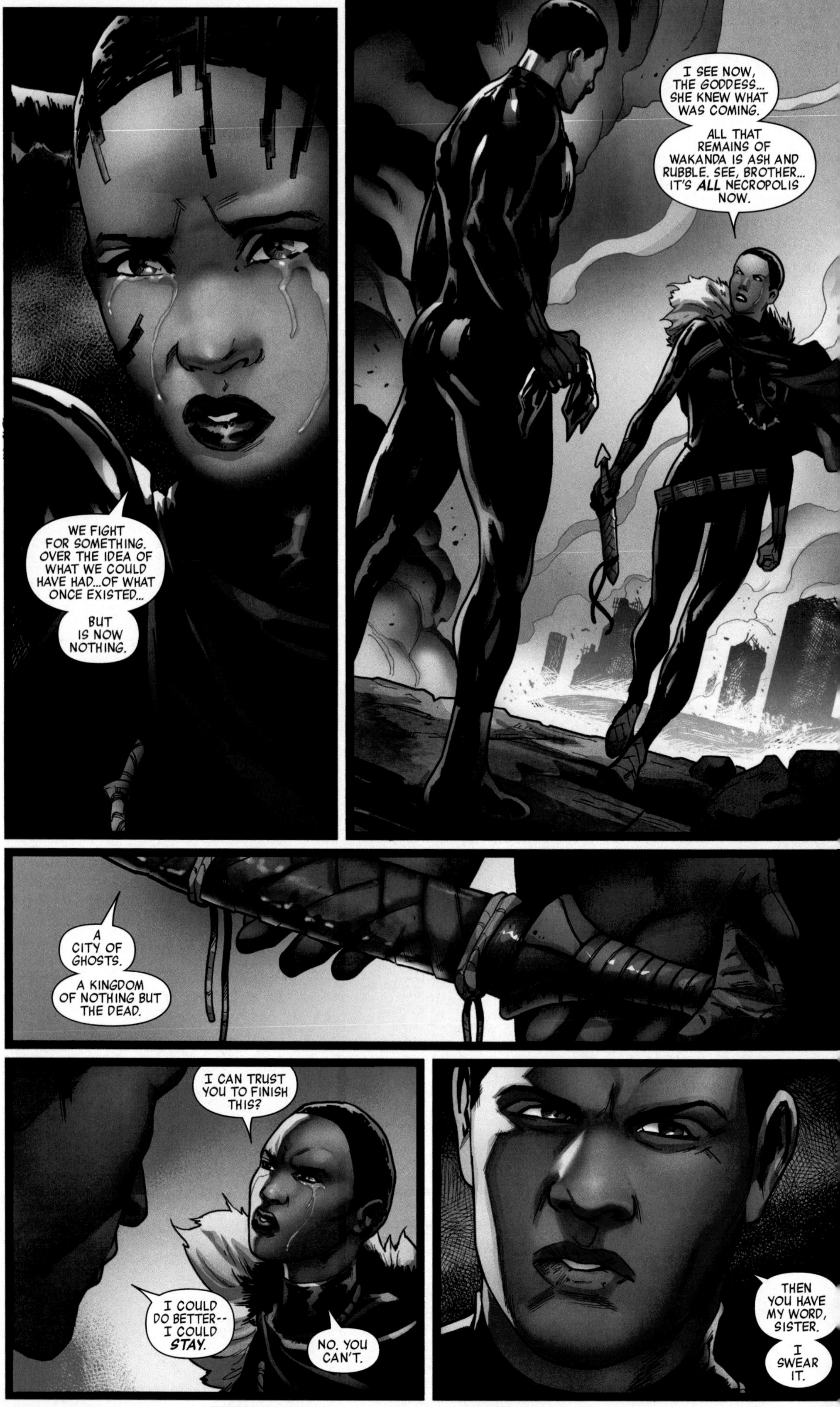
WE FIGHT FOR SOMETHING. OVER THE IDEA OF WHAT WE COULD HAVE HAD...OF WHAT ONCE EXISTED...
BUT IS NOW NOTHING.
I SEE NOW, THE GODDESS... SHE KNEW WHAT WAS COMING.
ALL THAT REMAINS OF WAKANDA IS ASH AND RUBBLE. SEE, BROTHER... IT'S **ALL** NECROPOLIS NOW.
A CITY OF GHOSTS.
A KINGDOM OF NOTHING BUT THE DEAD.
I CAN TRUST YOU TO FINISH THIS?
I COULD DO BETTER-- I COULD **STAY**.
NO. YOU CAN'T.
THEN YOU HAVE MY WORD, SISTER.
I SWEAR IT.

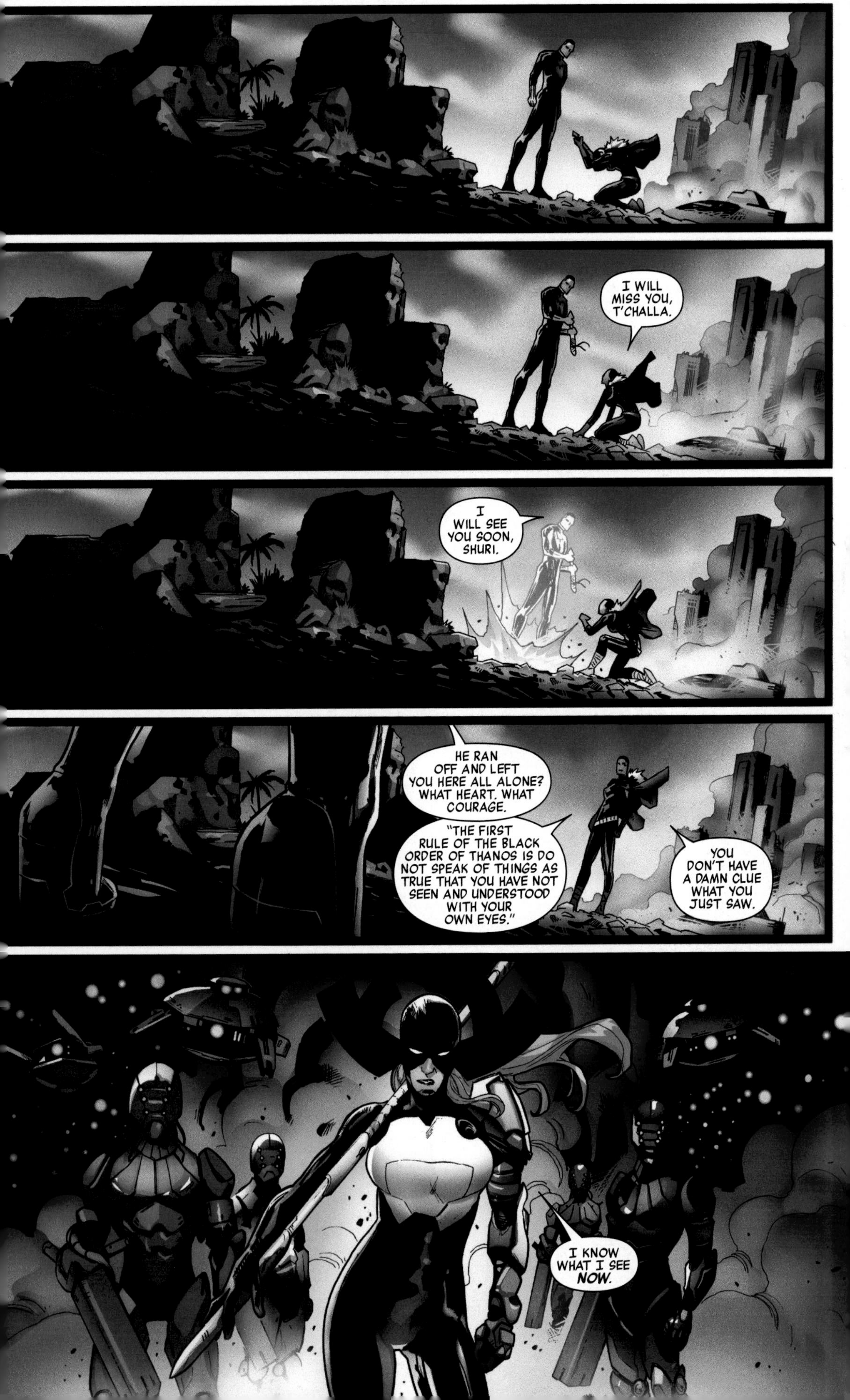
I WILL MISS YOU, T'CHALLA.
I WILL SEE YOU SOON, SHURI.
HE RAN OFF AND LEFT YOU HERE ALL ALONE? WHAT HEART. WHAT COURAGE.
"THE FIRST RULE OF THE BLACK ORDER OF THANOS IS DO NOT SPEAK OF THINGS AS TRUE THAT YOU HAVE NOT SEEN AND UNDERSTOOD WITH YOUR OWN EYES."
YOU DON'T HAVE A DAMN CLUE WHAT YOU JUST SAW.
I KNOW WHAT I SEE *NOW*.

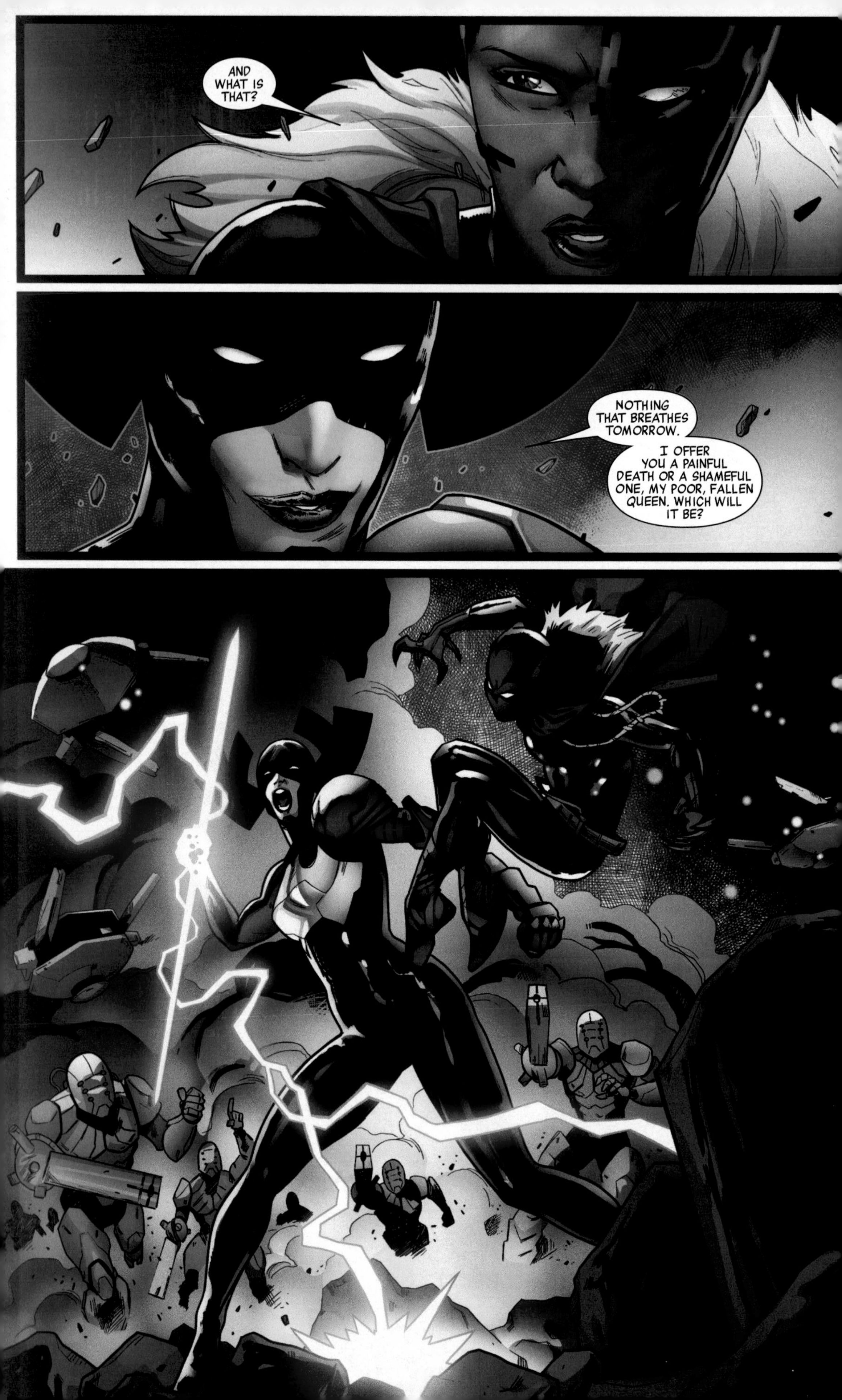
AND WHAT IS THAT?
NOTHING THAT BREATHES TOMORROW.
I OFFER YOU A PAINFUL DEATH OR A SHAMEFUL ONE, MY POOR, FALLEN QUEEN. WHICH WILL IT BE?

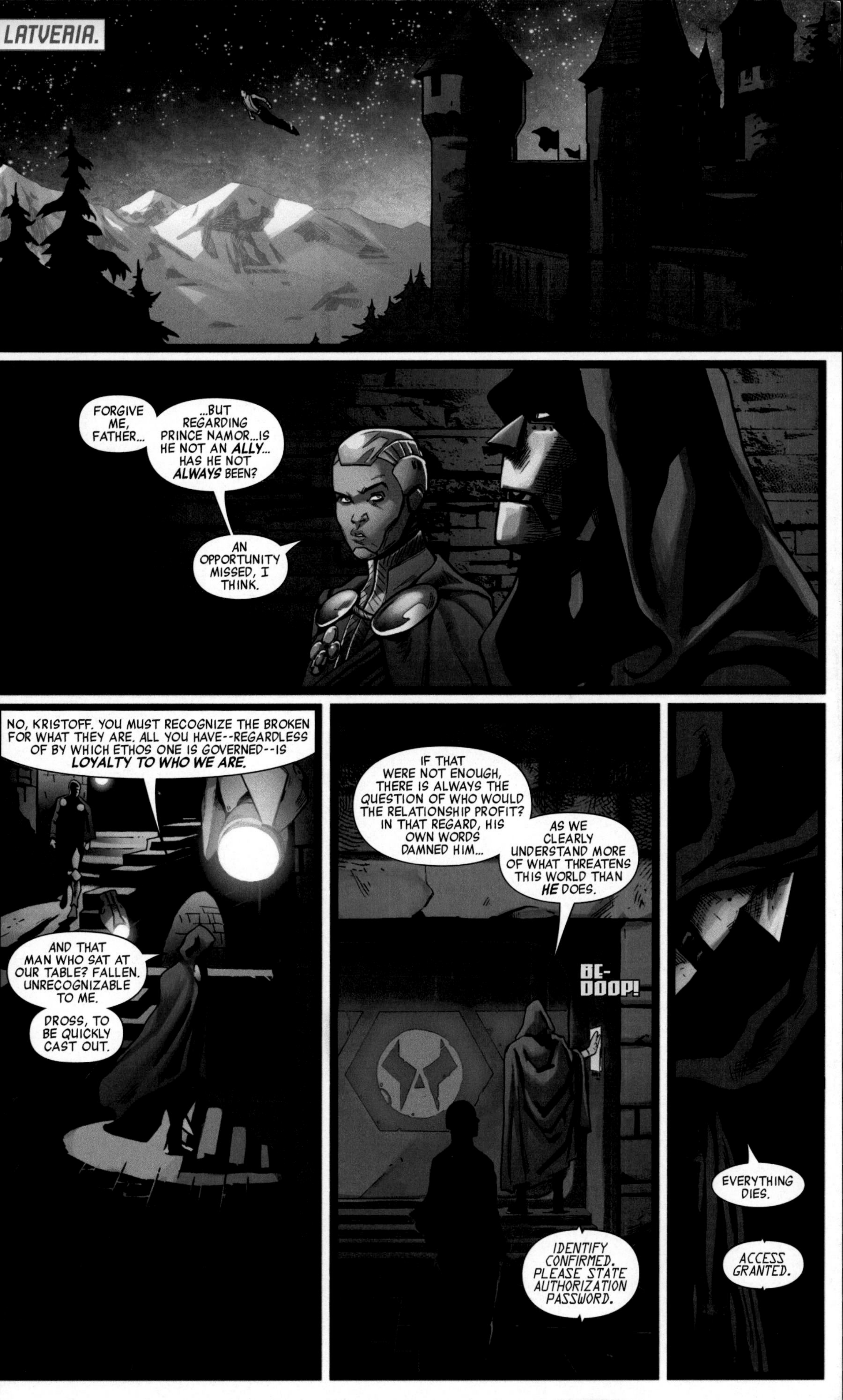
LATVERIA.
FORGIVE ME, FATHER...
...BUT REGARDING PRINCE NAMOR...IS HE NOT AN ALLY... HAS HE NOT ALWAYS BEEN?
AN OPPORTUNITY MISSED, I THINK.
NO, KRISTOFF. YOU MUST RECOGNIZE THE BROKEN FOR WHAT THEY ARE. ALL YOU HAVE--REGARDLESS OF BY WHICH ETHOS ONE IS GOVERNED--IS LOYALTY TO WHO WE ARE.
AND THAT MAN WHO SAT AT OUR TABLE? FALLEN. UNRECOGNIZABLE TO ME.
DROSS, TO BE QUICKLY CAST OUT.
IF THAT WERE NOT ENOUGH, THERE IS ALWAYS THE QUESTION OF WHO WOULD THE RELATIONSHIP PROFIT? IN THAT REGARD, HIS OWN WORDS DAMNED HIM...
AS WE CLEARLY UNDERSTAND MORE OF WHAT THREATENS THIS WORLD THAN HE DOES.
BE-DOOP!
IDENTIFY CONFIRMED. PLEASE STATE AUTHORIZATION PASSWORD.
EVERYTHING DIES.
ACCESS GRANTED.

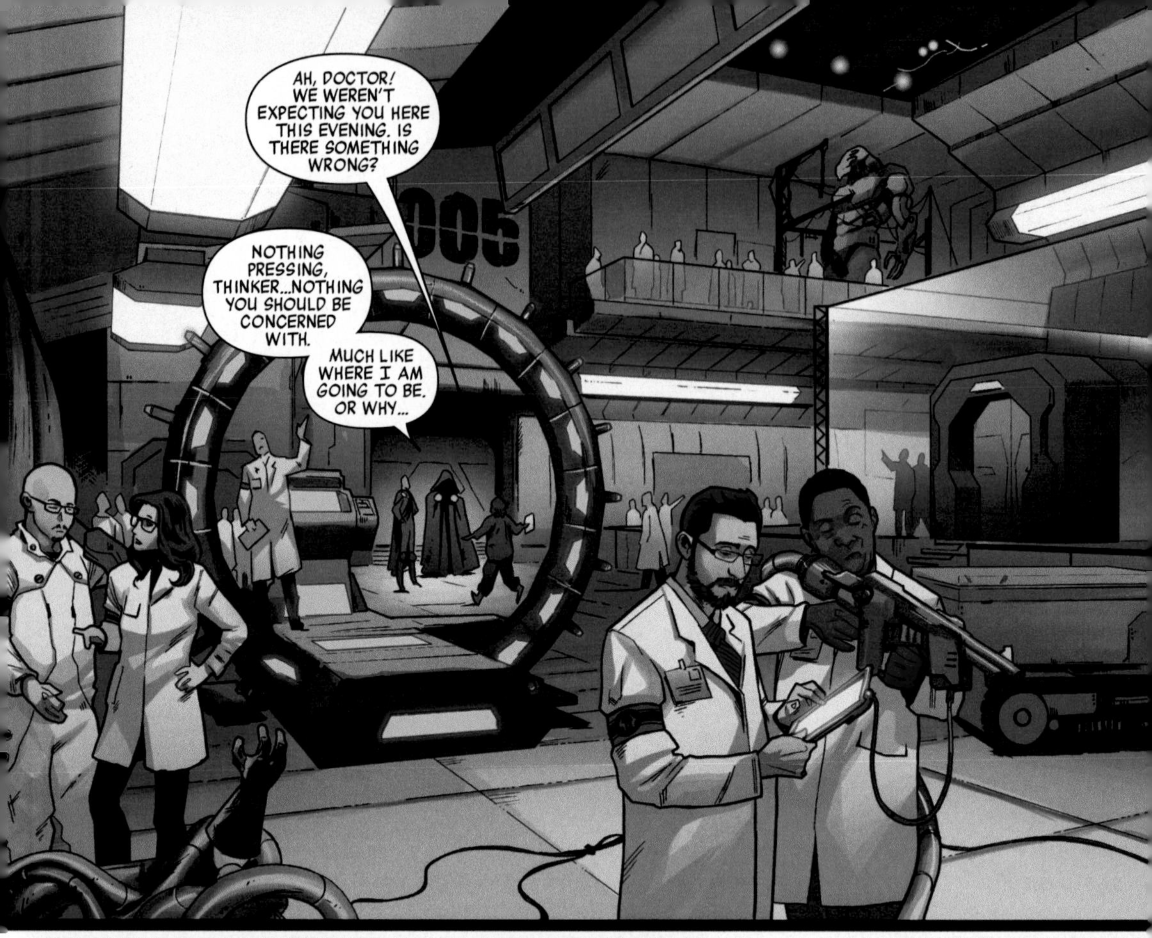
AH, DOCTOR! WE WEREN'T EXPECTING YOU HERE THIS EVENING. IS THERE SOMETHING WRONG?
NOTHING PRESSING, THINKER...NOTHING YOU SHOULD BE CONCERNED WITH.
MUCH LIKE WHERE I AM GOING TO BE. OR WHY...
0005

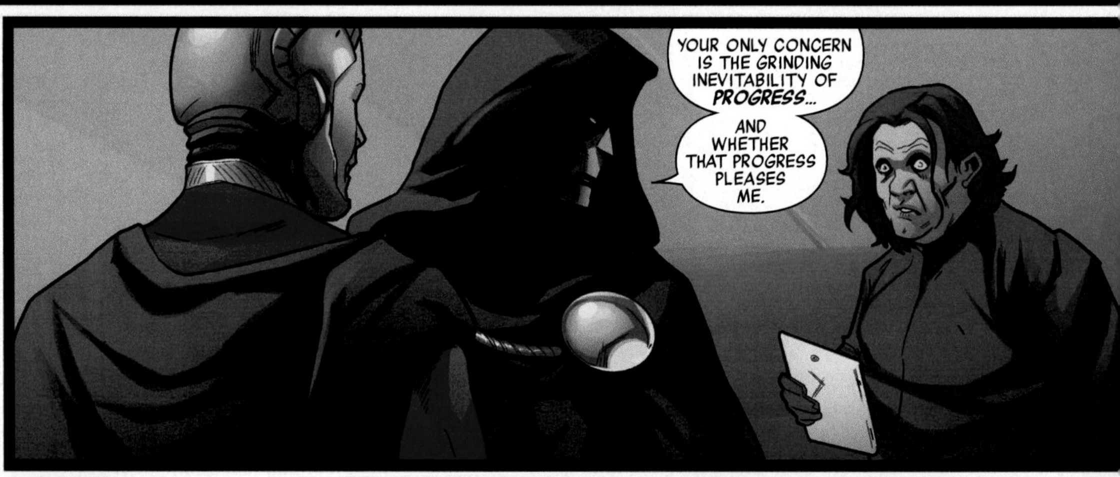
YOUR ONLY CONCERN IS THE GRINDING INEVITABILITY OF *PROGRESS*...
AND WHETHER THAT PROGRESS PLEASES ME.

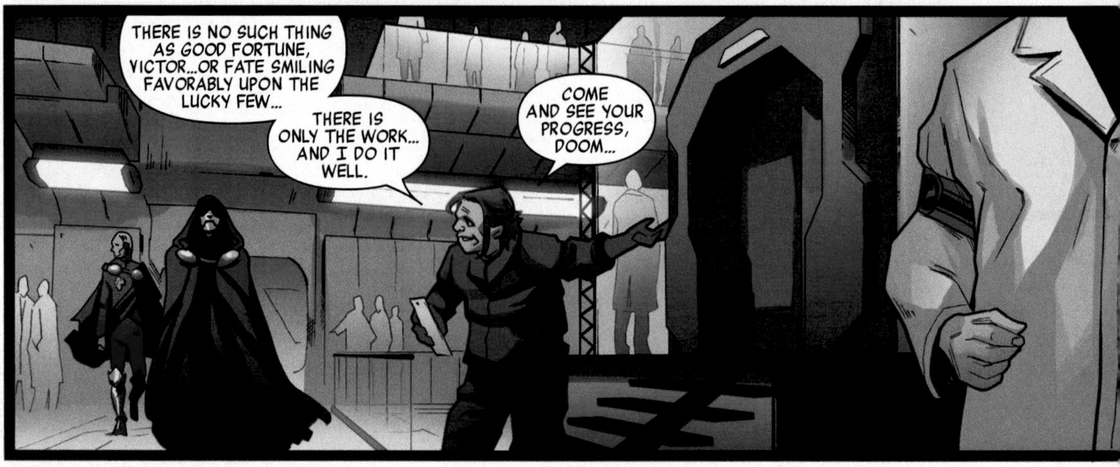
THERE IS NO SUCH THING AS GOOD FORTUNE, VICTOR...OR FATE SMILING FAVORABLY UPON THE LUCKY FEW...
THERE IS ONLY THE WORK... AND I DO IT WELL.
COME AND SEE YOUR PROGRESS, DOOM...

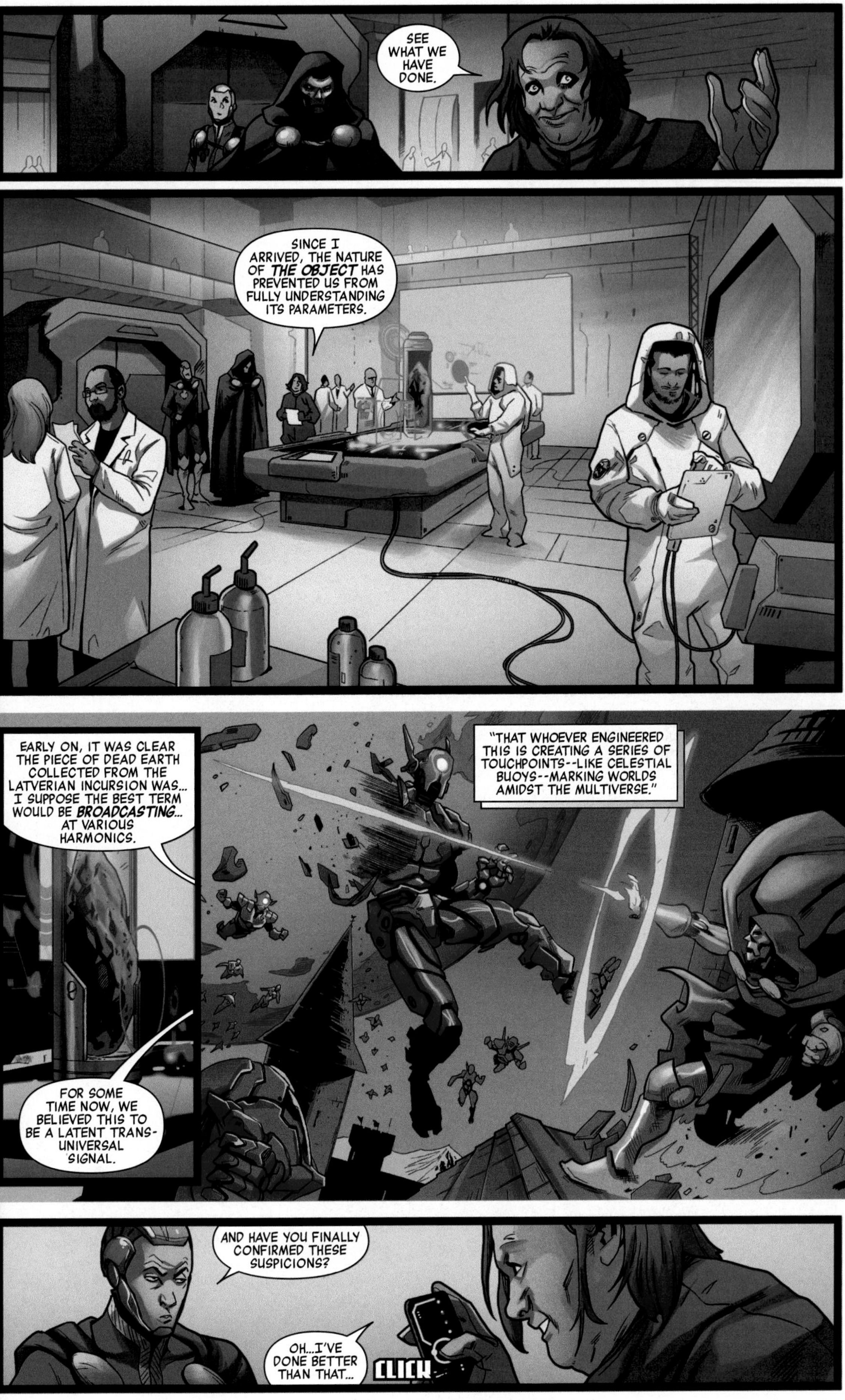
SEE WHAT WE HAVE DONE.
SINCE I ARRIVED, THE NATURE OF THE OBJECT HAS PREVENTED US FROM FULLY UNDERSTANDING ITS PARAMETERS.
EARLY ON, IT WAS CLEAR THE PIECE OF DEAD EARTH COLLECTED FROM THE LATVERIAN INCURSION WAS... I SUPPOSE THE BEST TERM WOULD BE BROADCASTING... AT VARIOUS HARMONICS.
"THAT WHOEVER ENGINEERED THIS IS CREATING A SERIES OF TOUCHPOINTS--LIKE CELESTIAL BUOYS--MARKING WORLDS AMIDST THE MULTIVERSE."
FOR SOME TIME NOW, WE BELIEVED THIS TO BE A LATENT TRANS-UNIVERSAL SIGNAL.
AND HAVE YOU FINALLY CONFIRMED THESE SUSPICIONS?
OH...I'VE DONE BETTER THAN THAT...
CLICK

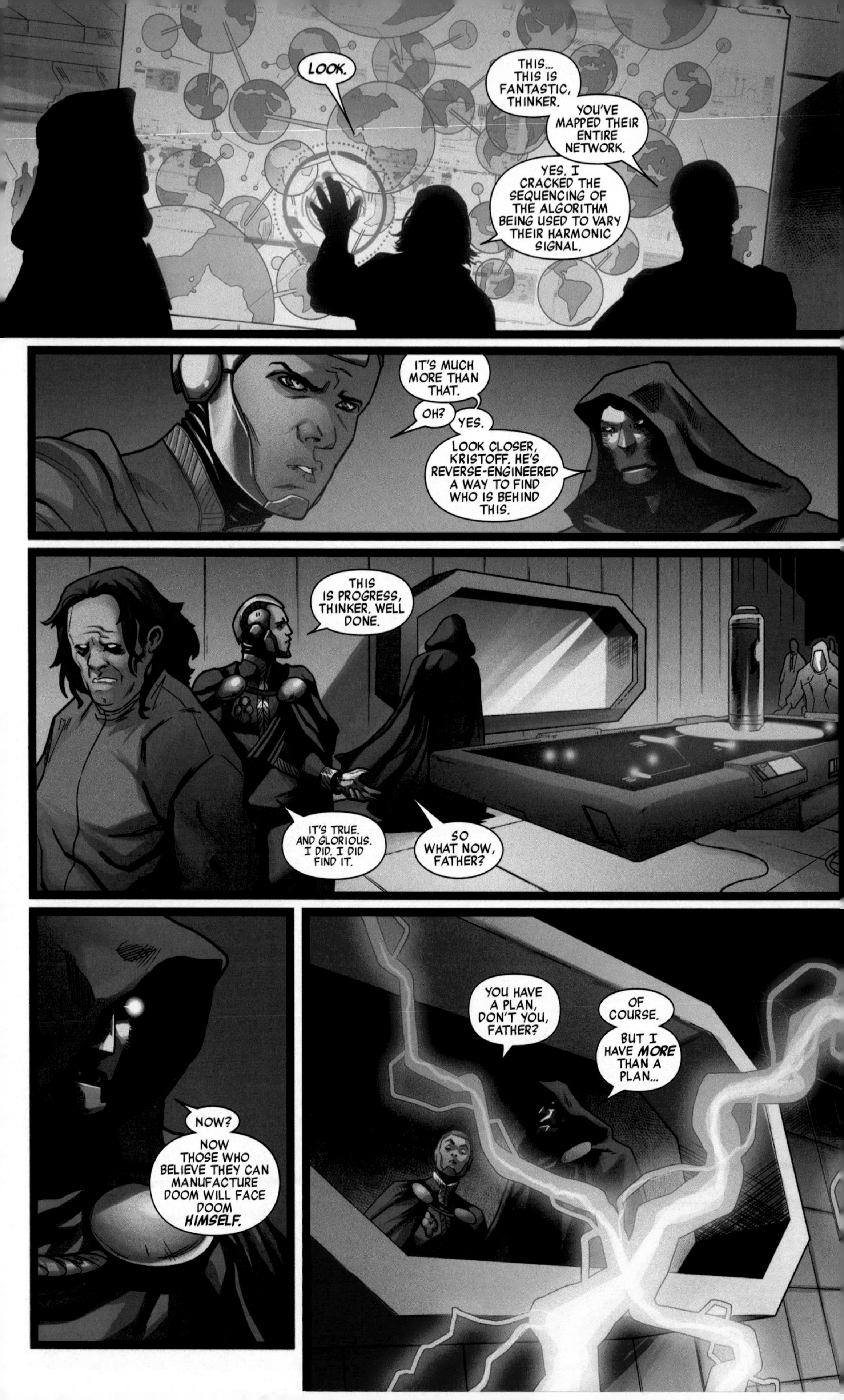
LOOK.
THIS... THIS IS FANTASTIC, THINKER.
YOU'VE MAPPED THEIR ENTIRE NETWORK.
YES. I CRACKED THE SEQUENCING OF THE ALGORITHM BEING USED TO VARY THEIR HARMONIC SIGNAL.
IT'S MUCH MORE THAN THAT.
OH?
YES.
LOOK CLOSER, KRISTOFF. HE'S REVERSE-ENGINEERED A WAY TO FIND WHO IS BEHIND THIS.
THIS IS PROGRESS, THINKER. WELL DONE.
IT'S TRUE. AND GLORIOUS. I DID. I DID FIND IT.
SO WHAT NOW, FATHER?
NOW?
NOW THOSE WHO BELIEVE THEY CAN MANUFACTURE DOOM WILL FACE DOOM *HIMSELF*.
YOU HAVE A PLAN, DON'T YOU, FATHER?
OF COURSE.
BUT I HAVE *MORE* THAN A PLAN...

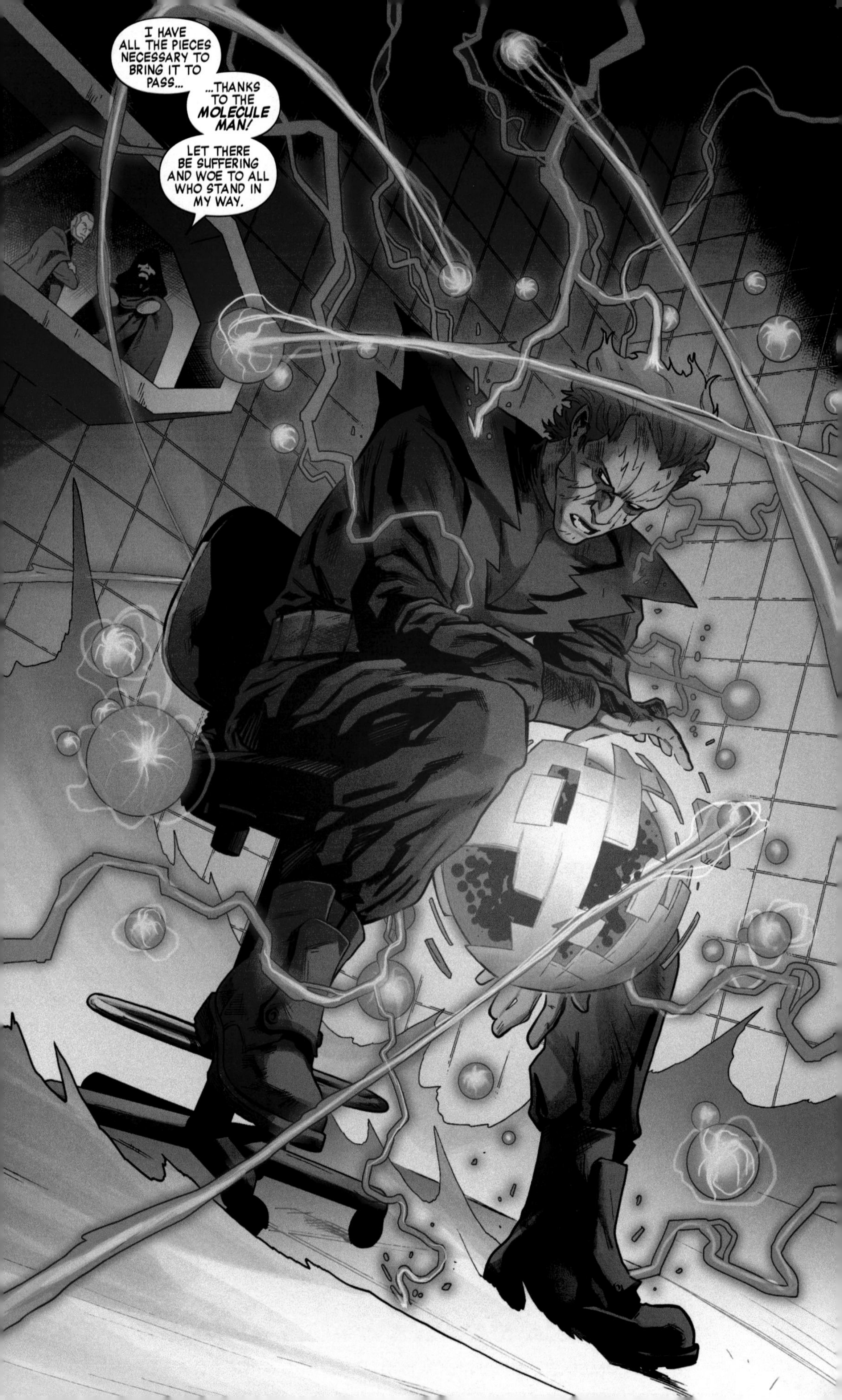
I HAVE ALL THE PIECES NECESSARY TO BRING IT TO PASS...
...THANKS TO THE *MOLECULE MAN!*
LET THERE BE SUFFERING AND WOE TO ALL WHO STAND IN MY WAY.

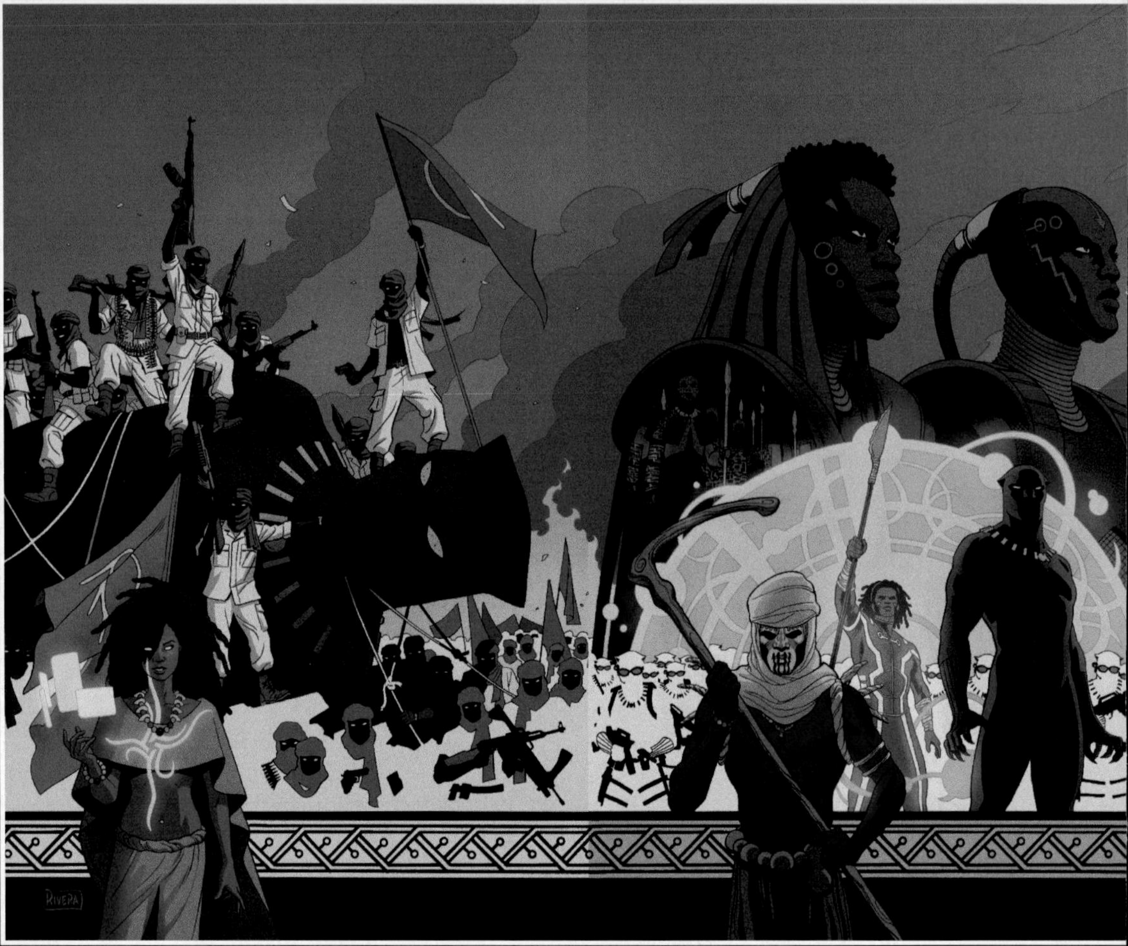
RIVERA

#9-12 COMBINED VARIANTS BY **PAOLO RIVERA** & **JOE RIVERA**

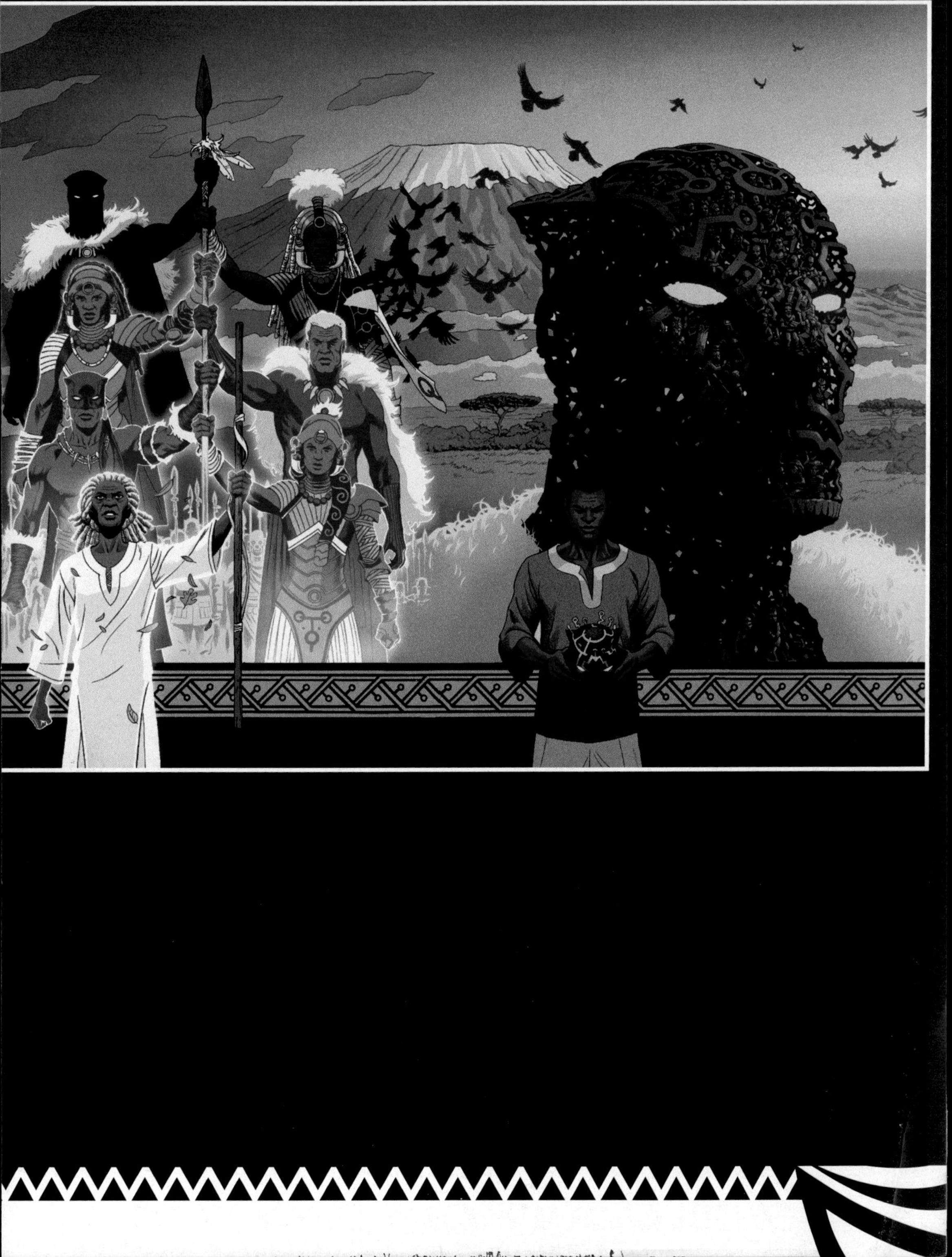

#11 CORNER BOX VARIANT
BY **JOE JUSKO**

#12 VENOMIZED VARIANT
BY **ELIZABETH TORQUE**